THE ENCYCLOPEDIA OF
TRACKS & SCATS

THE ENCYCLOPEDIA OF
TRACKS & SCATS

A Comprehensive Guide to the Trackable Animals
of the United States and Canada

By Len McDougall

THE LYONS PRESS
Guilford, Connecticut
An imprint of the The Globe Pequot Press

Copyright © 2004 by Len McDougall

ALL RIGHTS RESERVED. No part of this book may be reproduced or transmitted in any form by any means, electronic or mechanical, including photocopying and recording, or by any information storage and retrieval system, except as may be expressly permitted in writing from the publisher. Requests for permission should be addressed to The Lyons Press, Attn: Rights and Permissions Department, P.O. Box 480, Guilford, CT 06437.

The Lyons Press is an imprint of The Globe Pequot Press.

10 9 8 7 6 5 4 3 2 1

Printed in the United States of America

Designed by Maggie Peterson

Library of Congress Cataloging-in-Publication Data

McDougall, Len.
       The encyclopedia of tracks and scats : a comprehensive guide to the trackable animals of the United States and Canada / by Len McDougall.
       p. cm.
       ISBN 1-59228-070-6 (trade pbk.)
       1. Animal tracks—United States—Identification. 2. Animal tracks—Canada—Identification. I. Title.

QL768.M436 2004
591.97—dc22
                                                       2004057760

DEDICATION

This book is dedicated to Chakota, Nahanni, and Kenai,
the magnificent gray wolves who have been my companions, my teachers, and
a constant source of inspiration these past several years.

TABLE OF CONTENTS

INTRODUCTION

Of the many reasons people have for being interested in the natural world, none is more intriguing than the almost universal fascination we feel for the animals who live there. More than any other facet of nature, we humans are enthralled with creatures that can be born and live a full life that begets more like themselves, but without regard for the activities of people. Wild creatures great and small prosper in a world where they are co-dependent on one another while remaining independent of our own, and it tantalizes us to see how truly insignificant a role *Homo sapiens* plays in the normal business of life on this planet. If a single species of mosquito were to disappear, its loss would have adverse, perhaps even disastrous, consequences for dozens of other species. Yet if humankind were to suddenly become extinct from the earth, no wild creature would have cause to regret our passing. It's a sobering realization.

Maybe it's because we hate to feel left out of a world in which we perceive ourselves as the dominant species, or maybe it's because we feel that by better understanding the natural world we can better understand our own reason for being here, but humans have a driving curiosity to track, observe, and learn about their wild cousins. That innate curiosity motivated me to write this book. My goal in its pages is to help readers attain at least a basic understanding of the trackable animals of North America, by providing as much data as a single volume can hold.

From an author's viewpoint, compiling such a work is a daunting task. Despite an earnest attempt to answer as many questions as possible with established data and personal observations, this book cannot be complete. Worldwide, contemporary biology recognizes more than 3,000 species of reptiles, 4,800 amphibians, 9,600 bird species, and 5,000 mammals. And in North America, there are more than 400 species of mammals alone. Covering them all is simply not possible.

Instead, readers should note that there are many generic characteristics (covered in Section One) that apply to all members of a given group. These are the same characteristics that are used to classify animals into their respective scientific groups, and while it would be virtually impossible to remember every detail of every species, it is possible to commit general characteristics of each group to memory, and to apply them to similar species. All weasels, for example, have five toes on each foot, and all are carnivorous. All cats show four toes in each track, usually without claws, while all canids show four toes with claws in their tracks. All rabbits and hares are herbivorous, have four toes on the forefeet, five on the hind, and leave a distinctive double exclamation point (!!) track pattern. All frogs and toads must breed in open water, all snakes shed their skins several times each year, and all birds molt in summer. Even these generics entail studying if they're to be memorized, but knowing them means that a researcher who has studied cougars in North America can apply much of what he or she knows about cats to a study of leopards in Africa.

This book also cannot be complete because our knowledge of nature is still incomplete. Sorting through the library of information that has been accumulated by pioneers like the legendary tracker Olas J. Murie, and which has often been contradicted or changed by other researchers, is a task in itself. Add to that the environmental changes that have occurred over the latter half of the twentieth century, the continual adaptation by living things in response to them, and the frustrating realization that there still remains a huge amount of research to be done, and even the most comprehensive encyclopedia of animal facts is merely an update.

But perhaps that's actually the strength of this work, because only by first determining what is known can one see the questions that remain to be answered, and maybe highlighting the holes that exist in our current wildlife database will fire the curiosity of a new generation of field researchers. A wildlife biologist who can solve the riddle of how a denned black bear converts toxic nitrogen urea into useable proteins may well find the cure for kidney disease in humans. Learning how an air-breathing snapping turtle can remain underwater for hours by absorbing oxygen through its skin could lead to real advances in underwater exploration. And if science can figure out how a peeper frog can literally freeze solid during hibernation without sustaining cell damage, the implications for cryogenics and space travel might well change life as we know it.

Yet, while I hope that this encyclopedia will contribute to posterity by serving the community of professional biologists and field researchers, I have made an earnest attempt to keep it useable by amateur and hobbyist trackers. Folks who spend time in nature just because they enjoy it vastly outnumber the few who get paid for being there, and more than a few research projects have been launched because a recreational outdoors lover discovered something that the professionals had missed. For that reason, this book has been written to be useful to people who don't have a biology degree; use of unnecessarily large words, and their many synonyms, have been kept to a minimum, and where scientific terms are used, they've been defined in the text.

On a personal note, I hope that this treatise becomes a valued addition to the reference library of everyone with an interest in nature. No author gets wealthy from a book such as this, but my goal here is to attain far greater riches by encouraging others to explore the wonders of an environment that we all share under a common sky. In the latter half of the second millennium, our kind exhibited an almost obsessive drive to dominate the natural world, crushing forests, carnivores, and anything we perceived as being in the way of progress beneath our collective heel. Only now, when it's already too late to recover many of the habitats and animals that have been destroyed by our often thoughtless push toward changing the entire planet to suit our desires, is it slowly beginning to dawn on our species that we've made serious, potentially fatal, mistakes in judgment. No worldly treasure could be greater, no literary success sweeter, than knowing that my efforts have inspired even one of my fellow humans to exercise greater concern for this wondrous planet on which we all live.

THE ENCYCLOPEDIA OF
TRACKS & SCATS

PART ONE

ANIMAL CHARACTERISTICS
AND CLASSIFICATION

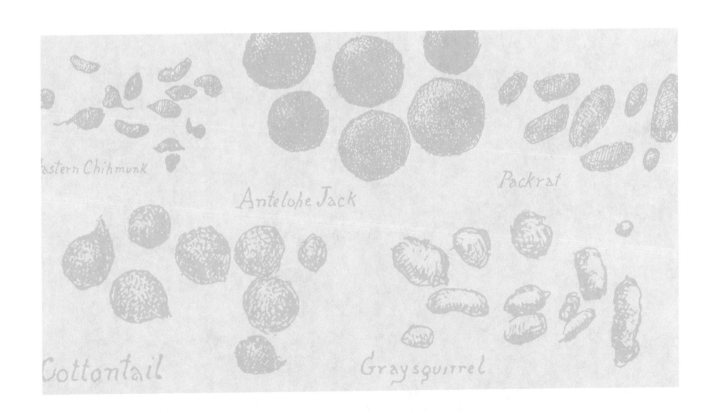

CHAPTER 1

GENERIC CHARACTERISTICS OF ANIMALS

All life on planet Earth shares certain traits that are generic. Every species is carbon-based, all need oxygen to breathe, and none can sustain life without water. That same broad philosophy of generic attributes also holds true when applied to tracking wildlife: All life must possess the means to migrate from a habitat that is lacking in some way to another, friendlier place where it will be easier to thrive. And all living organisms must leave some evidence of their passing as they move through the world. We humans often lack the sensory tools to detect some of the disturbances, known collectively as sign, that a particular creature leaves behind, but every animal's activities makes some sort of change to its environment. The science of tracking is perhaps most simply defined as the ability of a human being to detect, recognize, interpret, and follow the markings left by another creature's passage.

To track animals effectively, we first need to know the fundamentals of animal behaviors and physiology, especially those that are generic in nature. Every creature has needs that must be met by its environment if the species is to survive there, and few of its activities are random; rather, they are aimed toward satisfying those needs. Otters, for example, live only near water, so dry hardwood forest and prairie are poor choices for a researcher to seek them. (Specific information on individual species appears in Part Two, beginning on page 29.) Tracking and wildlife biology are not mutually exclusive disciplines, and the more a tracker knows about the way a species lives, the more effective he or she will be at tracking down its members.

The nature of any science is to establish hard-and-fast rules that will always apply to a given discipline, but wildlife biology deals with creatures that have been designed through millions of years of evolution to adapt to changes in their environment. While it is possible to establish reliable guidelines about what to expect from any species, it's also true that there are exceptions to nearly every rule. For instance, it was once believed that gray wolves would never interbreed with coyotes, which have historically been considered to be the natural enemy and prey of wolves; yet genetic testing of wolves in Minnesota at the turn of the millennium proved that roughly 75% of the wolves there have coyote blood in their lineage. As important as it is for a wildlife biologist to learn data that has already been established through research, it's also vital that he or she also accept that nature is fluid and always changing.

One rule that is always true is that nothing in the natural world occurs without good reason. Human ego makes us tend to believe that a phenomenon we can't explain must be an undecipherable mystery, but every physical attribute and behavior in the natural world is a logical result of ageless experimentation in a laboratory as wide as all outdoors. A logical answer is always there; we just need to find it.

GENERIC CHARACTERISTICS OF ANIMAL BEHAVIOR

Fortunately, many animal behaviors are nearly universal. All species operate from the need to feed and drink, to procreate, and to survive. All other activities are rooted in these basic needs. The Ojibwa proverb, "To find an animal, you must first find its food," is a truism that can also be applied to water, to breeding, and to other aspects of a species' habitat. Like hunters and trappers of old, the field researcher who enjoys the most success at finding and observing wild animals will always be one who knows his subject as intimately as possible.

Timetables

Unless disturbed, all animals tend to be creatures of habit, traveling the same well-worn pathways every day at approximately the same times. Like humans, animals have a penchant for falling into routines that are regular and predictable, because following the same route to do the same things every day for as long as circumstances permit requires less energy.

A few species are diurnal, or active during daylight hours, especially birds and cold-blooded reptiles that need outside warmth to function normally, but most mammals tend to be nocturnal. A good reason for being active at night is that humans usually avoid wild places during darkness because our eyes are evolved to see more into the infrared spectrum, where most colors occur. After sunset, the most prevalent ambient light is in the ultraviolet portion of the spectrum, of which we humans perceive very little. Animals that operate mainly at night see ultraviolet wavelengths very well, which gives them a natural night vision, but at the expense of the color perception that goes with an ability to see infrared light.

Trails

A real benefit of having established trails is that they permit high-speed travel through terrain where running flat out would be hazardous without them. A deer or rabbit surprised by a predator will always head for a trail that it knows intimately enough to run at top speed. Knowing every tree, stump, and knoll along a trail means less stumbling, allows for a faster pace, and greatly lessens the likelihood of surprising an animal that walks it every day.

A generic feature of animal trails is that they become more numerous the closer one gets to a bedding, denning, or foraging site. The reason for that is because animals tend to be more active at all times of day around these havens of relative safety, but the resulting proliferation of trails also serves to protect them from enemies. A whitetail being pursued by a puma will always head for its bedding ground in the deep forest, where visibility is limited to a few yards and it can defeat the cat's sharp eyesight behind dense thickets, leaving the predator with a maze of worn trails that all smell of the deer it was chasing. That same phenomenon helps to make a wolf den with pups safe from bears, and a rabbit burrow safe from foxes.

Too, more than one species of animal will tend to use the same trails. Large, heavy animals have the most impact on terrain, and they leave the best trails, so smaller species tend to travel them as well. Subsequently, the same well-worn trail is likely to be dotted with scats, tracks, and sign from many species that use it for the sake of convenience, while inadvertently protecting one another with a plethora of scents that work to confuse predators.

Territories

With few exceptions, every adult wild animal has a territory that it lays claim to and will defend against others who might compete with it for food and water, mates, and shelter.

Many biologists have tried to establish arbitrary distances for territorial ranges of different species, but the actual size of any animal's territory depends on the availability of those things that it requires to live and procreate. The whitetail deer, for example, is widely accepted as having a lifetime territory that encompasses only about 1 square mile. Yet in at least one place, Whitefish Point in Michigan's Upper Peninsula, whitetails make a seasonal autumn migration of more than twenty miles because that area lacks winter browse.

Likewise, the seasonal migration of one species can have an impact on the territorial ranges of others with whom it shares a symbiotic relationship. When whitetails move southward from Michigan's Whitefish Point in late fall, they're followed by gray wolves that need to hunt them for winter sustenance, just as caribou in Alaska and northern Canada are followed by Arctic wolves during their seasonal migrations. Conversely, coyotes that make small rodents a large part of their winter diets do not follow the deer, and are sometimes more populous in areas vacated by wolves who normally regard the smaller cousins as both competition and prey.

Any territorial animal must enforce its claim to a territory against intruders with similar diets and needs, or face the depletion of resources that are needed to keep it strong and resistant to disease. To hold a territory, its claimant must be stronger or more fierce than those who challenge that claim, which serves to insure that only the healthiest, most able individuals are permitted to breed. When a dominant animal becomes too old or sickly to defend its domain, its space and its place within a balanced ecosystem will typically be usurped by a younger and stronger challenger, and the process begins anew.

In fact, territorial disputes are relatively infrequent and seldom as dramatic as they're sometimes portrayed to be. Overpopulation especially can cause members of the same species to battle viciously over territory, but every wild animal harbors an instinctive revulsion against injuring its own kind. In a practical sense, fighting in earnest virtually guarantees that both combatants will be seriously wounded in an environment that doesn't forgive disabilities, and causing the death of one's own isn't at all conducive to survival of the species.

For those reasons, most territorial battles are limited to determining which animal is the strongest. Male deer lock antlers and try to shove the head of their opponent to the ground; wolves try to put a challenger on its back; snakes entwine one another in a test of strength; turtles attempt to flip an opponent upside down; frogs pummel one another until one withdraws; birds peck and slap with their wings. In nearly every instance the battle is finished as soon as it becomes apparent which combatant is the stronger, before a debilitating injury occurs to either.

GENERIC CHARACTERISTICS OF ANIMAL PHYSIOLOGY

As with behavioral traits, there are many physical characteristics among animals that are generic. All hooved animals exhibit similar walking patterns; all predatory mammals have elongated canine teeth; every serpent seeks shelter in a cold rain; and females of most species are pregnant in spring. Memorizing all the physical traits of 4,675 known mammal species, 9,702 bird species, 6,700 reptiles, and 4,780 amphibians is impossible, especially since the list of known species grows longer—particularly among reptiles and amphibians—with each passing year. But consolidating that vast library of information under generic headings such as "Only mammals have hair," "All birds have three forward toes," and "All amphibians are born in water" can help greatly in committing to memory the traits that are most common among different classifications.

Body Sizes

In most instances among larger animals, and especially among mammals, there exists a marked size difference between males and females, with males generally being the larger and stronger of the sexes. This difference, known as sexual dimorphism, occurs because a smaller female requires less food to remain healthy, particularly when pregnant. Conversely, larger and stronger males, which are typically outnumbered by females by more than 3 to 1, are more capable of traveling to breeding females, and of defending them against potential enemies.

Differences in body size also occur with changes in latitude. Individuals residing in southern latitudes tend to be smaller than individuals of the same species that live in more northern regions. This difference, which is common in every mammal species, results from a need to maintain body heat in cold climates. Larger bodies with more mass and fat are better able to retain heat in temperatures low enough to induce hypothermia. This phenomenon is exemplified by the whitetail deer, which reaches an average weight of just 50 pounds in the Florida Keys, while its otherwise identical counterparts in Maine can exceed 300 pounds. In recent years, researchers have been able to document this size difference as it happens by observing the northward migration of American opossums. This species ranged only as far north as Pennsylvania when the first Europeans settled in the New World and weighed about 6 pounds, but today it has migrated to the northern boundaries of the United States, and it weighs upwards of 12 pounds there.

Eyes

The placement of an animal's eyes is indicative of its role in the environment in which it lives. Species that have evolved in response to being preyed on by meat eaters have eyes positioned at either side of the head to provide a panoramic field of vision. Being able to observe a wider area lessens the possibility that a predator will be able to approach without being noticed. This trait is seen in all prey animals, from mice and birds to deer and rabbits.

A broader field of vision isn't without disadvantages, though. Having the eyes positioned at either side of the head means that they operate independently of one another, with little visual overlap except at the frontal periphery. The result is that prey animals are physically incapable of having binocular vision, where both eyes simultaneously focus on and compare the same image to determine precisely how far away one object is from another.

Predatory species that make their living by accurately judging distances require precise depth perception to strike efficiently, so the eyes of bobcats, wolves, raccoons, and otters are positioned at the front of the head. This design narrows the owner's field of vision, but results in sharper eyesight because both eyes are comparing slightly different viewing angles of a single image at about 60 times per second. The result is an acutely accurate sense of distance that allows predators to identify prey animals partially hidden behind camouflaging foliage, and then pounce with lethal exactness.

One example of how these two forms of vision work when pitted against one another is that of a cougar stalking a deer grazing in an open meadow. If the deer, with its wide range of vision, detects movement from the cat, it will be alerted and probably flee before the hunter can approach to within striking distance. But an experienced cougar will advance a few stealthy steps at a time, moving only when the deer has its head down to feed, its vision obscured by grasses, and freeze whenever the deer raises its head. Lacking good distance perception, the deer will probably not be aware that the motionless object it sees only as a blurred shape has moved closer since the last time it was observed. If the cat can continue to move closer only while its prey is unable to see, and not alert the deer with motion, it can often get close enough to pounce before the deer realizes its danger. This same technique has long been used to good effect by human hunters and photographers.

Many mammals lack color vision, but rather than being thought of as a disadvantage, their inability to perceive color might better be seen as a good trade-off. Since most are active primarily during the dim hours between dusk and dawn, their eyeballs are evolved to have more ultraviolet-sensitive rods than infrared-sensitive cones.

Bright colors become visible only when infrared light is present, meaning that they can be seen during daylight hours, but become indistinguishable at night. Humans, most birds, honeybees, and probably squirrels have good color discrimination because they're most active during the day, while deer, rabbits, and raccoons have eyes that see well into the ultraviolet spectrum, the most prevalent wavelength after sunset. Color-blind animals can see well in daylight, while color-sighted animals are virtually blind in darkness.

Most forest-dwelling animals are also nearsighted, but this too is less of a disadvantage than it might appear to be. Living in a close environment makes long-range vision unnecessary, so forest dwellers like bears have developed more acute senses of smell and hearing to compensate for an inability to see long distances.

Likewise, animals that inhabit wide open spaces tend to possess sharper long range vision because they need to see farther to avoid approaching danger. Pronghorn antelope are perhaps the best example of this phenomenon, with an ability to perceive movement from a distance of 2 miles.

TRACKS

Tracking gets its name from the impressions left in earth by the weight on an animal's feet, and although tracks are in fact just one of the signs used to profile and follow the creature, they're probably the most important. A well-traveled trail or a furrow through tall grass is a sure indication that something walked that way, but a clear track can conclusively identify the species. Tracks can also reveal an animal's weight and size, giving a good indication of its age, and perhaps even the individual.

Foot Placement

Nearly all terrestrial animals above the insect level possess four limbs that serve as their primary means of locomotion, and most land animals, including higher primates, walk on all fours. There are several commonalities with the quadrapedal design, meaning that even dissimilar species can be expected to exhibit many of the same physical characteristics and mannerisms when walking, trotting, or running.

Track Patterns

The way in which an animal's tracks are arranged as it travels is called a track pattern. Defined as the way an animal's tracks are grouped on a trail as it moves forward, track patterns reveal how fast an animal was moving, whether it was relaxed or afraid, if it has an injury or limp, and sometimes the identity of an individual animal.

Track patterns change as the speed at which an animal is traveling changes, and each of the walking, trotting, or running gaits has an identifiable grouping of individual tracks (gaits are explained in greater detail later in this section). The same patterns will repeat with minor variations between track sets for as long as the animal maintains the same pace. When it changes pace, as in slowing from or accelerating to a run, so will the track pattern change.

Weight Placement

Four-legged animals that make their living by running fast, whether in pursuit or in flight, tend to lean forward as they walk, with most of their weight on the toes. This trait, which is somewhat equivalent to a human walking on tiptoes all the time, insures that they're constantly in position to move away at top speed. Having body mass leaned forward helps to lessen the inertia that would otherwise slow its transition from motionlessness into fast-forward motion. That translates into a small reduction in the time it takes for an animal to go from stationary to its top running speed, which in the wild can make the difference between getting a meal or becoming one.

A tiptoe walk is also quieter, just as it is in humans, because less of an animal's foot is making contact with the earth, so there's less chance of stepping onto a dry twig that might snap and reveal its presence. Walking in a state of constant readiness and stealth would be exhausting to humans, but carnivores that must catch prey to eat and the animals that must run fast to escape them are conditioned to walk this way.

I have noted that this forward lean tends to diminish among animals that are relaxed. Whitetail deer that live in urbanized areas where there are few predators are literally less on their toes than deer living in wilder places where there are large carnivores to contend with.

Four-legged animals that walk plantigrade, or flat-footed, are always relatively slow-moving creatures who aren't easy prey. This category is diverse, including powerful animals like bears, ferocious animals like badgers and raccoons, well-armored creatures like porcupines and armadillos, and historically well-armed humans.

Another notable characteristic of animal tracks from nearly every four-legged species, hooved or pawed, is that most weight is carried on the outsides of the feet, and that the largest toe is to the outside. This is opposite the human design, where the big toe is innermost and most weight is carried to the inside, ostensibly because of our bipedal walking mode.

Terrain Differences

Wet mud, especially clay, is the best medium in which to find a clear track. As anyone who's ever walked barefoot in it can attest, mud molds itself to the contours of an object pressed into it, leaving a three-dimensional imprint that can be used to determine not only the size of the animal leaving it, but its approximate weight, idiosyncrasies as faint as a scar or a limp, and enough definition to clearly discern front and rear tracks in the same print.

Snow is the favorite tracking medium of most field biologists, largely because it covers everything, and any animal walking on it leaves some disturbance to denote its passing. The problem is that there are different types of snow, and all of them affect how well or poorly an animal's foot registers a track.

Fresh wet snow in ambient temperatures that are near the freezing mark usually leaves a very good track. Good for making snowballs, this type packs well under pressure and often registers a near-perfect print. The drawback is that this form of snow tends to "grow" a track, especially in direct sunlight where outside warmth causes the imprint to melt and expand outward. Depending on outside influences from freezing rain, sun, warm air, and of course the time it spends exposed to those factors, a track might grow to half again its original size.

Fresh powder snow in temperatures below 20°F is as dry as dust, and impressions left in it may be as indistinct and formless as tracks made in desert sand. Under such conditions it might prove impossible to identify any track characteristics without following the trail to a softer, more conforming medium. This is also an example of conditions under which length of stride and width of straddle can help to identify an animal's species and size. Deep snow, where tracks may be at the bottoms of holes and equally impossible to see, requires the same interpolative approach.

Hardpack snow that has compressed under its own weight to a solid surface may also fail to register a readable track. On this medium it may be necessary to inspect prints from very close up, looking for clawmarks, hoof edges, and other disturbances that can be assembled like a puzzle into a complete picture.

Sand can register either a perfect print or an unidentifiable track, depending on how wet it is when an animal walks over it. In dry, dusty sand an animal's tracks may be little more than blurred indentations, while wet sand can yield a perfect track. Whenever possible a tracker should try to follow a trail through dry sand until he can find an identifiable track in more revealing soil. Streambanks and lakeshores are good places to find prints that are defined well enough to make a plaster cast.

Forest humus is the toughest of tracking media because it seldom registers more than a portion of any track and what does leave a mark will soon disappear. Hooved animals tend to leave more obvious prints, but even then the impressions are likely to be little more than a sharp-sided indentation in dead leaves.

Pawed animals typically leave only faint, slightly flattened marks on leaves and humus as they walk over it, but very often their claws will obviously displace leaves and other forest debris. A twig displaced from a depression where it has laid long enough to make its own print indicates that an animal rolled it underfoot while traveling in the direction opposite that of the roll. Dry leaves that have slid away to reveal moist leaves beneath do the same, and frequently a pawed animal's clawmarks can be seen as perforations in dead leaves that have not been displaced.

Stride

The definition of stride varies significantly from one tracking text to another, but for our purposes here a single stride will be defined as the distance one foot travels from its most rearward position on the ground to the point where it again contacts the earth in its forward position.

The length of an animal's stride is significant because it gives a clue as to how long the animal's legs are, which helps to determine its size, probable age, and maybe even its species. However, stride length tends to vary in different types of terrain, just as it does for humans. A deer walking along a flat two-track road at a relaxed pace may take advantage of the easy terrain by stretching its stride distance to cover more ground. That same deer walking over a debris-strewn forest floor will take shorter steps to insure that the weight on one foot can be immediately shifted to the other three, thus preventing possible injury from having most of its weight on a single leg should it fall into a hole or trip. On slippery snow or wet clay the stride tends to shorten even further.

Straddle

Straddle is defined as the distance between the inside of an animal's left track and the inside of its right track. This measurement is significant because it shows the relative width of the animal's body. All things being equal, the wider the straddle, the larger the animal making the tracks.

But width of straddle seldom corresponds directly to the width of an animal's body, because nearly all wild mammals walk with their legs pointed inward. This trait is an adaptation to walking uneven terrain that may be strewn with holes or tripping hazards, where the smaller the area an animal steps on, the less likely it is to sustain an injury to feet or legs. A narrower trail also means that fewer twigs and other noise-making objects are stepped on.

This pointed-in characteristic becomes comparatively more pronounced the longer an animal's legs are; a 200-pound whitetail leaves a trail that's about 5 inches across, while a 1,000-pound wapiti using the same trail will widen it little, if at all. The same goes for coyotes, which have a straddle width of about 4 inches, while a gray wolf twice its size has a straddle of only 5 inches.

Gaits

Gaits are defined as differences in pace, generally segregated into the three categories of walking, trotting, and running. The different gaits denote the speed at which an animal is traveling, and a tracker can easily determine which of those was being used by differences in foot placement.

Walking—An almost universally common characteristic in the walking gait of four-legged animals is a tendency for the hind feet to step precisely into tracks left by the forefeet. This is a learned trait that becomes more pronounced in longer-legged animals, particularly those living in terrain that's treacherous enough to break a leg. Because no quadrapedal animal can see where its hind feet make contact with the earth, they all learn from experience to avoid holes and tripping hazards by placing the front foot, which they can see, on good footing, then automatically stepping into the same track with the hind foot.

This trait also serves to make an animal travel more quietly. Twigs and other objects that might make noise underfoot have already been snapped or displaced by the time the hind foot touches down. The result is that less noise is made during casual travel, which means predators are more likely to get within striking distance of prey before they're detected, and prey animals are less apt to be noticed by carnivores.

It should be noted that this characteristic, while nearly universal, applies only when an animal is moving at a casual walk. At faster paces—a trot, canter, or gallop—placement of all four feet changes to accommodate the need for increased speed.

Trotting—The trotting gait is a normal pace for many animals that must cover a lot of ground as part of their daily routines, including peccaries, coyotes, and wolves.

An almost universal characteristic of four-legged animals moving at a trot is that each foot registers independently, leaving four separate tracks that do not overlap. The explanation is that all four legs come into play at this gait, each of them working in succession to contribute an easy forward momentum that requires as little effort as possible, and can be sustained much longer than a full running gait.

Running—Most animals avoid running unless prompted to do so by fear or in pursuit of prey. Running is a high-energy gait, so it's usually reserved for those times when maximum speed is necessary.

The track pattern of a four-legged running gait is almost universal. Sometimes referred to as a "rocking horse" gait, the forefeet are planted firmly and close together to act as a fulcrum while the hind feet are brought far forward on either side of them. When the hind feet simultaneously make contact with earth, the animal uses the tensed muscles of its arched back to spring forward in a leap that, in the case of a whitetail deer, may span a distance of more than 20 feet. At the end of this leap the forefeet again make contact with the ground, supporting the runner's weight as its hind feet are brought forward to either side, and the process begins anew.

Depth-of-trough is defined as the distance an animal's body sinks into the medium over which it passes. In most instances that medium will be fresh, deep snow, or, more rarely, soft mud at the shorelines of ponds and rivers.

Although depth-of-trough is considered a legitimate part of the tracker's database by some biologists, its real importance is negligible. The biggest problem is that you'll seldom find a trough, because most animals intentionally avoid walking through terrain where their movement is hampered and travel is strenuous. Those that must walk over soft ground will generally have legs long enough to reach solid footing without dragging their chests, or feet large enough to displace their weight and keep them from sinking that deeply.

SCAT

Scat, a generic term for the solid excreta of living creatures in general, can tell a tracker numerous important things about the animal that left it. The revulsion we humans feel toward handling feces of all kinds is probably instinctual, because normal humans seem to understand from a young age that poop is bad. Today, we understand that scat can sometimes be a vector for several parasitic and microbial diseases, and we know simple ways to avoid infection from all of them.

Perhaps most important is to never handle animal scat with your bare hands when you can avoid it by wearing plastic or rubber gloves. Aside from bacterial infections like E. coli and salmonella that might be contracted, scat in general is a known vector for many parasitic organisms, some of which are dangerous to humans. Keep hands and under the fingernails clean, and wash your hands religiously after handling scat, even if you were wearing gloves. The danger of contracting an infection is really quite low, but by observing a few simple tenets of hygiene those odds can be kept at zero.

Scat Characteristics

While scats from most species are often consistent enough to identify at least the order of the animal that left it, there are numerous seasonal and dietary influences that can cause real differences in samples from the same species, or even the same individual. The theory is that by studying the contents and other characteristics of an animal's droppings you can see what it had been eating, approximately when it ate, and then extrapolate where and when it had been feeding. The more clues that can be gleaned from a scat, the more a tracker knows about the animal and its habits.

One generic fact about animal scat is that it carries an olfactory fingerprint of the animal leaving it, and even different species can learn to relate the scent of a scat to an individual.

Most carnivores avoid their own scat, which is typically more foul and quicker to decay than the fibrous pellets or flattened "pies" of vegetable eaters, as well as being a vector for diseases that are especially infectious to the species that deposited the sample. Probably this common aversion to feces from one's own kind, an aversion shared by humans, is a recognition at the instinctive level that scat from one species of animal will offer the greatest possibility of contracting a parasitic, bacterial, or viral sickness from others of the same species. The normally pellet-shaped scats of wild vegetarians, from rodents and rabbits to whitetails and moose, is notably less detested by all species, including a few human trackers who seem to handle it bare-handed with both impunity and immunity (not a recommended practice, however).

With the exception of marmots and a few other species, which actually excavate a bathroom into the rear of their dens, and porcupines that build sleeping platforms made from their own dried and compressed scat pellets, few animals defecate in their own dens, and no carnivore does.

Scat as a Boundary Marker

Most animals, and carnivores especially, tend to mark their territorial boundaries with scat because it carries with it a large amount of information about its owner. Science has only begun to quantify the information contained in a scat, but we do know that its scent is unique to its maker, much like a fingerprint. Other animals can use that smell to determine not only the maker's species, but its identity as an individual, its size, gender, sexual disposition, and probably its age and state of health.

Because this fecal calling card contains so much information, it helps to prevent chance encounters between animals of the same species and same sex, who would regard one another as competitors. The same scent marker works to advertise the presence of its maker to potential mates.

Predators also exhibit a habit of defecating directly onto the consumed carcasses of large prey animals. This is only done after the edible portions have been consumed and the predator is finished with the remains. The reason behind the practice is largely a matter of conjecture, but it is common among all carnivores from bears and bobcats to wolves and wolverines. Probably the scat serves to make the remains unattractive to other carnivores that might take up residence and compete for the same prey, but it also seems likely that it's a territorial marker.

Scat as Scent Camouflage

While it might seem counterproductive for a hunter to make itself known to prey by marking its own trails with scat, the reverse is actually true. By spreading its scent around, a predator is also making it difficult for even the most acute sense of smell to determine where it is at any given time. Some human deer hunters employ a variation of this strategy by urinating all around their hunting sites several weeks prior to the season's start, thus giving resident deer time to get used to human scent, while at the same time creating so many olfactory images of themselves that an animal can never be sure if it smells an actual person or not.

Prey animals, most notably deer and rabbits, also use scat to camouflage their presence. But instead of using scat as a scentpost to mark the boundaries of a territory, these animals leave scat randomly along trails, near feeding areas, and around bedding grounds. Presented with such a maze of prey odors, a bobcat in pursuit of a hare need only lose sight of its prey for a second to have lost it entirely.

Scat Size

All things being equal, the size of a scat corresponds directly to the size of the animal that left it. The diet and scat of a coyote may be exactly the same as that of a much larger timber wolf, but the wolf will eat more before getting a bellyful, and its colon is larger to enable passage of a larger scat. Likewise, the diet and the pelletlike scats of a moose may be identical to those of a whitetail deer, except that a moose dropping is nearly twice the size of a deer scat.

Instances where scat size might not be helpful, or might be indeterminable, include early spring, when herbivores are making the transition between dead, dry foods to richer green succulents. The switch causes a bit of gastrointestinal overload until the animal's system once again adapts to metabolizing fresh greens, and during that period the bowels are likely to be loose with watery, incomplete scat deposits left sporadically along a trail, where they wash away quickly with the first rain. (See page 46.)

But while small scats may come from a large animal, large scats can come only from large creatures. A carnivore scat 1 inch in diameter probably originated from a coyote or a large bobcat, while a scat 2 inches in diameter could only have come from a wolf or mountain lion.

SIGN

Sign is a collective term for marks left on the environment by a creature as it passes from one place to another. This includes tracks, but tracks are excluded here because they're covered in greater detail elsewhere. For that reason, our discussion of sign is devoted especially to those marks that are made with some intent in mind. These disturbances are usually easy to identify because they were meant to be seen, and they can reveal a good deal about the animal that made them.

Territorial Marking

Most animals mark their territories as a warning to others who might try to usurp its resources. Scat is usually predominant as a territorial stake, but a number of other signs are also used by territorial animals wanting to advertise their presence.

Among carnivores the sign of choice is clawmarks. All dominant canids, from wolves to dogs, tend to scratch the earth with all four feet after relieving themselves, leaving a visual representation of how large they are, as well as a scent signature from interdigital glands located between the toes. Bears stand erect and scratch as high up as they can reach on a tall tree, leaving large, obvious parallel gouges that tell other bears how large and formidable it is. Cats scratch the earth after defecating in a perfunctory effort to cover the odors from their scat, but also to leave a territorial scent from interdigital glands as they scratch with claws extended and toes wide apart. Felids are also well known for their scratching posts on trees.

For animals not equipped with stout claws, there are alternative territorial markings, like the mud-and-stick scent-posts used by beavers and muskrats to lay claim to a section of shoreline. Males of the deer family scrape their antlers against trees to advertise their size and disposition, and elk are well known for the bathtub-size depressions, or wallows, they make to roll in at the edges of rivers and lakes. Even the feisty little red squirrel marks its territory with bits of pine cone, discarded after the seed has been eaten, that eventually form a considerable pile as the squirrel continues to feed in that same place day after day.

Other sign that can benefit a tracker in the field include urine. An average human nose can detect the musky odor of a rutting buck's scrape or the pungent aroma of a lynx's scent post (recognizable by probably every house cat owner) from several yards. On snow the yellow markings left by a coyote cocking its leg against a tree, or the yellow spray of a cat that backed up to the trunk to do the same, are apparent from several yards.

Some sign is inadvertent. A snake's shed skin or the feathers and scat dropped by roosting turkeys aren't left intentionally, yet they can confirm a researcher's suspicions that those animals are in the area. The furrow left by a deer as it moved through tall grasses is easy to follow, even without seeing tracks. The sliding troughs made by otters in muddy or snow-covered riverbanks are a definite clue to their presence, and the tail drag of many animals helps to identify their species and size.

A whitetail buck's "rub" made by scraping its antlers against a sapling is an example of territorial sign made during the mating season.

VOCALIZATIONS

Since the beginning of history, wide-eyed campers have been remarking about the variety of sounds they hear from the deep woods, especially at night when they can't see and most animals are most active. Sometimes, as when two beavers are squabbling about dam construction, the calls are difficult to identify as more than a series of squeals and chittering.

Some calls are distinctive, however, and learning to recognize as much about the vocal communications of a species under study can help to detect its presence, and sometimes helps to establish the travel patterns and meeting places of animals like coyotes and wolves.

Mating Calls

Calls issued during a species' breeding season are often the loudest and most distinctive because they're intended to broadcast their maker's presence over a wide area in an attempt to attract mates. The wailing yowls of male bobcats coming into heat in late winter has sent chills down the spine of probably everyone who's heard them. Follow the whistling bugle of a bull elk in autumn and you'll likely find an entire herd of courting bulls and cows.

Territorial Calls

Calls that advertise their maker's claim to a territory are normally less exuberant than mating calls. This is largely because most animals rely heavily on odors to warn others that an area is already occupied. The objective in this instance is to keep competitors out, not to draw mates in, so many animals depend on scentposts to warn away intruders while they go about their business in a near silence that alerts neither predator nor prey.

Exceptions to this general rule include pack animals like gray wolves, the dingoes of Australia, African wild dogs, and peccaries. Social species living in an environment where hunting or foraging successfully demands the strength and efficiency of a team tend to keep track of one another through vocalizations. This is especially seen among large canids, when the alpha animal initiates a kind of pep rally that serves to gather pack members together, gets them worked up about the night's hunt, and loudly informs potential intruders that they should stay away.

Food Calls

Solitary animals such as bears, cougars, and owls have no need of vocalizations that tell others of their species where to find food, but social animals ranging from ravens and turkey vultures to gray wolves and coyotes have loud calls that are meant to attract others of their group. A lone wolf that gets lucky enough to claim a deer already dead, or one seriously injured by a car or hunter, will communicate its success to other pack members with a long, monotonal "lone wolf" howl that all of them recognize as a demand to come here.

In a few cases, food calls serve an interspecies purpose. A raven that spies an injured deer foundering in snow can neither kill the animal nor tear through its tough hide to get at the meat after it dies. What that raven can and does do is call in other ravens, who then circle the wounded deer while making raucous high-pitched cries. Predators, most notably coyotes and wolves, have learned to keep an eye skyward and an ear cocked for flocks of these birds, as well as turkey vultures and crows that behave in the same way, because their gatherings indicate the presence of an easy meal. The larger predator then opens the carcass and consumes the meatiest portions, leaving plenty of easy pickings to reward the birds whose cries led it there.

SCENTS

The olfactory world of most wild animals is a dimension that we humans can only believe in because it's so far beyond our sensory frame of reference as to seem supernatural. There have been instances of blind whitetails surviving in apparent good health because they could detect and interpret objects in their environment by odor alone, even learning to recognize how close or far those objects are from its nose by the concentration of scent emitted from them. My own experiences with captive gray wolves has shown that they can smell a piece of cheese in my closed pocket at more than 50 yards, and turkey vultures are said to have the olfactory power to detect a deer-size carcass from 10 miles by scent alone.

The few smell receptors in a human's short nasal passages, further dulled by exposure to numerous artificial odors and pollution, can't comprehend the olfactory aspect of an animal's world from a sensory standpoint. But we do a know a few things about the way some scents exuded by animals correlate to behavior in themselves and to other animals within its territory.

Territorial Scents

Territorial scents, usually in the form of urine-borne hormones or glandular secretions from the anal region, are often undetectable by the human nose from even a few feet. Unlike sexual scents whose purpose is to bring in prospective mates from afar, territorial scents serve essentially as a fence that warns potential competitors not to cross this line.

Cats are the easiest to track down by odor, but determining if a male coyote recently cocked its leg against a tree in summer may require pressing one's nose close to the base of a suspect tree and inhaling deeply. Likewise, smelling for urine in the immediate area of a whitetail bed can reveal the animal's sex because does tend to step to one side to urinate upon rising, while bucks usually urinate directly onto the bed.

Male canids especially tend to urinate as high up on a tree as they can in an effort to make themselves appear as tall as possible to potential rivals. Whitetail bucks carry information about their size, sexual disposition, and perhaps more, in their urine, and it's probable that other species do the same.

Mating Scents

Odors emitted by an animal for the purpose of attracting a mate are frequently strong enough for a person to smell from several yards or more, because their intent is to broadcast the sexual availability of their maker over as wide an area as possible.

Nearly all sexual scents share a strong musky characteristic that has been described as skunklike by some and like the smell of house cat urine by others. Either way, mating scentposts are often fragrant enough to permit finding them by scent alone.

Danger Scents

Not much is known about the proverbial smell of fear except that it is indeed a reality in the animal world. What little hard information that exists has been established mostly about whitetail deer, because retail sales of hunting aids to whitetail hunters has become an industry profitable enough to fund the research and development of new products.

It is believed that interdigital glands located between a deer's cloven hooves exude a hormone that fellow deer recognize as fright. This would give other whitetails a heads-up that danger was recently there, and cause them to avoid that area in case a predator might still be lying there in wait.

The same kind of interdigital excretion can be seen in the sweaty palms of humans who are afraid, although we can't smell it, and it seems likely that prey animals especially would benefit from an ability to leave a trail of fear warning others of its kind that danger lurks in the area.

Camouflage Scents

Probably every dog owner has seen his or her pet rolling exuberantly back and forth on something we wish they hadn't touched. Rotting fish carcasses are preferred by all breeds, but sometimes scat or garbage also triggers the rolling behavior among wild canids and an occasional wild or domestic cat. One likely theory is that this behavior, which is common to carnivorous mammals, is meant to fool the short attention spans of most prey herbivores into believing that the hunter which is slowly moving in for the kill is already dead, and therefore not a threat.

CHAPTER 2

TAXONOMY AND DENTAL CLASSIFICATION

AN EXPLANATION OF TAXONOMIC PRINCIPLES
Genus and Species: The Linnaean Binomial System

To understand animals, one needs first to understand the logical progression of their relationships to one another. The creation of our current, but continually evolving, system of classifying all life on planet Earth is credited to Dr. Carl Linnaeus (1707–78) of Sweden. Before Linnaeus, classification was a disorganized affair, with plants and animals named for the botanists who discovered them, and sometimes for friends or relatives. Further confusing things were sometimes superstitious myths like the Doctrine of Signatures, which postulated that plants were designed by God to resemble the medicinal use for which He had provided them. A plant with a uterus-shaped flower became known as wombwort, and was used to assist women in the pains of childbirth, although it appears to have no real analgesic qualities.

So it went, with living things being almost haphazardly classified with no established standards of organization, until Linnaeus perfected his *Systema Naturae* in 1758. In the *Linnaean binomial system,* which is still valid today, living things are grouped by shared characteristics from least specific to most specific, ending with a precise definition of what an animal is with a two-part name that's always in Latin, the common language of biologists worldwide. This two-part name consists of a genus name, like *Canis* (dog), followed by a species name, such as *familiaris* (domesticated). A mountain lion, for example, is known as *Felis concolor,* with the term *Felis* denoting that it's a kind of cat.

Felis sylvestris is also a cat, but the second part of its name distinguishes the 10-pound house cat from its 200-pound wild cousin.

Linnaeus's binomial system of naming organisms by a standardized common grouping made it much easier to keep track of the many species that could not easily be broken down further into categories. When a researcher sees the word *Mustela* preceding a species' name, he knows that it must be a member of the weasel family, even if he isn't familiar with that particular species. Likewise, *Lepus* tells a biologist the animal is a hare, and *Sciurus* identifies an animal as being one of the tree squirrels.

Higher Classifications: Kingdoms, Phyla, Classes, Orders, and Families

Perhaps even more important, Linnaeus standardized the higher, more general groups. In the Linnaean system, genera, such as *Felis* and *Canis*, are classified in the families Felidae and Canidae, which includes all cats and all dogs, even if a particular species' genus name doesn't indicate that. For example, *Canis latrans,* the coyote, is immediately recognizable as a member of the dog family by its genus name, but the gray fox's scientific name, *Urocyon cinereoargenteus,* gives no indication that the animal is a canid until you see that family name Canidae.

Families are further classified into orders. Because both canids and felids subsist primarily on meat, and both prey on other species to get it, they fall into the order Carnivora, the order of meat eaters in mammals.

Orders such as Carnivora and Artiodactyla (cloven-hooved animals that include pigs, cattle, and deer) are grouped into classes, which in this instance would be Mammalia, the class of warm-blooded animals that possess hair or fur, bear live young, and nurse them with milk.

Classes are further grouped into a phylum (plural, *phyla*), whose members share only the most generic commonalities. All mammals, for example, are members of the phylum Chordata, the phylum of animals that possess a spinal cord; but so too are reptiles, amphibians, and fish.

Phyla are further grouped into kingdoms, of which there are five. These consist of Monera, Protista, Fungi, Plantae, and Animalia. This work concerns itself solely with Animalia—the kingdom of so-called higher animals, those with an actual brain, nervous system, and some form of limbs to propel them from one habitat to another. (For a brief description of the other kingdoms, see the Glossary on page 411.)

Kingdoms, in their turn, fall into a realm known as the three domains of living things. This broadest of biological categories includes the domains of Archaea, Bacteria, and Eukarya. All plants and animals fall into the domain Eukarya: living things that are comprised of multiple, usually specialized, cells that have nuclei. (See the Glossary on page 411 for more information.)

Lumpers versus Splitters

Most recently there has been a division among the ranks of biologists, paleontologists, and other researchers over whether the standard categories of life given here are specific enough. The two sides of this argument are known loosely as lumpers and splitters.

Splitters would like to segregate the existing categories of life into even more specific groups, based on new discoveries—many of which have only been made possible by new technologies. For example, the category of order by itself could be split further to include subcategories like parvorder, nanorder, hyporder, minorder, suborder, and infraorder. In some instances, further subdivision seems to make sense, but often, the practice reaches the point of making taxonomic classification confusing and overcomplicated. We know that the red fox will sometimes be born with a black, gray, or mottled red-and-black coat, but should these color variations be considered simple aberrations, or are both the black and mottled coated individuals representative of two separate subspecies?

Lumpers usually want to maintain the status quo of taxonomic identification, claiming that further divisions are meaningless. Unfortunately, some of the more extreme lumpers are disillusioned with the Linnaean system as a whole and would like to abolish any category above genus. A few would even like to do away with genus, which would of course also dissolve Linnaeus's binomial system of species classification.

Beyond the lumper-splitter issue are numerous other taxonomic disagreements about which animal belongs in which category. The opossum has fifty teeth, more than any other land animal on Earth, and it possesses defined canines for killing prey and rending flesh into edible portions. Yet opossums are also marsupials, and have been deemed different enough to be classed in the order of Didelphimorphia, whereas it could be argued that they more rightly belong in the order Carnivora.

Perhaps the bottom line is that when a researcher is dealing with living organisms that are not only capable of evolving physically to meet the demands of changing environments, but that *must* do so at some point to continue existing, hard and fast rules are difficult—even impossible—to establish. But some sort of guide is necessary to keep the huge number of obviously different animals on this planet in a perspective that follows a logical progression—even if that logic may be a bit flawed at one point or another. The standard Linnaean system of taxonomy is currently the best guide available, and for that reason it is used to classify all of the animals described in this book.

PRINCIPLES OF DENTAL CLASSIFICATION

Trackers frequently find the bones and skulls of wild animals that have died, and these remains can reveal a great deal about the area in which they were found. Thick bones that have been crushed to get at the fatty marrow inside tell of large carnivores with long, powerful jaws, which usually rules out members of the cat family. Bones with chisel-shaped gouges in their outer surfaces reveal the gnawings of a rodent in search of calcium and other nutrients contained in bone, and the size of these gnawings are indicative of the size of the animal that made them.

None of these skeletal clues is more revealing than the dental structure in an animal's skull. Fundamentally, there are four basic types of teeth in the jaws of toothed animals: incisors, canines, premolars, and molars. The primary purpose of teeth is for rending large chunks of food into smaller pieces that can be swallowed and then passed through an animal's digestive system. (In many species, particularly carnivores, some teeth are also modified to serve as weapons for holding and killing prey.)

The purpose of a tooth can usually be determined by its shape. Sharply pointed canines, or fangs, aren't found in herbivores whose front teeth need to be shaped for cutting or tearing vegetation. Likewise, flat-topped grinding molars whose purpose is to reduce tough plant fibers to a digestible mass won't be found in the jaws of meat eaters. Modern monotremes (the order of egg-laying mammals, like the platypus) differ from most mammals by growing permanent adult teeth, without going through the temporary milk teeth stage.

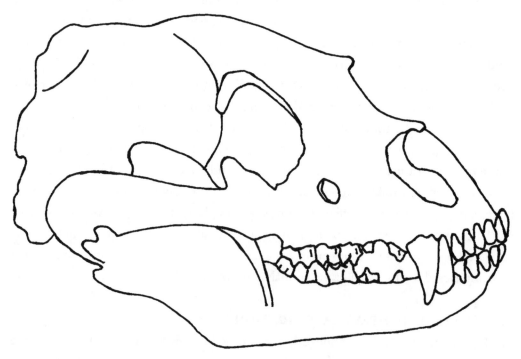

Black bear (Ursus americanus) *skull showing this omnivore's multifunctional jaw structure, with powerful mandibles, long canines for killing, strong incisors for biting, sharp carnassials for cutting, and heavy molars for crushing.*

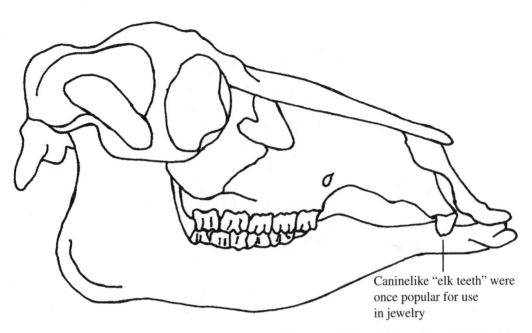

Caninelike "elk teeth" were once popular for use in jewelry

Wapiti, or American Elk, skull. Note lack of upper incisors, which is typical of deer and cows. Vegetation is pinned between lower incisors and hard upper palate, then torn free.

CHARACTERISTICS OF TEETH

The number and location of teeth in an individual's jaws can identify the family to which it belongs, and often its individual species. By identifying teeth in the four sections, or quadrants, of the upper left, upper right, lower left, and lower right sides of the jaws, a biologist can determine not only its family and species, but relative age and state of health.

Incisors

These are the most anterior, or frontal, teeth. Incisors are usually simple teeth, though the crown is sometimes lobed. And in most species, incisors are used as pincers for grasping or picking, both in feeding and in grooming.

Incisors have been modified by nature to serve a number of functions. Most successful, in terms of the number of species that have them, is an enlarged chisel design that works well for gnawing and scraping. Chisel incisors are often generally reduced in number, compared with other mammals—usually occurring in pairs that are bordered on either side by a toothless gap called a diastema. Chisel incisors are a feature of rodents and lagomorphs (rabbits and hares). They also appear in some primates like the aye–aye.

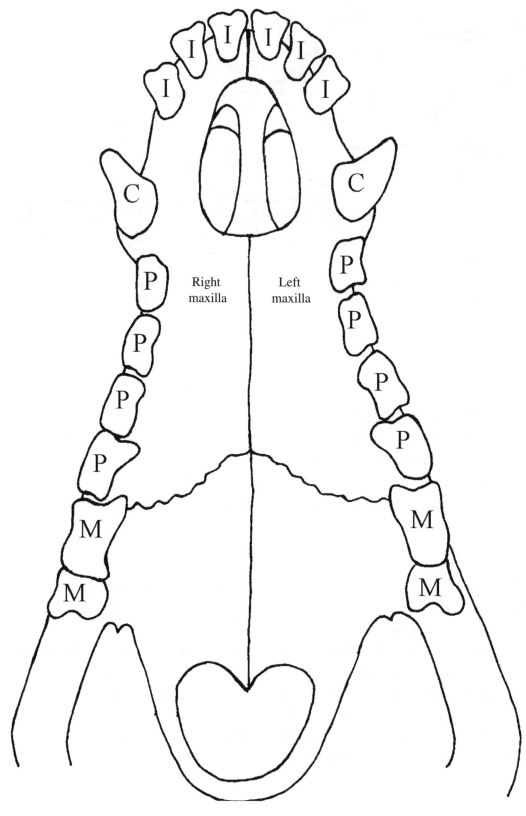

Right maxilla

Left maxilla

Typical mammalian dental structure. Dog (Canis familiaris) *shown. I = Incisor, C = Canine, P = Premolar, M = Molar.*

Other modifications of incisor teeth include the scalpel-like slicing incisors of vampire bats, an elephant's tusks, the shovel-shaped lower incisors of hippopotamuses, and the lateral third incisors of bears, which resemble smaller, stabbing canine teeth.

Canines

These teeth are normally located in the corners of the dental quadrants, at either side of the incisor rows. Some animal families, such as their namesake canids, have four elongated canines at each corner of the upper and lower jaws for holding and killing prey animals. In some species, particularly male baboons, the canines are spectacularly oversized for use both as weapons and as displays of status. Herbivorous hooved animals like deer and bovids have only two small, incisorlike canines in the corners of the lower jaw, while rodents and lagomorphs lack canines altogether.

When present, upper canines are the first teeth in the maxillae (the two bones that form the upper jaw in mammals). They tend to range from moderately long to very long, usually consisting of a single cusp (point) and just one root. Configurations range from the daggerlike, piercing fangs of the cat family to the stouter, blunter gouging designs that raccoons and bears use to tear open decaying logs and get at the insects inside.

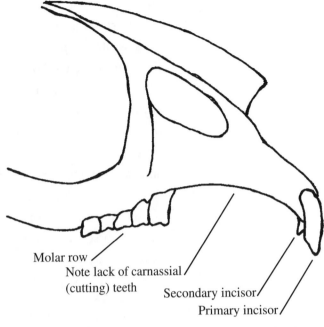

Molar row

Note lack of carnassial (cutting) teeth

Secondary incisor

Primary incisor

Lagomorph (rabbits, hares) upper skull showing dental structure.

Premolars

The premolars lie immediately to the rear of the canines. They can vary greatly in size and shape, from a tiny peg in shrews to massive crushing teeth in the jaws of a wolf. Premolars are usually smaller and simpler than the molars that follow them, and they are distinguished from molars because premolars are deciduous, beginning in young animals as milk teeth that are lost, then replaced by permanent teeth at adulthood.

Premolars differ in shape and function in different types of animals. A coyote's premolars are sharp and come together with a scissorlike action that can cut tough hide. This design, known as *carnassial* teeth, is nearly universal among carnivorous mammals. The premolars of a bison are comparatively flat for grinding coarse plant fibers into digestible pulp.

Molars

The most posterior (rearward) teeth in the jaws of mammals are molars. As with premolars, they vary in size, shape, and function with the species of their owners, but are always the most massive teeth in a dental structure. In herbivores, the molars are flattened grinding instruments that work to render tough plant fibers into a digestible mass, while the molars of carnivorous species have sharply pointed cusps and are designed for crushing bone.

Molars are the last teeth to erupt in an animal's jaw, and their appearance is usually delayed until an individual reaches adult size. For that reason, the presence or lack of molars is a reliable and fairly accurate indicator of an individual's age. Whitetail deer, for example, grow molars in their second year, so lack of them tells a researcher that the animal under study is a yearling.

Molars can also provide a good estimate of the age of an adult animal based on the amount of wear they exhibit. In general, adult molars remain clean, with sharply pointed or squared cusps, for the first 2 or 3 years after their emergence. As more years pass, these teeth become increasingly worn, chipped or broken, and duller on the edges, and they take on progressively browner stains from plaque.

PART TWO

COMMONLY TRACKED ANIMALS
OF NORTH AMERICA

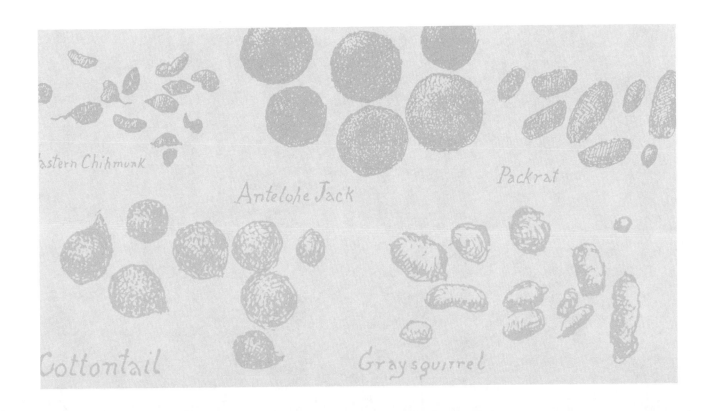

CHAPTER 3

HOOVED ANIMALS

THE DEER FAMILY (FAMILY CERVIDAE)

The family Cervidae, or deer family, are ungulates (hooved animals) of the order Artiodactyla (hooved animals that have an even number of toes). All cervids have a split hoof, which is actually a pair of modified, heavily nailed toes in front and a pair of small mostly useless toes, called dewclaws, located slightly above them at the rear of the foot. All species leave a relatively heart-shaped track that's split in the middle, where the hoof halves meet, and dewclaws may print behind the hooves in softer terrain like snow, mud, or wet sand. All deer are herbivores, and none have upper incisors, only a hard upper palate that causes them to rip food plants loose by pinning them between lower teeth and palate and pulling, rather than neatly snipping them off like a rodent or hare. All have an efficient digestive system that can extract nurients from rough vegetable fibers, and only caribou are known to migrate with the seasons for any great distance.

All males, and a small percentage of females, grow antlers in early spring. Antlers are covered with "velvet," a thin hairlike skin that nourishes and grows antlers until they mature in late October, and is then shed by rubbing against trees. Polished, mature antlers are used in ritual mating battles between males in contests for mates. Serious injuries and a rare fatality can result from these battles, but they're essentially shoving matches, where the objective is to push an opponent's head to the ground, whereupon the vanquished contender will quit and leave to find a receptive female that's less well-guarded.

Cervids are reproductively geared to lose at least half of their populations every year, and need to have their numbers diminished by that much to insure that plenty of

New World Moose.

food exists for all. All members of the deer family, primarily the young, the old, and the sickly, are preyed on by wolves, pumas, bears, and occasionally a large, usually very hungry, bobcat or pack of coyotes, and cervid reproductive rates have evolved against them to precisely match losses with increases.

But large predators are unwelcome around human habitations, while whitetails in particular have learned to regard suburbia as a safe haven. The upsurge in whitetail numbers since the 1940s has been followed by an apparently weakened herd that seems susceptible to a number of diseases that were formerly not seen in deer, like Bovine Tuberculosis, Chronic Wasting Disease, and probably Bovine Spongiform Encephalitis (Mad Cow Disease).

New World Moose (Alces alces)

The largest member of the deer family, the American moose is actually the same animal as the elk found in Finland, Sweden, and across northern Russia. It was apparently misnamed because the first explorers to the New World reported seeing huge elk, and those who came later to officially catalog them applied that name to the first really large deer they encountered, the wapiti. The wapiti was thereafter known as the American elk, while the true American elk became known as the moose.

Geographic Range

In North America, moose are found throughout the northern United States bordering Canada, throughout southern Canada and into Alaska, and downward along the Rocky Mountains into Colorado.

Habitat

Moose prefer coniferous forests with plenty of water nearby. Pines offer year-round protection from driving winds and snow, while river willows, elkslip, and other aquatic browse can usually be found in abundance along riverbanks and shorelines. The winter browsing of moose herds, which includes softwood bark and conifer buds, can negatively affect the regrowth of those trees in places that have been clear-cut for timber.

During the blackfly and mosquito hatches of spring and early summer, moose in mountain country tend to migrate upward to higher elevations where rivers and ponds are swollen with melting snow, sunlit meadows are lush with vegetation, and stronger breezes keep biting insects from landing on a victim.

In winter, moose stay in pretty much the same areas they summered in, moving only as conditions demand to find a location that offers adequate protection from weather, an ample supply of food until spring, and water. Mountain moose move lower to protected valleys, and forest moose gravitate toward secluded beaver ponds and floodings where spring-fed inlets never freeze entirely and there are always willow twigs and bark to feed on.

Physical Characteristics

Mass: Moose are the largest deer in the world, weighing 1,400 pounds or more at maturity. Cows are roughly 10% smaller than bulls.

Body: Shoulder height 5 to 6 feet, occasionally taller. Body length 8 to 10 feet from tip of nose to tail. Horselike body with long legs, thick rump, and broad muscular back. Heads of bulls, and a small percentage of cows, are adorned with palmated antlers from early spring to the following winter, when old antlers, which can span more than 4 feet across, are shed and new ones begin to grow in their place.

The face of a moose is distinctive and easily recognizable, with a long thick muzzle that's nearly the same diameter as the animal's head out to its big overlapping nose and large drooping lower lip. A fold of loose skin, called a dewlap, hangs beneath the jaws of mature males, becoming more elongated and tail-like as its owner ages. Large, normally erect ears are prominent and pointed, but may not be visible behind the large antlers of an adult bull.

Moose have excellent senses of smell and hearing, but their vision is very nearsighted. These traits aren't unlike those of other deer that live in a close environment where acute long-range eyesight is of less importance than an ability to smell or hear potential predators well in advance of their arrival.

Tail: Thin and relatively inconspicuous in relation to other deer species, similar to that of a domestic cow but shorter, with a length of about 8 inches.

Tracks: Moose tracks are easy to locate and identify on most terrain. Being very heavy and having a hard hoof, they tend to leave clear tracks in the most packed soil. The split-heart shaped hoofprint is very similar to that of the whitetail, and unlike the more circular and concave wapiti track, but the hooves are nearly twice the size of a large whitetail's, measuring 4 to 5 inches long, 7 to 8 inches if dewclaws are included in measurements. Note, however, that moose walk weight-forward, like all deer, and on hardpacked dirt roads or trails only the foremost portions of hooves leave an impression, resulting in shorter tracks that can be mistaken for those of a whitetail.

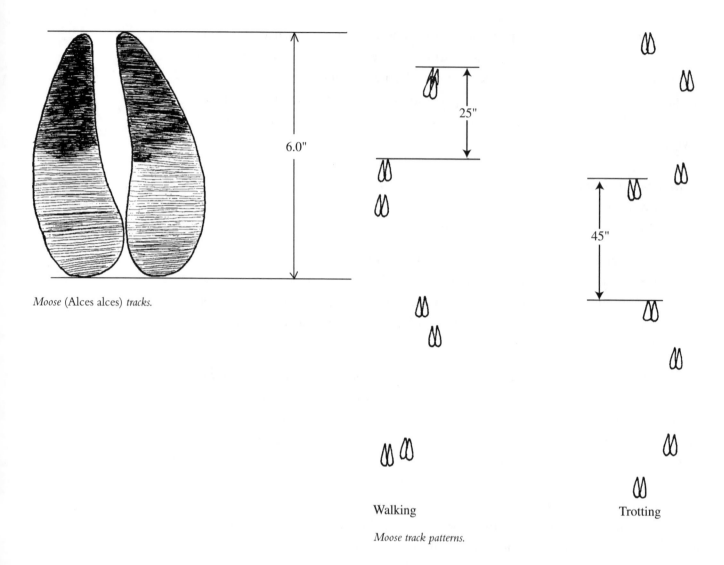

Moose (Alces alces) *tracks.*

Walking

Trotting

Moose track patterns.

Scat: Normal moose scat is typical of the deer family, consisting of packed brown pellets that are usually egg- or acorn-shaped, ranging in length from 1 to almost 2 inches, or twice the size of a whitetail or mule deer.

Variations in moose scat occur with changes in diet, with masses of soft manure that re-semble a cowpie when an animal is making the spring transition between eating bark and woody shrubs to green succulents, or when it has been feeding at the bait pile of a whitetail hunter.

A unique scat configuration is the somewhat mushroom-shaped dropping that appears most common in moose that have fed on long-fibered grasses. No other animal has a scat like this one, and finding a mushroom scat is proof of a moose having been there.

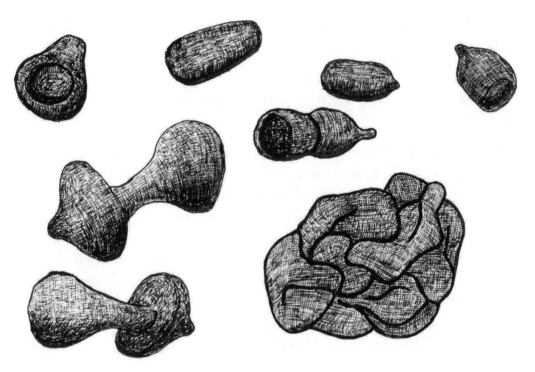

Variations of moose scats.

Coloration: One color, no apparent markings. Short fur, dark brown, sometimes nearly black, tending to become grizzled (interspersed with gray) as the animal ages.

Sign: Being so large, moose leave numerous identifiable marks on the environment where they live. The paths they plow through willow and dogwood browsing thickets are obvious from the way even larger shrubs have been pushed aside by a tall, massive body to form a V-shaped trail. Shrubs and plants at trailside are often broken and up-rooted when bulls begin practicing with their antlers in late summer and early autumn, and during that period there may be scraps of discarded antler velvet in evidence at these places. Moose beds are also easily identifiable as horse-size impressions of compacted plants and soil that have been compressed under massive weight for a period of time.

While moose aren't so fond of wallowing in mud as elk, their entry and exit points into a mucky bog to find succulent water plants is often marked by a visible trough that can be as wide as the animal's body, depending on how deeply it sunk in the mud. Following the trail to firmer ground often yields cast-quality hoofprints.

The most obvious winter sign of moose (and elk) are the gnawings they leave in the smooth bark of poplar, aspen, and young birch trees that serves as one of their winter foods. In moose wintering grounds, or yards, these trees are heavily scarred in large areas of 10 inches or more, becoming scabbed over with rough black bark as the wound heals.

Vocalizations: Like most wild creatures, moose are generally silent as they conduct their daily business, moving slowly through their territories with no particular place they need to be.

When a moose does vocalize, as with a cow calling for a calf to join her, the voice is a soft lowing sound, much like the mooing of a domestic cow. A cow mother may also emit a sharp huffing sound or grunt to warn intruders, animal and human alike, that they've approached too closely and she's feeling threatened.

During the autumn mating season, or rut, moose become more vocal, especially amorous bulls. During the rut, males are loudly boisterous and virtually fearless, and have been known to charge people, livestock, automobiles, and at least one railroad locomotive. Bull moose in heat may be heard grunting like hogs, bellowing like a domestic bull, huffing, and mooing. Cows and immature moose are less noisy, continuing to communicate mostly through soft lowing sounds.

Lifespan: About 10 years in the wild, up to 27 years in captivity.

Diet

An adult moose requires about 10 pounds of edible plant material every day. Like all ruminants, moose possess a complex and efficient digestive system that allows them to process and use rough vegetable fiber as food.

During the summer months moose are replacing fat burned during the previous winter, and the animals are most often found near open water. Browse found along the shorelines of remote lakes, beaver ponds, and slow rivers includes pond lily, water lily, marsh marigold, horsetail, and rough grasses. I've also observed moose near the Mosquito River in Michigan's Upper Peninsula eating quantities of jewelweed (*Impatiens capensis*) tops, a plant known best to us as an effective fungicide against athlete's foot and a good remedy for poison ivy. Moose can swim well, but their long horselike legs also permit them access to marshy places with several feet of muck, where the preferred water plants grow thickest.

In winter moose eat a rougher diet consisting primarily of willow and red-osier dogwood twigs, poplar and aspen bark, and the shoots of woody plants. Long legs allow moose to wade through snows too deep to be negotiated by shorter deer to reach marshy shorelines and snowblown meadows where the best winter browse is found.

Mating Habits

Moose become sexually mature at 2 years, and mating among them occurs from September through October, with each cow remaining in heat for about 30 days, or until she becomes pregnant within that period. Cows begin the rut by giving off strong sexual pheromones in their urine and from tarsal glands inside the knees of the hind legs. To reinforce the invitation to mate, cows moo more frequently while in heat to alert bulls that might not have gotten the message.

Male moose tend to become extremely territorial and possessive during their time in the rut. Increased levels of testosterone causes their muscles to swell, especially around the neck, and their behavior can become hostile, even dangerous, toward intruders large or small. Researchers should always keep a safe distance from antlered bulls, especially in autumn.

After impregnation, cow moose undergo an 8-month gestation period before giving birth to one or two calves in April or May, with twins being an indication that food has been abundant. If the cow is unhealthy or underweight, she may spontaneously abort the developing calf during the winter, a phenomenon not unusual in nature, where offspring can be more easily replaced than fertile mothers.

Moose calves are born gangly and clumsy, but within 2 days they can outrun a fast man. They can keep up with their mother's normal pace by 3 weeks, and are weaned at about 5 months, in September or October. Wolves, bears, and mountain lions prey on young calves, seeking to inflict a fatal wound to the offspring before its mother, who is too large for any but the largest and hungriest predators to tackle, can come to its defense. Left with a calf that's fatally wounded or dead, the cow has no option except to go about her business, leaving the calf's carcass to the waiting predators.

Moose calves stay with their mother for at least a year after birth, until the next spring's calves are born. Calves lack the spots that are characteristic of most offspring in the deer family, being some shade of darker brown from birth to death.

Behavior

Moose are most active during the hours of dawn and dusk (crepuscular), with more nocturnal habits in places where they might be likely to encounter humans by day. In wilder places moose may be active at all times of day, especially during the autumn rutting season.

Moose bedding areas are typical of most deer, which prefer secure thickets in regularly used places where the vegetation offers plenty of concealment, and an abundance of deer scents helps to confuse a predator's nose. Whenever possible, bedding thickets will be close to or within feeding places, including dense growths of river willow, dogwoods, and poplar saplings.

Except for the rutting period, adult moose are solitary animals, keeping to themselves as they feed quietly along shorelines and in nearby forests or glades. Exceptions include females with calves (which are usually noticeably smaller in stature than their mothers), and an occasional incidence of two or more feeding in a particularly lush spot where there's too much food for one moose to eat.

In North America, moose are generally not migratory, but in Europe, particularly across Russia, moose have been known to journey as far as 200 miles between summer and winter habitats. They're strong swimmers, able to cross swollen rivers, and their long legs permit travel in deep snow, but moose normally travel alone, as opposed to migrating herds of caribou, bison, and pronghorns.

Moose can be very dangerous to humans. Mothers are extremely protective of their calves, and with a running speed that can exceed 35 miles per hour they present a danger not only to people, but to even large predators. Sharp front hooves, used to hammer those a moose perceives as enemies, are the primary weapons of either sex, although rutting bulls have been known to scoop up and toss humans who've gotten too close. One photographer on Lake Superior's Isle Royale National Park proved this point when he was forced to spend 3 long winter days and nights in the branches of a tree before the cow he'd offended grew tired of keeping him there and left the area with her calf.

Despite their solitary nature and a potential for being dangerous, moose have been domesticated for meat and milk, and in places like Yellowstone National Park, moose herds have been conditioned to live together in winter by handouts of hay and other food from local farmers.

Bull elk (wapiti).

Wapiti, or American Elk (*Cervus elaphus*)

A close cousin of the European red deer, or roebuck, the wapiti is the second largest deer in the world. Elk were successfully transplanted in eastern states from existing herds in the western United States, most notably Yellowstone National Park, on three occasions throughout the twentieth century, after unrestricted hunting led to extirpation over much of their original range. With little fear of predators, elk make easy targets, and native populations were hunted to extinction in Indiana (1830), Ohio (1838), New York (1847), and Pennsylvania (1867) before hunting seasons and game laws were enacted to preserve remaining herds. Unfortunately, these preventative measures came too late to save the eastern subspecies of forest-dwelling elk, *Cervus elaphus canadensis*, which is now extinct. Today elk are not endangered, thanks to good management, and in large part to their financial value as a game animal.

Geographic Range

Wapiti were once common throughout much of the Northern Hemisphere, but today large populations are found only in the western United States, from Canada through the eastern Rocky Mountains to New Mexico. A small herd of approximately 900 animals also exists in the Pigeon River Valley section of Michigan's Mackinac State Forest, and these seem to be expanding their range.

Habitat

Just as whitetail deer gravitate toward dense thickets where being nearsighted isn't a disadvantage, so do elk prefer open prairies and mature woodlands where their relatively good vision permits detection of impending danger by sight as well as scent. After centuries of unrestricted hunting that decimated the species from much of its original range, elk have learned to become comfortable in dense unbroken forests, too. Elk have a greater tendency to migrate long distances in search of fresh territory than do whitetail or mule deer, but migrations are only as far as is required to find a suitable place to live.

Physical Characteristics

Mass: 900 to more than 1,100 pounds. Males about 20% larger than females.

Body: Shoulder height 4.5 to 5 feet. Six to more than 9 feet in length. Stocky, more barrel-shaped than a whitetail, with muscular humps at the shoulders and flank. Hindquarters typically stand several inches higher than the shoulders, giving the elk a jacked-up silhouette.

Tail: Short, surrounded by a dark-bordered light brown to blonde colored patch that covers most of the rump in an inverted teardrop shape.

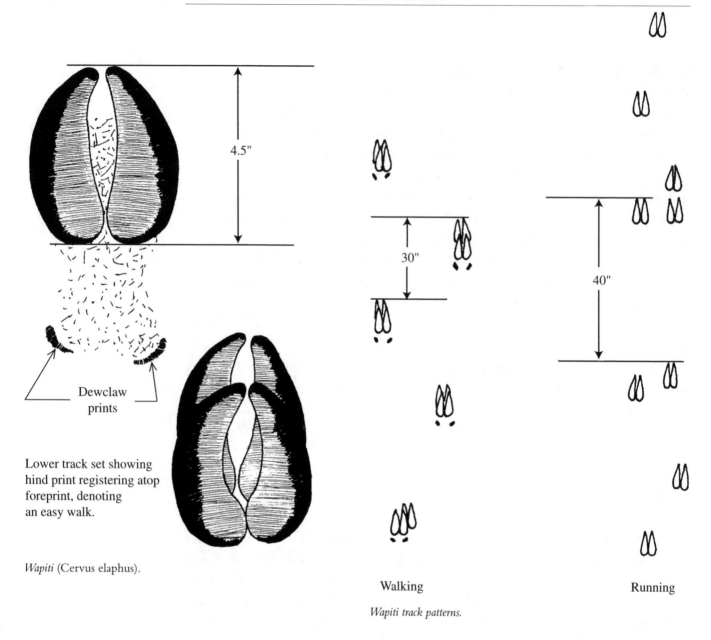

4.5"

Dewclaw
prints

Lower track set showing
hind print registering atop
foreprint, denoting
an easy walk.

Wapiti (Cervus elaphus).

30"

40"

Walking

Running

Wapiti track patterns.

Tracks: 4 to 4.5 inches long, discounting dewclaws. Cloven, but much rounder than those of a whitetail or mule deer. Hooves tend to be concave, which results in tracks that are more deeply impressed around their outer perimeters than in the center.

Scat: Dark brown pellets, sometimes acorn-shaped, 0.75-inch to 1-inch long.

Coloration: The wapiti was known by Indians as the "ghost of the forest." Both cows and bulls have a dark brown head, neck, and legs, with a lighter, almost blonde body that stands out when the animal is in shadows, and lends it an almost ghostly appearance during twilight hours. Both sexes have a prominent blonde rump patch that provides a visual beacon for herd members to follow when running, especially calves following behind their mothers.

Sign: The most obvious of elk sign is the species' signature mud wallow. These bathtub-size depressions are created by the animals as they roll back and forth in muddy earth near streams, lakes, or marshes to dislodge shed fur and parasites, or just to cool off on a hot day. Suspected wallows can be positively identified by the presence of light-colored hairs and tracks in the mud within and around them.

Like moose, wapiti also feed on the smooth bark of poplar, aspen, and cottonwood trees during winter months, leaving the trunks scarred with their bottom-teeth-only gnawings. As these scrapes heal over the following years, they become covered with a rough black bark "scab" that contrasts against the tree's smooth, lighter colored bark.

Vocalizations: Best known among elk voices is the autumn "bugle" call of a mature rutting bull. This very loud, high-pitched call, intended to be heard by receptive cows over long distances, begins as a low grunt, then abruptly becomes a hollow squeal that spans several seconds and repeats two or three times.

Breeding male wapiti can also make coarse grunting, almost growling, sounds that are reminiscent of domestic cattle. These calls are heard only between elk bulls, particularly during the rutting season when they're vying with one another for mates.

The alarm call used by either sex is a piercing squeal, heard most often from mothers that believe their calves are in danger.

Other wapiti voices are less notable. A low, cowlike mooing between cows and their calves serves to keep them close to one another, and pairs of cows will occasionally box with their front hooves while making softer squealing or grunting sounds.

Lifespan: 8 to 10 years in the wild, longer in captivity.

Diet

Although a strict vegetarian, the elk's diet is varied enough to give it numerous food options. In summer, they eat most types of grasses and forbs in open country, marshland plants like marsh marigold, and its namesake elkslip. In winter the diet becomes rougher and more fibrous, even woody, including the bark, twigs, and buds of aspen, poplar, beech, cottonwood, basswood, staghorn sumac, cedar, and most evergreens.

Elk are true ruminants, meaning that they feed on vegetation, then retire to a usually concealed resting place where the partially digested "cud" in their primary stomach is regurgitated to be rechewed and broken down further into usable nutrients. This typically cervid characteristic is also seen in bovids, like domestic cattle and bison.

Like other deer, and most animals, elk are especially active during the twilight hours at dawn and dusk. Human presence may dictate that they feed primarily by night then sleep and ruminate under cover by day, but elk that are left undisturbed tend to be daytime grazers, and may spend all of their time in the same place.

Mating Habits

Mating season for wapiti coincides with that of other deer, beginning in late August through September with a gathering of mature bulls and cows, peaking in October and November, when the actual mating season occurs. Both sexes reach sexual maturity at 16 months, but bulls less than 2 years old, or bulls that are physically less than prime, will probably not mate due to competition from stronger males.

Although it seems that bulls initiate the rut by bugling loudly to attract receptive cows, the cows actually start the mating period by emitting pheromonal scents. A wandering bull seeking out its own territory might attract young cows to itself, thereby establishing a new herd, but it appears that more often males will travel to females. Bull elk are known for the harems they gather, but cows generally play a passive role in courtship rituals, and harems are usually maternal families consisting of a dominant female and her offspring. A typical harem consists of one bull, six adult cows, and four calves.

Like other deer, courtship battles between rutting elk are typically shoving matches in which the competing males lock antlers and attempt to shove one another's head to the ground, whereupon the weaker animal submits and withdraws to seek out a mate elsewhere. The objective isn't to harm an opponent, although injuries sometimes occur when a pair of half-ton bulls exert all of their considerable strength against one another.

Bull elk mate with as many cows as possible, then withdraw at the end of the rut. Gestation for impregnated females lasts 8 to 9 months, with a single 35-pound spotted calf being born in April or May. If mothers are healthy and food is abundant, cows might have twins, but this is unusual.

Calves and mothers live separately from the family herd for about 2 weeks, and calves are weaned at about 60 days. Probably due to their low reproductive rate, cows are exceptionally protective of calves. Predation by wolves and bears is common, but few less powerful carnivores are willing to brave the sharp hooves of a protective mother elk. Coyotes, and even eagles, have been blamed for preying on elk calves because they've been seen feeding on carcasses, but healthy elk calves have little to fear from them.

Male calves leave their mothers at sexual maturity, if not voluntarily, then by banishment, to prevent inbreeding that might weaken the gene pool. Females may stay with the family herd for their entire lives.

Behavior

The most social of deer, wapiti spend their lives in the company of their own kind. Except for the mating season, they normally run in same-sex herds of males and females that may number from just a few to several hundred. The "bachelor" herds get along well among themselves and are willing to accept wandering strangers—i.e., young bulls ejected from their maternal herd—into their company. There's no apparent hierarchy among them, and no animosity except during the autumn rut.

Wapiti herd consisting entirely of non-breeding cows.

Cows are a bit less social, and despite the often majestic appearance of bulls, the dominant animal in every gathering of elk in every season is a female. Cow and bachelor herds frequently share the same feeding and bedding areas, but the sexes do not socialize outside of the rut. If alarmed, a gathering of elk will split into two distinctly same-sex herds as the animals run to safety.

Dominant cows are more territorial than bulls at all times of year, protecting the feeding areas they require to nourish their family herds from migrating cows with flailing front hooves. Territorial battles between cows aren't common, but the herd matriarch will protect her claimed area against any usurper, and fights are often more violent than mating contests among bulls.

Whitetail Deer (*Odocoileus virginianus*)

The whitetail deer, alternately known as the Virginia or flagtail deer, is the most popular game animal on the planet. Its value to sport hunters has spawned an entire industry of clothing, tools, and gadgets designed to get humans within shooting range, and no wild animal has been more widely studied, mostly because no other game species is so commercially valuable.

Nearly wiped out from unrestricted hunting by the 1940s, whitetails have made a strong comeback, with an estimated 11 million animals in the United States alone. Today the resurgence of whitetail deer is counted as one of our most successful efforts at wildlife management.

Geographic Range

Whitetail deer are common throughout the United States, inhabiting all but the most arid regions, and extending northward throughout southern Canada. Their range to the south includes Mexico, Central America, and the northern portion of South America.

Whitetail doe.

Habitat

The most successful and widespread of deer, whitetails can make a living in virtually any habitat that provides sufficient plant browse, water, and concealment. Although sometimes seen grazing in meadows and open fields, they will never be far from the dense cover that provides them with an escape from predators and a safe place in which to sleep.

Whitetails are the least migratory of deer. Typically, a whitetail deer will spend its entire life in an area of about 1 square mile, moving between open feeding areas and concealed bedding places, and an animal can be expected to be intimately familiar with every facet of its habitat.

One unique exception is the Whitefish Bay area of Michigan's Upper Peninsula, near the tiny village of Paradise. Whitetails there summer around the thickly forested southern shoreline of Lake Superior, browsing on grasses and aquatic plants from the area's many lakes and rivers. In late November they abandon the region wholesale, traveling more than 20 miles southward, because the jackpine forests of Whitefish Bay provides almost none of the cedar trees on which whitetails depend for their winter browse.

Physical Characteristics

Mass: 150 to 200 pounds, occasionally in excess of 300 pounds in the far north. Subspecies like the Key deer of Florida and the Coues deer of Arizona average 50 pounds and 75 pounds, respectively.

Body: Muscular and less barrel-shaped than those of other deer species, 4 to 7 feet from chest to rump. Shoulder height: 3 to 4 feet. Powerful hindquarters with strong, slender legs that can propel them through dense, rugged terrain at speeds in excess of 30 miles per hour.

Whitetail antlers are configured with a single main tine, or "beam," extending from the top of the head on either side, forward of the ears, from which single "point" tines extend. Antlers are shed in January and begin to grow again in April.

Whitetails and other deer have interdigital scent glands between the two halves of their hooves which carry a signature scent and secrete alarm scents when the animal is frightened. Bucks more than 2 years of age have antlers most of the year (about 1 in 15 does grow antlers). Metatarsal glands on the outside of each hind leg and a larger tarsal gland on the inside of each hind leg at the knee are used for olfactory communication, with musk from them becoming especially pungent during mating season.

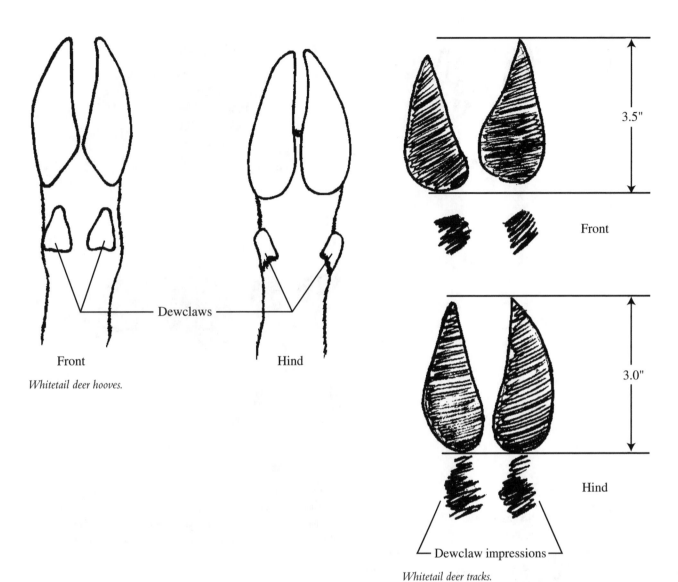

Whitetail deer hooves.

Front

Hind

Dewclaws

3.5"

Front

3.0"

Hind

Dewclaw impressions

Whitetail deer tracks.

Tail: 4 to 5 inches long, brown on top with white underside. The tail is held erect when the deer is fleeing from danger, exposing its white underside, and giving rise to the common name "flagtail."

Tracks: Cloven hooves that leave a split-heart impression when the toes are together, 2 dewclaws behind and slightly above. Length: 3 to 3.5 inches without dewclaws.

Scat: Typically oval-shaped pellets, sometimes acorn-shaped, 0.5 to 0.75 inches long, dark brown color, lightening with age.

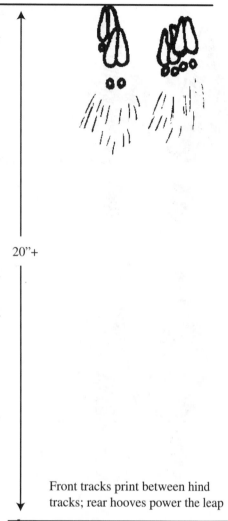

20"+

Front tracks print between hind
tracks; rear hooves power the leap

Spray of earth or
snow thrown to rear
of tracks denote a fast
gait with forceful leaps

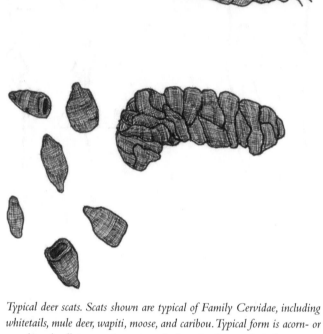

*Typical deer scats. Scats shown are typical of Family Cervidae, including
whitetails, mule deer, wapiti, moose, and caribou. Typical form is acorn- or
egg-shaped pellets, sometimes massed when the diet consists of green succulents, but sometimes a flattened disc when the diet has been especially
rich in fruits.*

Coloration: Reddish-brown coat in summer, becoming gray in winter. White chest and belly. Nose black with white band running around muzzle, white chin, white circles around the eyes.

Sign: Raggedly torn grasses. Saplings with bark scraped from them by a buck's antlers—called "rubs"—seen especially in early autumn. Patches of pawed-up earth, called "scrapes," seen prior to and during the mating season.

Vocalizations: Normally silent. Alarm call is a forceful exhalation, much like a sudden release of pressurized air. Does bleat softly to fawns, but the sound rarely carries more than a few yards. Mortally wounded deer bleat with a goatlike sound.

Lifespan: About 8 years in the wild; up to 20 years in captivity.

Diet

Like most deer, whitetails have crepuscular feeding patterns, meaning that they tend to feed mostly during the twilight hours before dawn and after dusk. Favorite summer browse includes all types of grasses, alfalfa, clover, elkslip, and sometimes aquatic plants. Winter browse consists of buds and tender twigs of evergreen trees, especially cedars, as well as bark and buds of staghorn sumac, river willow, beech, and dead grasses found in hummocks along stream and river banks. In more arid country they can subsist on prickly pear, yucca, and other tough, fibrous shrubs. Few plants are beyond the whitetail's ability to digest.

Mating Habits

The whitetail's mating season coincides closely with that of other deer, beginning in September and October with a pre-estrus rutting period during which bucks 2 years and older polish their antlers against young trees and advertise their availability to does through a urine-scented "scrape" of pawed-up earth. During this pre-breeding period adult bucks will spar with one another, usually far back in the woods, in what are essentially elimination rounds to determine which of them can lay claim to a particular area and the females that live within. As with other deer species, these battles consist primarily of shoving matches in which contenders lock antlers and try to push one another into submission. Occasional injuries result from these contests of strength, and in a few rare instances both bucks have died because their antlers became inextricably locked together, but the intent is not to injure an opponent, just to drive it away.

By the time the actual mating season begins in mid-October, bucks will have established their territorial boundaries. From then until the rut ends in mid to late November (as late as December in southern regions), breeding males will be fixated on little else except mating, and during that period they may be active at any time of day. Receptive does, which may mate in their first year, play a passive role in breeding rituals, stopping only to deposit pheromone-scented urine onto a buck's scrape as they travel between feeding and bedding areas. If does are to be pregnant through the coming winter they'll need to gain as much body fat as possible to insure a healthy birth in spring, so it's up to a buck to check its scrape for pheromonal messages, then to pursue the female that left its scent there.

Like other deer, whitetail bucks are polygamous, mating with as many receptive does as possible during the 30 to 45 days of the rut. Occasionally a buck will remain with the same female for several days, usually waiting for her to come into estrus, but as soon as she becomes pregnant (does seem to know instinctively when this occurs), the male will move on to another fertile doe. Does that enter gestation spurn further advances from rutting males, instead concentrating their energies toward feeding to support twin fawns as they develop through the coming winter.

Does are typically in heat for a single day, which may explain the urgency bucks exhibit about mating. If a doe is unmated during her day of fertility, she will come into heat again approximately 28 days later. In the unlikely event that this second heat passes with a doe still not pregnant, she will not come into heat again until the following October.

Gestation lasts through the following winter, with a duration of 6 to 7 months. Does bred for the first time normally give birth to a single spotted fawn in April or May, with twins being the norm in subsequent years, sometimes triplets or even quadruplets if food is especially abundant.

Fawns are able to stand and walk within hours after being born, and within a week they've begun to nibble on vegetation. Mothers leave their fawns hidden in deep grasses or underbrush while they graze nearby, checking on them from time to time and eating their feces to help prevent predators from detecting them by scent. If a carnivore should approach too closely to a hidden fawn, the mother will usually try to distract the predator and lead it in the opposite direction, but she won't risk her own life to save her offspring.

Weaning occurs at approximately 6 weeks, but fawns remain with their mothers for the rest of the summer, and sometimes through the winter, even though their mothers are likely to be pregnant with next spring's fawns.

Behavior

Whitetails are generally nocturnal, traveling from secluded bedding areas to feeding places at dusk, then returning to the safety of dense thickets or forest at dawn. They may move about within the seclusion of these bedding areas at any time during the day, and in places where they're unmolested they may be seen grazing in the open during daylight hours, but they can be counted on to avoid contact with humans.

When winter snows cover the fields and meadows where whitetails graze, they move into protected yards where pines and especially cedars provide both a windbreak and browse. In probably most places winter yards are the same as summer bedding areas, enabling deer to use the same established trails year round.

As with elk, whitetail does are the most dominant deer, and they're more territorial than bucks at all times of year because survival of themselves and their offspring demands securing a habitat with enough food, water, and shelter to support them. Territorial disputes are settled with flailing front hooves, and the contests are often quite violent.

Whitetail deer are mostly solitary throughout the summer months, but an abundance of food, especially farm crops such as beans, alfalfa, and corn, can cause them to herd together in large numbers. Agriculture has caused whitetail populations to explode in farming regions where predatory species are historically unwelcome, with the result being overpopulation, disease, and an increase in car-deer accidents.

Mule Deer (*Odocoileus hemionus*)

Mule deer represent the second most popular large game animal in the world. Subspecies include the black-tailed deer of America's northwest coast.

Geographic Range

Mule deer are found from southwestern Saskatchewan through central North and South Dakota, Nebraska, Kansas, and western Texas, with isolated sightings in Minnesota, Iowa, and Missouri. Gaps in their distribution occur in the arid regions of southern Nevada, southeastern California, southwestern Arizona, and the Great Salt Lake desert region.

Habitat

Nearly as adaptable as the whitetail deer, with whom its range overlaps, *O. hemionus* occupies a wide range of habitats, including California woodland chaparral, the Mojave Sonoran desert, the Interior semidesert shrub woodland, the Great Plains, the Colorado Plateau shrubland and forest, the Great Basin, the Sagebrush steppe, the northern mountains, and the Canadian boreal forest. Mulies prefer open grassland for grazing, and are rarely found far back in the woods.

Mule deer buck and doe.

Physical Characteristics

Mass: 110 to more than 400 pounds, with those in southern regions being typically smaller than those in the North. Males about 25% larger than females. Shoulder height 3 feet, sometimes more.

Body: More stocky and barrel-shaped than that of the whitetail, 4 to more than 6 feet from chest to tail. Very large mulelike ears, 4 to 6 inches long. Buck's antler spread about 4 feet. Antlers differ from the whitetail's in that the main beam forks into points, rather than having points growing individually from the main beam. Being a creature of open plains and mountain country, *O. hemionus* has good binocular vision and distance perception, and probably much keener eyesight than a whitetail.

Tail: 5 to 9 inches long, dark brown or black above, white below, tipped with a black or sometimes white tuft.

Tracks: Very similar to the split-heart print of the whitetail, but usually larger in adults, measuring about 3.5 inches long, discounting dewclaws.

Scat: Similar to the whitetail's, being pellet- or acorn-shaped, with individual pellets averaging about 0.5 to 0.75 inches long. Sometimes pellets will be massed together when browse has been succulent.

Coloration: Dark brown to red during the summer months, becoming more gray in winter. The rump patch is white in younger individuals, becoming more yellow as the animal ages. The throat patch is white. A dark V-shaped mark that is more conspicuous in males than females extends from between the eyes upward to the top of the head.

Sign: Similar to the whitetail, consisting of saplings from which bark has been scraped by bucks rubbing their antlers. Mule deer bucks make urine-scented scrapes during the rut, much like a whitetail buck. Occasionally, both sexes will wallow in mud like an elk, leaving depressions that are smaller than the elk's.

Vocalizations: Alarm call is similar to the blowing of a whitetail, but tends to be more prolonged and ends with a high-pitched whistle. Mule deer are more vocal than whitetails when grazing together, communicating among themselves with a variety of grunts, snorts, mooing sounds, and soft squeals.

Lifespan: About 10 years in the wild.

Diet

Although the mule deer is a cud-chewing ruminant like other members of the deer family, it appears to have a less efficient digestive system than its cousins, requiring more

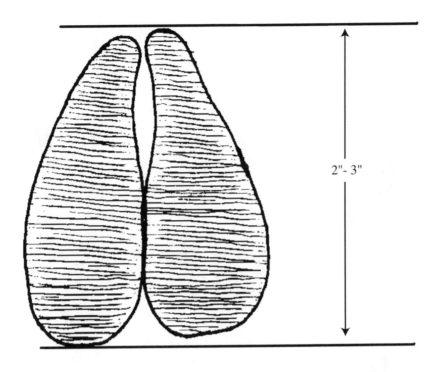

2"- 3"

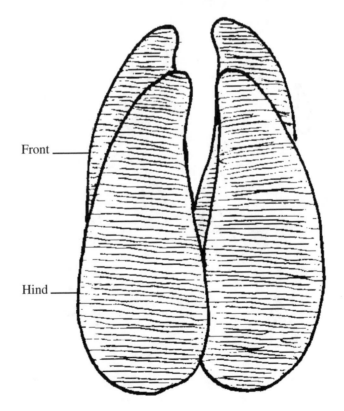

Front

Hind

Mule deer (Odocoileus hemionus).

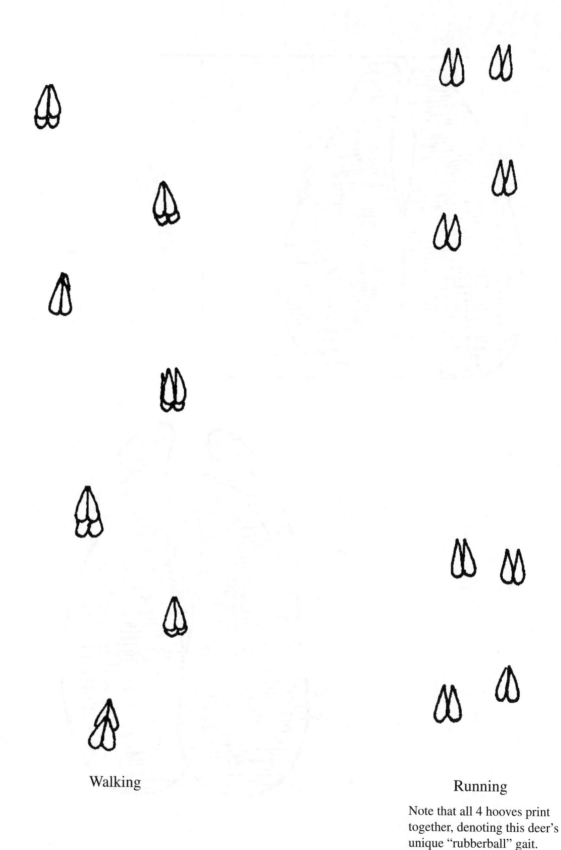

Walking

Running

Note that all 4 hooves print together, denoting this deer's unique "rubberball" gait.

Mule deer track patterns.

easily digestible green plants in its diet. This explains in part why the whitetail, which has a remarkable digestive system that can extract proteins and nutrients from woody browse and dead grasses, has expanded into the mule deer's range, but not vice-versa. To counter the deficiency of green browse in winter, *O. hemionus* feeds with more urgency than other deer during the summer months to put on enough fat to sustain it through winter. Green grasses, acorns, legume seeds, berries and fleshy fruits are among the preferred foods.

Mating Habits

Mule deer tend to breed slightly later than whitetails, with the rut beginning in October and peaking from November through December. As with whitetails, mating is largely initiated by the bucks, which create urine-scented scrapes of pawed-up earth that receptive does urinate onto as they pass between feeding and bedding areas. When the buck returns to its scrape to check for olfactory messages and finds that a doe has left a pheromonal calling card, it immediately sets out in pursuit.

Like other deer, mule deer bucks are polygynous, having more than one mate per breeding season. Bucks are known to remain with a single doe only so long as it takes to make her pregnant, or until displaced by a competitor, but there is no lasting bond between males and females.

Bucks competing for mates engage in pushing matches by locking their antlers and shoving hard against one another until the weaker opponent surrenders and withdraws. Injuries sometimes occur, but as with all wild species the objective is to establish which male is the stronger, not to harm one another.

O. hemionus females are less likely to mate in their first year than whitetails. First births usually—and sometimes second—produce a single fawn, with twins being the norm thereafter. Gestation lasts about 29 weeks, with most fawns born from mid-June to early July. Fawns weigh from 6 to 10 pounds at birth, with twins typically weighing less than singles, and males slightly heavier than females. Fawns can walk within a few hours after being born, and begin nibbling at vegetation within a few days. Fawns are weaned by 16 weeks, and attain full skeletal development at 3 years for females, 4 years for males, although both continue to grow until the ages of 8 and 10 years, respectively.

Behavior

Mule deer prefer a small home range that provides for their needs in every season, but they can be migratory when weather and other conditions dictate that they seek out a more suitable habitat.

Bucks are driven away by their mothers at about 2 years of age to prevent inbreeding, and most will travel 5 or 6 miles in search of their own territories. Seasonal movements can also be prompted by hatches of biting insects, lack of water in arid regions, and deep winter snows.

Although mule deer prefer to bed down during the daylight hours in concealing thickets, they're less nervous about being in the open than whitetails because they possess better long distance vision. Major predators include mountain lions and wolves, with bears, coyotes, and golden eagles preying on fawns. By feeding and bedding in open areas, mule deer can see these predators coming from as far away as 400 yards, and with a head start their running speed of more than 30 miles per hour gives them an edge in escaping. If surprised at close range, a mule deer's powerful hindquarters and its ability to instantly change direction allows it to evade most predators, although this defensive maneuvering is often unsuccessful against the drill team precision of a wolf pack.

Female mule deer are more territorial than males at all times of year, defending their home range against other does that might intrude and start their own families, thus depleting an area's resources. Fights between contentious does are often violent, consisting of pummeling blows from their sharp hooves. Bucks are spurned by females except during mating season, traveling alone or in bachelor herds for most of the year, but they aren't subject to the sometimes fierce territorial battles that ensue between does.

Mulies often run afoul of timber companies by browsing on economically important trees like the Douglas fir and Ponderosa pine, which serve as the species' winter browse. This has prompted state governments to purchase tracts of land that provide suitable winter habitat, which in its turn has created a public stir among citizens who object to their governments buying private properties.

O. hemionus is subject to a variety of viral, bacterial, and parasitic diseases. Gastrointestinal nematodes (worms) are known to cause death among them, particularly in instances of overpopulation, with resultant malnourishment. Infection by the parasitic meningeal nematode can cause sometimes fatal neurological complications, also more common in herds that have become overpopulated in relationship to available habitat. Livestock may infect mule deer that graze the same pastures with viral infections like hoof-and-mouth disease (characterized by blistering of the mouth and feet), or bacterial diseases like bovine tuberculosis.

Caribou (*Rangifer tarandus*)

Caribou are best known as reindeer, especially among children who recognize them as the animals that pull Santa's sleigh at Christmas. In fact, caribou have been domesticated to pull sleighs and wagons, as well as for their milk, and they've historically been an important source of food in northern aboriginal cultures.

Caribou bull in velvet. Photo by Steve Kaufman. Courtesy of U.S. Fish & Wildlife Service.

Geographic Range

Historically, caribou were native to all northern latitudes, but extensive hunting by humans (who initially and erroneously blamed gray wolves) has made this most northern of deer extinct over much of its original range. Large herds can still be found in Alaska, Canada, Scandinavia, and Russia, but unrestricted hunting is now a thing of the past.

Habitat

Caribou are most at home in arctic tundra, where they migrate long distances in response to changing seasons and availability of food. They also adapt well to temperate forest and rainforest, but require open plains and cold winters.

Physical Characteristics

Mass: Bulls roughly twice as large as cows. Males weigh from 275 to 600 pounds, females from 150 to 300 pounds.

Body: Shoulder height 3 to 3.5 feet; 4.5 to 7 feet long. Stocky build with thick legs and unusually large knee joints. Large snout and nose pad. Both sexes are antlered, with males having the largest and most branched antlers.

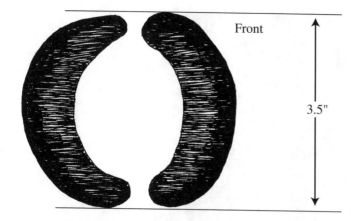

Front

3.5"

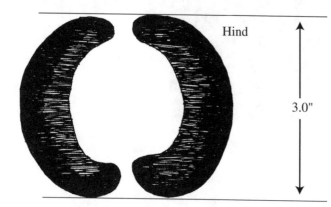

Hind

3.0"

Caribou (Rangifer tarandus). *Hind hooves normally print atop foreprints when walking. Note concave design in which only the outer edges of the hooves print on hard ground, leaving a track that resembles paired parentheses ( ).*

Tail: Relatively short at 4 to 6 inches, darker colored on top, white below.

Tracks: Cloven hooves leave almost round impressions, 4 to 5 inches long, with males leaving larger tracks than females. The feet are slightly broader than they are long, and flat with deeply cleft hooves; this hoof design presumably allows them better stability in winter snows and spongy arctic tundra. The pad between hoof halves is larger in summer to provide better traction against soft, often slippery terrain, but shrinks in winter to help conserve heat.

Scat: Acorn-shaped pellets, about 0.5 inch long, sometimes clumped together in a mass that can measure more than 3 inches in length when the animal has been feeding on succulent browse.

Coloration: The coat is very heavy with dense, wooly underfur. Coat color is predominantly brown to olive, with whitish chest, buttocks, and legs. Coloration often varies with geography; some populations in Greenland and northeastern Canada have nearly white coats.

Sign: Browsed reindeer moss (Cladina rangiferina) lichens, a staple in the caribou diet that's seldom eaten by other deer species. Shed antlers often found on open tundra.

Vocalizations: Gutteral grunts, squeals, and whistles. Caribou are especially vocal during seasonal migrations when large groups prompt a variety of individual communications. Cows often moo softly to young calves.

Caribou have thick tendons that snap across a bone in the foot when they walk, producing a clicking sound. This sound is alluded to in the Christmas carol lyrics, "Up on the rooftop, click, click, click; down through the chimney comes old Saint Nick." Hunters often use this noise, which can be quite loud in a moving herd, to locate the animals.

Lifespan: 4 to 5 years in the wild, up to 13 years in captivity.

Diet

Caribou are strict herbivores that can digest most available types of vegetation, including green leaves, evergreen buds and foliage, and fine twigs. When other types of browse are unavailable, caribou may feed predominantly on their namesake reindeer moss (Cladina rangiferina), a hardy lichen that grows in carpetlike masses and is common to open, otherwise barren places around the globe.

Mating Habits

Mating season occurs through the month of October, with northern populations coming into rut earlier than those in the south. Caribou are able to breed at 2 years, although competition from dominant bulls will likely keep males from mating until their third year. Like whitetail does, caribou cows are seasonally polyestrous, meaning that those not impregnated during the first 10-day period of estrus will come into heat again 10 to 15 days later. Like elk, caribou bulls gather a harem prior to mating; harem size may exceed 12 cows, but is largely dependent on competition from other bulls.

In May or June, after a gestation of about 8 months, a single calf is born. Twins may occur when food is abundant, but this is not common. Calves weigh 12 to 19 pounds at birth; they can follow their mothers within an hour of being born, and can outrun a human by the end of their first day.

Behavior

Caribou are diurnal (active during the day) and gregarious in nature, forming herds that can number from 10 to more than 1,000 individuals, increasing to as many as 200,000 animals during seasonal migrations. Caribou are the most migratory of deer, traveling as far as 1,000 miles between northern summer habitats to more southerly winter grazing areas. Migrations happen abruptly, with smaller herds coalescing into sometimes huge herds that can number more than 20,000 animals per square mile and travel more than 30 miles per day.

Caribou are the fast runners in the deer family, able to reach speeds of 50 miles an hour for short distances, which means a healthy animal can quickly outdistance its most common predator, the Arctic wolf. They cannot so easily escape human hunters, and had been hunted to extinction over most of their European range by the 1600s, and were becoming scarce over much of their Canadian range by the latter half of the twentieth century. Today there are 30 wild herds known to exist in North America; the smallest of these are in Idaho and Washington state, numbering about 30 animals each, while the largest in northern Canada and Alaska may number more than 50,000 animals. Strictly enforced hunting laws have helped to preserve existing populations, but oil exploration may yet prove to be a threat.

THE COW FAMILY (FAMILY BOVIDAE)

Bovids are characterized as cloven-hooved mammals that are herbivores and ruminants, and which possess a pair of usually permanent horns on top of their heads. They're

Domestic cattle. Photo by George A. Robinson, courtesy of USDA.

further typified as grazing herd animals with large bodies, short, thick legs, and poor running speed, relying on size, individual strength, and numbers as protection from predators. Members of this family include all domestic cattle and oxen, the Cape buffalo of Africa, the American bison, muskoxen of the Arctic, and the water buffalo of Asia. Like deer, all of these lack upper teeth at the front of their mouths, having instead a hard upper palate, or dental pad, and heavy rear molars that are designed for grinding coarse plant fibers.

Domestic Cattle (*Bos taurus*)

Wild bovids were first domesticated in Asia about 8,000 years ago. Domesticated cows have played a key role in the development of human civilization, providing meat, dairy products, leather, and the power needed to pull wagons, plow fields, and operate early machines. Today they still provide those services to the human economy, as well as materials for the manufacture of glue, medical serums, fertilizer, and soap products.

Geographic Range

Like most domestic animals, domestic cows are found throughout the world.

Habitat

Domestic cows are common throughout the world. Most are born and raised on grassy rangelands that require no care from humans.

Physical Characteristics

Mass: Varies with the breed, but ranges from about 600 pounds to more than 1,000 pounds.

Body: Domestic cows are large barrel-shaped animals having short, thick necks, folds of loose skin (dewlaps) that hang loosely below the throat, short heavy legs, and a pair of permanent hollow horns atop their heads. Shoulder height from 4 to more than 5 feet.

Tail: 12 to 20 inches long and comparatively thin, tufted at the end, used for shooing away insects.

Tracks: Cloven-hooved, about 4 inches long, sometimes larger depending on breed and size.

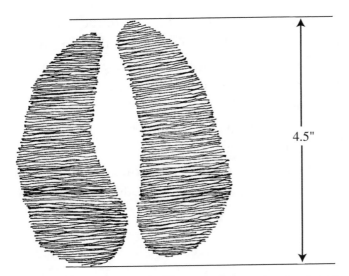

4.5"

Domestic cow (Bos taurus) *Tracks typical of the order Artiodectyla, with cloven hooves that leave a roughly split-heart impression.*

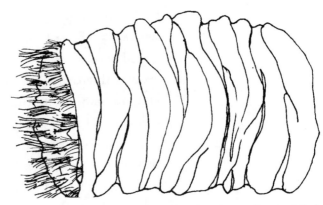

Typical scat of family Bovidae. 6"-7" long. Scat shown reflects a relatively dry diet of rough grasses. A more succulent diet is indicated by flattened disclike scats, or cowpies. Typical of domestic cattle, bison, muskox, and pronghorn antelope.

Scat: Cowpies; typically semiliquid masses, or clustered segments when feeding on dry browse, measuring 8 to more than 12 inches in diameter.

Coloration: The body is covered with short hair which can be mostly solid or patterned with colors that include black, gray, white, reddish, brown, and blonde. Spotted patterns are like a fingerprint, with no two cows having exactly the same arrangement.

Sign: Heavily trodden trails. Grasses and forbs browsed short.

Vocalizations: Usually comprised of low moos (lowing), sometimes punctuated by sharp, low exhalations if an animal is agitated. Bulls occasionally bellow loudly and snort as a warning or to assert dominance.

Lifespan: 8 to 10 years.

Diet

Grazing cows feed on grasses, stems, and other herbaceous plant material. Like wild bovids, cows first wind long grasses around their rough tongues to twist them into a mass, then pin the mass between their lower teeth and hard upper dental pad before tearing the mass free with a twist of the head.

All bovids are ruminants, or cud-chewers, with a sophisticated digestive system that permits them to break down coarse plant fibers and celluloids into usable nutrients. The stomach has four chambers, consisting of a rumen, reticulum, omasum, and abomasum. Grass passes through the rumen where it mixes with and is initially broken down by specialized bacteria. From the rumen it moves to the reticulum, where it's further broken down by digestive enzymes. From there, the partially digested mass, known as a cud, is regurgitated into the mouth where grinding molars crush and separate remaining plant fibers. Upon being swallowed a second time, the cud mass moves into the omasum and, finally, the abomasum, where it's completely digested and nutrients are absorbed. The entire process requires between 70 and 100 hours, depending on the coarseness of the cud, making it one of the slowest digestive processes in any species. The benefit is that even the most undigestible plant materials can be metabolized into usable nutrients, giving bovines a real advantage over most other herbivores.

Mating Habits

Cattle are social animals that live in herds dominated by a single bull. Bulls are polygynous, mated to a group of females rather than to a single female, and only one male is permitted to breed within a herd.

Although the mating habits of wild bovids are predictably seasonal, domestic cattle may breed throughout the year, with a single calf (twins are rare) being born after a gestation period of approximately nine months. Calves are precocial, usually able to stand and walk within 2 days after birth. Calves suckle for about 6 months, with females reaching sexual maturity at 1 year, remaining fertile for up to 12 years.

Behavior

Like wild bovids, domestic cattle herds are structured by a dominance hierarchy, with a leader (usually a bull) and a subordinate herd of cows and calves that have their own hierarchy. Bulls maintain their dominant status until supplanted by a younger and stronger bull. Calves typically inherit their mother's status within the hierarchy, but maternal care of them is often shared among female herd members. Dominant bulls are fiercely protective of their territories and of their herds.

Mother cows are normally quite protective of their offspring, chasing away anything that threatens them, but neither sex is willing to risk its own life to defend young against large predators.

Cattle ranching continues to have a serious negative impact on the environment, especially in places like the American west where overgrazing by domestic herds that often number in the thousands threatens the food supply of wild herbivores.

Another negative aspect of domestic cattle ranching is a disease called bovine spongiform encephalopathy (BSE), which is perhaps better known as mad cow disease. Mad cow disease is a fatal degenerative brain disease caused by feeding cattle processed foods that have been made using by-products from other cattle. The catalyst is a protein atom known as a prion, which causes the infected animal's brain tissue to become porous (spongiform), thus leading to an irreversible loss of cerebral functions and creating an effect similar to rabies. People who ingest meat from cows suffering from BSE are also at risk of contracting the disease, which in human form is called Creutzfeldt-Jakob disease, or CJD. The symptoms are the same in either case: The victim's brain becomes porous, creating a rapidly progressing form of dementia, increasingly severe neurological damage, and death. Numerous outbreaks of CJD in Canada and Great Britain at the end of the twentieth century led to an international ban on the importation of beef products from those countries.

In addition, there exists a genuine concern that the disease might be passed on to wild herbivores that ingest contaminated bovine feed, and to wild carnivores that scavenge the bodies of cows killed by BSE.

Bison, or New World Buffalo (*Bison bison*)

The largest terrestrial species in North America, bison are the native wild cows of North America. As the common name implies, this species is the New World cousin to the water buffalo of Asia and the Cape buffalo of Africa.

The American buffalo, or bison, is North America's largest bovine.

Geographic Range

Prior to the "Indian Wars" of the nineteenth century, bison numbers were as high as 60 million and the species was widespread from Alaska to northern Mexico. After decades of unrestricted slaughter that included shooting from trains, bison were very nearly exterminated in the wild. By 1900, fewer than 1,000 remained. Today the bison remains endangered, with about 30,000 remaining in Wyoming's Yellowstone Park and Wood Buffalo Park in Canada's Northwest Territory. A number of commercial herds also exist to provide meat and hides for consumers, and bison have been successfully bred with domestic cattle.

Habitat

Like domestic cattle, bison are primarily grazers of open prairie grasslands, although some of them, called timber bison or wood buffalo, once inhabited mature forests where there were sufficient grasses and forbs. Today the species' vastly diminished population, along with fences, roads, and competition from domestic cattle herds, restricts their range and numbers to small, heavily controlled environments.

Physical Characteristics

Mass: 1,000 to more than 2,000 pounds, females about 15% smaller than males.

Body: Massive, sloping downward from humped, heavily muscled front shoulders to short, thick hind legs that give the animals a pronounced front-heavy appearance. Body length 10 to more than 12 feet. Shoulder height for mature bulls can exceed 6 feet, 5 feet for cows. Large, blocky head with short, heavy muzzle and large black nose pad. Both sexes have black horns, which are larger on males, that curve upward and inward from the brow to end in sharp tips.

Tail: Much like that of domestic cattle, about 16 inches long with short hairs except for a tuft at the tip which serves to shoo away flies.

Tracks: Cloven-hooved, about 6 inches long for bulls, 5 inches for cows. Similar to the tracks of domestic cattle, except more rounded at the sides and wider. On hard soil the cleft between hoof halves may not show clearly, and can be mistaken for a horse hoofprint.

5.0"

Bison (Bison bison) track. Similar to the tracks of muskox, domestic cattle, and other bovids, except that the bison hoof is typically more circular in its outline, being as wide as it is long.

Scat: Soft, rounded mass 8 to more than 10 inches in diameter, with undigested grasses and coarse plant fibers in evidence. Similar to and easily mistaken for the dung of a domestic cow.

Coloration: Fur color varies from dark brown to nearly black. Bulls especially exhibit darker and thicker fur along the head, neck, shoulders, and back, with shorter and sometimes lighter-colored fur covering the rump and underbelly.

Sign: Large mud wallows near water, lined with shed fur. Rubbed bark on trees and saplings. Shed fur might also be found on or around boulders, especially during the spring shedding season.

Vocalizations: Grunts and snorts, frequently mooing sounds, much like domestic cattle. Bulls may bellow when threatened or when competing with other bulls for territorial rights.

Lifespan: About 25 years in the wild.

Diet

Bison graze the year round, pawing through snow to reach grasses, and migrating as necessary to find suitable grazing areas. The animals feed primarily on grasses, forbs, and plant tops, but if these are scarce, they can subsist on the buds and ends of woodier browse, particularly sagebrush. On average a bison consumes 15 to 30 pounds of vegetation per day, or about 1.5% of its body weight. Being ruminants, they chew cuds of partially digested plant fibers, and can survive by eating coarse vegetation.

Mating Habits

Bison cows typically reach sexual maturity at 2 years. Bulls are sexually mature at 3 years, but seldom mate until at least 6 years of age due to competition from larger and stronger herd bulls.

Mating season begins in late June and lasts through September, with just one lead bull mating the cows within its harem. July marks the peak of the territorial season for males, when mature bulls charge head-first into one another from distances of about 20 feet, slamming together using their massive skulls, not their horns, until the weaker combatant withdraws, usually without real injury.

Cows are in heat for 24 hours, but those not impregnated will experience 3-week breeding cycles (seasonally polyestrous) throughout the mating season until they become pregnant.

Gestation lasts roughly 280 days, with a single calf, or occasionally twins if food has been abundant, born in mid-April or May. Cows give birth in brushy isolated areas that provide good concealment from predators and are more defensible than open range. Newborn calves have a reddish coat and weigh from 30 to 50 pounds, depending largely on how healthy and strong the mother was during her pregnancy.

A bison calf is able to stand and nurse within 30 minutes after being born, and after 1 or 2 days is strong enough to rejoin the herd with its mother. Calves begin nibbling grasses within a few days, but nurse several times each day for their first 7 to 8 months, becoming fully weaned by the end of their first year. Bison mothers are fiercely protective of their young, but herd bulls will typically do nothing to defend calves.

Behavior

Bison are gregarious animals, but the composition of their herds changes with the seasons. Cow groups in the nonbreeding months contain usually related females, males under 3 years of age, and an occasional older male. Mature bulls join the cow herd as mating season approaches, but in every season the herd leader is a dominant cow.

Adult males may live alone or in bachelor herds of up to 30 animals during the nonbreeding months, coexisting peacefully, but with a linear hierachy that extends downward in rank from a single dominant bull. During this period relatively gentle mock battles occur among them, and these seem to be an important training exercise for young bulls that are not yet of breeding age.

Migrating bison tend to travel in a narrow line. This habit appears to be an ingrained behavior that lessens the amount of damage inflicted on valuable grazing habitat by the animals' hooves, and their narrow trails provided the first explorers to the New World with an easily seen guide for finding navigable passes through mountain ranges. They swim well enough to cross most rivers, but early accounts of plains Indians tell of hundreds of drowned bison being scavenged from swollen rivers for meat and hides during the spring thaw.

Although adult bison have little to fear from most predators, newborn calves are preyed on by coyotes, bears, and, historically, wolves. When a calf is threatened its mother will defend it by charging the intruders, but if the attackers are pack animals that cannot be fended off by a single cow, the entire herd may try to escape by running away at speeds of up to 45 miles per hour, which most adults can maintain for about a mile.

Bison are less farsighted than most plains animals, probably because they have so little to fear from predators, but they can distinguish large objects—like a truck—from more than half a mile, and detect movement from more than a mile. Their hearing is good, and the bison's olfactory senses are acute enough to detect water and grazing land from perhaps several miles.

Muskox (Ovibos moschatus)

This species was in danger of extinction due to unrestricted hunting by the beginning of the twentieth century, but was brought back from the brink by effective management programs. Inuit tribes have historically depended on the muskox for their hides, meat, and horns, and a limited number of hunting permits are still being granted to native peoples. Muskox hides were a trade commodity in Canada until 1917, when the government passed protective legislation.

Muskox. Courtesy of U.S. Fish & Wildlife Service.

Geographic Range

Natural populations occur in the high arctic areas of northern Canada and Greenland, with introduced populations doing very well in northern Europe, northern Russia, and Alaska. Muskox populations are now estimated at 66,000 to 85,000 individuals worldwide, and introduced herds are increasing their numbers more quickly than had been anticipated.

Habitat

Muskox always live in very cold Arctic tundra areas, but habitat varies with the season. During the summer months they tend toward low wetland areas that include river valleys, marshlands, and lake shores. In winter they migrate to higher grounds where colder temperatures keep snowfall to a minimum.

Physical Characteristics

Mass: Males 600 to 900 pounds, females 400 to 600 pounds.

Body: Massive head with a thick, short muzzle that is nearly as wide as the skull. The neck is short and thickly muscled. Short, very stout legs and large hooves. Shoulders are thick and humped, more so on bulls than cows. The entire body is covered with long shaggy hair that hangs nearly to the ground. Shoulder height ranges from 3 to 5 feet, with males 30% to 50% larger than females. Body length 6 to 8 feet.

Both sexes have large, permanent horns at maturity, but the horns of a bull are typically massive, curving downward and forward from the skull to end in points in front of the face. The horns of a cow are shorter and more straight, extending outward from either

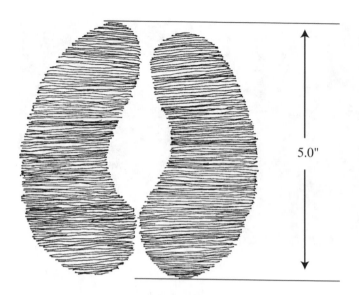

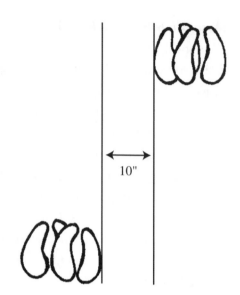

Muskox (Ovibos moschatus). *Track is cloven-hooved, leaving a split-heart imprint common to members of order Artiodactyla. Tracks closely resemble those of domestic cows and bison.*

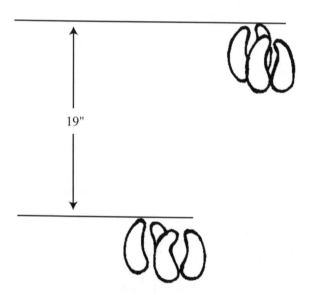

Muskox track pattern.

side of the skull. These characteristics give the muskox a uniquely distinctive appearance that make it nearly impossible to mistake for any other species.

Tail: 2 to more than 6 inches.

Tracks: Cloven hooves, rounded sides. Very similar to the tracks of a bison, but the hoof halves are more pointed at their fronts. Tracks about 5 inches long.

Scat: Disc-shaped, 6 to 8 inches in diameter. Much like the droppings of domestic cattle or bison, with plant fibers evident. Winter scats tend to be smaller and drier because there is less drinking water available and most moisture comes from ingested snow.

Coloration: Long shaggy fur, dark brown to black, with a nearly white saddle-shaped patch on the back. There is also a whitish patch atop the head of both sexes, a whitish patch around the end of the muzzle, and whitish fur on the lower legs.

Sign: Well-trodden trails left by migrating herds. In spring and early summer muskoxen may also wallow in mud to loosen and help shed their winter coats.

Vocalizations: Bisonlike, consisting of snorts, grunts, and bellows from excited bulls.

Lifespan: About 20 years.

Diet

The muskoxen's summer diet consists of arctic grasses and sedges, horsetails, reeds, and almost any other available plants. In winter the diet changes with the availability of browse, consisting largely of reindeer moss lichens.

When snow covers the ground, muskox clear large circular patches of ground with their hooves to expose edible vegetation. These exposed patches are rigorously defended against other muskoxen.

Mating Habits

Muskox bulls reach sexual maturity at 5 years, females after 2 years. The breeding season peaks in mid-August, after a herd's most dominant bull has driven out the other adult males to form a harem. During this time the musky-scented urine for which the species is named grows more pungent in the males. Displaced males form bachelor herds or wander away in search of another group where they might be able to achieve dominant status. Fights for dominance consist of threatening gestures like head wagging, loud bellows, pawing at the ground and snorting, and, finally, head butting at high speed.

Cow muskoxen typically breed every 2 years unless their calf is killed, which prompts them to breed sooner, during the next mating season. Gestation lasts about 8 months, with a single calf being born in late April through May. Twins are uncommon, but may result from a mother who is especially healthy and well-fed. The calf is weaned after one year but may eat vegetation as quickly as a week after birth.

Behavior

The muskox is a social species that normally congregates in herds of 10 to 20 animals, but sometimes more than 100. Herds may include individuals of all ages and both sexes, particularly in winter, but there is only one dominant bull among each herd, and the real leader is always a dominant cow.

Muskoxen are superbly adapted to life in very cold climes, surviving approximately 8 months of every year in subzero temperatures with no sunlight. The species' range is overlapped in places by moose, but only the caribou can survive the extremes of cold and sparse tundra browse that muskox can not only thrive on, but also prefer.

Muskoxen get their common name from their musky urine, the scent of which grows more pungent during the breeding season. Unlike deer, muskoxen have no external musk glands, but the scents contained in their urine appear to play the same role in identification of individuals, their size, social rank, and mating status.

Although muskoxen are considered migratory because they move between summer and winter feeding grounds, they seldom range more than 50 miles. Like all animals, they migrate only as far as conditions demand to find sufficient food and water to survive or mate, and if a habitat were to provide for these needs year round, the herds would probably not migrate at all.

Muskox are best known for their unique defensive behavior. When threatened by predators, primarily the Arctic gray wolf, the herd bunches into a tight circle, with the largest and strongest animals facing outward toward the threat. Calves and adolescent herd members are kept to the inside of the circle, where they're protected by the encircling wall of more powerful adults. If a predator approaches too closely, one of the surprisingly fast and agile adults charges, head down like a domestic bull, and attempts to gore it, then fling it into the air with a toss of its powerful neck. This defensive behavior is effective against wolves, but it made muskoxen the proverbial sitting ducks for humans armed with rifles, which led to the species' near extinction.

SWINE AND PECCARIES (FAMILIES SUIDAE AND TAYASSUIDAE)

Wild Boar and Domestic Pig (Sus scrofa)

For our purposes here, the wild boar, feral hog, and domestic pig will be lumped together as the same species. The true wild boar of Eurasia is the forebear of domestic swine, but both of them share the same general behaviors and physical characteristics, and wild boars have been widely transplanted as game and farm animals around the globe since before the Middle Ages. Wild boar and domestic pigs interbreed freely, and in places where both exist they've hybridized into a third type of swine that shares the markings, coloration, and other physical traits of both.

Geographic Range

Wild pigs are found in numerous places throughout the world, including Pacific islands, Australia, Europe, Asia, and Africa. In many regions they were imported either as game animals or for domestication, and escaped captivity to become established as part of the ecosystem, sometimes with severe negative impact on native species. Of all members of the pig family, *Sus scrofa*, the large wild boar from which all domestic pigs were spawned in approximately 3,000 B.C., occupies the largest range.

Originally, there were no pigs in the Americas except the peccaries of South America, Mexico, and the southwestern United States, which are not considered true swine. The first domestic pigs arrived with European immigrants, and these were not able to survive on their own

Wild pigs. Courtesy of USDA.

in the vast wilderness of the New World, so there were no feral populations until 1893, when 50 wild boar were transplanted from Germany's Black Forest to a hunting preserve in New Hampshire's Blue Mountains. These were followed in 1910–12 by a release of Russian wild boar in North Carolina, near the Tennessee border, and another in 1925 near Monterey, California. A few were also released on California's Santa Cruz Island.

Habitat

Although *S. scrofa* is now found in a variety of habitats as a result of domestication and introduction to new areas, the typical wild habitat consists of marshes, forests, and shrublands, where acorns, grasses, and roots are abundant. The species is poorly suited to travel and forage in deep snow, and are not furred well enough to withstand subzero temperatures, so wild pigs are not found in northern areas with heavy snowfall. Temperatures below 50°F are uncomfortably cold to wild pigs, although many do survive in places where there is mild snowfall. Conversely, swine don't do well in very hot climates, where their lack of a protective coat makes them prone to sunburn and heatstroke; those that do live in warm places seek shade during the heat of midday, and frequently wallow in mud to cool themselves.

Physical Characteristics

Mass: 160 to 450 pounds, females about 20% smaller than males.

Body: Barrel-shaped and very stout; short, thick legs; 4.5 to 6 feet long. Shoulder height up to 3 feet. Large head with short, massive neck and long muzzle ending in a flat, disc-shaped snout with large nostrils. Eyes are comparatively small in relation to head size.

S. scrofa has an advanced sense of taste and a very good sense of smell. Long-range eyesight is believed to be poor. Interbreeding between feral and true wild pigs has led to a variety of ear shapes, ranging from small and erect to large and folded over at their fronts. Most prominent is the flat disc-shaped snout of tough cartilage, used for rooting in soil.

Although considered an omnivore, pigs have canines that might classify them as carnivores. The upper canines grow out to curve backward into large, arced tusks that function as tools for digging and as weapons; length may range from 3 inches to 9 inches, with longer tusks denoting older animals. The upper and lower canines continue to grow throughout the animal's life, but are so closely set that they're honed to sharp points against each other by the pig's jaw movements.

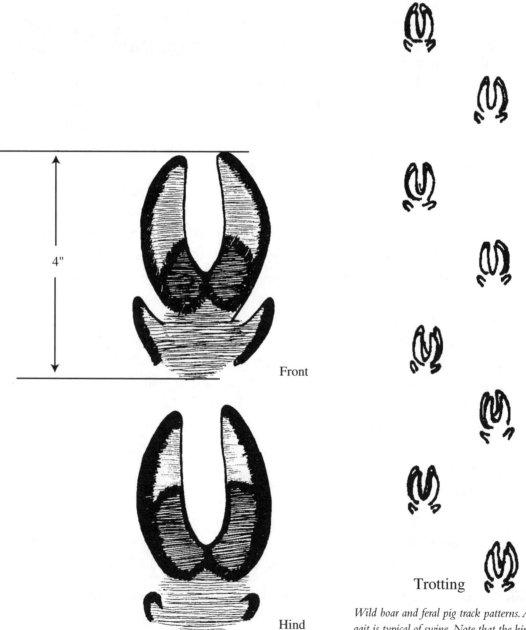

4"

Front

Hind

Trotting

Wild boar and feral pig (Sus scrofa).

Wild boar and feral pig track patterns. A trotting gait is typical of swine. Note that the hind hooves register almost precisely atop foreprints, and that the track pattern is regular and very straight.

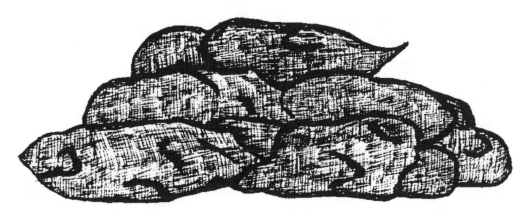

Wild boar/ feral pig scat.

Tail: Tail lengths vary, but average about 8 inches. True wild boar have a straight tail with a tufted end, while domestic swine tend to have coiled tails; hybrids usually have some combination of both.

Tracks: Cloven-hooved with dewclaws usually printing to the rear and to either side of hoofprints. Tracks 2 to 4 inches long, shaped like a deep U. Dewclaws in front track are longer and more prominent than hind dewclaws.

Scat: Usually large pellets, similar to those of a deer, but ranging from 3 to more than 6 inches long, sometimes massed together. When the animals have been feeding on succulent vegetation or rich meat, scats may become soft and disc-shaped, much like a cowpie. Recognizable content includes undigested plant fibers, insect legs and carapaces, seeds, and small bones.

Coloration: True wild boars possess a dark grizzled coat of dark brown to nearly black with whitish guard hairs that is typically longer and shaggier than that of hybridized feral pigs. Feral pigs often exhibit the same splotched skin colors of domestic hogs.

Sign: Well-traveled trails made by herds of traveling pigs. Rooted soil with grasses and roots neatly clipped free by the animals' sharp teeth.

Vocalizations: Grunting, oinking, and squealing when excited or threatened. Some researchers believe that *S. scrofa* speaks a rudimentary language, but specifics have yet to be identified.

Lifespan: About 20 years.

Diet

Swine are believed to represent a primitive condition of ungulates because they have a comparatively simple digestive system with a two-chambered stomach that processes tough plant fibers less efficiently than most hooved mammals. Pigs are omnivorous, with a diet that includes fungi, leaves, roots, bulbs, fruit, snails, insects, snakes, earthworms, rodents, eggs, and carrion. They use their tough snout, tusks, and forefeet to unearth food plants.

S. scrofa's broad diet has enabled the species to survive in a variety of environments, from deserts to mountainous terrain, so long as winter snows there are shallow enough to permit the short, heavy pigs to travel without foundering. Their herbivorous diet brings swine into direct competition with black bears, and in some states, most notably Tennessee, both species have been known to kill one another over territory.

Wild pigs aren't the gluttons that they're purported to be, and are typically much leaner than farm-raised hogs. Being self-sufficient and forced to live from the land, they're more active than domestic pigs, and they tend to subsist on a more natural and less fatty diet. Like domestic swine, feral hogs and wild boars carry parasitic infections that are transmittable to humans through eating their undercooked meat and from contact with their scats, including trichinosis, cysticerosis, and brucellosis.

Mating Habits

Swine become sexually mature at 18 months, but continue to grow until 5 or 6 years. Being herd animals, only one dominant male (boar) is permitted to breed, so most males leave the herd to find their own mates and territories at 2 or 3 years of age.

Mating season runs from mid-November to early January, peaking in December. The rut can be a violent time, and large boars frequently inflict serious, even mortal wounds on one another while battling for a harem that may number up to 8 females (sows). Extra-thick skin covering the chest, shoulders, and underbelly offers some protection against stab wounds for the prize of a sow, but mating fights are often bloody.

Sows are in estrus for 3 weeks, and are receptive to copulation for about 3 days during that period. Females that aren't impregnated during that time will probably come into heat again before the mating season ends. In northern regions, sows may birth one litter per year, but in warmer climes breeding may take place year round.

Gestation lasts about 4 months, with litters of 3 to 16 (5 is average) piglets being born in April. Piglets are 6 to 8 inches long and have brown fur patterned with 9 or 10 paler longitudinal stripes on the back. Sows withdraw from their herds to a secluded and easily defended grass- or leaf-lined nest a day or so prior to giving birth. Few predators are powerful enough to challenge a ferociously protective mother sow, but boars have been known to kill and eat their own newborn, while coyotes and larger birds of prey are quick to snatch piglets if they can take advantage of the mother's incapacitation. On average, only about half a litter can expect to reach maturity.

Sows rejoin their herd 1 to 2 days after giving birth, and by 1 week the young are able to travel with the group. The young begin feeding on solid foods almost immediately, but suckle from their mothers for 3 months. The piglets' stripes fade slowly, until they're completely gone at 6 months and the animals take on the color and pattern that will remain with them for the rest of their lives.

Behavior

Wild *S. scrofa* in Europe sometimes congregate in herds, called sounders, of up to 100 individuals, although 20 or fewer is more normal. Large sounders usually result from 2 or more dominant females joining their herds to feed in places where food is especially abundant. Sows tend to coexist peacefully at all times of year, while males 18 months and older band together in bachelor herds or sometimes live alone during the nonbreeding months. Outsiders may be challenged by dominant animals of either sex, particularly if food is in short supply, but herd members are generally very tolerant of one another.

Although wild and feral pigs aren't known to be more migratory than is necessary to find suitable habitat, they can easily cover 10 miles a day. The normal gait is a trot of roughly 6 miles an hour, and pigs seldom walk except when feeding. At a fast run the average adult can reach speeds in excess of 20 miles per hour.

In ancient times, pigs served not just as food but also as farming animals. A plot of rough land could be tilled and made ready for planting crops just by turning a herd of pigs loose, where the animals' rooting and pawing would loosen the soil nearly as well as a drawn plow. Early Egyptians are said to have used swine hoofprints in loose soil as planting holes for their seed, and pig dung is among the best fertilizers.

S. scrofa's extremely acute sense of smell, which some think is superior to that of a tracking dog, has also been exploited by humans. In Europe, where fungi known as truffles are considered a delicacy, pigs have been trained to sniff out these and other mushrooms. Pigs have also been used experimentally for tracking people lost in the wilderness, and for finding dead bodies, although the species' temperament and lack of agility make it more difficult to work with than a dog. In medieval times, pigs were sometimes trained to hunt game, but most often swine have themselves been the subject of a hunt.

Collared Peccary (Dicotyles tajacu)

Peccaries are New World pigs, related to the warthog of Africa and the wild boar of Eurasia, though more diminutive than either of these. Peccaries, which are members of the family Tayassuidae, have fewer teeth than true swine and a two-chambered stomach that appears to be transitional toward the order of ruminants (cud chewers).

Collared peccary. Photo by Tom Stehn, courtesy of U.S. Fish & Wildlife Service.

There are two major species: the collared peccary and the white-lipped peccary, with fourteen recognized subspecies in North and South America. All of them are known by the alternate name "javelina," which is a reference to the species' sharply pointed straight tusks that fit together tightly enough to be honed with each jaw movement.

Geographic Range

Collared peccaries are found only in warmer climates, occurring from northern Argentina, throughout Central America, and northward to southern Arizona, New Mexico, and Texas.

Habitat

In South and Central America, the collared peccary inhabits tropical rainforests and lower mountain regions. In the southwestern United States and northern Mexico, the preferred habitat includes rocky deserts of saguaro and mesquite. Collared peccaries are also becoming common in residential areas, where they appear to be learning to rely on human handouts of food.

Physical Characteristics

Mass: 30 to 65 pounds.

Body: Typically piglike, with a stout barrel-shaped body on short legs. Large head with long, tapered muzzle, ending in a disc-shaped snout designed for rooting in soil. Shoulder height 20 to 22 inches. Body length 35 to 40 inches.

Collared peccaries have short, straight tusks that fit together tightly enough to hone one other down with every jaw movement. This razor sharpness gives this species its common name: javelina ("javelinlike"). Javelinas have a distinct dorsal gland on the rump that emits hormonal scents used in communication. The species possesses poor eyesight and good hearing, which are believed to contribute to the very vocal nature of this species.

Tail: Short and inconspicuous, about 3 inches long, and straight, not coiled like domestic swine.

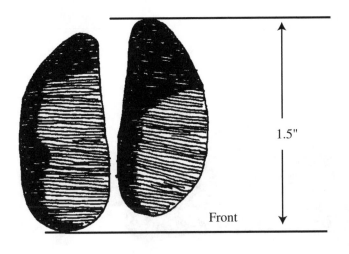

1.5"

Front

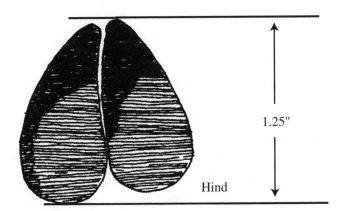

1.25"

Hind

Collared peccary (Dicotyles tajacu).

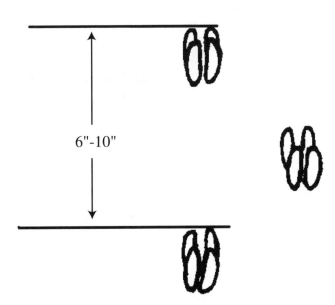

6"-10"

Collared peccary trotting track pattern.

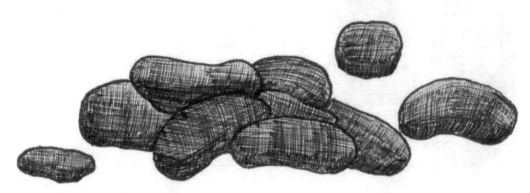

Collared peccary scats. Pellets, sometimes massed, 1"-2" long. Some disclike and flattened, like very small cowpies.

Tracks: Cloven hooves on all four feet, tracks 1 to 1.5 inches long. Stride is a short 6 to 10 inches, with hind hooves usually registering in front tracks. Despite their similarities to true pigs, collared peccaries comprise their own Artiodactyl suborder by having two dewclaws on the forefeet, one on the hind feet; true swine have two dewclaws on all four feet.

Scat: Typically large, almost pellet-shaped segments, much like the pellets of a deer, but larger at 2 to 3 inches long. When the peccary has been feeding on especially rich or succulent plants, scats may take on a flattened disc shape similar to a cowpie. Scat may contain small bones of rodents or birds, and insect carapaces and legs.

Coloration: The peccary's coarse-haired coat is grizzled gray to nearly black with white guard hairs that give it a salt-and-pepper appearance. There is a yellowish patch on the cheeks and a collar of yellowish hair encircling the neck just ahead of the shoulders. Males and females are nearly identical in size and color.

Sign: Regularly used trails made by several animals. Feeding areas of disturbed earth, rooted up by the animals' tough snouts as they dig for roots. Chewed cactus, especially prickly pear. There will often be a strong odor of musk from the animals' urine and from a scent gland located in the middle of the back above the flanks.

Vocalizations: Grunts, squeals, growls. Peccaries are sometimes thought to be especially vocal because they possess poor long distance vision and hearing, but it appears more likely that herd members communicate vocally to keep contact with one another in thick, brushy terrain where visibility is limited. The alarm vocalization is a coughing sound. Peccaries can squeal like a pig, but do so only when in mortal danger.

Lifespan: 15 to 20 years; up to 24 years in captivity.

Diet

Collared peccaries are primarily herbivorous, with complex stomachs for digesting coarsely chewed plant material, but like other swine they will generally eat anything they can. Prickly pear cactus leaves, spines and all, are a preferred food in arid regions because the succulent cacti provide both food and a valuable source of water, but the species will also eat frogs, snakes, lizards, the eggs of ground-nesting birds like the roadrunner, and all manner of roots, fungi, and fruits. They will also eat carrion, and sometimes destroy vegetable gardens with their rooting.

Mating Habits

Male collared peccaries reach sexual maturity at 11 months, females at 8 to 14 months. The species does not have a set mating season, but instead responds to changes in climate, particularly rain, that initiate the breeding cycle. In wet weather there is a greater abundance of food, which helps to insure that pregnant mothers are well-fed and healthy, so most mating occurs during heavy rains. Conversely, in years of prolonged drought, very few young will be born.

Peccaries are herd animals, and like other social species they have a fairly rigid hierarchy. The dominant male in a herd is the only male permitted to breed. Nonbreeding subordinate males are permitted to remain with the herd when breeding is initiated, but are not allowed to approach females in estrus. As a result, bachelor herds don't exist as they do in most herd species.

After a 4-month gestation period, two to four piglets are born, with twins being the norm, and larger litters usually the result of an exceptionally well-fed mother. In contrast to most other social species that are predominantly female, the ratio between sexes is approximately equal.

Pregnant females withdraw from the herd just prior to giving birth, seeking out a protected cave or other suitably sheltered location in which to have their litters. If they don't retreat from the group they run the risk of having their young killed and possibly eaten by other herd members, especially if food is scarce. However, the risk of cannibalism is of short duration, and after one day the mother rejoins her herd, where she provides such fierce protection for her offspring that other group members leave them alone.

Peccary young are a yellowish brown color with a black stripe down the back. They follow their mother everywhere, but are sometimes nursed by older sisters from a previous litter, the only other herd members that are allowed near the suckling piglets. Female peccaries have four nipples, but only the rear pair produce milk. This forces the mother to nurse from a standing position, and the piglets must suckle from behind her, rather than from the side as is normal with true swine. Piglets begin to feed on vegetation within a week of being born, but are not completely weaned until they reach 2 to 3 months of age.

Behavior

Collared peccaries live in herds of five to fifteen individuals of all ages and both sexes. Herds are notably cohesive, with members eating, sleeping, and foraging together, but there is a definite hierarchy in which a dominant male leads and the remainder are ranked primarily by size. Exceptions are the old, the terminally ill, and those seriously injured, all of which appear to withdraw voluntarily from the group, possibly to avoid being killed and eaten by other herd members.

Although peccary herds avoid contact with groups or individuals outside their own, and will defend their territories against intruders, feeding subgroups are often formed within the same herd. These subgroups of males, females, and young sometimes form the nucleus of a new herd, which breaks off from the parent herd to establish its own territory.

Peccary group territories range in size depending on herd numbers and the availability of food and other resources. Territorial boundaries are claimed by the herd leader, which rubs oily fluid from the musk gland on its rump against rocks, trees, and other prominent landmarks. Scats are also used to mark territorial boundaries, especially at trail intersections, and these will be refreshed periodically. When herd members meet one another after having been apart, they rub one another head-to-rump, each scenting the other with its own scent, thus verifying that both are members of the same group.

Herd members of either sex actively defend their territories against intruders from outside herds. First comes a warning that includes laying back the ears, raising the hair along the spine (hackles) to involuntarily release musk from the rump gland, and clacking the teeth together rapidly to make a chattering sound. If an intruder fails to withdraw, the defending peccary charges, attempting to knock the adversary off its feet, biting with its fanglike canines, and sometimes locking jaws with its opponent. Fights may be bloody, but are seldom fatal to either combatant because the weaker animal will normally withdraw as soon as it becomes apparent that the other is stronger.

Collared peccaries are sensitive and responsive to environmental changes, including precipitation, ambient temperatures, and length of day, and feeding behavior changes with the seasons. In winter, night foraging begins earlier in the evening and ends later in the morning as temperatures become more tolerable, and herds that would normally seek shade under which to sleep through the heat of the day in summer may forage for food at midday.

Despite their status as a game animal, especially in Arizona, collared peccaries have become habituated to residential areas, and often frequent locations where they know they will be fed, frequently making a nuisances of themselves by rooting up gardens or raiding trash cans. Their major predators, coyotes, pumas, jaguars, and bobcats, avoid human habitation, which may explain the peccary's penchant for living near people. The species is resilient and not in danger of depopulation, although about 20,000 are killed in Texas each year by sport hunters. Some subspecies living in the tropics of South America are threatened by rainforest destruction and the resultant loss of habitat.

OTHER HOOVED ANIMALS

Pronghorn Antelope (*Antilocapra americana*)

Antilocapra americana is unique among all other species. Fossil data indicates that the species dates back to the Miocene period and is the sole surviving member of at least thirteen genera that existed in the Pliocene and Pleistocene periods. Historically, the pronghorn antelope was classified as a goat. Today, it is the sole member of its own family—Antilocapridae—but some scientists would like to place it in the bovine family. However, the pronghorn antelope sheds its horn sheaths annually, about a month after breeding, whereas most bovids do not.

Pronghorn antelope mother and calves.

Pronghorns are the fastest runners in North America, able to achieve speeds of up to 70 miles per hour and maintain that pace for up to 4 minutes. More remarkably, pronghorns can sustain speeds of 30 miles per hour for 30 minutes or longer, making them the best long-distance runners in the world.

Geographic Range

A. americana is native to the western plains of North America, from southern Alberta and southern Saskatchewan in Canada, throughout the western United States into the western portion of Sonora, Mexico.

Habitat

The pronghorn makes its home on prairies and grassy desert. It will not be found in forest, where its ability to run is hampered, and it avoids slippery mud or deep snow for the same reason.

Physical Characteristics

Mass: 75 to 140 pounds, males about 15% larger than females.

Body: Nose-to-rump length averages 4 to 5 feet. Shoulder height 3 to 3.5 feet. Both sexes grow a pair of inward-curving black horns at maturity, but the buck's horns are longer at 12 to 20 inches and have a forward-facing tine, or prong. Does' horns typically don't exceed 4 inches in length, and lack the prong. Does usually have four mammae, but six have been recorded in some individuals. The long, woolly undercoat is covered by coarser guard hairs.

Tail: Tail length 3 to more than 6 inches, relative to an individual's size.

Tracks: Cloven-hooved and deerlike. No dewclaws. Prints average 2 to 2.5 inches long. Average stride about 12 inches at an easy trot. Straddle typically narrow, measuring 4 to 6 inches.

Scat: Deerlike pellets, about 0.5 inch long, occasionally clustered when feeding on succulents.

Coloration: Reddish-brown or tan above and white below. The neck bears a short black mane and two white stripes across its anterior portion. The rump is white. Males have a black mask and black patches on the sides of the neck; females lack the mask.

Sign: Browsed grasses. Large areas of heavily tracked grassland where herds have fed, with body-size impressions where the animals lay down to sleep and ruminate.

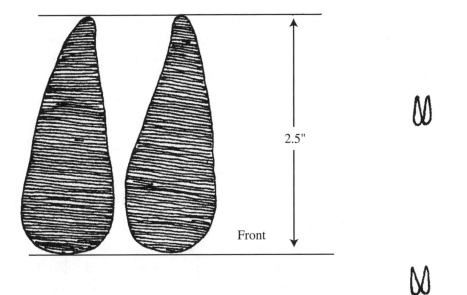

2.5"

Front

2.0"

Hind

Pronghorn (Antilocapra americana). Slender but extremely strong legs built for running very fast, with no dewclaws.

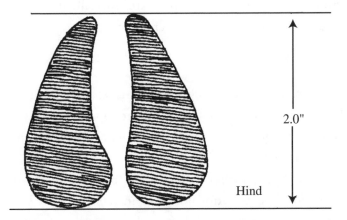

Slow run

Pronghorn antelope track pattern.

Vocalizations: Several vocalizations and visual signals are common among pronghorn: Calves bleat when separated from their mother, mothers grunt when seeking their calves, males roar during fights, males and females blow through their nostrils when angered, and the hairs of the white rump patch are erected in warning.

Lifespan: Captive individuals have lived longer than 11 years.

Diet

Pronghorns are distributed over several habitat types, and diet reflects the availability of food plants. A 1964 study estimated that two-thirds of antelope lived on open grassland, while the remaining third inhabited more arid areas of sagebrush and bunchgrasses. Only about 1% lived in desert regions. A study of pronghorns in Kansas estimated that cactus makes up about 40% of the animals' diet, various grasses 22%, succulent forbs 20%, and woody browse about 18%. Like deer, they will dig through shallow snows using their front hooves to reach browse, but avoid deeper snows that inhibit running.

Antelope seldom drink from open water unless its foods are especially dry, being able to extract most of the moisture their bodies need from green browse.

Mating Habits

In the northern part of the pronghorn's range, breeding normally takes place during a 3-week period between mid-September and early October. Antelope living in the southern range begin mating as early as late July. Females usually mate in their second year, but males seldom mate until their third year.

Although male pronghorns attempt to gather harems prior to mating, and will sometimes lock horns with competitors in conventional shoving matches, they are best known for staring one another down, a uniquely nonviolent method of settling territorial disputes.

After mating, females hold their fertilized ova in stasis (delayed implantation) for about 1 month before the fetus begins to grow, and will abort the egg if a mother is malnourished or in poor health. Like deer, females typically give birth to one calf at the end of their 7-month gestation periods, with twins being the norm thereafter. Newborns are unspotted and weigh an average of 6 pounds at birth. The young have a grayish coat until 3 months old. At 3 weeks, fawns begin feeding on plants, but continue to suckle on their mothers' fat-rich milk for a month or more.

Behavior

Pronghorns may be diurnal or nocturnal, with their most active times being in the twilight hours of sunrise and sunset (crepuscular). Daily movements depend on need and the availability of resources, and animals may not travel at all so long as an area provides for their needs. In winter when browse is more scarce they may range 2 to 7 miles each day, again depending on environmental resources, and sometimes migrate 100 miles to escape deep snows. From late autumn to spring the animals congregate in loose herds of up to 1,000 individuals of both sexes and all ages. In spring these herds separate into smaller groups that are segregated by sex, much like wapiti. Female herds are not territorial, and travel freely during the summer months, while males 3 years old or older ready themselves for the coming autumn rut by engaging in mock combat.

A typical summer territory encompasses about 2 square miles, contains a water source, and is bounded by mountains, high fences, or other obstacles that males use in an attempt to keep female herds nearby. Dominant males scent their territories with urine to keep intruders from outside their own bachelor herd from claiming females. Bachelor herds of younger, nonbreeding males are permitted to wander freely between territories, but maturing males will be driven off by the dominant male if they show sexual interest in claimed females.

After the mating season, horn sheaths are shed and pronghorns of either sex become less hierarchical, once again forming loose herds.

Pronghorns once numbered about 35 million, but they were seen as a competitor for grasslands by early cattle ranchers who killed them indiscriminately. By 1920, there were only 20,000 of them left in North America. Today, legal protections have allowed their numbers to increase to about 500,000, but cattle ranching still poses the biggest threat to population growth and range with fences that are too high for a pronghorn to jump. In Mexico, habitat destruction in the forms of strip mining and oil exploration is threatening that country's population, which now numbers only about 1,200 animals.

Domestic Horse (*Equus caballus*)

The horse is arguably the most important animal that has ever been domesticated. *Equus caballus* has served for millennia as a biological source of power for pulling or carrying loads too heavy for humans to manage, to draw the plows and other farm implements needed to turn large tracts of land into valuable crops, and even for war.

Horses are members of the family Equus, which comprises several of the most important animals in the evolution of human history. Unlike the other hooved animals in this book, who are even-toed (order Artiodactyla), equines have hooves with an odd number of toes, which places them in the order Perissodactyla. And in the case of the equine family, one large toe covers the entire

Domestic horses. Photo by Ken Hammond, courtesy of USDA.

bottom of the foot. This family includes donkeys, horses, zebras, and the rhinoceros. Mules, another member of family Equus, are not a true species because they are actually a hybrid of horse and donkey, and all mules are born sterile.

Geographic Range

Wild horses originated in the vast grassland, or steppe, region that extends from Poland to Mongolia, and it was there that the species was first tamed and trained by humans for use as working animals. No species of horse was found in the New World until after 1492, when a few of those brought by Spanish explorers escaped and soon thrived on rich prairies that already supported bison, elk, and antelope. Today domesticated, horses are found throughout the world, while feral populations exist on Australian savannahs, along the coasts of Spain and France, on the Outer Bank Islands of North Carolina, and in the Great Basin region of the western United States. Feral populations are typically small.

The only true wild horse, Przewalski's wild horse (*Equus caballus przevalskii*) was officially discovered by Russian naturalist Nikolai Michailovitch Przewalski in 1879 while he was exploring the Mongolian steppes. Too small to be considered a good riding or work animal, Przewalski's horse was hunted for meat, and was thought to be extinct from its natural habitat by 1968 due to overhunting, loss of grazing areas to domestic cattle, and through hybridization with feral horses. A few Przewalski's horses still survive in zoos.

Habitat

Because they are grazing animals, horses require large tracts of grassland. Suitable habitats include semiarid savannah, open plains, and mountainous steppes. They can be found at elevations up to 8,000 feet, so long as the habitat there provides sufficient grazing and water.

Physical Characteristics

Mass: 650 to more than 4,000 pounds, depending on the breed.

Body: Size varies considerably with individual breeds. Length ranges from 7 to 10 feet. Shoulder height 3 to 6 feet. The general body pattern includes long legs, a robust barrel-shaped body, a comparatively long and slender neck with a ridge (mane) of longer hair extending along its top from skull to shoulders, and a large head with a long muzzle. The large ears are always pointed and erect. Unlike deer or bovines, horses have incisor teeth in the top front of the mouth, instead of a hard palate, which allows them to bite off foliage as opposed to tearing it free.

Tail: Length varies with the size of the animal, but tails are relatively short with long hairs growing from them in a brushlike pattern. Tails function as a swatter to chase away flying insects.

Tracks: 4 to 8 inches long. The pattern is distinctively U-shaped because horses have a single uncloven hoof on all 4 feet, with rounded portion of the U pointing in the direction of travel. Stride varies with an individual's size, but straddle, like the straddle of other hooved animals, is always narrower than the horse's actual body width because the legs point inward. Also, unlike wild hooved mammals, the tracks of a walking horse tend to print individually, rather than with the hind hoof registering in the front track.

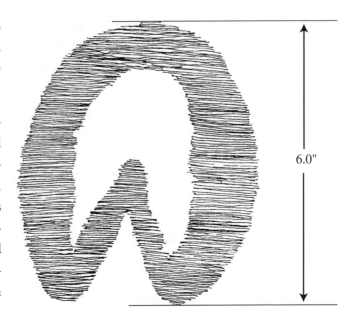

6.0"

Domestic horse track (Equus caballus).

Scat: Very similar to a cowpie, except that horse dung tends to be drier and with more obvious rounded segments.

Coloration: Highly variable, with individual coats ranging from solid white, tan, brown, reddish, or black to splotched patterns consisting of any or all of these.

Sign: Grasses and forbs neatly cut near to the ground, not torn free as with bovines or deer. Heavily impacted trails that are relatively narrow compared to the number of animals using them.

Vocalizations: Neighs, whinnies, and snorts in varying frequency ranges. When alarmed, the animals issue a blowing sound similar to that of the whitetail deer.

Lifespan: 20 to 30 years, occasionally longer.

Diet

Wild and feral horses are grazers of open grasslands, walking as they feed and biting off mouthfuls of grasses, sedges, clovers, and alfalfa as they're encountered. They also like domestic grains, including corn, wheat, and oats, as well as fruits like apples.

Mating Habits

Horses are seasonally polyestrous, with mares typically coming into heat in April and repeatedly coming into heat once every month thereafter until October, or until the mare is impregnated. Mating is initiated by the mares; stallions (studs) are physically capable of breeding throughout the year. Mares become sexually mature at about 18 months, with stallions usually reaching puberty at 2 years.

Gestation for horses is a comparatively long 11 months, with one offspring, or foal being born in spring or summer. Size and weight of foals varies with that of the mother, being much smaller in pony-size horses than in large workhorses. Foals are able to stand and walk within minutes after birth, and remain at their mothers' sides for at least the first week of life. Weaning takes place at approximately 7 months, but mares that are not impregnated the following year may allow their foals to suckle until they're 1 year old.

On reaching puberty, males normally leave the herd, forced out by the lead stallion, and find a mate by enticing sexually mature females from another herd. Unlike most animals, inbreeding is fairly common among feral horses.

Behavior

Like bovids, horses live within a harem-type social system, where one dominant male leads a herd consisting of several females and their offspring. There is only one leader in a herd, and he will defend his harem against usurpers by rearing on hind legs and boxing and biting a challenger until one of them retreats. Defeated males may then follow the herd, attempting to steal away females with which to begin another herd, or they might strike out to find another herd that isn't so strongly defended.

Like other plains grazers, horses avoid deep snows, and will migrate as necessary to find ample food supplies and water. Typical migrations seldom exceed 50 miles.

CHAPTER 4

PAWED ANIMALS

THE DOG FAMILY (FAMILY CANIDAE)

Members of the family Canidae, or dog family, are characterized by having four feet with four toes each—discounting a dewclaw high up on the forefeet that doesn't show in tracks—each toe tipped with a single nonretractable claw. A long tail is universal, as are long canine teeth designed for inflicting mortal wounds to prey animals. All are digitigrade, meaning they normally walk and run weight-forward, on their toes, so the heaviest impressions in a track will be from the toes and claws, with heel pads printing more faintly. All are meat eaters, although all require at least some vegetable matter in their diets. Wild species have erect pointed ears that can be rotated to precisely home in on the location of sounds, and all have an acute sense of smell.

Domestic Dog (Canis familiaris)

Any treatment of the family Canidae should probably begin with the member that's most familiar to all of us: the domestic dog. Dogs have been the constant companions of humans since before recorded history began, so the beginning of their lineage is a matter of some conjecture.

Some researchers think that the dog and wolf began as two separate wild species, one of which shunned humans, while the other became first a scavenger of human settlements, then a domestic servant. Others believe the dog branched directly from the gray wolf, learning as a matter of necessity to live with people in exchange for a steady supply of food.

In either case, the free-living gray wolf, the epitome of wilderness, has had many centuries of persecution in which to learn to avoid humans, while the dog has been selectively bred to enhance the characteristics and traits that are most important to human needs. Selecting a dog these days can be complicated, because there are hundreds of breeds with different looks, temperaments, and sizes from which to choose. The modern dog is indeed so far removed from the gray wolf as to be considered an entirely different branch of the family tree.

What we do know about this canine that has been genetically manipulated to serve our purposes is that it's unconditionally loyal, protective of its adopted family, and that its acute senses of hearing, smell, and night vision can detect impending danger far in advance of our own. It thrives on human affection, and every breed can be expected to give its life to protect a kind owner. Today dogs are trained to be the eyes of people who are blind, to find hikers who become lost, to find people trapped under rubble, and even to retrieve or manipulate objects for owners who are confined to a wheelchair.

Geographic Range

Dogs are common throughout the world. Rarely can a dog survive to reproduce in the wild, so they can be expected to be found only near human habitation, where even unowned dogs can survive by scavenging through human garbage. Domestic dogs can be found in every culture on earth.

Habitat

Worldwide.

Physical Characteristics

Mass: Varied

Body: Varied. There exists a diversity of sizes, colors, temperaments, fur types, and physiques that is beyond the scope of a book not dedicated entirely to dogs. The different subspecies, or breeds, reflect several millenia of selective breeding, the result of which is that only a few dog breeds bear more than a passing resemblance to wild canids.

Tail: Varied, usually long, averaging about 50% of body length.

Tracks: Size varies, from about 1 inch to more than 5 inches for large breeds. Four toes in all tracks. Heel pad variable in shape, but usually with two or three rearward-pointing lobes. Claws always show in tracks.

Scat: Because the diet of a dog differs greatly from that of any wild canid, consisting almost exclusively of processed foods, the scat it leaves is easy to identify. The shape is generally cylindrical, segmented, and tapered at the end, much like the scat of wild canids, but there will almost never be evidence of fur or bone fragments. Instead the scat of a dog is generally smooth, perhaps a little grainy from the cereals contained in commercial dry foods. Color varies from brown to black, depending on the foods eaten, becoming gray, then white and crumbly as organic materials within it decompose.

Size of a dog's scat generally matches the size of the animal, with larger dogs leaving larger deposits than smaller dogs. However, like most animals, diameter and mass can vary with content, the amount eaten at the animal's previous meal, and with the volume of water in its digestive system.

Coloration: Varied.

Rottweiler front track in wet sand.

Sign: Scratch marks made by the animal's paws as it scrapes its feet against the ground after urinating or defecating. Dogs are also prone to chewing and gnawing, especially against softer materials like plastic and wood.

Vocalizations: Domestic dogs are far more vocal than their wild cousins. Barking is the most recognized form of communication among them, but they also growl, whine, and sometimes howl, although some individuals seem incapable of howling.

Lifespan: About 10 years.

Diet

Like wild canids, dogs are primarily carnivorous, requiring a predominance of meat proteins and fats in their diets. But like their wild cousins, dogs also need to eat vegetation to obtain vitamins, minerals, and sugars not found in meat. Tastes tend to vary with individuals, but most dogs will eat uncooked green beans, blueberries, cherries, raspberries, potatoes, and apples.

Pups require about 50 calories per pound of body weight for their first year, after which energy requirements drop back to about 30 calories per pound of body weight for average-size animals. Small, energetic dogs might actually require more than 40 calories, while larger, and typically less active, breeds may need as few as 20 calories per pound of weight.

Dogs like table scraps, largely because of the high concentrations of calories found in people foods, and they exhibit a tendency to become overweight, whereas wild canids seldom eat more than their bodies require to maintain health, even in captivity. Dogs overfed with fat, including bone marrow, run the risk of contracting pancreatitis, a serious and often fatal condition in which the pancreas loses its ability to metabolize fats. Human foods that can be toxic to dogs include chocolate, onions, and foods that have gone moldy.

As with wolves and coyotes, a dog is genetically designed to endure short periods of starvation, and may lose up to 40% of its body weight without suffering permanent harm.

Mating Habits

Dogs of either sex reach fertility at 6 to 12 months, with smaller dogs typically becoming sexually active sooner than large breeds. The age at which a dog breeds also depends on social factors, including competition from other dogs, health, and the level of confidence an individual possesses.

Unlike wild canids, male dogs are prepared to breed at any time, and, like all male mammals, they're prompted by the scent of female sex hormones, or pheromones. Female dogs, or bitches, come into their breeding period, or "heat," about every 6 months, a characteristic that's known as seasonally monocyclic. The breeding cycle has four stages: anestrus, proestrus, estrus, and diestrus. The anestrus, or non-breeding, period lasts about about 4 months, followed by the proestrus stage when a bloody vaginal discharge appears. Proestrus is the initial stage of heat, and may last from 9 to 28 days. Pheromonal scents emitted during the proestrus cycle are intended to attract potential mates, and this period normally ends with the bitch's acceptance of a partner.

Estrus is the stage at which a female becomes sexually receptive and may become pregnant. Bleeding from the proestrus period may or may not continue during the estrus period. Ovulation occurs about 24 hours after copulation, but eggs (ova) can remain fertile for 4 days after ovulation, making it possible to have two or more fathers within the same litter of pups. If a female in heat fails to become pregnant, the mating period ends with a diestrus stage in which uterus and ovaries are swollen and may make the female appear to be pregnant. This "pseudopregnancy" passes in a few days as the reproductive organs return to their anestrous state.

Behavior

Like wolves and coyotes, dogs are essentially pack animals, which helps to explain why they tend to do so well as members of a human family. When allowed to live together, as in a sled dog team or bear hunting pack, there's usually at least an initial struggle to determine which animal is dominant.

Unlike wild animals, which possess an innate reluctance to inflict debilitating injury to members of their own kind, battles between dogs are often bloody, and sometimes fatal to one or both combatants. Much of the problem is created because team dogs are generally not all from the same family, whereas wild packs of wolves and coyotes are nearly always related to one another. In the best case, battles end when one of the dogs submits by rolling onto its back to expose its vulnerable underside and averts its eyes.

Body language exhibited by dogs can reveal an animal's mood or intent. When relaxed, a dog's tail is down, but not between the legs, ears are erect or loosely laid back, and the mouth may be open or closed, depending on whether the dog is "tasting" scents in the air.

When wary, as with meeting another dog for the first time, the ears are usually back, tail between the legs to protect the genitalia, and hackles (fur along the spine) may be erect. The legs will probably be stiff and body movements are likely to be quick and a bit jerky.

An alerted dog will typically hold its tail erect to make itself look larger, its hackles raised for the same reason, and the ears will likely be fully up to enhance its hearing. Body movements are fluid, almost prancing, as the dog decides whether to flee or fight. This dog will probably bark constantly in an attempt to make the potential aggressor flee. Humans are often amused when this behavior is directed at inanimate objects that the dog doesn't recognize.

An aggressive dog that's ready to fight pulls back its lips to expose as many teeth as possible. The ears are pulled tightly back to keep them from being injured, hackles are fully raised, and the tail is held stiffly up or down, but not between the legs. Vocalizations include snarling, deep growls, and intermittent barking.

Dogs that live in close contact with people often learn human mannerisms. One of the most misinterpreted is the smile. Pet dogs frequently pick up on the way humans smile at one another on meeting, and many adopt the same behavior when meeting people, baring their front teeth and sometimes frightening strangers. The act is sometimes made more confusing by dogs that have learned to "talk," growling a greeting to people they perceive as friends. Body language, which includes a relaxed posture, a loosely held tail that will likely be wagging, and unraised hackles help to distinguish a smile from a snarl.

Gray Wolf (*Canis lupus*)

Gray wolves are believed to be the ancestor of all domestic dog breeds, including feral breeds that include Australian dingoes *(Canis lupus dingo)* and New Guinea singing dogs

Gray wolf trotting on hardpack snow. Note: This photo is of Chakota, alpha male of our captive pack of gray wolves. Photo by Cheanne Chellis.

(Canis lupus halstromi). Genetic evidence indicates that gray wolves were domesticated by humans at least twice, and possibly as many as five times.

Geographic Range

The gray, or timber, wolf is the largest of 41 species of wild canids worldwide, and although all wolves in North America (except the red wolf, *Canis rufus*) are considered to be Canis lupus, some biologists believe there may be as many as 32 regionalized subspecies.

Along with the coyote, gray wolves were once the most prevalent of wild canids, occupying most of the northern hemisphere from the Arctic through central Mexico, North Africa, and southern Asia. Today there are an estimated 2,600 wolves living in the lower 48 United States, with approximately 2,000 of those living in Minnesota. Most of the balance live in Michigan, with a small planted population in Yellowstone National Park. In Canada there are an estimated 50,000 wolves, Alaska claims about 7,000. Both Canada and Alaska permit wolf hunting, and in 2002 the status of gray wolves living in the Eastern Management Region of Michigan, Wisconsin, and Minnesota was downlisted from Endangered to Threatened.

In Europe, where wolves were once common, there are now only a few populations in northern Russia, Poland, Scandinavia, Spain, Portugal, and Italy. A few also survive in Japan and Mexico. The species was exterminated from Great Britain in the sixteenth century, and nearly so in Greenland during the twentieth century. Thanks to good conservation efforts, Greenland's wolf populations appear to have regained their original strength.

Left unmolested, wolves have shown that they can thrive in the face of advancing civilization, even expanding their range across Michigan's Straits of Mackinac in 1997 to become established at the northern tip of that state's Lower Peninsula.

Habitat

Gray wolves are perhaps the most successful of land animals, able to make their livings in a broad variety of climates and conditions, from Arctic tundra to dense forest, desert, and even prairie. Few large animals, including muskoxen, bison, and moose, are beyond the scope of a wolf pack's prey base, and they seem capable of feeding themselves in almost any environment where suitable prey can live.

The territorial range of a pack can encompass hundreds of square miles, but there are no arbitrary ranges because, like most animals, wolves range only as far as environmental factors demand. If an area provides plenty of prey and water with little competition from other large predators, a resident pack's territory may be no larger than a few square miles. In regions where a pack's food supply is migratory, as it is with caribou herds on the Arctic tundra, wolf packs may travel hundreds of miles.

In the latter half of the twentieth century it was widely believed that wolf numbers were kept low from loss of habitat due to construction of roads and other human encroachments on the wilderness. Today it appears that roadways hamper gray wolf populations very little, and the only real restriction on where they can live comes from the poisons, traps, guns, and human prejudice that exterminated them from most of their original range in the first place.

Physical Characteristics

Mass: 60 to 135 pounds, with northern populations tending to be larger than those in the south. Females average about 10% smaller than males.

Body: Very much like that of a large dog, but with proportionally larger head, more massive muzzle, and heavier legs. Body length (tip of nose to base of tail) 40 to 50 inches. Shoulder height 26 to 38 inches.

Tail: 14 to 20 inches long, bushy, darker on top than below. Note that the tail of a gray wolf never curls, but is always held straight down when the animal is relaxed, straight back when it's running, or straight up when it feels challenged. All domestic dogs, including wolf hybrids, curl their tails. Wolves differ from dogs in that they walk or trot using only their legs for locomotion, keeping the spine very straight. This adaptation helps to keep a traveling wolf less noticeable to prey that it hasn't seen yet, and is markedly different from the rocking gait of a dog.

Tracks: Front: 4 to more than 4.5 inches; hind: 3.5 to more than 4 inches. Forepaws typically about 10% longer than hind paws. Tracks always show claws and are 15 to 20% larger than those made by a dog of the same weight. Straddle 4 to 6 inches. Walking stride 26 to 30 inches.

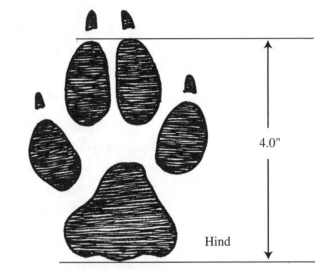

4.0"

Hind

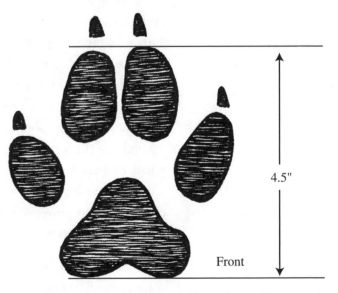

4.5"

Front

Gray wolf tracks (Canis lupus).

The tracks of a gray wolf are notably different than those of a coyote, and can usually be distinguished from those of a domestic dog by their larger size and physical characteristics. Like all canids, they have four toes on each foot tipped with heavy nonretractable claws, and a heel pad behind. The heel pads of the hind feet have three distinct lobes to their rear, which is fairly typical of canines, but the front heel pads show only two lobes in their tracks and leave a chevron-shaped imprint that is easily differentiated from the three-lobed front tracks of a coyote, fox, and most dogs.

Some dog breeds, like the Samoyed or malamute huskies, also display a chevron-shaped foretrack, but these animals are generally smaller than a gray wolf, and their feet are always much smaller. Gray wolves have very large feet to help distribute their weight over a wider area on soft surfaces, much like a snowshoe, and the front track of a 90-pound wolf will measure at least 4 inches in length, while a dog of the same weight will normally have a front paw that measures 3.5 inches or less. Larger feet give wolves an ability to pursue prey over deep snows at speeds that can reach 35 miles per hour.

Scat: Irregularly cylindrical, usually segmented, tapered at both ends. Size varies with diet, but typically 1.5 to 2 inches in diameter, 6 to 8 inches long. Fur and bone fragments are normally in evidence, with most fur wrapped in spiral fashion around the outside. Fresher scats are darker in color, in varying shades of brown or black, becoming gray as organic matter decomposes.

The scat of a gray wolf is nearly identical to that of other wild canids because all share similar diets, except that the wolf's is generally much larger in diameter and longer because the animal making it is larger. A typical scat is cylindrical and tapered at one or both ends, its outside covered in animal hair that runs longitudinally along its length. The fur, which wraps the outside of the scat in spiral fashion as it moves through the digestive system, serves a useful function by surrounding small bones and bone fragments that might otherwise scrape or even perforate the animal's lower intestine. Wolf scat especially is wrapped predominantly with deer hair, but may be covered with finer fur from rabbits, raccoons, and other smaller prey.

Inside the scat will be the bones of whatever animals the animal has been eating. Smaller bones may be whole, but an adult wolf can exert roughly 1,500 pounds per square inch to crush large leg bones to get fat-rich marrow that's inaccessible to smaller canids with less powerful jaws. These large chunks of crushed bone are an identifying characteristic of wolf scat.

Coloration: Varied, but North American gray wolves tend to exhibit three distinctive color phases. The common gray phase is typified by varying combinations of white (especially the coarser guard hairs) with black, gray, red, and brown on the upper body and head. The back is usually more black, with most reddish fur occurring around the muzzle and ears. The underside is typically light gray to white, with a concentration of black over the tail gland, and a black-tipped tail.

The black phase is normally seen in young animals, and always lightens toward gray as the animal ages, with black hairs becoming progressively more interspersed with gray or white, often with spots of reddish fur around the head and neck. Black wolves appear to be always low in the pack hierarchy.

Completely white coats are most often seen on Arctic subspecies in the far north, where the coloration is best suited as camouflage, and then usually on older adults. Comparatively few wolves living in the Arctic are white, however, and the normal gray and black phases are most common there. Wolves in every phase tend to lighten in color with age.

Coyotes are sometimes mistaken for gray wolves, especially in the north where coyotes may weigh in excess of 60 pounds, and most often in winter when the coyote's seasonal coat is thicker and tends to be more gray. Distinguishing characteristics include the gray wolf's much larger size, which is typically about double that of the coyote, a comparatively heavier build with stouter legs, a broader less-pointed muzzle, and shorter less-pointed ears. Coyote tracks rarely exceed 3 inches, and where clear prints are evident the coyote's front heelpad will show three distinct lobes at its rear, where the gray wolf's front heel pad has only two, and leaves a V-shaped imprint.

Sign: Digging for ground squirrels and other burrowing animals is one of the most obvious signs left by gray wolves. Bears also dig for burrowed prey, as do coyotes and badgers, but bears aren't active in winter, and the loose soil excavated by this activity will usually hold a track imprint that identifies the digger.

Scentposts, usually in the form of trees and stumps that have been urinated on, are one of the wolf's territorial advertisements, and an indication of its social status. Males try to urinate as high up on a tree as possible to demonstrate, and even exaggerate, their size. Females may also urinate at these scent posts, usually squatting, but sometimes actually cocking one leg like a male, especially during the late-winter mating season when young migrating adults are trying to meet one another.

Wolves make a habit of transporting deer-size prey away from the place where they were killed to a more secure location, where the animals can eat in peace. Gray wolves seem to have little trouble picking up a deer weighing nearly as much as themselves in their powerful jaws, and carrying it a half-mile or more, leaving traces of deer hair where the prey was scraped against a tree, sometimes dragmarks where its hooves slid over soil. If the prey is too large to be carried, or if the wolves are in a pack, killed animals are often dismembered before being carried off, which may also leave sign in the form of blood trails and fallen hairs.

The places where wolves take prey to be eaten are also good places to find sign. In one instance, I found the remains of five deer that had been taken up onto a flat ridge overlooking the surrounding woods, indicating that this was a preferred and regular dining location where the wolves felt safe enough to relax and eat.

Vocalizations: Like most wild animals for whom being too noisy can mean not eating or getting eaten, gray wolves are normally silent. However, they're still one of the more vocal species because a social lifestyle demands communication.

Howling is the wolf's most recognized sound. Prior to a pack hunt, the alpha male, and occasionally the alpha female, will sound a "lone wolf" howl to gather members together. This mostly monotone howl, which some humans have classified as sad or even eerie, is heard mostly in the early evening, and usually from the same tall hill or ridge, until the pack moves on to new territory. Gathering howls also serve to warn other wolves (and coyotes) that might be in hearing distance that this territory is claimed.

Upon gathering, a chorus of howls sounds from the meeting place as packmates have a kind of pep rally to get themselves worked up for a strenuous night of hunting. These community howls are purposely multi-pitched and of different timbres to help convince larger predators and competitors that the pack's numbers are greater than they really are. Some howls may be higher-pitched than others, and often they'll have a wavering quality, but never the high-pitched yapping of coyotes.

Wolves rarely bark, and never exhibit the repeated barking of a dog. All wolves can bark, however; one of these is a short, muted alarm bark, almost a huffing sound, that is intended to alert other pack members to potential danger. The other is a louder and more prolonged bark, usually accompanied by deep growls.

Lifespan: About 8 years in the wild; up to 15 years in captivity.

Diet

Gray wolves are primarily meat-eaters, but like most carnivores they require at least some vegetable matter in their normal diet. Wolves in captivity are usually fond of green beans, especially in winter, while those in the wild eat blueberries, grasses, and other fruits, both for nutrition and as dietary fiber to keep their colons healthy.

Gray wolves are probably best known as hunters of large prey, ranging from whitetail deer to moose to muskoxen in the far north. The drill-team precision exhibited by a hunting pack as it maneuvers larger prey into a vulnerable position is the stuff of stories, but in fact wolves rarely take on prey capable of injuring one of their number because a flailing hoof can seriously injure the strongest wolf, thereby weakening the entire pack. In every case the prey of choice will be a small, immature animal or an adult that has been weakened through old age, disease, or one that has been wounded by human hunters. Deer that are near death from starvation are not eaten, because acids that accumulate in muscle mass when it cannibalizes itself are toxic.

When wolf packs split up in mid-winter (when the alpha pair leaves to mate and seek out a den), they may regroup periodically to hunt larger prey, but mature pack members may strike out to find their own mates and territories. These "lone" wolves haven't the means to bring down larger animals, so much of their diets consist of mice and voles, squirrels, rabbits and hares, small raccoons, and most other small animals that can be easily caught and killed.

Mating Habits

Gray wolves mate between January and March, with those in the south breeding first because spring comes to them earlier. Only the parent, or Alpha, pair will mate within a pack, which is itself a family unit, to prevent the possibility of inbreeding. Adult offspring may leave the pack to find a mate and establish their own territories at 2 to 4 years of age, but some weaker "omega" wolves may remain with the pack their entire lives.

Like dogs, the females' breeding cycle has four stages: anestrus, proestrus, estrus, and diestrus. The estrus stage, when the female actually copulates, lasts 5 to 14 days, about half that of a domestic dog. Breeding male wolves come into heat at the same time their mates do, and, unlike dogs, their testicles, which are retracted and inactive for the rest of the year, will descend only during this period.

About 2 weeks prior to mating, the alpha pair separates from the rest of their pack to find or create a den, which will always be near a source of fresh water. Like coyotes and foxes, wolf dens normally consist of a body-size tunnel, roughly 18 inches in diameter and 10 feet long, excavated into the soil of hillside. This opens into a chamber which is typically 4 feet high by 6 feet long and 6 feet wide, and usually at a higher level than the entrance tunnel to prevent flooding. The chamber floor is usually covered with grasses and other plant material. Dens may also be made in small caves or cracks in mountainous terrain, so long as these afford protection from weather and large bears, which are known to prey on pups. A good den may be used year after year if left unmolested.

During the denning period adult offspring may strike out to find their own mates, while those that remain with the pack frequently adopt younger siblings and teach them to catch rodents. Except for the alpha male, pack members aren't allowed at the den site until pups are weaned, but the alpha male may regroup them for a hunt by howling. As the alpha female becomes more pregnant and more vulnerable, she will spend more time in the den, and her mate will bring her food.

Gestation lasts about 60 days, with most pups born between March and May, again depending on how long winter lasts in that area. Average litter size is about 6, sometimes more, sometimes less, depending on how healthy and well-fed the female is during her pregnancy, and pups weigh about 8 ounces at birth. If the female is very hungry or sickly during her pregnancy, her body may spontaneously abort the entire litter.

Newborn pups are blind and deaf. They remain in the den, completely dependent on their mother for nourishment and warmth for about 8 weeks, and for their first 3 weeks she will stay with them constantly except for infrequent outings to drink and to expel waste. She will take at least some of her meals in the den, but its interior will be fastidiously clean and free of refuse that might bring disease to her young. During the denning period pups grow fast, putting on about 3 pounds of body weight every week.

For several weeks after leaving the den pups will be fed regurgitated meat by pack members returning from a hunt, stimulating the adults to throw up the predigested flesh by licking at the corners of their mouths, a habit that is also seen in dogs. Predigested meat is easier for the young pups to assimilate, and adults can carry more meat more easily in their stomachs than in their mouths.

Pups are completely weaned by 9 weeks, freeing their mother to join her packmates on hunts. Pups may leave the den to play-fight with one another at this time, watched over by a "babysitter," a task usually assigned to the weakest member of the pack, but youngsters don't stray far from the safety of the den because of coyotes, bears, bobcats, and other large predators. By 10 months of age the pups have grown to about 65 pounds and are old enough to hunt with the pack.

Female pups reach sexual maturity at 2 years, and may leave the pack to find their own mates at this age. Males typically don't reach full maturity until age 3.

Behavior

Gray wolves are among the most social of animals. Pack size may number from just 2 animals when an alpha pair is establishing its own family territory, to more than 30 in the far north. A typical wolf pack is comprised of family members, usually the alpha pair and their offspring, but it isn't unheard of for a pack to take in unrelated individuals, and orphaned pups are always adopted.

A defined hierarchy exists within each pack. Alpha males are normally the most dominant, although a few packs have been led by a widowed alpha female. All other members are subordinate to the alphas. If one of the alphas is seriously injured or killed, the other may leave the pack to seek out a new, unrelated mate, leaving the Beta, or second strongest male in charge. Alternately, if the alpha female is killed, the alpha male is likely to take one of her sisters, who joined the pack when she did, as his new mate.

It has been noted that newly paired alpha mates seeking out territories in which to establish their own pack will often travel with a third female wolf, usually a sister of the alpha female. This practice helps to insure that a new alpha pair has the strength to take down larger prey, but also provides the alpha male with a backup mate should the original alpha female be killed. If all goes well, the secondary female will serve as a babysitter for the alphas' first litter of pups.

Members of a wolf pack virtually never fight one another, because to harm a member of what is essentially a team weakens its ability to hunt. Alphas are almost never challenged, and the pack hierarchy is strictly followed, with alphas and pups eating first, followed by betas, then subordinate pack members, and finally by the omega, or lowest ranking wolf. Pups that reach adulthood and wish to begin their own families must leave the pack to find mates, thus preventing inbreeding. Alphas and other pack members are cared for and fed if they become injured or grow too old to participate in hunts, but these wolves often leave the pack voluntarily.

All gray wolf packs have an annual stationary and nomadic phase. The stationary phase occurs during spring and summer, when pups are too small to travel with their pack. The nomadic phase occurs from autumn to the late winter, when packs must travel to follow migratory or yarded deer herds. Depending on terrain and necessity, a pack may travel upward of 100 miles in a day, most of it covered during the hours of darkness at an easy lope of about 15 miles per hour.

Despite historical prejudices that persist even into the twenty-first century, gray wolves are a critical part of the ecosystem in North America and around the globe. Whitetail deer, for example, are genetically geared to lose one-third of their population each year, and in fact need to lose that many individuals to maintain a strong, disease-free herd. Increased bag limits for hunters have helped, but even combined with the number of whitetails killed by cars, humans account for less than 1% of the mortality rate required to keep deer herds healthy. The result, which has become increasingly apparent as deer populations exceed the capacity of their diminishing habitat to sustain them, is a weakened, disease-prone herd.

Other arguments against increased wolf populations include livestock predation and the potential danger to humans. Real data gathered in recent years has shown that livestock losses are neglible, despite being exaggerated, and there has never been a single verifiable instance of a healthy wild wolf harming a human of any age.

Although this is the most popular image of a gray wolf, the species is actually harmless to humans. Photo by Cheanne Chellis.

Red Wolf (*Canis rufus*)

Very little is known about this canid and its habits, because by the time any serious scientific research was committed to it the red wolf was already on the brink of extinction. Red wolves were placed on the Endangered Species List in 1967.

There exists some controversy about the validity of classifying *Canis rufus* as an individual species. Some biologists believe that red wolves are too different from coyotes and gray wolves to be a member of either species, while others think red wolves are merely the result of wolves and coyotes interbreeding, which current DNA evidence has shown is more commonplace than had been previously believed. This might also help to explain why the red wolf is currently endangered, which has been in large part because it readily interbreeds with coyotes, thus diluting its own bloodline. Currently only about 200 red wolves exist, despite efforts at reintroduction.

Geographic Range

The original range of red wolves included most habitats in the southeastern United States, but today this species' range is limited to extreme southeastern Texas and southwestern Louisiana. Attempts are being made to reintroduce red wolves in other areas of their historical range at Alligator River, South Carolina, in North Carolina, and in Tennessee's Smoky Mountains.

Physical Characteristics

Mass: 40 to 90 pounds. Males about 10% larger than females.

Body: More slender and smaller than a gray wolf, about 50% larger than a coyote. Shoulder height about 15 inches, body length 55 to 65 inches, nose pad much larger than a coyote's, measuring about 1 inch across. Pointed ears are slightly smaller than the coyote's, slightly larger than the gray wolf's. Muzzle more squared and stronger than a coyote's, less massive and blocky than a gray wolf's.

Tail: 14 to 16 inches. Very bushy, grizzled gray with reddish tinge on top.

Tracks: 4 toes on all 4 feet, claws always show in tracks. Front and hind prints about 4.5 inches long. 2 lobes on front heel pad leave a chevron shape similar to the foreprint of a gray wolf, 3 lobes on rear heel pad. Outermost toes on either side are much smaller than the center toes, opposite that of a gray wolf or coyote, both of which have larger outer toes.

Scat: Easily mistaken for coyote, but much smaller than that of a gray wolf. 3 to more than 4 inches long, segmented, tapered at both ends, about 1 inch in diameter. A diet of rodents and deer carrion will reveal small bones wrapped spirally inside the prey's own fur to protect the wolf's intestinal tract.

Coloration: Grizzled gray back and flanks made up of interspersed hairs of white and black. Some red on shoulders and neck, with reddish ears, and red on top of the muzzle. Legs rust-colored. Gray wolf lacks red legs, coyote is similar in coloration, but usually much smaller and more slender.

Sign: Carcasses with gnawed joint ends.

Vocalizations: Howling similar to that of a coyote, with yapping not heard among gray wolves, but more deeply toned than the shrill barking of coyotes. Researchers have described red wolf vocalizations as being in between those of coyotes and grey wolves.

Lifespan: Uncertain, but probably about 8 years in the wild. One individual in captivity lived to 14 years.

Habitat

Red wolves were originally native to mountains, lowland forests, and wetlands—virtually any environment where a coyote or gray wolf might live, except with a more southerly range. Today, red wolves are nearly extinct, with only a few reintroduced packs living in swamplands and mountains of the southwestern and southeastern United States.

Diet

Like coyotes, red wolves subsist mainly on rodents and other small prey that can be overtaken by a 40 miles-per-hour running speed. In lean times family members may form a pack to take down larger prey like deer. Most often prey will consist of rodents and small mammals.

Like gray wolves, red wolves seldom consume larger prey animals, like deer fawns, where they were brought down, but transport them to a more secure location where they can eat in peace. These dining places are usually on a ridge or other high ground that affords a good view of the surrounding area.

Mating Habits

Female red wolves are ready to mate at 2 years, but males will probably not breed until age 4. Males take a single mate and typically remain with her until one of them dies. Breeding season takes place from January to March. The gestation period is 2 months, with litters of 3 to 6 pups born between March and May in dens whose locations might range from streambanks to hollow trees to existing dens that have been appropriated from coyotes and badgers. If left unmolested, especially by humans, the same den may be used the following year.

Like gray wolves and coyotes, both male and female red wolves take an active role in rearing young. So long as the female is confined to the den by her nursing duties, her mate will hunt alone and bring her food, and will look after the denned pups while she leaves to drink from a stream or pond that will always be nearby.

Behavior

Red wolves are believed to be primarily nocturnal, although it seems likely, as with other species, that this behavior is a result of being harassed by humans during daylight hours. The size of a red wolf pack's home range in the wild is virtually unknown, but it seems likely that they, like coyotes or gray wolves, travel no farther than is required to find the necessities of life.

Red wolf packs usually consist of a mated pair of adults and their offspring. Larger packs of related individuals have been reported, but the average pack will seldom number more than 8 animals. Red wolves coexist harmoniously within their own pack, but are reportedly quite aggressive toward strangers of their own species.

Red wolves tend to be more continually nomadic than gray wolves, hunting a small portion of territory for about 1 week, then moving on. This behavior stems from a diet that consists largely or entirely of rodents. With a reproductive system that is geared toward being prey for many species of predators, mice and voles breed prolifically throughout the year, and have been known to reach population densities as high as

20,000 small rodents per acre. A red wolf simply stays in one place so long as mice remain plentiful enough to be easy prey, then moves on to a fresh hunting ground when the pickings get slim.

Like gray wolves, red wolves have been blamed for killing livestock, but also like gray wolves, reports of predation have been exaggerated, sometimes grossly. Like all wild canids, red wolves may kill pet dogs and cats, but this threat is also unlikely to occur because of the species' low population.

Coyote (*Canis latrans*)

This species gets its common name from the Nahuatl Indians who called it *coyotl*. With the disappearance of other large carnivores, coyotes have become the dominant terrestrial carnivore in North America. Despite having been subjected to the same poisons, traps, and human prejudices that successfuly exterminated red and gray wolves from most of the continent, coyotes have thrived in virtually every environment. In fact, it might be argued that removing wolves from the ecosystem not only played a role in the coyote's rise to dominance by removing its most serious competitors, but also contributed to the overpopulation and disease that afflicts the species today.

Geographic Range

Coyotes are native only to the Americas. The species is found from Central America throughout Mexico and the lower 48 states, northward into central Canada and Alaska.

Habitat

Coyotes have proved to be very adaptable over a broad range of environments and climates. They thrive in the jungles of southern Mexico, in the desert southwest of the United States, and in the sometimes bitter winter cold of northern forests. The species is extraordinarily amenable to living in the vicinity of humans, having learned to recognize people as a potential food source, and in many suburban areas it has made a pest of itself by raiding garbage cans.

Coyote (Canis latrans).

Physical Characteristics

Mass: 30 to more than 60 pounds, with the largest specimens occurring in the far north.

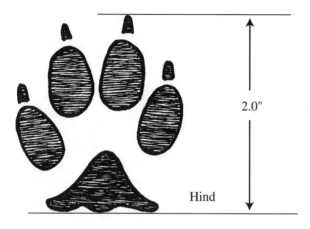

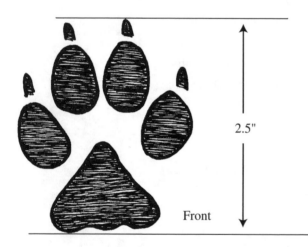

Coyote (Canis latrans). *Note that the heel pads of all four paws have three lobes at the rear, but that those of the hind feet tend to print only partially, leaving a "mustache" imprint.*

Body: Lanky and more slender than the gray wolf. Body length 40 to more than 50 inches, height at shoulder 23 to 26 inches. Large pointed ears. Narrow tapered muzzle ending in a small black nose pad, less than 1 inch in diameter. Slender legs and body. The coyote is about half the size of a gray wolf and much larger than any fox. Like wolves, the eyes have a yellow iris and round pupil. The molars are structured for crushing small bones, and the canines are long and narrow.

Tail: The tail is roughly half the body length, measuring 20 to 25 inches, bushy (especially in winter), and brush-shaped with a black tip. Like all canids, including dogs, there is a scent gland located on the dorsal base of the tail. Note that a coyote's tail droops normally, and is held below the back when running, while a gray wolf's tail is nearly always held straight back, in line with the spine.

Tracks: Compared to wolves, the feet of a coyote are relatively small for its body, averaging about 2.5 inches for the forepaws, with hind paws roughly 10% smaller. In northern forests there have been tracks as large as 3.5 inches recorded, but these are extraordinary. Unlike gray or red wolves, a coyote's heelpads have three lobes on all four feet, whereas wolves have only two lobes on the forefoot, three on the hind. Walking stride about 14 inches, straddle 4 inches.

Scat: Varied in color from black to brown, or a combination, growing lighter and more gray as the scat ages. Length 3 to more than 4 inches, cylindrical, segmented, about 1 inch in diameter. May be composed largely of blueberries when these are available, giving the scat a purplish color, but usually covered with fur or hair wrapped around small bones of prey animals.

Coloration: The coyote's fur varies from gray-brown to yellow-gray on the upper part, often with some rust-colored patches around neck, shoulders, and flanks, and usually grizzled on the back. The throat and belly are lightly colored, sometimes white. Forelegs, sides of the head, muzzle, and feet are reddish brown. There is one molt per year, beginning with profuse shedding in May and ending in July. The new, heavier

Accumulation of coyote scats of varying ages indicates that this spot is a regularly refreshed territorial scentpost.

winter coat begins to grow in late August, September in the coyote's more southerly range.

Sign: In winter, urine-scented tree trunks and stumps, marked by male individuals at a height of about 8 inches above the ground, or about half as high up as a gray wolf. Gnawed rib ends and cartiliginous joints on deer carcasses; large leg bones will be intact, not crushed as they would be by a gray wolf.

Vocalizations: Shrill howling, barking, and yapping, almost a screeching at times, especially when the animals congregate at dusk or in the early morning. The scientific name, *Canis latrans*, is Latin for "barking dog," a reference to the coyote's vocal nature.

Lifespan: 8 to 10 years.

Diet
Coyotes are mostly carnivorous, but their diet is broad enough to include almost any type of meat, including the occasional lizard, snake, or fish. Some have been observed killing and eating venomous snakes, but even though a coyote is sometimes bitten during the kill, the species appears to have considerable resistance to venom.

Most often the coyote diet consists of smaller mammals like squirrels, rabbits, and especially mice and voles. One of the best mousers in nature, coyotes can often be seen standing in the middle of a field or meadow, cocking their heads and ears from one position to another as they pinpoint the exact location of a scurrying rodent using their extremely acute sense of hearing. When a mouse has been located, the coyote leaps into the air, often clearing the ground with all 4 feet, and pounces onto its prey with the forefeet. This hunting technique is especially effective in winter, when rodents travel under hardpack snow through tunnels that a coyote can cave in by jumping onto the snow, thus trapping its prey. Once caught, rodents are swallowed whole.

The opportunistic coyote will also eat carrion, especially deer, which are normally too large and strong for even a pack of coyotes to bring down. Coyotes are often seen by hunters who bait deer, because the little wolves have learned to associate hunters with wounded deer and a large meal of venison.

In winter coyote families sometimes form a pack to hunt deer, particularly after the alpha pair retreats to a secluded denning site to mate, but only if smaller, more easily obtainable game like rabbits and hares are in short supply. Deer represent a large and potentially dangerous adversary to even a pack of coyotes, whose members are typically one-third the size of an adult whitetail. A sharp-hooved kick to the jaw or ribs can be fatal if it prevents a predator from eating or running fast, so deer are typically at the bottom of a coyote's list of preferred prey, and those they do hunt will always be small, weak, or wounded.

Coyotes are particularly fond of fruits, especially in autumn, when blueberries, wild grapes, elderberries, and other sugar-rich fruits help them to put on precious fat stores as a hedge against the coming winter. In a good blueberry area the scat of coyotes and foxes will often be purple between the months of August and October.

Mating Habits

Coyotes become sexually mature at about 12 months, but, like wolves, may not mate until they leave the parent pair and find their own mates. Mated pairs are usually monogynist, but will infrequently split up to find other mates, even after being together for several years, probably from an instinct to diversify the gene pool. Male coyotes who attempt to usurp another male's mate will likely find itself being run off by both of the mated pair.

Coyote pairs retire to a secluded denning site in January, probably using the same site year after year if it goes unmolested. Dens are excavated, usually in the side of a ridge or rise, sometimes under the roots of a large tree, always near water, but always in a place where good drainage will keep the den from flooding during the spring thaw or rains. Dens are very much like those of the gray wolf, consisting of a narrow tunnel about 12 inches in diameter that extends 5 or 6 feet inward, sometimes more than 10 feet, terminating at a roomy nursing chamber that measures roughly 3 feet high, 3 feet across, and about 4 feet long.

Mating occurs during a period between late January and March, and is usually initiated by the female, who paws at the male's flanks to indicate she's in estrus. Female coyotes are monoestrous, and remain in heat only about 5 days, so there is some urgency to become pregnant.

Male coyotes are not fertile most of the year, and like wolves, their testicles remain retracted until mating season prompts them to descend. Spermatogenesis, the maturation of sperm cells, occurs between January and February, and requires an average of 54 days before a male becomes sexually fertile.

Actual coitus between coyote pairs occurs between February and March. Gestation is 60 days, with a litter of 1 to as many as 19 pups being born in April or May. Pups weigh about 7 ounces at birth. At 10 days the pups will have doubled in mass and their eyes open for the first time. At 3 to 4 weeks the pups begin emerging from the den to play under the watchful eyes of their parents, who protect them from birds of prey, bobcats, and even bears that consider coyote pups a delicacy. During this period the male brings food to his mate and offspring, feeding the young regurgitated meat, and occasionally babysitting while the mother leaves to drink or relieve herself. At 35 days the pups will have reached 3 to 4 pounds and are weaned.

Coyote pups grow up quickly; by 6 months they will have reached a weight of nearly 30 pounds, and are able to fend for themselves. By 9 months the male pups will have typically left the parents to strike out on their own, while female pups may remain to form the basis of a pack, and to look after next year's pups, for 2 years or more.

Although the coyote is an individual species with its own identifiable genetics, there exists a marked propensity for it to interbreed with other canids. The red wolf (*Canis rufus*) is thought to be on the verge of extinction partly because it breeds readily with coyotes, thus causing its own genetic distinctions to fade. Dogs, particularly those with pointed ears and generally coyotelike physical characteristics, have also mated with coyotes in the wild, producing a sometimes hard-to-identify animal known as a "coydog." Most recently, the increased use of DNA testing in field biology has revealed that perhaps most of the gray wolves in Minnesota exhibit some coyote genes in their bloodlines, dispelling any doubt about interbreeding between coyotes and wolves.

Behavior

Coyotes are less likely than wolves to form a pack, largely because coyotes are so very well-equipped to catch rodents, while the larger and more powerful wolf is adapted to working in a team against larger prey animals. Coyote packs form up at dusk, with the gathering initiated by a prolonged howl from the alpha male, which is then joined by high-pitched yaps and barks from other members as they join him. Pack members may split up during the nightly hunt, communicating the find of a deer carcass or another meal large enough to be shared to the rest of the pack with a prolonged but broken howl that is unlike the low, monotonal howl of the gray wolf. Nightly hunts typically encompass an area of about 3 square miles.

Coyote territories are only as large as is required to provide for their needs, but generally range from 6 to 12 square miles. Territories will always include a source of fresh water, particularly near den sites during whelping periods, and will typically include fields and meadows where mice and voles prefer to live. Territories are bounded by olfactory scentposts consisting of urine sprayed onto trees and other landmarks, and scat deposits left on regularly used trails, especially at intersections where two trails cross. Most scent marking is done by males, but alpha females may also scent claimed territories.

There exists a very old myth that claims the coyote and the American badger *(Taxidea taxus)* will sometimes hunt cooperatively, with the coyote using its acute sense of smell to locate burrowing rodents and squirrels, and the badger then using its powerful claws to dig them out so both predators can share the meal. The truth behind this charming fable is more pragmatic; the coyote and badger do indeed conspire against burrowed prey, but the badger's keen nose needs no assistance from the coyote, and the two do not share meals. Instead, the comparatively intelligent coyote has learned to position itself near the escape tunnels that are common to most burrowing species, waiting patiently while the single-minded badger excavates inward toward its prey. Thus trapped, the burrowed animal can wait until the badger reaches it, or it can try popping out of an escape tunnel and past the waiting coyote's lightning fast jaws. In either instance only one of the predators is likely to be successful.

Gray Fox (Urocyon cinereoargenteus)

Gray foxes are native to the New World, and they were the reason that red foxes, which are not native, were brought here from Europe. When the first immigrants to America attempted to practice the nobleman's sport of fox hunting from horseback, they quickly learned that this continent's largest native fox had an ability that was unique among canids: it could extend its semi-retractable claws and climb trees like a cat. This characteristic made for a short chase in the vast forests of the New World, so the red fox, which cannot climb trees, was imported for sporting purposes.

Geographic Range

Gray foxes are found throughout most of the southern half of North America, their range extending from southern Canada to northern Venezuela and Colombia. This

Gray fox. Photo by Dave Schaffer, courtesy of U.S. Fish & Wildlife Service.

species does not inhabit the more mountainous areas of the northwestern United States, the Great Plains, or eastern Central America.

Habitat

Gray foxes are most often found in deciduous forests where their unique ability to climb trees serves them in escaping predators, but may sometimes be seen in adjoining fields where they forage for grasshoppers, rodents, and berries. Unlike red foxes, gray foxes tend to avoid open agricultural areas, and are much less likely to be seen by humans.

Physical Characteristics

Mass: 7 to 13 pounds.

Body: Gray foxes are typically foxlike in appearance, with long bushy tails, short legs, and a comparatively elongated body. Body length 31 to 44 inches, shoulder height about 14 inches. The head is wide, with widely spaced temporal ridges that distinguish it from other North American canids. The muzzle is narrow and tapered, ending in a small black nose pad. Ears shorter and less pointed than the red fox. Males only slightly larger than females.

Tail: Bushy, black-tipped, 8 to 17 inches long, typically shorter than that of the red fox.

Tracks: About 1.5 inches long for all four feet, hind foot slightly narrower than front. Claws semi-retractable—unique among canids—but usually show in tracks. Three lobes on heel pads of front and hind feet, but in a clear track only the outer edges of the outermost lobes will show for the hind foot.

Scat: About 2.5 inches long, 0.5 inch in diameter, segmented, tapered at one end, sometimes both. Often covered with fine rodent fur. Similar in shape and size to red fox scat,

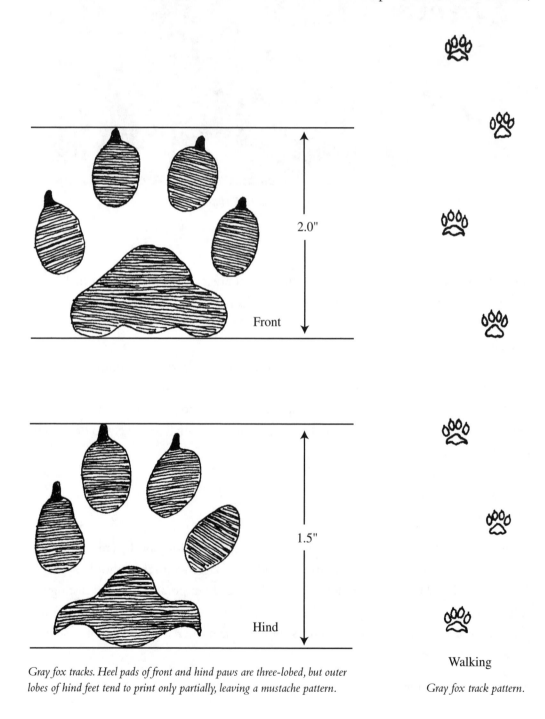

Gray fox tracks. Heel pads of front and hind paws are three-lobed, but outer lobes of hind feet tend to print only partially, leaving a mustache pattern.

Walking

Gray fox track pattern.

except that gray foxes normally eat a more vegetarian diet of berries and fruits, making their scats darker, and showing a predominance of seeds and undigested berries when these fruits are in season.

Coloration: Although most likely to be confused with a red fox, especially those in a "cross phase" of mottled red, gray, and black fur, there are identifiable differences between the coloration of red and gray foxes. The gray fox is grizzled gray and black along its back, neck, and the upper tail, much like a typical coyote. The upper head and muzzle are grizzled, with a contrasting patch of white at the tip of the muzzle, on the cheeks, and along the underbelly. Sides of the neck, legs, body, and tail are rust-colored.

Sign: Food caches buried in shallow holes and marked by loosely piled soil, sometimes with tracks evident, or wide, shallow holes left by removing cached foods. Trees that have been marked with urine at a height of about 8 inches, leaving yellow stains on snow.

Gray foxes are unusual among wild canids because they tend to den throughout the year, usually in natural shelters under tree roots, in rock crevices, or in hollow trees, and will often have several dens within their territories. Dens are normally much smaller than those used by coyotes, largely because coyotes prey on gray foxes, and are likely to be marked with snagged fur, bones too large to swallow, and tracks around their entrances.

Vocalizations: High-pitched barks, yaps, and growls, much like a small dog. Less vocal than the red fox.

Lifespan: 8 to 10 years.

Diet

Like all of the most successful species, gray foxes have a broad and varied diet. They're good hunters, able to pounce on mice in fields or catch rabbits in brushy swamps, but the gray fox's diet has an added dimension because it can climb trees to snatch roosting birds at night, or to rob nests of their eggs. They also prey on frogs, grasshoppers and locusts, eat carrion, and appear to possess some ability to catch small fish.

Gray foxes also eat a good deal of vegetation, probably more than any other species of wild canid. Blueberries are a favorite when these are in season, but the gray fox can also climb into the upper branches of fruiting trees, particularly wild cherries, to get at rich fruits that are beyond the reach of its non-climbing cousins.

Mating Habits

Gray foxes mate in late winter, usually in March in the northern extreme of its range, and in February in the warmer south. (In habitats shared by both gray and red foxes, a rule of thumb is that gray foxes mate about 1 month after red foxes). Mated foxes are presumed to be monogamous, though many facets of this species have yet to be researched.

The gestation period lasts about 50 days, with up to 7 pups born in a secluded woodland den in April or May. The young nurse for about 3 months, and during that time the father will bring his mate food, and babysit while she leaves the den to drink or relieve herself, but he takes no active role in parenting during the suckling stage, and doesn't enter the den.

Gray fox pups are probably the most precocious of North American canids, growing very quickly both physically and mentally. Immediately after weaning they leave the den and begin hunting with their parents. A month later, at 4 months of age, the pups will have all of their permanent teeth, and weigh an average of 7 pounds. At this time the pups leave their parents to fend for themselves, and the mates separate to resume a normally solitary lifestyle until the next mating season, when the pups will also be mature enough to breed. Radio telemetry data indicates that separated family members remain within their own established territories, so inbreeding is unlikely.

Behavior

Gray foxes lead a solitary existence for most of the year, and a researcher who sees one in the wild should count himself lucky. The species is naturally reclusive and less vocal than other canids, keeping to secluded dens in the shadowed woods most of the day and hunting primarily at night. At least part of the reason for their secretive behavior is explained by the fact that so many species, from large raptors and owls to coyotes to even domestic dogs consider them prey.

The gray fox has been well-equipped by nature to fend for itself. Its light weight allows it to run across snow that larger carnivores would find too soft for easy travel, while its good night vision, excellent olfactory senses, and effective camouflage make it a formidable predator of smaller prey animals. Its most important advantage, however, is an ability to use its sharp, curved semi-retractable claws to climb trees and escape enemies that it couldn't outrun on the ground. This unique climbing ability also helps to explain why gray foxes can run neither fast nor far.

Occasionally gray foxes have been labeled as chicken killers, but instances where this rarely seen wild canid has actually been guilty of raiding a henhouse are rare. Most often the real culprit is a red fox, if it was a fox at all, and in many instances farmers have simply presumed that the predator must have been a fox, without ever seeing it first-hand. Such erroneous leaps of logic are made all the more believable by adages like "a fox in the henhouse" and "sly as a fox." Meanwhile, skilled chicken and egg thieves, most notably raccoons, often go undetected.

Red fox. Photo by V. Bern, courtesy of U.S. Fish & Wildlife Service.

Red Fox *(Vulpes vulpes)*

The red fox is not native to North America, but was brought here from Europe so that gentle-born immigrants could continue to enjoy the nobleman's sport of fox hunting with hounds from horseback. The native gray fox, with its extendable catlike claws and an ability to climb trees, was poorly suited to this pastime, so red foxes were imported to the New World. Before long the transplanted red foxes, whose adaptability to the most hostile environment is equalled only by the coyote, had escaped captivity to become firmly established as part of the American ecosystem.

Geographic Range

Although native to Europe and the British Isles, the red fox has thrived in almost every location where it was transplanted, or simply escaped to the wild, throughout the world. Today, red foxes are common throughout the continental United States, in all but the most frigid regions of Canada and Alaska—where it overlaps the range of the Arctic fox—in Australia and Japan, and across nearly all of Asia.

Habitat

Red foxes are able to make their homes across an extraordinary range of habitats that includes deciduous and pine forests, Arctic tundra, open prairies, farmland, and residential districts. The species is becoming increasingly common to suburban areas, where it preys on rats, mice, and other small animals with more efficiency than a house cat. The most preferred habitats will have a diversity of plant life, particularly fruits and berries, and especially blueberries, grapes, and cherries. Unlike the more reclusive gray fox, red foxes are frequently seen in open places.

Physical Characteristics

Mass: 7 to 15 pounds, with the largest individuals occurring in the far north.

Body: Slender build with a comparatively elongated body length and short legs. Body length 35 to 40 inches; shoulder height about 15 inches. The erect directional ears are remarkably long and pointed, with black-colored backs. The muzzle is very long and slender, tipped with a prominent black button nose that is often exaggerated in caricatures. Like most wild canids, the eyes of mature animals are yellow.

Tail: Very prominent and very bushy. Rust-colored, 13 to 17 inches long, with a white tip. Like most canids, red foxes have a scent gland located on the dorsal base of the tail, identifiable by a patch of dark fur covering that area.

Tracks: Usually larger than those of the gray fox, but with smaller toe pads. About 2.5 inches long, hind foot slightly smaller and more narrow. 4 toes on each foot, with claws showing. In the north, feet are heavily furred in winter. Heel pads of all 4 feet are two-lobed, leaving a chevron-shaped print. The most distinguishing characteristic is a ridge that runs across the heelpad, also in a chevron shape, that prints more deeply than the rest of the pad.

Scat: Very similar to the scat of other canids, being cylindrical, segmented, and tapered at the ends, but with a predominance of berry seeds and vegetable matter when green foods are available. Often with an outer covering of rodent fur wrapped around small bones. About 0.5 inch in diameter by 4 inches long.

Coloration: Rust-colored to deep reddish brown on the upper parts and white to light gray on the underside. The lower part of the legs is usually black, and the tail has a white, occasionally black, tip.

A typical red fox is unlikely to be confused with any other animal, but there are two cross phases that sometimes occur, in which most or all of the fur is not red. One phase is an almost startling grizzled coat of rust-colored and black fur that covers the upper body, head, and tail. In this phase the legs are usually black and the underside reddish. There is usually a black dorsal stripe extending the length of the back, and another across the shoulders, forming the T shape that gives this color phase the name "cross fox."

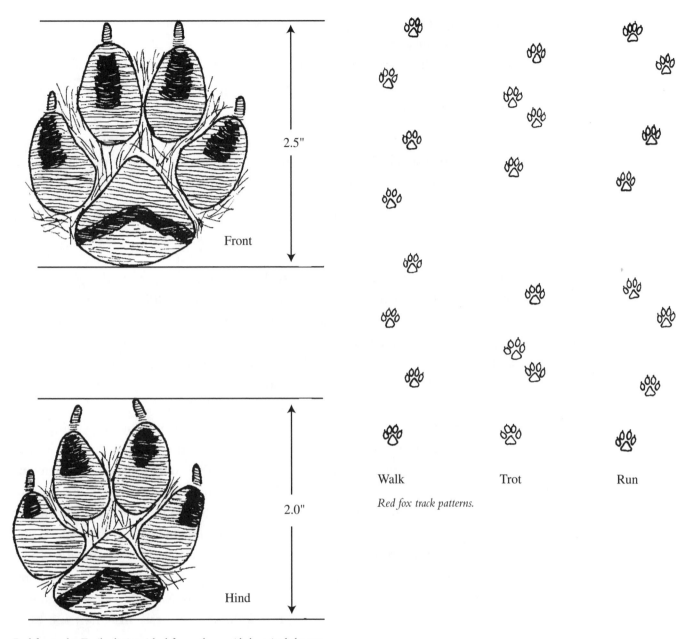

Red fox track patterns.

Walk   Trot   Run

Red fox tracks. Easily distinguished from other canids by raised chevron-shaped ridge on heel pads, and furry soles.

The other phase, prized by furriers, is the silver phase, in which the upper body is silver-gray with a black mask around the eyes, black ears, and dark gray to black legs. Exactly what causes these color variations is a matter of conjecture, but they might stem from interbreeding with gray or Arctic foxes, or possibly from an evolutionary adaptation to different environments. Both phases are too common to be considered mutations, with cross foxes making up about 25% of a given population, and silver foxes about 10%.

Sign: Spring birthing dens excavated in the sides of hills, usually in sand, and marked by a fan of loose soil around a main entrance that may measure 12 inches across. There will always be smaller escape holes branching from the underground chamber, usually within 10 feet of the main entrance. Small mounds or holes where food was cached will usually be evident near the den.

Vocalizations: Usually silent, but more vocal than the gray fox. Calls include high-pitched yapping and barking reminiscent of a small dog. The alarm call is a single sharp, high-pitched bark that sounds almost like a short shriek.

Lifespan: 8 to 10 years, sometimes longer in captivity.

Diet

Although the red fox's predatory habits classify it as a carnivore, its diet is essentially omnivorous. It hunts rodents, rabbits, catches an occasional fish from shallow streams, and can make a meal of grasshoppers, but when fruits and berries are available it may forgo meat almost entirely. Blueberries are a perennial favorite, but grapes, pears, apples, and other orchard fruits are well-liked. With the high metabolic rate typical of small canids, an adult red fox may need to eat more than 10% of its body weight each day, and the sugars contained in fruits are a valuable source of calories.

Red foxes are also skilled hunters, especially of rodents. With a technique very much like that of the coyote, a fox will stand motionless in a meadow, cocking its head from one side to another and swiveling its acutely sensitive directional ears as it pinpoints the location of a mouse scurrying under the grass or snow. When the fox is sure of its target, it springs high into the air, all four feet leaving the ground, and comes down hard onto the rodent with both forefeet, stunning the prey and pinning it to the earth.

Red foxes also eat carrion when it's available and not already claimed by larger carnivores. One remarkable behavior occurs during the deer hunting seasons, when red foxes, which are more bold than most canid species, have learned to associate humans and gunshots with the rich venison liver, kidneys, and heart that most successful hunters leave behind.

Mating Habits

The red fox's annual mating season depends greatly on the arrival of warm weather, and varies by as much as 4 months from one region of North America to another. In the Deep South, mating generally takes place in December and January; in the central states from January to February; in the far North between late February and April.

The annual estrus period of female, or vixen, red foxes lasts for a period of about 6 days. As with other canids, ovulation is spontaneous and doesn't require copulation to occur, but females signal their readiness to prospective mates through pheromonal excretions for several days prior to coming into heat. During the pre-heat period males fight more or less bloodlessly to compete for breeding status. Like vixen, male red foxes have an annual cycle of fecundity in which they produce fertile sperm, being sterile the rest of the year.

Copulation lasts about 15 minutes and is usually marked by barking and yapping, mostly from the male. Females may mate with more than one male, probably to help insure impregnation by the strongest genes, but will pair off with only one of them at the end of breeding season. In a process called delayed implantation, which is common to many species, the fertilized egg doesn't attach to the uterine wall for 10 to 14 days after mating. This delay helps to insure that the female is physically fit to develop and bear pups; if she isn't, the fertilized egg will spontaneously abort.

On becoming pregnant the female pairs off with, usually, her strongest suitor, and they retire to a secluded location to excavate her birthing den. Although he works to dig it and make it ready, the male doesn't enter the den after its completion. Gestation lasts 49 to 56 days, with the shorter period indicating a healthy, well-fed mother, and for several days prior to giving birth the female stays close to the den, leaving only to drink from a nearby water source.

In a period between February and May, depending on latitude, the female births a litter of pups, or kits, which typically number 5, but may be as many as 13. Kits are born blind and weigh about 3 ounces, but grow quickly. By 14 days their eyes will have opened, and at 5 weeks the pups will be playing around the outside of the den, immediately running back inside to safety in response to an alarm bark from their mother. Kits are fully weaned by 10 weeks, and the father, who has up to this point faithfully provided food for his mate and regurgitated meat for his offspring, will leave to resume a normal solitary lifestyle. The kits will remain with their mother, who teaches them to hunt and forage, until the following autumn when the pups disperse and sometimes travel more than 100 miles before taking a mate for themselves at 10 months of age.

Behavior

In 1966, when I was a boy of 10, I recall being publicly berated by a schoolteacher because I argued the validity of a short story my class had been assigned to read about foxes that formed packs and killed calves on the author's farm. That story, and many more like it, reflected the ignorance of an era when wild animals were generally regarded as enemies, and too many people went to ridiculous lengths to find any justification for killing them.

In fact, I was right to dispute that bit of public school propaganda; foxes have never run in packs. Red foxes, like gray and other species of fox, are solitary creatures. The only exceptions to that rule occur when the sexes join during the spring mating season, and with mother foxes that are guiding young through their first summer of life.

As with other territorial species, the range of a red fox depends largely on how slim or fat the pickings are where it lives. Plenty of rodents to eat will help to keep an individual's territory small, but the nearly omnivorous red fox diet demands berries and other rich fruits, as well as a good year-round source of water. Generally speaking a red fox's territory will range from 3 to 9 square miles in places that provide for those needs.

Although fights between red foxes are rare, a good home territory will be defended against intruders, especially by females with kits. Battles are seldom more than a nip and a chase, with the resident fox having the proverbial home field advantage.

Although red foxes don't den as regularly as gray foxes, the species habitually has several dens throughout its territorial range, each connected to the others and to buried food caches by a series of trails that are patrolled daily or nearly so. In the case of a vixen, at least one of these will be a maternal den that's used year after year, so long as it remains undisturbed, especially by humans. The others, all of which have an escape exit, provide the animal with a place to duck out of reach if chased by a predator, including coyotes, wolves, and bobcats. With a running speed of about 30 miles per hour, a healthy fox has a good chance of reaching safety before being overtaken by a faster carnivore.

Red foxes are known to take an occasional chicken from farmyards, but their predation is limited to small farm animals, and it has been exaggerated. Simply having a dog will discourage not only foxes but also coyotes and most other meat eaters that might be tempted to raid a chicken yard, while good fencing and modern materials can further reduce predation by them to zero.

THE CAT FAMILY (FAMILY FELIDAE)

Family Felidae is a family of hunters that paleontologists believe split off from other mammals during the Eocene period, about 40 million years ago. All species within this group are endowed with acute senses of smell, hearing, and vision, as well as sensitive whiskers that can detect slight changes in air currents, and possibly more. Members are well-armed with very sharp retractable claws on all four of their toes, as well as a front dewclaw that can be used like a thumb to further maintain a solid grip on prey. All species are extremely stealthy, with lightning fast reflexes, sharply pointed canines that kill almost instantly with a well-aimed bite to the base of a victim's skull, and unrivaled agility. Most prefer to hunt at night, when their well-developed night vision and binocular eyesight gives them a distinct advantage over less well-equipped creatures. Few eat carrion, and none eat animals that have been dead long enough to decay, the way coyotes and bears are wont to do.

House Cat (Felis silvestris)

Domestic cats are descendants of a wild cat species, *Felis silvestris libyca,* that originated in Africa and southwestern Asia. Cats were probably first domesticated in Africa, but the earliest known records of cats as pets date back to 1500 B.C. in ancient Egypt, when these proficient predators were used to protect the granaries from rodents. From there domestic cats spread to other cultures; the first record of domestic cats in the Old World was in Britain in the year A.D. 936, when a law was passed in Wales for their protection. By the mid-1700s, domestic cats had become estabished in the New World.

Geographic Range

Domesticated cats are presently kept throughout the world as pets and as tools to control rodents. Perhaps the only domestic species generally capable of survival in the wild, feral cats are also established in a few places around the world.

Habitat

Domestic cats are found throughout the world in urban and rural areas. About 45 million cats are kept as pets in the United States alone and about 2 million live in Canada. House cats that have gone feral typically gravitate toward civilization, often living in outbuildings and barns. The species is capable of surviving climates that range from tropical to temperate, and most domestic cats are able to live in bitterly cold temperatures so long as they can find shelter and food.

Physical Characteristics

Mass: 4 to 10 pounds, occasionally larger.

Body: The domestic cat is very strong and muscular for its size. The average height of an adult cat is about 8 to 10 inches at the shoulders. Long, powerful bodies with rounded heads, short muzzles, and erect triangular ears are typical of all feline species. Females have four pairs of mammae.

Cats have true fur, with a downy insulating undercoat covered by a coarser outer coat. The ears of a cat can rotate independently of one another to precisely locate the source of minute sounds, such as those made by a scurrying mouse, and can detect ultrasonic frequencies up to 25,000 cycles per second. The eyes of cats are located on the front of the head, giving them excellent depth and range perception, while large elliptical pupils permit very good night vision. Cats lack eyelashes, but have an inner eyelid, or nictitating membrane, that prevents drying of the eyeball and protects it from foreign objects.

The teeth are highly specialized, with long, sharply pointed canines that extend straight downward from the upper jaw and are curved inward in the lower jaw to permit stabbing and holding prey. The molars are pointed and specialized for cutting like scissors. None of the cat species has molars that are designed for crushing bone, as in the canid family, nor do cats have the jaw pressure of longer-muzzled carnivores.

Cats have AB blood groups, much like humans, and are subject to a form of AIDS called feline immunodeficiency virus, or FIV. House cats, especially older individuals, can also be victims of cancer, most notably feline leukemia, but in probably most cases the disease is curable.

Tail: All but two domestic breeds have a long tail that extends from the spine to a length equaling about 75% of total body length, usually 8 to 10 inches. The tail is used for balance, much the way a human tightrope walker uses a long pole to amplify his own sense of balance, and is largely responsible for the house cat's legendary ability to walk over very narrow surfaces at great heights.

Tracks: Cats have four toes with retractable claws at the front of each forepaw, with a thumblike clawed toe to the inside rear that permits a more secure grip when climbing or holding prey. The hind paws also have four toes with retractable claws. All toes are nearly the same size and length, leaving a track whose outer dimensions are nearly round. Hind paws are only slightly smaller than front paws, in contrast to most other animals, which have larger forefeet than hind feet. Track lengths from 0.5 inch to 0.75 inch.

Scat: Segmented, cylindrical, 1 to 3 inches long, about 0.5 inch in diameter. Sometimes with rodent hairs or insect parts evident on the outer surface.

Coloration: Coat length and colors can vary greatly, depending on the breed. Most domestic cats are black, gray, yellow, white, or "tabby," with dark stripes or swirls on a paler background. Tortoiseshell, or calico, markings are a piebald mixture of black, white, rust, and yellow that's normally seen only in females; males born with this pattern are rare and nearly always sterile. The eyes are normally yellow, and cats that have blue or mixed color eyes, especially those with white fur, are often born deaf. Cats with white fur and pale skin are prone to sunburn and cancer.

Sign: Vertical clawmarks in trees, posts (and sometimes furniture). Scratching posts are not so much for sharpening claws as they are for depositing territorial scents exuded from interdigital glands in the underside of the cat's paws. Cats may also urinate on scentposts to mark territory, leaving a very strong odor reminiscent of

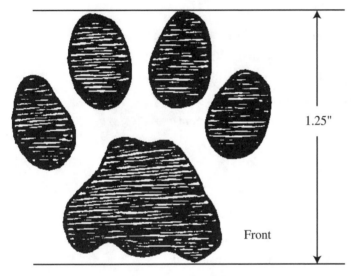

1.25"

Front

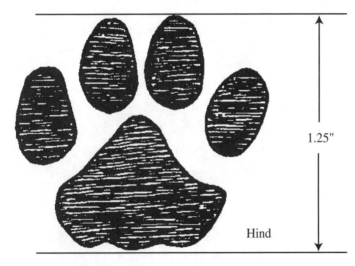

1.25"

Hind

House cat (Felis silvestris).

musk and ammonia. Look, too, for scratch marks in loose soil where a cat buried its feces, sometimes mounded soil with a strong urine odor left as territorial marking.

Vocalizations: Purring when content, but also when the animal is in pain. Mewing sounds for general communication and to get attention. Low growls when the animal feels threatened or is frightened. Yowling sounds, sometimes likened to the wailing of a small child, when an individual is mating or fighting over territory.

Lifespan: About 10 years, often longer.

Diet

Domestic cats, like all felids, are not only carnivorous but also superb hunters. Most house cats enjoy a regularly fed diet of processed pet foods, but most will supplement this with fresh meat from small animals that include mice, birds, squirrels, and even frogs. A few rural house cats have been known to take down prey larger than themselves, including rabbits and muskrats. Some humans dislike house cats because of their strong hunting instincts, and some cat owners try to supress it, but a cat's need to take prey is literally the nature of the beast.

Because cats lack both the tooth structure and jaw pressure required for crushing bones and other hard foods, they prefer softer foods (i.e., flesh) that can be rendered into smaller pieces by slicing them with scissorlike molars. The upper surface of a cat's tongue is covered with tiny hooklike projections, called papillae, that are used for rasping meat from bone, as well as for grooming.

Although domestic cats are primarily meat eaters, most like to have at least some vegetation in their diets. All will occasionally eat green grass, which is then either vomited out with indigestible matter like bones and fur, or passed through the digestive system as scat to help scrub it free of waste matter and parasites. A notable physical characteristic of domestic cats is a large intestine that's comparatively bigger than those found in wild felids, which allows the house cat to better digest vegetable matter.

Mating Habits

Domestic cats have no fixed mating season, and may mate at any time throughout the year. Males become sexually mature at 10 months, females usually at 7 months. Female house cats may have 2 to 4 litters per year, with litter sizes ranging from 1 to 6 kittens. If a female is prevented from mating during the estrus period, she will come into heat again shortly thereafter, and will continue to come into heat until she becomes pregnant.

Unlike wild felids, female house cats do not squirt urine to attract a mate, but tomcats are able to detect their sexual disposition by pheromonal scents anyway. When a female begins to come into estrus, she will likely attract attention from every unneutered male within a mile or more, and the noisy, yowling, frequently violent competion among them can last for a week or more.

The gestation period for domestic cats is approximately 2 months. Kittens are born blind and deaf, and weigh about 4 ounces. Their eyes open after about 7 days. Mother cats give their young very good care until the kittens are weaned at 8 weeks, then resumes the lifestyle she had before becoming pregnant.

Behavior

With the exception of African lions, house cats are the most social of felids. Rural farms often have more than a dozen "barn" cats that serve to keep rodent populations low, and these typically live together in relative harmony. As with African lions, there exists a definite hierarchy among groups that cohabitate, but after a pecking order has been established by means of a series of ritualized fights, especially among the males, groups tend to get along peacefully. Males and females seldom exhibit animosity toward one another, even when meeting for the first time.

Felis silvestris is one of the most expressive animals in terms of using body language that can be interpreted by humans. A cat that flops onto its side, and sometimes waves a paw, has placed itself into a position of submission, and is inviting its owner to play. A tail that twitches erratically, often just at its tip, is a sign of anxiety or discomfort. A strutting walk with tail held vertically to better disperse perineal scents from the anal area is a demonstration of dominance. A casual walk with the tail hanging down indicates calmness.

Both house cats and their wild cousins are known for sleeping a lot. This seemingly lazy behavior is the trademark of a family of predators that obtains most of its food by hunting, and thus conserves calories whenever it isn't doing something worthwhile. As most house cat owners can attest, the sleep of a cat is usually light enough to let the animal be aware of its surroundings, and even the most slothful feline can go from fast asleep to moving fast in the space of a heartbeat.

House cats are known to prey on a diversity of wild species that includes birds up to and including ruffed grouse, chipmunks, red squirrels, and other rodents, and even a cottontail rabbit or small hare larger than itself. Because domestic cats and wild cats alike have the hunting instinct of animals that can keep fed only through predation, the act of stalking and killing prey brings felines of all species a great deal of pleasure. There's nothing evil about this love of hunting, it's merely an adaptation that helps cats to ignore hardships like pain, cold, and hunger that are counterproductive to survival. A few naturalists have expressed fear that predation by pet cats could have a negative impact on certain wild species. Others believe that limited predation in urban or suburban environments might on the whole help to make small native species smarter and healthier by killing off those that are dumb and sickly.

Mountain lion. Photo by Larry Moats, courtesy of U.S. Fish & Wildlife Service.

Mountain Lion *(Puma concolor)*

Known alternately as cougars, pumas, painters, and catamounts, mountain lions are the New World's second largest felids, next to the jaguar of Mexico and South America, and probably the most maligned large cat in American movies. These once wide-ranging predators are nearly always portrayed as dangerously aggressive in novels and movies, and, to make matters worse, there have been a few extraordinary instances where an individual puma under extraordinary circumstances has actually attacked humans. Usually the cat is an old one, with bad teeth, failing health, and perhaps debilitating arthritis that keeps it from catching large game—namely small deer—as well as it used to.

Human victims are always small people who are alone in rural areas, and at least most have been engaged in an activity that excites the feline hunting instinct the same way a wriggling string triggers a compulsive instinct to attack in house cats. Lady joggers and running children are among the few people who've been attacked, but skiers, snowshoers, and backpackers virtually never are because they appear too large to be easy prey; as always, the objective of any hungry predator is not to fight, but to obtain food with as little danger to itself as possible.

Geographic Range

The mountain lion once had an extensive range that spanned most of the New World from southern Argentina to northern Canada, and coast to coast across the continental United States. Because pumas, like brown bears, posed a threat to livestock and a potential threat to humans, they were trapped, poisoned, and killed on sight for centuries, until only a few remained in the wildest, least traveled places. Today cougars are mostly restricted to mountainous areas in the American west, with isolated populations in South Carolina, southern Florida, Georgia, western Tennessee, and Michigan's Upper Peninsula.

Not to be confused with native populations, a number of cougars have been transplanted illegally from California and Oregon to keep them from being hunted after those states lifted a ban on killing them. The conflict between cats and people arose as a result of increased housing development along the Pacific coast in the early 1990s, which moved humans into areas that had historically been the domain of pumas. This brought the big cats into conflict with homeowners, and state authorities ruled against the mountain lion, permitting them to be killed. Animal rights groups responded by live-trapping cougars, and by 1994 the animals were being spotted in Pennsylvania, Wisconsin, and Michigan's Lower Peninsula—places where the species had long been extinct. It's doubtful that these few transplanted cats will establish populations, but most appear to be living well in their new habitats.

Habitat

Given the freedom to do so, mountain lions can utilize a broad range of habitats, from jungle and northern evergreen swamps to alpine forest and desert mountains. Deep snows, craggy rock, and thick undergrowth are not limiting factors. Essentially, the species is capable of existing any place where they can find water, concealing cover, and enough deer-size prey to keep them well-fed.

Physical Characteristics

Mass: 75 to 275 pounds.

Body: Mountain lions are large, muscular, and lithely built, very much along the same lines as a domestic cat. Body length 60 to 108 inches. The legs are short, thick, and muscular, with longer legs in the rear and powerful hindquarters that give the species a jacked-up appearance. The skull is broad and short, with a high arched forehead, and a broad rostrum (nasal bone). The nose pad is large and triangle-shaped. Ears are comparatively short and rounded. The mandible is powerfully constructed, the carnassial (flesh-cutting) teeth are massive, and the long canines are built for making quick kills on large prey. The mountain lion's upper jaw holds one more small premolar on each side than either the bobcat or the lynx. More so than canids, the molars have a scissorlike fit, not designed for crushing bone, but for cutting hide and flesh.

Tail: About one-third of the animal's total length, 21 to 36 inches long, tawny brown with a distinctive black tip.

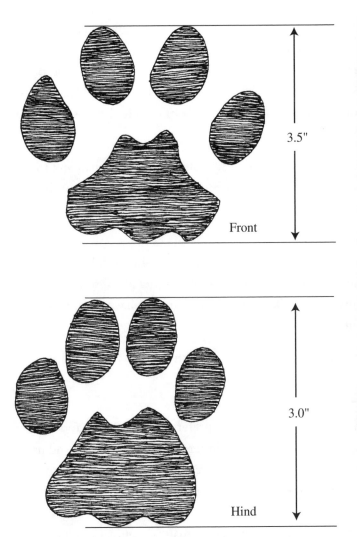

Cougar front track in wet sand.

Cougar (Puma concolor). Four toes on all paws, claws not showing. Three lobes on all four heels. Foreprints less rounded than those of a bobcat.

Tracks: Prints more round than the elongated tracks of canids. Front prints 3 to more than 4 inches long, hind tracks about 10% smaller. Four large toes showing in all tracks (front dewclaw doesn't register), but normally with no claws showing because of retractable claws. Heel pads of front and hind feet have three lobes, but the front pads are more blocky, less rounded. Walking stride about 20 inches, straddle about 8 inches.

Scat: Similar to that of canids, being segmented, cylindrical, and tapered at one or both ends. About 5 inches long by 1 to 1.5 inches in diameter. Deer hair is usually predominant, wrapped around the outer surface in spiral fashion to prevent sharp bones from scratching the intestines.

Coloration: The pelage, or fur coat, of a mountain lion is short and fairly coarse. Color of the upper body ranges from tan to reddish brown in summer, becoming darker and more gray during the winter months. The chest, underbelly, and mouth portion of the muzzle are white to yellowish. The backs of the ears and tip of the tail are black. A dark stripe extends downward around the muzzle at either side of the pinkish nose. The eyes of adults range from bright yellow to gray-yellow.

Sign: Claw marks in trees that serve as territorial scratching posts, the span and thickness of which are much broader than those of a bobcat or lynx. Scats haphazardly covered with soil will show clawmarks that are usually from the same direction in which the cat was traveling.

Vocalizations: Mountain lions purr when they're content, or when mothers are suckling kittens, and can mew like house cats. Other vocalizations include hisses, growls, and the trademark loud snarl. Kittens mew like domestic kittens, but have a loud chirping cry that gets their mother's attention.

Lifespan: About 10 years in the wild, up to 20 years in captivity.

Diet

Like all felids, the mountain lion is a carnivore that prefers to kill its own food rather than eat carrion. Superbly equipped to be a hunter in terms of stealth, speed, and natural armament, a puma can take down prey larger than itself, usually leaping onto the backs of large animals and killing them with a brain-piercing bite to the base of the skull.

Although best known for preying on deer-size animals, a mountain lion also eats most smaller animals, from mice and muskrats to raccoons and rabbits, and can survive well on a diet that doesn't include large animals. When the prey is large, a puma prefers to concentrate its efforts on immature or sickly individuals that won't put up a hard fight. Annual food consumption for an adult cat is estimated at approximately 600 to 900 pounds.

Mating Habits

Mountain lions are normally solitary, and when they do get together for mating, it's a polygamous relationship, with both partners typically breeding with more than one mate. Both sexes are ready to breed at 2.5 years, but males will not take a mate until they've established their own territories, usually at about 3 years. Males are said to remain sexually fertile for up to 20 years, females to about 12 years. Mating is preceded by a period of courtship that allows the pair to become accustomed to one another, but there is no fixed mating season. However, courtship and mating generally take place from December to March. Males respond to the pheromone scents, yowling, and other vocalizations from females with their own eerie caterwauling, sounding very much like large alley cats.

Female mountain lions mate every other year, because for the first year of her cubs' lives a mother is devoted to teaching offspring the skills of survival. The estrus period lasts for 9 days, but if the female hasn't achieved pregnancy before a heat passes, she will come into estrus for another 9-day cycle.

Mating battles between males vying for a female are relatively nonviolent. Most competitions consist largely of body language, and when two males do fight, the contest is largely one of physical strength. Some injuries do occur, but, like all wild species, mountain lions harbor an instinctive revulsion against harming their own kind, and their decidedly lethal claws and canines are not used with the violence that they could be.

Gestation periods last from 82 to 96 days, with mothers giving birth in a secluded, existing cave or den within the father's territory. Litter sizes range from 1 to 6 cubs with 3 or 4 being average. A cub's weight at birth averages between 1 and 2 pounds, and each will be blind and completely helpless for its first 10 days of life. The cubs first teeth erupt immediately therafter, and they begin to play. The cubs' father may bring the incapacitated female gifts of food during the denning period, but takes no active role in rearing his offspring. At about 40 days the cubs are fully weaned and begin to accompany their mother on short hunting forays away from the den.

Male cubs remain with the mother for approximately 1 year before wandering away to establish their own territories, female cubs may remain with her for up to 2 years. Male cubs that wander off together will probably remain together for only a short time, using the strength of numbers to discourage would-be predators, then will separate to find their own home ranges.

Behavior

Mountain lions are solitary animals whose lone lifestyles are interrupted only by breeding and rearing young. Territorial ranges vary from more than 60 square miles to as small as 9 square miles, depending on the availability of food and water. Residents of either sex mark their territories by depositing urine or fecal materials, usually at the bases of trees that have been used as scratching posts.

Mountain lions are primarily nocturnal, with excellent night and binocular vision. Their main sense is that of sight, followed by sense of smell, and then hearing. Pumas typically have summer and winter home ranges in different locations because they follow the migratory habits of deer, their main prey.

Mountain lions are hunted as sport and their pelts have considerable trophy value as rugs or wall hangings. The species is considered to be a threat to domestic animals, but they tend to stay far away from human habitation, and livestock losses are typically exaggerated. Also exaggerated are the few extraordinary cases in which an old or sickly, and usually starving, individual has attacked small-statured humans.

Jaguar (Panthera onca)

Once revered as a forest god by pre-Columbian civilizations in southern Mexico, Guatemala, and Peru, the jaguar's name is an Indian word that means "kills in a single bound." The species is comprised of eight subspecies, all of them threatened, and some are extinct except in zoos. The greatest threat to this largest of American cats comes from the illegal fur trade, which places a premium on the jaguar's beautiful spotted pelt, and the clearing of old growth forest where the cat's dappled coat has evolved to give it good camouflage. Little data has been established about the way these reclusive felids live in the wild, and most of what is known has been recorded from zoo specimens.

Geographic Range

Panthera onca is native to warmer regions in the Americas. It once ranged as far north as southern Texas, but is now extremely rare, and perhaps nonexistent, in the United

Jaguar. Photo by John and Karen Hollingsworth, courtesy of U.S. Fish & Wildlife Service.

States. Today, most sightings occur in South America, mostly in Argentina, Brazil, and as far south as Patagonia.

Habitat

Jaguars require a habitat that provides not only large prey and plenty of water, but forest cover where their spotted coats are hard to distinguish among undergrowth and dappled sunlight from forest canopy. Dense jungle and scrub forest, reed thickets along waterways, and shoreline forests are preferred, but in times past the species was occasionally found in open country, so long as tall grass and rock formations offered sufficient cover for hunting.

Physical Characteristics

Mass: Males 120 to 300 pounds, females 100 to 200 pounds.

Body: Stoutly built cat, slightly larger and stockier than a mountain lion, with a spotted coat, thick limbs, and a massive head. Body length about 4 feet, shoulder height 2.5 to 3 feet.

Tail: 18 to 30 inches, spotted with a black tip. The jaguar's tail is comparatively shorter and thinner than the mountain lion's, probably because it tends to hunt from the ground or in the water, and requires a less acute sense of balance.

Tracks: Forefoot 4 to 4.5 inches, nearly as wide as it is long, leaving a print that's almost round. Hind prints slightly smaller. Toes are much smaller and heel pads much larger than those of the mountain lion. Heel pads of all four feet are three-lobed, but the two outermost lobes in a jaguar's front track are larger than the center lobe and extend more rearward, whereas the three lobes in a mountain lion's front track are of nearly equal size. Walking stride about 20 inches, but can vary greatly in the cat's overgrown habitat; straddle 8 to 10 inches.

Scat: Often indistinguishable from the mountain lion, being cylindrical, segmented, tapered at one or both ends, and often exhibiting an outer covering of fur wrapped around the scat in spiral fashion. About 5

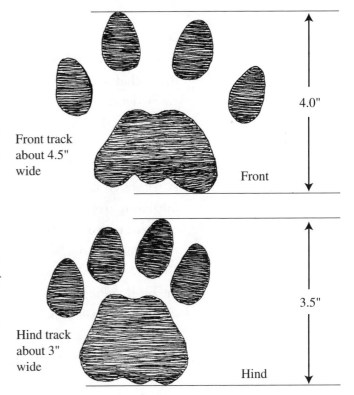

Front track about 4.5" wide

Front

4.0"

Hind track about 3" wide

Hind

3.5"

Jaguar (Panthera onca). *The only felid that makes a habit of swimming and hunting along waterways, the jaguar's very large forepaws make it the best swimmer in the cat family.*

inches long by 1.5 inches in diameter. Notable differences may be evident from the jaguar's tendency to prey on aquatic animals, including alligators and fish.

Coloration: Jaguars are normally yellow and tan with a mottling of black rings, many of which have a single black dot inside each of them. The cheeks, throat, underbelly, and insides of the legs are white. It's also common for a jaguar to be black, a color phase in which the cat is known as a black panther. Black panthers are also spotted, but the mottling is subdued by a coat that's nearly as dark as the spots.

Sign: Scat deposits at trail intersections, usually near trees that have been clawed and marked with pungent urine as territorial boundaries. Alligator remains near water. Large cat tracks on riverbanks or lakeshores that enter and exit the water.

Vocalizations: Jaguars are the only cat in the Americas that can roar. The sound is different than the roar of an African lion, though, being more like a series of loud coughs rather than a single unbroken roar.

Lifespan: Jaguars have lived up to 22 years in captivity, lifespan in the wild is unknown, but probably 12 to 15 years.

Diet

P. onca is carnivorous and very much the predator. It feeds on medium to terrestrial prey that includes deer, peccaries, and alpacas. As the only wild felid that actually prefers to swim, jaguars also prey on aquatic animals that include nutria (a large rodent related to muskrats), fish, frogs, and even alligators up to 5 feet in length.

Mating Habits

Jaguars reach sexual maturity at 3 years of age. Females breed once every 2 years. Those inhabiting tropical regions may breed at any time of year, while those living in the northern part of the range tend to mate in December or January. Females are thought to be monogamous, accepting a single mate per breeding season.

The recorded gestation period for jaguars is 93 to 110 days. Just prior to giving birth the mother, who is still accompanied by her mate, retires to a den that may consist of a small rock cave or crevice, a hollow beneath the roots of a large tree, or another suitable secure and dry refuge. Like all cats, jaguars are poor diggers, so dens are naturally occurring or appropriated from other species, rather than excavated by the cats.

Litter sizes are relatively small, with 1 to 4 cubs born blind but furred, and weighing 1.5 to 2 pounds each. Mothers remain with their cubs nearly all of the time until they're weaned at about 40 days, leaving the den only to urinate, defecate, and drink while her mate guards the den. During this period the father jaguar brings her food and keeps close watch on the den, but does not enter.

When cubs are grown enough to travel with their mother at roughly 2 months of age, the parental pair splits, the male taking no role in the rearing of his offspring. The cubs will have become proficient hunters of small animals at 6 months of age, but remain with the mother for the next year before going off on their own. Female cubs may remain with the mother for 2 years, but are emancipated before she mates again.

Behavior

Jaguars are solitary animals, with interaction between the species occurring only during the mating period. The big cats are known to live within a territorial radius of just 3 miles, but if food is scarce they may roam as far as 200 miles in search of a more suitable habitat. Jaguars are fast runners, but tire quickly. They climb trees very well, but are also proficient swimmers, and prefer habitats with plenty of fresh water. Jaguars have been deemed a keystone species in tropical ecosystems, where their predation on herbivorous and granivorous mammals helps to control overpopulation of species whose feeding might negatively impact native flora.

Like all wild cats, jaguars will kill domestic animals for food, but livestock predation is usually the result of clearing forest to move farms into areas already occupied by the cats. Jaguars have a reputation for being man-eaters, but the Miskito and other Indians have coexisted with them in relative peace for centuries, and the actual danger appears to have been greatly overexaggerated. The Amazonian Indians tell stories of jaguars emerging from the forest to play with village children, while Mayan tribes believed that the jaguar was God of the Underworld, helping the sun to travel beneath the world each night, and insuring that it rose again each morning. Incidents of humans being followed through the jungle by lone jaguars are probably attributable to a catlike sense of curiosity, and perhaps an intent to frighten intruders from their territory.

Bobcat (Lynx rufus)

The bobcat is the most dominant wild felid over most of North America, largely because this highly adaptable cat species is also the most prevalent in a broad range of habitats. Having been hunted with dogs and trapped or poisoned to near extinction in many states, bobcats are extremely shy of humans, and are rarely seen even in places where they abound. That secretiveness may lessen, however, as housing development continues to invade bobcat habitats and bring humans closer to where the animals live.

Bobcat (Lynx rufus). *Reddish brown coat spotted with dark markings, short tail, stocky build, ears slightly tufted.*

Geographic Range

Bobcats are found throughout North America from southern Mexico to southern Canada, and from the Atlantic coast to the Pacific. Population densities in the United States are much higher in the forested eastern region than they are in western states. Perhaps significantly, the species is rare or nonexistent in the large agricultural regions of southern Michigan, and throughout Illinois, Indiana, Ohio, and Pennsylvania.

Habitat

Bobcats are extremely adaptable to a wide variety of habitats, including dense forests, wet swamps, semiarid deserts, forested mountains, and brushland. They prefer plenty of cover with trees large enough to climb for the purpose of observation or escape. The species seems well-adapted to cold and snow, but isn't found in most of Canada.

Physical Characteristics

Mass: 14 to more than 68 pounds, with the largest specimens occurring in the northern part of the cat's range.

Body: Much like a domestic cat; lithe, well-muscled, and built for agility. Cheeks and ear tips are tufted, though not to the extent of the lynx. Head and body length 28 to 50 inches, height at shoulder 15 to more than 20 inches.

Tail: Short, black-tipped, 3 to 6 inches long. Longer than that of the lynx, looking much like the tail of a house cat, but less than half as long.

Tracks: Usually 1 to 2 inches long, with some as long as 3.5 inches in the northernmost portion of the species' range. Four toes on each foot, no claws showing. All four feet approximately the same size. Stride 10 to 14 inches, straddle 6 to 7 inches. Hind prints noted for registering precisely inside front tracks, leaving a track pattern that appears to have been made by a two-legged creature. Front of heel pad, toward toes, is concave, and distinctly different from that of any of the canids.

Scat: Cylindrical, segmented, tapered at one or both ends. Length 2 to 6 inches, diameter 0.5 to 1 inch. Always with a predominance of rodent, rabbit, and occasionally deer fur wrapped in spiral fashion around small bones encased within. Scats are indistinguishable from those of the lynx, which has an identical diet, and easily confused with those of a coyote or fox, except that canids typically don't attempt to scratch soil over their scats.

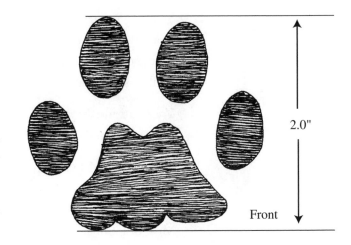

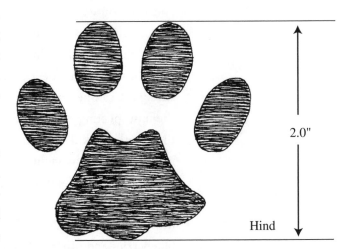

Bobcat (Lynx rufus). *Note that the front and hind paws are the same length, while the forefeet of most species are larger than the hind feet. Also, individuals living in the north tend to be larger, frequently with tracks that can exceed three inches.*

Unlike cougars, which tend to scratch soil from the direction they'll be traveling when covering scats, bobcats scratch from all directions, leaving raylike patterns of scratch marks all around the scat deposit.

Coloration: The bobcat's coat can be quite variable, and it changes with the seasons. The normal summer coloration is darker brown spots against a coat of brown or reddish brown. In winter, the coat tends to become darker, with less evident spots, ranging from dark brown to almost gray. In all seasons the insides of the legs, the underbelly, and throat are cream-colored to white, mottled with brown spots. The short tail is also spotted, and tipped in black.

Sign: Deep scratches in smooth barked tree trunks, about 2 feet above the ground, often scented with the cat's pungent urine. Soft pines seem to be the preferred scratching posts, possibly because the sticky, heavily scented sap helps to conceal the bobcat's scent while it's hunting.

Vocalizations: Very much like those of a domestic cat, consisting of soft mews, purring, low growls, and childlike wailing or yowling during the breeding season.

Lifespan: 8 to 10 years in the wild.

Diet

Most of a bobcat's diet consists of prey that ranges from small rodents to rabbits to an occasional small deer. The species rarely eats carrion, preferring to kill its own food, and, like house cats, bobcats have an uncanny ability to sneak within striking distance of prey. Even larger birds like bluejays, grouse, and an occasional small goose are caught before they can take wing and escape this wildcat's lightning fast attack.

Small yearling deer may be taken by large bobcats in deep winter snows, where a strong cat can perch on a tree branch and lie in wait for a yearling deer to pass. When the unsuspecting deer comes within range, the cat pounces onto its back, anchors itself there with hooklike retractable claws, and drives its long, sharp upper and lower canines into the base of its victim's skull. The wound quickly kills the prey either by piercing the brainstem or the spinal cord.

Although sometimes said to be strictly carnivorous, bobcats supplement their mostly meat diets with a few fruits and some vegetable matter. Sugar calories from blueberries and other rich autumn fruits are favored for putting on fat against the cold of an approaching winter, as well as for the vitamins and nutrients they contain. Grasses and sedges are also eaten because their coarse fibers help to dislodge hairballs accumulated through grooming, and because they help to clear the animal's colon of undigested waste matter.

Mating Habits

Bobcats in the northern part of the species' range typically mate in February or March, but those in the southern range may mate throughout the summer, and in especially warm areas females may produce two litters in the same year. The breeding season is initiated by the scent of a female coming into heat, which in turn attracts several suitors. After a contest that consists mostly of caterwauling, growls, and an occasional scuffle, the strongest male mates with the receptive female, and the pair sets off to find a suitable birthing den in a rock crevice, hollow log, or under the roots of a large standing tree. Like all felids, bobcats are not well-designed for excavating, so dens are made from existing shelters.

After a gestation period of 60 to 70 days, a small litter of two or three blind kittens, each weighing about 8 ounces, is born in late April or May. After nursing for 10 days, the young open their eyes and begin to move about the den. The mother stays with her kittens nearly all of the time for their first 2 months, leaving only to drink and to relieve herself. During this vulnerable time, her mate, who doesn't enter the den, brings her food, watches over his offspring while she's out of the den, and protects his family from predators that might eat the kittens.

Bobcat kittens are weaned in June or July, and the parental pair separates, the male taking no further role in the rearing of his offspring. Kittens begin traveling and hunting with their mother, learning the finer points of catching a meal and avoiding danger, until they reach 8 months of age, usually in December or January. Now nearly full grown, males are the first to leave, followed within a month by the females. Adolescents may disperse widely, taking up residence several miles distant, but generally travel no farther than is dictated by habitat requirements and competition from other bobcats. Emancipated kittens will likely take, or at least compete for, a mate in their first breeding season.

Behavior

Like all wild felids in the Americas, bobcats are normally solitary, interacting only to mate and during the summer months when mothers are training their young. Females are more apt to live discreetly, especially if they have kittens that might fall prey to bears, coyotes, and large birds of prey, but males freely advertise their claim to a territory that might encompass several square miles. Partly buried scat deposits left pointedly at the intersections of trails usually delineate territorial boundaries, while pungent sprays of urine on tree trunks that may also be marked by clawing serve to warn passersby that this area is claimed.

The home range of a dominant male bobcat typically overlaps the smaller ranges of several females, giving the resident male a better chance of detecting when one of them comes into estrus before an intruder can usurp his claim. Occasionally the territorial boundaries of two males will overlap, but this seldom leads to conflict except during mating season.

Although bobcats don't normally live in dens, there are usually several refuges sited throughout an individual's range. The dens serve a shelter for escaping foul weather that also drives most prey into hiding, or for eluding larger predators that might view a bobcat as competition or food, like pumas, wolves, and bears.

Occasionally a human, who is always alone at the time and who always seems to be an armed sport hunter, will claim that he was attacked by a bobcat. In none of these supposed attacks has a claimant been so much as scratched by the cat, which could easily ambush a human, but in every instance the bobcat ended up dead. In one case that was published in a recognized hunting magazine, a hunter claimed to have been attacked by several bobcats at once, whereupon the intrepid nimrod proceeded to shoot the mother and her entire litter. Having spent many hundreds of days and nights in places where bobcats live, I personally dispute these tales as the product of adventuresome imaginations and an individual's need to be glorified. It simply defies logic that any lone predator would attack an adversary that's 3 or more times its own size, especially one that for centuries has given all carnivores so much reason for fear.

Lynx (*Lynx canadensis*)

This slightly smaller cousin to the bobcat is one of the most reclusive species in North America, and perhaps the world. Known variably as *Lynx lynx, Felis lynx,* and *Lynx canadensis,* this cat is supremely adapted to life in the dense forests and deep snows of the far north.

Despite its shyness, lynx pelts with their long, silky fur have become increasingly valuable to the fur trade since restrictions were placed on the importation of exotic cat

Lynx. Photo by Erwin and Peggy Bauer, courtesy of U.S. Fish & Wildlife Service.

pelts in the latter half of the twentith century. Fortunately, the current market demand for fur is low, and there seems to be no danger to lynx populations from overtrapping.

Geographic Range

Although never overabundant in any locale, the largest populations of lynx are found throughout Canada and in the northernmost regions of Montana and Idaho. There are small populations in New England, northern Wisconsin, and in Michigan's Upper Peninsula. With a pronounced aversion to humans and a habitat that shrinks with each passing year, it's unlikely that lynx will ever be common.

Habitat

Native to North America, the lynx will occasionally be seen on tundra or in rocky areas in the far north, but never far from the deep old growth forests and thick swamps that are its required habitat. The species is superbly adapted to life in deep snow, and it has a pronounced tendency for avoiding humans, so a researcher who sees one in the wild can count himself lucky.

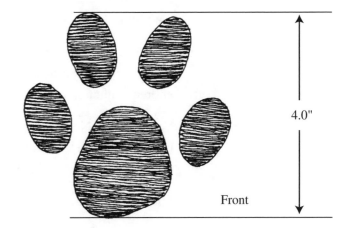

Physical Characteristics

Mass: 11 to 40 pounds.

Body: Long-legged with large furry paws adapted for travel in deep snow. Body length 29 to 41 inches. Males about 10% larger than females. Pointed ears tipped with long tufts of fur, cheeks also heavily tufted, giving the appearance of thick sideburns. Height at shoulder 15 to more than 20 inches.

Tail: Shorter than the bobcat's, 2 to 5 inches long.

Tracks: Four toes on each foot, no claws showing in tracks. The paws are large and well-furred, especially in winter, making tracks appear larger than they actually are, but giving this fast runner more flotation when pursuing prey over deep snow. Foreprint 3 to 4.5 inches long, hind prints about 10% smaller. Hind print with three lobes at rear of heel pad, front print with three lobes on heel pad, but two outermost lobes extend more to the rear at

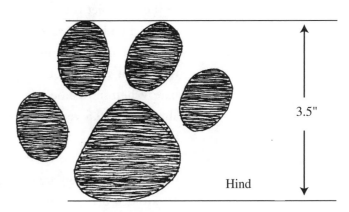

Lynx (Lynx canadensis). *Like all cats, and unlike members of the canine family, claws are normally retracted, and don't show in tracks. Misshapen, undefined heel pads are a result of the lynx's heavily furred soles, which tend to blur a track's details.*

either side, leaving a chevron-shaped impression unlike the three equal-sized lobes made by the front heel pad of a bobcat. Stride 14 to 16 inches, straddle 5 to 7 inches.

Scat: Usually indistinguishable from that of a bobcat, being cylindrical, segmented, and tapered at one or both ends. Length 2 to 6 inches, diameter 0.5 to 1 inch. Scats are usually partially buried under soil or snow, and typically have an outer covering of fine hare or rabbit fur wrapped spirally around an inner core of small bones.

Coloration: There is some variation in the color of different individuals, but the usual lynx coat is yellow-brown in summer, becoming more gray in winter, and much longer than the fur of a bobcat. Some individuals have dark spots, but lynx generally lack the heavily spotted appearance of a bobcat's coat. The ear tufts and tip of the tail are black, with whitish throat, underbelly, and insides of the legs. The eyes are yellow.

Sign: Scentposts on smooth-barked trees that have been clawed and sprayed with urine, partially covered scats left at the intersections of trails. Large prey that cannot be eaten entirely will often be cached by burying it beneath forest debris or snow.

Vocalizations: Normally silent except during the mating season, when males especially utter a loud shriek or scream the ends with an echoing wail that some woodsmen have described as eerie, or like the wailing of a woman.

Lifespan: Probably 8 to 10 years in the wild.

Diet

Lynx are more carnivorous than most felids, although they too eat grasses to help clear their digestive systems of hairballs and other undigestible matter. A key species in the lynx diet is the snowshoe, or varying, hare (*Lepus americanus*). Being at least as proficient a hunter as its larger cousin, the bobcat, the lynx is capable of catching rodents, spawning fish, and may even take a small yearling deer given the right opportunity, but survival of this particular felid is linked heavily to that of the snowshoe hare. When snowshoe hare populations peak and then fall off dramatically, as they do about every 9.5 years, lynx populations also fall due to disease and starvation 1 year later.

Lynx will also eat carrion, but only if the meat is fresh and undecayed. Deer wounded by hunters are often eaten, especially in cold weather, but road-killed animals are avoided because they're too close to places frequented by humans.

Mating Habits

Like northern bobcats, and unlike southern bobcats, female lynx come into heat only once a year in March and April, and raise only one litter per year. Prior to selecting her mate, a receptive female normally has several suitors that accompany her everywhere with much wailing, caterwauling, and an occasional fight that's marked by hissing, spitting, and growling, but not much bloodshed. After about 1 week of this competition, the female undergoes an estrus period of just 1 to 2 days and selects a mate. After mating, the pair leaves to find a secluded birthing den in a hollow log or rock crevice.

After a gestation period of about 9 weeks, the pregnant lynx gives birth in May or June to two, sometimes as many as five, blind kittens, each weighing about 7 ounces. As always, larger litter sizes are a product of an especially healthy mother and an abundant supply of food.

Except for short departures to drink, urinate, or defecate, the mother lynx remains with her young almost constantly for their first month of life, relying on her mate to bring food and keep watch against enemies. After 1 month the kittens begin eating meat scraps, but continue to nurse for 5 months, with most weanings occurring in October or November.

After weaning, when the kittens are grown enough to travel and learn to hunt, the male lynx leaves them, and takes no part in the training of his offspring. The nearly grown young remain with their mother until January or February before setting off on their own, with males usually leaving first. Freed of her charges, the mother will come into heat again about 1 month later. Her female kittens won't reach sexual maturity until they're 21 months old, males at 33 months.

Behavior

Lynx are normally solitary animals, and adults avoid one another except during the mating season. They appear to be territorial, but the boundaries of females may overlap, and, like bobcats, a male's home range is likely to infringe on the territories of one or more females. Ranges may vary in area from 7 to more than 200 square miles, depending on the availability of food and other resources.

Lynx are primarily nocturnal hunters, with excellent night vision and keen directional hearing. They might lie in wait for several hours along a game trail, overlooking it from a tree branch or hiding behind brush, or they might stalk a prey animal to within a few yards, then pounce onto its back. Long canine teeth deliver a fatal bite to the base of the victim's skull, piercing its brainstem or spinal cord.

Females with young sometimes hunt cooperatively for snowshoe hares, spreading themselves to form a skirmish line and moving through brushy areas until one of them jumps a hare from hiding. This hunting technique appears to be learned rather than instinctual, but it's a regular part of the training that females give their offspring.

Lynx frequently take shelter from foul weather in rough dens under rock ledges, in caves, under fallen trees, or in hollow logs. There are likely to be several such refuges scattered throughout an animal's territory.

THE WEASEL FAMILY (FAMILY MUSTELIDAE)

Family Mustelidae is the family of weasels, which includes such diverse species as skunks, the wolverine, the badger, and otters. All members are characterized by having five toes tipped with sharp, sometimes retractable, claws on each paw; short but powerful legs; muscular bodies; and perineal (anal) glands that emit a strong musky odor. All are carnivorous and predatory, although none are fast runners. Some, like the badger and skunk, can dig through soil with amazing speed, while the fisher and pine marten bound through treetops with the same agility as the squirrels they pursue. Still others, like the sea and river otters, swim well enough to catch fish, while the wolverine makes its way out of sheer ferocity.

Sea Otter (Enhydra lutris)

Largest of the weasels, and the only one that makes its living in the Pacific Ocean, the sea otter is a keystone species that plays an important role in its environment by controlling herbivorous invertebrates, mainly the sea urchin (*Strongylocentrotus sp.*). Sea urchins feed on kelp, and in coastal areas where otters are absent, the spiny creatures tend to overpopulate and deplete the area's kelp forests. Where sea otters are present, urchins and benthic (sea bottom) feeders are kept in check by predation, and kelp forests are healthy.

Sea otter.

Sea otter pelts were highly valued by the fur trade from the late 1700s to 1911, when the species had been depleted to less than 2,000 animals worldwide, and the International Fur Seal Treaty was signed between the United States, Russia, Japan, and Great Britain. The United States' Marine Mammal Protection Act of 1972 further reinforced sea otter protection against hunting, and today sea otter populations are estimated to be as high as 150,000 animals worldwide. The California sea otter (*Enhydra lutris nereis*), which currently has a population of about 2,200, is listed as threatened under the Endangered Species Act, where it will remain until a population of 2,650 is recorded for 3 consecutive years. Biologists are concerned that another oil spill like that of the 1989 Exxon Valdez incident, which killed an estimated 5,000 sea otters, could wipe out the entire population of California sea otters.

Geographic Range

Historic distribution of the sea otter once included Japan's Hokkaido Island, north through the Kuril Islands and the eastern coast of Kamchatka, east through the Commander Islands and Aleutian archipelago, and southward along the Pacific coast of America from Alaska to Baja, Mexico. Unrestricted hunting during the eighteenth and nineteenth centuries greatly reduced the distribution of the sea otter. Natural boundaries include sea ice that limits their northern range to below 57 degrees North latitude, while availability of kelp forests keeps the species north of 22 degrees North latitude.

Today there are three recognized subspecies of *E. lutris*. *E.l. lutris* is found from the Kuril Islands north to the Commander Islands in the western Pacific. *E.l. nereis* inhabits the coast of central California. *E.l. kenyoni* lives throughout the Aleutian Islands and southern Alaska and has been reintroduced to the Pacific coast in several locations from Oregon to Alaska's Prince William Sound.

Habitat

Sea otters are native to the Pacific Ocean, specifically the kelp forests along its shoreline, where most of the marine life they rely on as food can be found in abundance. They prefer temperate waters with rocky or sedimentary bottoms less than 1 mile from shore, and avoid places where the surface freezes in winter.

Physical Characteristics

Mass: 25 to 80 pounds.

Body: Elongated, stoutly built, and streamlined, much like its smaller relative, the river otter. Length 30 to 71 inches. Short powerful legs, hind legs longer than front. Small

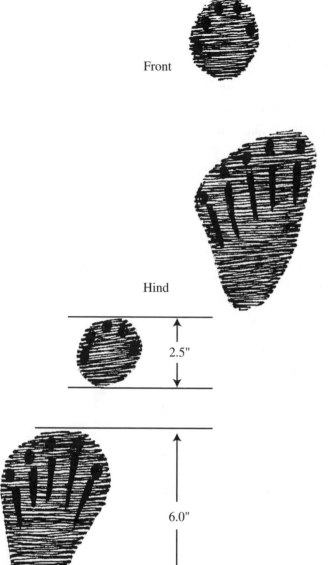

Front

Hind

2.5"

6.0"

Sea otter tracks as they might appear on wet sand. Trackers should note that sea otters feed, mate, and even sleep in the water, and tracks on shore are not common.

rounded ears, short muzzle, long whiskers that droop like a mustache from either side of a large nose pad. Males slightly larger than females. Females have only two mammae. Sea otters are the only mammalian carnivores that have just four lower incisor teeth.

Tail: Broad and well-furred, comparatively shorter than that of the river otter, measuring 10 to 14 inches.

Tracks: Rarely seen, as this most aquatic of pawed mammals spends nearly all of its time in the water. Five toes on all four feet. Hind feet are elongated and webbed, much like flippers, with nonretractable claws, leaving fan-shaped tracks 5 to 6 inches long. Forepaws rounder, leaving dotlike tracks, about 3 inches long, which may show only four toes. Nonretractable claws on hind feet; retractable claws on forepaws.

Scat: Cylindrical, flat at one end, shaped almost like a cigar stub when fresh. Length 2 to 4 inches, about 1 inch in diameter. Composition is mostly small shards of crustacean and mollusk shells, with fish scales and bits of fish bones. This composition is similar to the regurgitations of seagulls, but with much more mass.

Coloration: Dark brown to reddish brown body with gray or yellowish head and neck. Long gray whiskers, large black triangular nose pad. Sea otter fur is the thickest of any species, with a density of about 250,000 hairs per square inch. Unlike seals and other aquatic mammals, sea otters do not carry a layer of insulating fat, but rely on their waterproof fur for warmth; this characteristic makes oil spills especially dangerous to them because petroleum oil robs sea otter fur of its insulation properties and subjects the animals to hypothermia.

Sign: Sea otters rarely come ashore, so there is very little sign left by them, and the few scats or tracks left when they do leave water are rare and quickly erased by the elements.

Scats of the weasel family. Typical of all weasels; size varies with size of animal. Note that most samples exhibit an outer layer of fur ingested from prey.

Vocalizations: Usually silent. The most common vocalization is heard among groups of foraging otters, which communicate with one another using a soft grunting sound that is repeated four or five times per call.

One distinctive sound often heard among sea otters is a clacking sound made when the animals use a stone taken from the ocean floor to pound the shells of mollusks and crustaceans until they break. These stone hammers appear to be selected with care for just the right size and shape, and good ones are often used over and over. When groups of sea otters gather to feed, the clacking of their hammers can sometimes be heard over several hundred yards.

Lifespan: Up to 23 years in the wild.

Diet

Sea otters are carnivores that have evolved to make their livings by hunting creatures in an ocean environment, and they will eat nearly any marine animals they can find in their kelp forest foraging grounds. The typical diet consists of marine invertebrates and filter feeders such as mussels, sea urchins, snails, and abalone, as well as crabs, octopus, squid, sea stars, and fish.

Individuals tend to specialize in their choice of prey, with one otter being partial to urchins and crabs, while another eats mostly fish or mussels, depending largely on an individual's hunting skills and the types of food available in a given area. Whatever its food, an otter must eat approximately 25% of its body weight each day.

Perhaps the sea otter's most interesting trait is its ability to use stones retrieved from the sea bottom as hammers to crack open mollusks and other shelled animals that serve as food. Floating on its back and using its chest as a table, the otter places a clam or crab on its belly, then, holding its stone hammer between both paws, pounds the shelled morsel until it breaks. Stone hammers are selected carefully for just the right size and flatness, and appear to be prized, because the same stone will be used many times. An alternate method sometimes used by otters to crack shells that are too large or too thick to be hammered open is to hold prey tightly to their chests, then propel themselves forward in the water to smash it against stationary rocks. Once the shell is broken, the otter picks out the larger shards, and washes smaller pieces from the edible flesh by rolling laterally underwater, returning to its original belly-up position.

Most of the water a sea otter needs to survive is obtained from food animals, but the species also has a rather unique ability to drink sea water.

Mating Habits

Female sea otters are capable of breeding at 4 years; males reach sexual maturity at 5 to 6 years, but may not mate until much later. Sea otters can reproduce at any time of year, but delayed implantation causes fertilized eggs to be carried within the female until weather, food availability, and other conditions are right for pregnancy. This means that gestation periods vary greatly, ranging from 4 months under optimal conditions to 12 months if environmental conditions are poor. Under good conditions, births tend to be at their peak in May and June among Aleutian Island populations and from January through March in the California herds.

The estrus period for female sea otters lasts just 72 hours, although females not impregnated during that cycle will come into heat again soon after. Males tend to breed with any females that come into their claimed territories, and will occasionally try to steal mates from the territories of others. Battles between males consist mostly of splashing and body language, with little real fighting.

Breeding males remain with their mates until the estrus period passes. Copulation takes place in the water, where the male holds his mate's head or nose firmly in his jaws while gripping her body with strong forelimbs. Ironically, this breeding ritual is more violent than mating battles between males, and females that have mated previously can often be identified by the scars on their noses and heads.

Female sea otters generally give birth once per year, although mothers that lose a pup will probably come into estrus again within a few months. Birth takes place in the water. Litter size is normally a single pup. In about 2% of cases twins will be born, although some biologists believe that mothers are capable of rearing just one of them. Pups may weigh from 2 to 4 pounds at birth, and are born fully furred, with teeth, and with their eyes open. Pups nurse while lying on their mother's belly as she floats on her back, and when she dives to forage on the sea bottom, youngsters float in one place until she resurfaces. If danger approaches—usually in the form of an orca, shark, or eagle—the mother otter wraps one forelimb around her pup and dives into the safety of the kelp forest. Pups begin eating solid food soon after birth, and by 2 months of age are diving on their own. Weaning typically occurs at 5 or 6 months, but this too can vary considerably depending on the strength of a pup at birth.

Behavior

Sea otters are both social and solitary, claiming territories, but living, feeding, and breeding in close proximity to one another. The social structure is herdlike, with males tending to congregate in groups, and females tending to stay apart from them except when mating. Both sexes can spend their entire lives in the water, but may rest on land when populations are high enough for them to enjoy safety in numbers.

Sea otters swim by using their webbed hind feet for propulsion, adding to the thrust from them with undulating movements of the tail and body, while forelimbs are kept tightly tucked against the chest. This swimming technique is efficient for the otter's streamlined body, and most adults can reach speeds of about 6 miles per hour underwater.

Sea otters are active during daylight hours (diurnal), with crepuscular (dusk and dawn) peaks in foraging activity. A typical foraging dive keeps the animals underwater for 50 to 90 seconds, but otters can remain submerged for more than 5 minutes. Depending on the abundance of food animals, foraging may use 15% to 55% of an otter's waking hours.

Sea otters locate and identify underwater prey with eyes located in the front of the skull that provide binocular vision and good depth perception, and the animals see well underwater. Once found, urchins, mussels, and other food animals are detached from their moorings with the otters' sensitive paws, and brought to the surface to be eaten.

Male sea otters are known to steal food from the smaller females if given an opportunity, so females tend to forage in locations that are separate from male herds. Herds of them often rest together, floating on their backs and grooming themselves by using claws as combs. When resting or sleeping, sea otters float on their backs, sometimes with forepaws held over the eyes to shade out sunlight, and anchor themselves in place by wrapping their bodies or their limbs with kelp, which is itself anchored to the bottom.

Despite a moratorium on harvesting them for the fur trade, populations of sea otters have been in decline since the 1990s. An overpopulation of orcas *(Orcinus orca),* combined with a reduction in seals, the orca's staple prey, is thought to have resulted in increased predation on sea otters. Other predators of sea otters that might also be responsible for current declines include the white shark *(Carcharodon carcharias)* and the sea lion

A family of river otters with the alpha female (mother) in a defensive posture.

(Zalophus californianus). Increasing populations of bald eagles *(Haliaeetus leucocephalus),* which prey on young otters, might also have a negative impact on sea otter numbers.

River Otter *(Lontra canadensis)*

River otters are the freshwater version of the sea otter. These large weasels are equally adapted to life as aquatic mammals, except that they've evolved to make their livings in inland rivers, lakes, and streams, and are better suited to cold environments.

Geographic Range

The North American river otter ranges from Alaska, eastward across northern Canada to Nova Scotia, and south to California and waterways in Arizona. Prized for their pelts, river otters were trapped nearly to extinction in the midwestern United States until the twentieth century, when laws were implemented for their protection. Today, the river otter has made a successful comeback in many of the areas where it was once rare.

Habitat

Rivers, ponds, and lakes, usually no more than a few hundred yards from water unless an individual or newly mated pair is migrating to establish its own territory. River otters can tolerate environmental extremes of heat and cold, so long as the terrain offers a year-round supply of fresh water.

The presence of river otters also serves as an indicator that a waterway is naturally clean and free of pollutants. The species isn't tolerant of pesticides, herbicides, and other chemical pollutants, and won't be found near industrial, agricultural, or other areas where these toxins are in the water.

Physical Characteristics

Mass: 11 to 30 pounds.

Body: Elongated, lithe, and streamlined, very much like the larger sea otter. Body length 35 to 51 inches. Legs comparatively short; wide, rounded head; short muzzle, small round ears. Nostrils can be closed while the animal is underwater. Long, silvery whiskers hang like a mustache from either side of the muzzle.

Tail: Tail length 8 to 12 inches. Well-furred, thick at the base and tapering to a point. Used as a rudder and for propulsion when the otter is swimming, helping the animal to make sudden changes in direction when pursuing prey underwater.

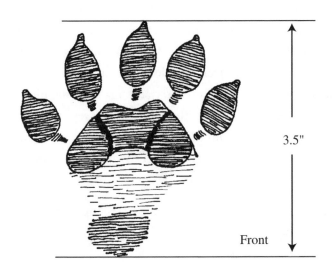

3.5"

Front

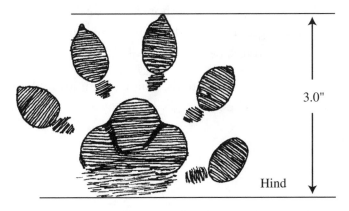

3.0"

Hind

River otter tracks. There are five toes on all four feet. Toes are webbed, but the webbing rarely shows.

Running

River otter track pattern. Track patterns as they might appear in soft mud or wet snow.

Tracks: Five toes on all four feet, toes widely splayed in tracks; ends of toes bulbous, making almost round impressions well ahead of the heel pads. Short nonretractable claws register as points at the end of each toe. Front tracks 3 to 3.5 inches long, nearly as wide as they are long; hind tracks slightly shorter. Four lobes pointing forward on the heel pad of each paw, but usually just three will register in tracks made by the hind feet; a fifth lobe, separate and to the rear of the others on the forefeet may register as round impression to the rear of the track on softer ground, but probably not on firm ground. Hind toes are elongated and webbed, much like a scuba diver's swim fins; webbing may show in tracks made in mud, but not on harder earth.

Scat: Segmented, cylindrical, 2 to 6 inches long by about 0.5 inch in diameter. Composed largely of fish scales, a few fish bones, and small pieces of crayfish shell. Always found near shorelines of rivers or lakes.

Coloration: Dark brown to near-black upper coat. Underside, cheeks, and throat lighter brown to blonde.

Sign: Opened mollusk shells and crayfish carapaces along shorelines—easily confused with raccoon sign. Twisted tufts of rough grasses along shorelines, normally scented with a musky, skunklike excretion from the otter's perineal scent glands.

Vocalizations: River otters make a variety of vocal sounds, ranging from grumbling chuckles and loud whistles to growls and screeches.

Lifespan: Probably 8 to 10 years in the wild.

Diet

The river otter's diet is comprised mostly or entirely from the water in which it spends much of its waking time. Able to remain underwater for about 8 minutes per dive, frogs, clams, crayfish, panfish like sunfish and bluegills, and a few small suckers or bullheads, are on this otter's daily menu. Beaver pups are also taken if an opportunity presents itself, especially in spring, when newborn beavers are still young enough to be stupid and small enough to handle easily.

In winter, when river otters use small holes through lake ice to forage for underwater prey, they will sometimes unearth hibernating frogs or small turtles and bring them up onto the ice, where the heads and limbs are gnawed off. Whiskers are dragged along the bottom when harvesting prey buried under mud, and they appear to be an important sensory tool.

Captured prey is usually brought onto shore, or onto the ice in winter, and eaten immediately after its capture. On ice, the otter is never far from a hole through which to escape back into the water, because all of them will learn that coyotes, bobcats, and even wolves have learned to take advantage of the otter's regular successes. An otter returning to enjoy a meal of panfish on the ice must be alert for skulking predators waiting to rush and try to steal a free meal.

River otters are often blamed for depleting game fish, but so far the prevailing reason that large bass, trout, and other angler favorites become scarce in fishing holes has been attributable to simple overfishing. Sport fishermen tend to pursue larger fish, while otters prefer smaller fish that are easier to catch, put up less fight, and are more plentiful.

Mating Habits

Normally solitary, although seldom violent toward its own species, male river otters that are at least 3 years of age seek out females 2 years or older for mating in March and April. Mating is initiated by females coming into heat, and it appears that they leave scentposts along river and lake shorelines to advertise their receptivity, often next to the twisted tuft of scented grasses that males use as a territorial claim. Once joined, neither sex seeks out another mate, and the pair remains together, usually within the male's territorial boundaries.

After a long gestation period of about 11 months, the result of a delayed implantation process that allows a female time to get healthy enough for a winter of pregnancy, or spontaneous abortion if she isn't, a litter of up to five pups is born in an excavated den in a river or lake bank. The main entrance to the den will usually be underwater, and an escape hole will normally be found farther up the bank.

Mated pairs remain together throughout the winter, frolicking and foraging together through holes in the ice when lakes and ponds freeze over. When the female reaches the point of giving birth in February or March, she retires to the leaf-and-grass lined den, where she will be watched over and provided for by the male for the next 3 or 4 months. Mothers won't allow their mates into the birthing den until pups are weaned, but he's never far away from his family.

Most river otter pups are weaned between May and July, when they leave the den with their mothers to learn the skills they'll need to survive. The father may remain with the family for another month or more, but the pair will likely separate before summer's end. Pups will be grown enough to survive on their own by the first winter, when they will leave the protection of their mothers. Those who don't leave voluntarily will be ejected by the mother before she mates again the following spring.

Behavior

Lontra canadensis is a normally solitary species, but mothers with pups might be seen throughout the summer and most of winter, mated pairs remain together until midsummer, and there's generally not much territorial animosity between otters living in the same area. Tolerance of one another is enhanced by rich foraging places that provide enough to share, but most neighbors whose ranges overlap will be of opposite sexes.

The territories of especially male river otters can encompass more than 60 miles of river, but are generally about 5 miles. As with any species, the amount of territory an otter must claim, then defend, to insure that it has the resources to survive will vary with how abundant or scarce those resources are in its habitat.

Otters have been described as being playful, but this phenomenon probably stems from the same reason that cats are playful: both are such efficient hunters that they have time and energy to spare. About half of an adult otter's waking hours are devoted to finding food, leaving the rest of the day open for doing anything else that comes to mind. In fact, the swimming, diving, and rolling behaviors that seem to be pleasurable activities for an otter with spare time serve a real purpose by honing the animal's hunting and other survival skills.

One of the river otter's best liked activities, for humans at least, is its penchant for sliding over slippery surfaces on its belly. The practice, which seems to be just for the fun of it most of the time, but also makes it more difficult for predators that might try to catch them, is most notable in winter, when river otters leave obvious troughs in snow-covered river and lake banks. If a larger predator threatens, the otter can zip away by sliding on its stomach, legs trailing under and behind the body, down well-polished runways to the safety of water. Otter slides are usually trough-shaped, but one I found in a snow-covered beaver pond bank was actually a tunnel that ran under the snow for a distance of approximately 10 feet before exiting at the waterline of the pond.

Fisher (*Martes pennanti*)

The fisher has always been a difficult subject, because the species is never numerous, and individuals tend not to show themselves. More data needs to be established through field research before humans can really know the fisher, so the information presented here is limited by what modern science does know of *Martes pennanti*.

Fisher. Photograph by Roger Barbour.

Although only half as large as a river otter, it's obvious that the fisher shares a common ancestor with its aquatic cousin. Both species have the elongated streamlined bodies, short legs, five-toed paws, and other physical characteristics shared by most members of the weasel family, and both are almost exclusively carnivorous.

Beyond those common physical traits, otters and fishers are distinctly different, because the fisher has adapted to making its living among the lofty branches of a mature forest canopy. In that arboreal environment the same long muscular body that makes the otter such an excellent swimmer allows a fisher to demonstrate impressive agility when pursuing prey through the treetops. That the otter and fisher could be so physically similar, yet so different in habitat, is indicative of how well the weasel design can be adapted to very different environments.

Geographic Range

Fishers are native only to North America, and there they will be found only in the most remote and vast of forests. The species ranges across the southern half of Canada, from Nova Scotia on the Atlantic coast to British Columbia on the Pacific coast, and north to the southernmost tip of Alaska.

To the south, fishers range from New England, across Michigan's Upper Peninsula and the heavily forested northernmost tip of its Lower Peninsula, from the Sierra Nevada in California to the Appalachians in West Virginia. The species is not found in prairie regions, or in most states south of the United States-Canada border. Populations have been in decline in the southern parts of the fisher's historical range in recent decades, mostly due to deforestation of its native habitat.

Habitat

Fishers live only in large tracts of mature forest. The habitat may be hardwood or conifers in the warmer months, but during months of snow most are found near swamps and especially in white pines, where their staple winter prey, the porcupine (*Erethizon dorsatum*), has migrated to feed through the winter on buds and tender bark.

Fishers are designed to hunt in the treetops, and while an experienced individual might take an occasional hare or rabbit on the ground, their required habitat is dense forest, where surefootedness and superb climbing ability makes them efficient predators of squirrels, small birds and eggs, porcupines, and an occasional small raccoon.

Fishers often take to a den to wait out storms and blizzards, and the ideal habitat will offer lots of hollow logs from large fallen trees whose less tough cores have rotted away to form a tunnel. Aboveground dens in large, standing, hollow trees that once be-longed to porcupines may be used as well.

Physical Characteristics

Mass: Up to 18 pounds.

Body: Elongated, muscular, with short legs, long bushy tail, pointed snout that isn't so blunt as the otter's, and short rounded ears. The fisher might easily be mistaken for a tree squirrel as it bounds through the treetops, except that its body length of 31 to 41 inches is 3 or 4 times that of a large squirrel. Male fishers average roughly 10% larger than females.

Tail: Bushy, long, squirrel-like, 11 to 17 inches long. Functional for maintaining balance in the treetops, much the same as a squirrel.

Tracks: Fishers have the weasels' trademark five toes on all four of their feet, but unlike most of their cousins, the fisher's sharply hooked claws are semi-retractable, able to voluntarily extend into grappling hooks for treetop pursuits. Tracks usually 2 inches or less in length, and typically wider than long, with widths between 2 and 2.5 inches, front

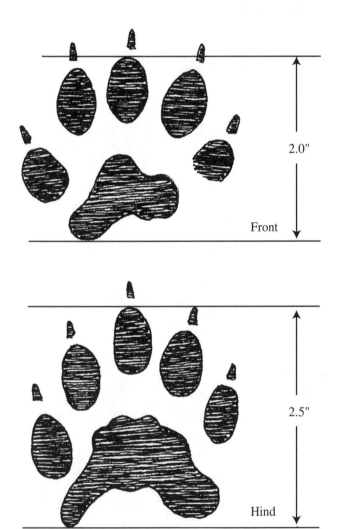

2.0"

Front

2.5"

Hind

Fisher tracks. Tracks shown are typical of what a tracker might find on wet sand or firm mud, but it should be noted that these are partial prints, and in wet snow, where the entire paw makes an impression, tracks may be about five inches long.

Fisher tracks in wet sand.

paws slightly larger than hind. The heelpads of both front and hind feet leave an irregular but roughly crescent-shaped impression that is also a trademark among long-bodied members of the family Mustelidae.

Scat: Cylindrical, tapered at one or both ends, 1 to 3 inches long, about 0.5 inch wide. Often with squirrel and rodent fur wrapped cylindrically around undigestible fragments of bone and, in spring, bird eggshell.

Most notable in fisher scat is the species' rare penchant for making porcupines a regular part of their winter diet. This fact is made obvious by the number of mostly intact porcupine quills that are evident throughout the big weasel's winter scats. The fisher's digestive system can pass these sharp, barbed spears without suffering damage, and although a usually very hungry coyote or bobcat might take an occasional porcupine, only fishers are noted for making a habit of the practice.

Coloration: The fisher's pelage ranges from medium to dark brown, with grizzled head and shoulders. Legs and tail are usually darker, often black. Some have a minklike whitish spot on their chests. Fur color and patterns may vary with the individual, the season (darker fur is more common in the winter coat), and possibly the sex or age of an individual.

Sign: Porcupine skins with most quills intact, but meat-bearing limbs eaten or carried away from the carcass. Porcupine kills are usually found well away from hiking trails, and often under large trees from which a fisher pushed them.

Vocalizations: Nearly always silent. If threatened a fisher may snarl, bare its teeth, and hiss like a cat.

Lifespan: Lifespan in the wild is unknown, but fishers have lived in captivity for more than 10 years. The species appears to have a remarkable resistance to disease.

Diet

Fishers are efficient predators. The typical diet includes small rodents, squirrels, rabbits and hares, and roosting birds. Bird eggs are stolen from nests during the spring brooding season, and snakes and frogs are eaten, as well. The fisher is not noted for catching fish, however, and it seems likely that the fisher's common name came after it was mistakenly ascribed skills that rightfully belonged to the similar but much smaller mink, which is a proficient predator of small fish.

Fishers are agile hunters, with ferocious weasel-like personalities, but while they are capable of tackling hares nearly as large as themselves, they prefer smaller, more easily handled prey. A persistent but erroneous belief that fishers take even small whitetail deer stems from exaggerated accounts from people who have seen them scavenging a deer carcass.

Fishers are also fond of fruits and berries. Their weasel-like metabolisms demand large numbers of calories that can be found in the raw sugars of fruiting bushes. Blueberries are a seasonal favorite, as they are with so many carnivores.

The fisher's best-known prey is the porcupine. Few predators are able or willing to tackle the porky's spiny defenses, but when porcupines take to the white pines in deep winter snows, the arboreal fisher follows. The porcupine's habit of sleeping the day away on a thick branch in the tree on which it might feed for a month, heavily quilled tail toward the trunk, is proof against most climbing predators, but the squirrel-like agility of the fisher allows it to climb around in front of the treed porky. There, face-to-face, the porcupine's unprotected head is an easy target for the fisher's sharp teeth and claws, and the fisher typically knocks the hapless porcupine to the ground, where it dies from the impact or is injured sufficiently to be easily dispatched.

Mating Habits

Fisher females breed at the end of their first year, usually in March or April, and once every year after. Males, which probably mate in their second year, after establishing their own territories, become sexually aroused in response to pheromonal scents from the females' perineal scent glands. Mated pairs may remain together for a short time after mating, but most evidence suggests that they part company as soon as the female is sure she's been impregnated.

Like many female mammals, female fishers enjoy the advantages of a reproductive process known as delayed implantation, which allows them to mate in spring when the warming world makes life easier, but carry the fertilized egg dormant inside their wombs until early autumn. If a female hasn't put on enough fat, or if she's otherwise physically unfit to bear young, the egg will spontaneously abort to reserve bodily resources for her own use. Delayed implantation causes females, which generally breed every year within 2 or 3 weeks after giving birth, to appear as if they're always pregnant or nursing.

Actual gestation, in which the fertilized egg becomes implanted on the uterine wall, and where it begins to draw nourishment from the mother and grow, most likely occurs in November or December. Just before giving birth to a litter of up to five blind pups in February or March, pregnant females retire to a secluded den, usually up high on a standing dead tree. A hollow log or rock crevice may also be employed as a birthing den, but the fisher's habitat provides pre-existing elevated dens that were created by porcupines. If a porcupine returns from a nightly forage to find its den occupied and scented by a birthing female fisher, its most dangerous natural enemy, the den will be given over to the fisher without a fight.

Fisher pups nurse within the den for about a month, but it isn't known if the father or older pups take part in bringing the mother food or watching the den while she's away to drink. Field researchers should note that denned fisher mothers are easily disturbed, and will move their entire litter to a different den if made to feel uneasy.

By the time pups are weaned in May or June, they will have become proficient climbers of the den tree. By the onset of winter, pups will have grown sufficiently to strike out on their own, leaving the mother, who is most likely pregnant, free to birth another litter, then breed again immediately.

Behavior

Like most weasels, fishers are normally solitary, quietly hunting high up in the shaded canopy where its agility equals that of the squirrels it pursues. Males appear to be territorial, judging from aggressive behavior toward intruders of the same sex, with territorial ranges averaging between 6 and 12 miles in diameter. Most of what little communication passes between fishers is through scents and scats deposited at regular places along a boundary trail, particularly at intersections.

In good weather fishers may sleep among tree branches, but the weasels are known to take shelter in hollow logs, porcupine dens, or in rock crevices during rain or snowstorms. In winter they sometimes sleep in snow dens, essentially long tunnels hollowed through hardpack snow, and may take possession of fox or other excavated dens used the previous spring. Tree nests constructed high up in the canopy using sticks and branches are used year-round.

Fishers are active both day and night. Frontal eye placement gives them good binocular vision and the depth perception needed to catch prey, and the species apparently has good night vision as well. Nested or roosted birds and their eggs, sleeping squirrels, and most rodents become easier prey at night, so the fisher has learned to hunt day and night.

In the past, overtrapping of the fisher for its fur depleted populations in some areas to near-extinction, but the harvesting regulations and good management practices have insured that the species as a whole was never endangered. In fact, recent upsurges in populations of both fishers and humans who develop their habitats has led to a few rare instances in which wild fishers from the surrounding forest have taken chickens, attacked pets, and frightened children. Fishers react aggressively when startled or cornered, or if a mother's den is approached too closely, so proper care and respect should be exercised when observing this species.

Pine Marten. Photograph by Erwin and Peggy Bauer. Courtesy of U.S. Fish & Wildlife Service.

Pine Marten (*Martes americana*)

The pine marten, known variously as the American marten or American sable, is a smaller cousin of the fisher. Like fishers, martens are weasels that took to the trees somewhere along their evolutionary process, except that while fishers prefer tall deciduous forests, pine martens are best adapted to coniferous forests.

Geographic Range

Throughout the northern forests of North America, across Canada from Newfoundland to British Columbia, and north to inhabit most of Alaska. Martens are found in most New England states, across Michigan's Upper Peninsula to northern Wisconsin and Minnesota, with a few populations southward through the Rocky and Cascade Mountain ranges.

Habitat

As its common name infers, the pine marten's preferred habitat is coniferous forest, where its rusty-colored fur provides good camouflage among dead pine needles, and small tree squirrels like the red squirrel and chickaree provide good hunting. Like the larger fisher, martens require expansive tracts of relatively unbroken forest, and like the fisher it spends much of its time in the treetops, where observers often mistake it for a fox squirrel. The species will not be found in plains areas or other environments that lack coniferous forest and snowy winters.

Physical Characteristics

Mass: 1 to 4 pounds, about the same size as a fox squirrel.

Body: Elongated, muscular, short legs, long tail, long shiny fur. Forward pointed eyes, pointed snout with catlike whiskers, small rounded ears. Body length 19 to 27 inches, females slightly smaller and lighter in color.

Tail: 5 to more than 9 inches long, fluffy, especially in winter, much like the tail of a fox squirrel.

Tracks: Five toes on all four feet, tracks in soft soil showing curved, sharp claws. Heel pads print in the U shape distinctive of the weasel family, and tracks are easily mistaken for those of the slightly smaller mink in places where their ranges overlap, or for those of the larger fisher. Front track about 1.25 inches long; rear about 1.5 inches. Tracks approximately as wide as they are long.

Scat: Irregularly cylindrical, tapered at one or both ends, 1 to 3 inches long, less than 0.5 inch in diameter. Dark brown or black when fresh, graying with age. Differs from mink scat by having more berries and vegetation in evidence. Scats are often deposited at regular places, especially as territorial markers at trail intersections, and refreshed periodically.

Coloration: Thick reddish pelage. Head whitish to gray, legs and tail darker with reddish fur grizzled with dark brown to black. A small patch on the front of the throat is grayish white to orange.

Vocalizations: Normally silent. Can hiss and snarl if threatened, the behavior usually accompanied by a pungent skunklike aroma from the marten's perineal scent glands.

Lifespan: Probably 6 to 8 years in the wild.

Diet

Although as much an arboreal acrobat as its larger cousin, the fisher, the marten appears to be a more opportunistic hunter, preying on just about every small animal that it can find in its coniferous environment. Mice and voles, red squirrels, birds, eggs, snakes, rabbits, and an occasional small porcupine make up most of the marten's diet.

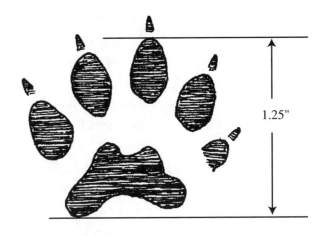

1.25"

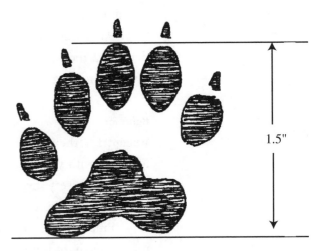

1.5"

Pine marten tracks are very similar to those of the smaller mink and the larger fisher, and in places where their habitats overlap, positive identification may rely on finding other sign.

The marten is ideally matched against its main prey, the red squirrel (*Tamiasciurus hudsonicus*), able to scamper up tree trunks and scramble from tree to tree through intersecting branches with an ease that equals the most nimble tree monkey. When the prey is finally run to exhaustion, or cornered in a den into which the lithe weasel can follow, a death blow is delivered by driving the upper and lower canines into the base of the victim's skull, piercing its brainstem or spinal cord.

Pine martens are more omnivorous in their diets than mink or fishers. The carnivorous diet is regularly supplemented by whatever fruits and berries are available, seeds and other signs of which are evident in scats.

Mating Habits

Pine martens reach sexual maturity at 15 months to 2 years of age, with females typically reaching puberty before males. Mating occurs during the period between June and August, when receptive females advertise their availability through skunky-smelling scentposts left on branches in a tree, or stumps and rocks on the ground. It appears that the normally solitary marten takes only one mate for the duration of courtship and mating.

After mating, the fertilized eggs are carried in a state of delayed implantation within the female's body, where they will remain until they attach to the mother's uterine wall and begin to develop in February and March, or may be spontaneously aborted if she's physically unfit to to bear a litter.

After becoming implanted to the uturine wall, the embryos develop quickly. After a brief gestation of about 30 days, as many as five young pups (or kits) are born blind and helpless in a leaf-lined den. The father may have already gone his own way by that time, and takes no part in the rearing of his offspring.

After nursing for roughly 40 days, the pups are weaned and leave the maternal den to learn the skills of survival from their mother. The young learn and grow fast, and by June they begin to wander off in search of their own mates and territories.

Behavior

Except for their brief late-summer mating season, martens are normally solitary. Mothers with young might also be seen from spring through summer, but in general the species is very shy of humans, and seeing one in the wild seldom happens to anyone but a dedicated observer.

Pine martens may be active at any time of day. Most tree squirrels are active during the daylight hours, so a marten in search of red squirrels must by necessity hunt during the day. Likewise, voles and most mice are active throughout the night, so a marten hunting small rodents must be nocturnal. The species' normal active times appear to be more crepuscular, with most hunting and mating activities being conducted in twilight hours at dawn and dusk, and sometimes on cloudy days.

Martes americana is territorial, especially males and females rearing young. Depending on prey densities, the availability of drinking water, and competition from other pine martens, a typical home range can vary from 5 to 15 miles. The claimed territories are marked by musky scent deposits, which are often among upper tree branches and undetectable by humans.

Like the fisher and mink, the marten is active throughout the year, as is its main prey, the red squirrel. The animal has warm fur and can lay up, or estivate, for several consecutive days in a hollow tree or appropriated den during periods of harsh cold.

Although not quite as aquatic as its smaller cousin, the mink, pine martens are at home near, and occasionally in, water. Being such versatile hunters, they can forage along shorelines for crayfish, clams, and small fish, or in nearby pine forest for rodents on the ground, or among the treetops in search of red squirrels and birds.

Marten pelts are luxurious, and in the past they've fetched as much as $100 for a prime plew, but today sell for less than $20. In a few places, overtrapping has threatened local populations, but the species in general has never been threatened. When left alone, this efficient predator has shown that it can overpopulate and become a threat to its own food resources, although the species' natural aversion to humans usually keeps it away from chicken yards.

Wolverine (Gulo gulo)

Largest of terrestrial weasels (only the sea otter is bigger), the wolverine epitomizes the characteristics that distinguish weasels from other animal families. A carnivorous hunter and scavenger, the wolverine demonstrates an almost unnatural feistiness, backed up by a powerful musculature, sharp teeth, and strong claws, that evokes respect from predators many times its own size.

Before being properly classified, the species was known variously as bearcat, because its physique and demeanor resembled both those animals, and sometimes as skunk bear, because its bearlike body is striped like that of a skunk, and it can emit a

Wolverine (Gulo gulo). *Largest of the family Mustelidae, the wolverine is known for its aggressive nature, nomadic lifestyle, and tendency to avoid contact with humans.*

strong skunklike odor from its perineal glands. The wolverine's scientific name, *Gulo,* which means glutton, is probably more descriptive.

The North American wolverine has also been referred to as *Gulo luscus,* as opposed to *G. gulo,* the Eurasian wolverine of northern Scandinavia and Russia's Siberia. In fact, they appear to be the same species, and probably most wildlife biologists now agree that the minor differences between them are no more than regional adaptations.

Geographic Range

Although generally thought of as a North American species, the wolverine's present range extends across northern Europe, through Siberia, and into the northern wilderness areas of the United States and Canada. The species' distribution was once more widespread, including the Rocky Mountain range down through Colorado, the forests of Indiana, Ohio, and Pennsylvania, and the Great Lakes region in general.

In recent years there has existed a controversy over whether wolverines ever lived in Michigan, once known as "The Wolverine State," and defended by a winning college football team called the Wolverines from Michigan State University. The controversy was spawned by a graduate thesis in 1987 that challenged whether wolverines would live in any part of Michigan, based on terrain, habitat, and food requirements.

In fact, wolverines did once (and possibly still do at its western end) inhabit the Upper Peninsula of Michigan, and, less recently, the heavily forested northern tip of its Lower Peninsula. Theories about whether or not the environment was suitable notwithstanding, I've seen old photos from the turn of the twentieth century in which Odawa Indians and white trappers showed off catches of wolverines they'd snared or trapped hung by the legs from a rope tied between two trees. The Elder Ojibwa and Odawa Indians I knew as a boy, most of whom could recall how to hitch and drive a team of mules, regarded the presence of wolverines in the back woods as common knowledge; many told stories of experiences they'd had with bold wolverines raiding their food stores, killing an occasional chicken, and stealing meat from baited traps without getting caught.

Habitat

Wolverines essentially require a wilderness in which to live and procreate. The aggressive nature of this species, and its tendency to roam throughout its life, make it unwelcome anywhere close to civilization, and its willingness to meet a confrontation head-on soon reduced wolverine numbers at the hands of gun-wielding settlers.

Given a large territory where it isn't likely to be trapped, shot, or to interact with civilization, wolverines can inhabit nearly any northern or high-altitude environment where there is snow in winter, vast tracts of forest, drinking water, and an abundance of small prey. Dens used by nursing mothers, or for weathering storms, consist of leaf- or grass-lined rock cracks, existing coyote or badger dens, and burrows excavated under the roots of large trees. In winter a nomadic wolverine might also wait out a blizzard inside a snow cave made by simply tunneling into a large snow drift, a job made easy by powerful muscles, large paws, and strong claws.

Physical Characteristics

Mass: 18 to more than 45 pounds. Females average 10% smaller and 30% lighter in weight than males.

Body: Second in size only to the sea otter among mustelids, the wolverine's body is wide and powerfully built, with longer legs than most weasels for traveling constantly and over long distances. Body length 31 to more than 44 inches. The head is large with a wide skull, short powerful muzzle, short rounded ears, and teeth designed for rendering animals from prey to food. Eyesight is thought to be poor at distances beyond 100 yards, but the wolverine's sense of smell is excellent.

Tail: 6 to 10 inches, bushy.

Tracks: Proportionally large, wide paws, with five widely splayed toes on each paw, each toe tipped with a heavy semi-retractable claw that makes the wolverine nearly as good at climbing trees as the fisher and marten. Foreprint 4.5 to more than 7 inches long, as wide as it is long. Hind feet slightly smaller than forefeet, with a heelpad shaped roughly like the outline of Lake Superior. Smallest, inside, toe often fails to print, leaving an apparently four-toed track that can be mistaken for that of a gray wolf.

Scat: Wolverine scat is also easily confused with that of a mountain lion, wolf, or coyote. Like the scats of these other predators, a typical wolverine scat is cylindrical, tapered at one or both ends, 4 to 6 inches long by 1 to 1.5 inches in diameter, and comrise primarily of bones and bone fragments wrapped inside a spiral twist of fur from prey animals.

Coloration: Wolverines have a long, thick coat, the color of which is largely a mottling of black guard hairs against predominantly dark brown. A lighter brown to blond band extends from the shoulders to the rump along either side of the spine, leading to the moniker "skunk bear." The top of the head and cheeks are light gray, with a dark mask extending from around the eyes to cover the entire muzzle.

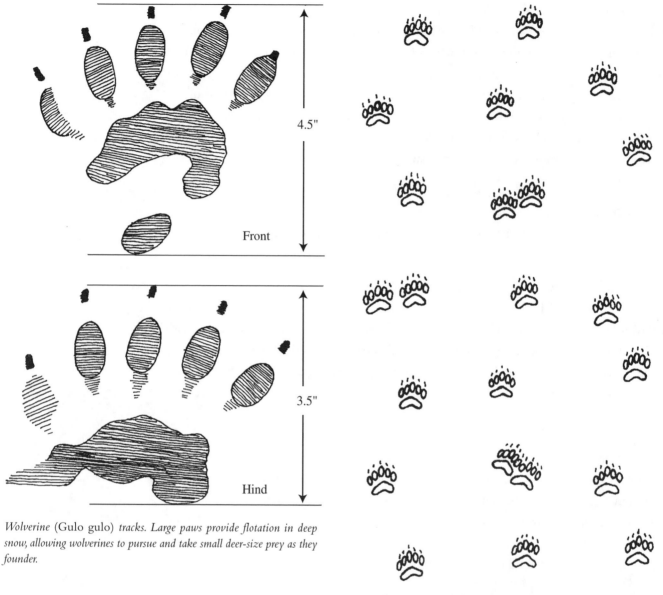

4.5"

Front

3.5"

Hind

Wolverine (Gulo gulo) *tracks. Large paws provide flotation in deep snow, allowing wolverines to pursue and take small deer-size prey as they founder.*

Walking   Loping   Running

Wolverine track patterns.

Typical wolverine scat. Scat length four to six inches, with an outer spiral of prey fur encasing small bones, teeth, and other indigestibles.

Sign: Skunklike scents emanating from the remains of larger animals that have been fed on, or carcasses that are in the process of being consumed. (Never, ever approach a carcass to less than 200 yards.) Excavated rodent burrows are also common, but easily confused as the work of a badger.

Vocalizations: Wolverines are normally silent unless agitated, with most vocalizations occurring during mating season. Voices include a low grunting sound that repeats, snarls, and screams.

Lifespan: Wolverines have lived up to 17 years in captivity, but lifespan in the wild is usually between 8 and 10 years.

Diet

The wolverine is a strong, well-armed predator with a willingness to fight that makes it more trouble than it's worth to even large carnivores. Despite being one-third the weight of a gray wolf, a single wolverine has been known to drive several wolves away from a deer carcass, and even bears have relinquished kills to an aggressive wolverine that was too quick to get a grip on, and too violent to ignore. Ownership of any prey too large to be carried away will probably be challenged by a passing wolverine. Once claimed, the wolverine urinates onto the carcass, leaving a pungent skunklike scent that won't stop it from consuming the meat, but repels other carnivores.

When carcasses aren't available to steal, the wolverine is a capable hunter in its own right. It can excavate ground squirrels from their burrows nearly as well as its cousin, the badger, and it has little trouble catching small rodents, snakes, or frogs.

Wolverines are also capable of taking down deer-size prey. Some biologists have estimated that a wolverine can successfully tackle an animal 5 times its own weight, and while this might seem a bit arbitrary, there's little doubt that an adult has the means to kill a small yearling whitetail. Able to climb trees and pounce from overhead branches, capable of running at speeds up to 30 miles per hour, and strong enough to outmuscle large prey while inflicting mortal injuries with powerful teeth and claws, the wolverine is a capable predator that seldom goes hungry.

Mating Habits

Wolverines become sexually mature at 2 years for females, 3 years for males. Females are monoestrous, coming into a prolonged heat once each year between the months of May and August. The long mating season allows time for these normally solitary and nomadic weasels to find one another. When a pair does mate, they remain together for only a few days before a natural animosity toward every other creature causes them to separate. Both may mate again before summer's end, a natural adaptation that helps to insure that a female is pregnant with the strongest genes available.

Although female wolverines come into heat and emit sexual pheromones to attract mates, they don't actually ovulate until release of a fertile egg is triggered by copulation. Females that don't mate simply don't ovulate, which means they lose none of their body's resources. Females that do mate successfully carry the fertilized egg in a state of diapause (called delayed implantation) for up to 6 months after mating to insure that the female is adequately healthy to carry young through the coming winter—if she isn't, the egg spontaneously aborts. When the eggs take root to the uterine wall between October and January, gestation takes 30 to 50 days.

Just prior to giving birth during a period between January and April, depending on geographic location, females excavate a den in snow if that medium is available, or enlarge an existing coyote or similar burrow for their own uses, or sometimes take refuge in a rock crack. After insulating the birthing den with grasses and dry leaves, mothers retire inside to birth up to six cubs, some of which may have had different fathers.

Wolverine cubs nurse continually for about 9 months. After weaning, the cubs learn the basics of life from their mothers for their first year, then the males begin to wander off to find their own ways, followed by female cubs shortly thereafter. By their second spring, all cubs will have gone, leaving the mother free to mate again.

Behavior

Wolverines are all-terrain hunters. They can travel up to 10 miles at a loping gallop of about 15 miles per hour, and cover 30 miles in a day, enabling them to move nomadically to a more suitable habitat whenever resources grow scarce. They swim well enough to cross swollen rivers, and they climb and move about the treetops with nearly as much agility as a fisher or marten. Few smaller animals are beyond the wolverine's predatory abilities, and even an occasional yearling deer can fall prey to this ferocious weasel.

Wolverines are notorious for patrolling traplines, stealing whatever animals they find caught, and incurring the ire of fur trappers for whom a prime pelt might represent a substantial increase in their next paychecks. In some cases the wolverine itself has been used as fur, but mostly for parka hood linings and boots, because while it has water- and frost-repellent qualities, it isn't a silky coat. Market demand for wolverine plews has never been high enough to justify trapping them, but trappers from the sixteenth century through the first quarter of the twentieth century tended to shoot them on sight, and most residents of the countryside applauded them for doing so.

Wolverines have also earned a little hatred from gold-panners, trappers, and folks who depend on a food cache to insure that they'll get through a hard winter in relative comfort. Strong, able climbers, the animals can scramble up a pole to get at an elevated cache like those used in Alaska, and they're both powerful enough and smart enough to get locks open. There have also been instances of wolverines breaking into vacant seasonal cabins, usually by breaking a window, to get at the food stores inside. Aside from the damage incurred, marauding wolverines tend to add insult to injury by defecating and spraying the cache with a skunklike scent that claims it as territory.

Unfortunately, the wolverine's bold fearlessness and its instinctively aggressive reaction to confrontation with potential enemies places it at a real disadvantage when facing humans. A wolverine that dared stand its ground when surprised in a chicken yard by a farmer toting a large-bore shotgun was seriously overmatched; the ferocity that served to help frighten off larger adversaries was of no use against an enemy that could kill with a single blow from a great distance. Within a few generations, farmers in the New World had all but eliminated wolverines from any but the wildest and most remote areas.

Depending on your perspective, an adult wolverine has either a huge territory or no territory at all. Left to itself the species appears to be nomadic in nature, wandering from one place to another throughout its life. There are no hard-and-fast rules concerning how long a wolverine might stay in one location, but a typical adult may range more than 500 miles in its lifetime.

Except for nursing females, wolverines aren't likely to den longer than overnight, and individuals have been observed going about their business in severe weather conditions. Some wolverines will take shelter from inclement weather to sleep in a dry place or to escape a howling wind, but shelters are rarely used for more than a single day.

American Badger (Taxidea taxus)

Second largest of North America's terrestrial weasels, the American badger is also the largest of its close cousins in the Old World. The common name refers to a medieval sport of "badgering," in which a squat and powerful dog, especially a dachshund or basset hound, was trained to crawl into a badger burrow and pull its resident out into the open. There, the two natural enemies could put on a spectacular show of fighting for human observers. The larger, more powerful, and definitely short-tempered New World badger soon made it obvious that no dog could enter its den without sustaining serious to fatal injuries, and the practice was abandoned.

Geographic Range

The badger is a very adaptable weasel. Its range covers nearly all of the United States west of a rough line extending from Michigan south to the Texas Panhandle. In the

American badger (Taxidea taxus). *Second in size to the wolverine in North America, this carnivorous species can reach more than twenty-five pounds, about twice the size of its European cousins. Like the closely related skunks, the more powerful badger has five toes on each paw, each toe tipped with a long, stout claw that enables it to rapidly bore into most soils after prey, or to escape.*

west its range extends north into Alberta along the Great Plains Basin, into parts of British Columbia, Manitoba, and southern Saskatchewan. The species is absent throughout the eastern United States and Canada, although it appears that Michigan badgers are migrating northward into Ontario.

Habitat

Left alone, badgers prefer open spaces, and they were once common throughout the Great Plains region, where prairie dogs (now threatened) provided a ready supply of food, and winters were usually warm in the lowlands. Prairie-dwelling badgers were especially feared by riders on horseback, because passing too closely to a den, or surprising one of the big weasels in the open, frequently led to snarling encounters in which horses sometimes threw their owners.

But badgers can also thrive in woods, deserts, low mountains, and even swampland, so long as the terrain provides enough high ground to accomodate mice, chipmunks, and ground squirrels that make up most of the badger diet. In times past badgers were trapped, their coarse fur used as bristles in shaving brushes, and they were typically killed on sight. Today, badgers are making a comeback.

Physical Characteristics

Mass: 8 to 25 pounds.

Body: Length 20 to 34 inches from head to tail. Short legs and a flat, heavily muscled back give the badger's wide, powerfully built body a flattened appearance. Short snout, somewhat upturned black nose pad, muzzle black on top, white below. Broad, flat-looking skull with short, rounded ears at either side.

Tail: Short, 3 to 6 inches long, covered with fur.

Tracks: Five toes on each paw. All toes heavily clawed, but front toes are tipped with un-usually long, almost straight claws designed for digging, reminiscent of a brown bear; front claws usually more than 1 inch long, three inner claws longer than outer claws. Foreprints 1 to more than 2 inches long, usually with all five toes and claw tips show-ing, although innermost small toe prints more lightly. Hind prints slightly narrower, but equally long, discounting shorter claws, all five toes usually show in tracks. Stride 6 to 12 inches, straddle 5 to more than 7 inches. Walking track pattern exhibits an extremely toed-in stride with the forefeet, leaving a unique trail in soft soil or snow that can be identified by inward-pointing clawmarks that may increase a track's overall length to 3 or more inches. Hind feet print on top of front tracks, usually at the same inward-pointing angle, making tracks appear longer because overall length of a paired track can exceed 5 inches.

Scat: From 4 to 6 inches long, cylindrical, segmented, about 1 inch in diameter. Usually wrapped in a spiraled layer of rodent, rabbit, or sometimes deer hair. Often by itself in-discernible from scats of a bobcat, coyote, or other medium-size predator.

Coloration: The badger's most outstanding and identifiable feature is its masked face, which is actually whitish, but broken by a pair of wide black stripes that run parallel to one another down the skull to the muzzle, leaving a white skunklike stripe between them. Interestingly, this white dorsal stripe ends at the shoulders in larger northern populations, but extends to the tail in badgers that live where winters are mild. Both cheeks have a black stripe that extends from the ears to under the chin. Fur on the back and flanks is a brindled coat consisting of a thick underlayer of whitish fur covered by coarser black, or sometimes auburn, guard hairs that are arranged in a way that gives the body a striped appearance from auburn to gray in older individuals.

Sign: Excavated burrows, sometimes extending several feet underground, where the badger tried to corner a ground squirrel or other rodent. Excavations, including badger birthing dens, reflect the size and shape of the digger's body, being elliptical, wider than they are high, and usually 10 inches or more wide.

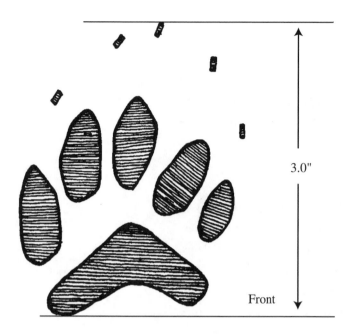

3.0"

Front

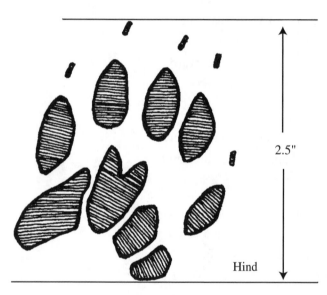

2.5"

Hind

American badger tracks. Very long claws, especially on the forefeet, are well adapted to digging.

American badger walking track pattern. Hind paw registers atop foreprint in normal walking gait. Note extreme toe-in pattern and very long claws built for digging.

Vocalizations: Normally silent, but quite vocal when the animal feels threatened. Voices range from hissing to a grating snarl that most folks find unnerving.

Lifespan: Probably 6 to 8 years in the wild.

Diet

Like most carnivorous species, badgers eat a variety of usually sweet berries and fruits when they come into season throughout the summer months, but the bulk of a badger's diet will always consist of meat in every season. Carcasses of larger animals may be fed on, especially during the lean winter months, providing the formidable badger can take possession from another, often larger, predator, but *Taxidea taxus* is well-designed to dig out mice, squirrels, and rabbits from their dens. No other species can excavate a tunnel into the earth so quickly, actually throwing a rooster tail of soil that also serves to keep an adversary at bay while the badger disappears underground, plugging the tunnel behind itself as it goes deeper.

With such tremendous digging speed, a badger can sometimes corner a ground squirrel before it can get away via its burrow's escape tunnel, but suckling litters are the more efficient prize. In winter, ground squirrels, marmots, and other hibernators may be dug out while they sleep, so long as the earth isn't frozen too deeply.

An old legend has it that the badger and the coyote hunt cooperatively, then share the results of their efforts. In fact, coyotes have at some time in the history of these two species learned to exploit the badger's efforts, stationing themselves at the escape burrow of a prey animal's den while the single-minded badger bores in through the main entrance. If an adult squirrel tries to escape, the coyote is there waiting to snap it up. If the den contains a litter of young, both predators can win an easy meal, but neither shares its catch with the other.

Other foods eaten by badgers vary with the environment and terrain, but include frogs, grasshoppers and other insects, fat-rich grubs dug from rotting stumps in the style of a black bear, turtle eggs, the eggs of ground-nesting birds, and an occasional snake.

Mating Habits

Badgers mate in late summer, beginning in late August and ending when all females have been impregnated, usually by October. Yearling females have normally reached puberty by 5 months, and may breed in their first year of life. Males will probably not be matured enough to mate until their second or third years, after they've established their own territories. Pairs of normally solitary adults join for a brief courtship before mating, then go their separate ways, often to mate with another partner, thus helping to insure that a female is carrying the strongest genes available in her environment.

Like other weasels, badger females carry fertilized eggs in their wombs until autumn, a process called delayed implantation, when eggs will implant to the uterine wall in late December through February, providing the female is healthy enough to bear a litter of young; if she isn't the fertilized eggs will spontaneously abort.

Actual gestation occurs over a period of just 6 weeks after the eggs have implanted, with litters of up to five well-furred but blind young born in a leaf-lined den in March or April. Dens are typically about 3 feet below the ground, with a 3- to 4-foot elliptical body-shaped tunnel leading into an enlarged sleeping and nursing chamber, and one or more additional tunnels that serve as escape exits.

Badger cubs nurse frequently until June, when they're weaned, and the mother takes them out into the world to teach them the skills of badger survival. By August, when the mating season begins, the young will have grown sufficiently to live on their own, and they disperse to seek out their own territories.

Behavior

Badgers are solitary with small home territories that range from 1 to 2 square miles, the larger territories usually belonging to adult males. Since most of the badger's diet consists of prolific breeders like mice and ground squirrels, territorial ranges can be kept small, permitting population densities of 5 or 6 peacefully coexisting adults per square mile. Territories are marked at trail intersections by scat deposits that are regularly refreshed, and often accompanied by a pungent odor of skunk musk. Despite exhibiting territorial behavior, badgers are quick to find a new territory should the one they have experience a drought or other phenomenon that limits its resources.

Badgers are most active at night, when their keen sense of smell and good night vision give them an advantage over squirrels that have retired to their burrows for the evening. The species is also active by daylight in places where it doesn't encounter humans, the most frightening of daytime predators.

In snowy or very cold weather, badgers may estivate, laying up in a den for several days at a time, but not actually hibernating. The animals are quite capable of unearthing enough food during harsh weather, but have adapted to taking long rests as a means of conserving energy. In a severe blizzard a badger may wait for better weather in a shelter it excavated in a snowbank, but there are usually sufficient dens within a badger's territory to provide good shelter.

Known for its aggressiveness and seemingly terrible temper, the badger will nearly always shy from a confrontation, and if pressed will dig itself out of sight. Tales of its ferocity in a fight stem from incidents in which the animal was cornered by dogs, or a female with young.

The badger also lives up to its image as digger to a sometimes surprising degree, emerging from tunnels it has dug upward through even asphalt-paved roads and driveways. Aside from creating road hazards, badger burrows are feared by horseback riders and by ranchers whose cattle could be injured by stepping into them. In one case, a local bounty on badger carcasses was raised after a prize stallion stepped into a badger hole and had to be shot.

Long-tailed Weasel (Mustela frenata)

Except for its notably longer tail and larger body, the long-tailed weasel in its summer coat is nearly identical to its close cousins, the short-tailed weasel (ermine), and the diminutive least weasel. This is the weasel of most cartoons in which the species is depicted as very energetic, fearless, and always hungry, and it has frequently borne out those caricatures by slipping into henhouses to eat eggs and an occasional small chicken.

Long-tailed weasel. Illustration by Bob Hines, courtesy of U.S. Fish & Wildlife Service.

Geographic Range

The range of the long-tailed weasel includes most of North America, encompassing all but the most arid regions of the southwestern United States and the Florida peninsula, extending north into southern British Columbia, Alberta, and Saskatchewan, and southward through Mexico to Bolivia. This species ranges farther south and less north than the closely related ermine and least weasel, and it has the largest distribution of any Mustelid in the Northern Hemisphere.

Habitat

Long-tailed weasels can survive in almoste any temperate to subtropical habitat that provides water, dry ground, and vegetation in which to hunt its main food, mice and voles. Fortunately, that habitat is also good for rodents, and predator and prey exist more or less harmoniously. These weasels tend to avoid dense forests where the ermine and least weasel do well, and they tend to avoid very snowy and cold environments.

Physical Characteristics

Mass: 3 to 9.5 ounces.

Body: Long and slender, but agile and muscular, 11 to 21 inches long, males about 25% larger than females. Short legs lend a squirrel-like appearance, and like squirrels, the long-tailed weasel runs by bounding, leaping from one point to another through the air. The skull is slender, with short rounded ears and a short but almost sharply pointed muzzle tipped with long horizontal whiskers. Small eyes set into the front of the head denote that this animal is a hunter, with sharp eyesight and sense of smell, and the depth perception needed to swiftly strike a death blow to prey that is sometimes larger than itself.

Tail: 5 to more than 10 inches long, measuring proportionally to about half its owner's body length. The tail is bushy and warmly furred, and probably serves as a balancing aid when running along branches.

Tracks: Five toes on all four feet, usually with claws showing in tracks. Smaller innermost toe may print lightly or not at all on firm ground. Like other weasels, *Mustela frenata* has an elongated hind foot that defines it as a plantigrade, or flat-footed, walker. But like other weasels, this one tends to walk weight-forward, on its toes, and the entire somewhat human-looking pad might not print except on soft ground or snow. Hindprints average almost 1 inch wide by more than 1 inch long, up to 2 inches if entire heel pad prints. Foreprints are slightly longer than hind, unless entire hind foot prints, averaging a bit longer than 1 inch and noticeably wider than hind tracks. The heelpad just behind the toes prints in a typically weasel U-shape, with the ends of the U pointing rearward.

Like all of the long-bodied weasels, long-tails move in leaps, shoving off with their hind feet to travel 12 inches at a normal gait, and up to 20 inches when in pursuit of prey. Straddle may reach 3 inches. Tracks tend to be paired when leaping because the animal's short legs move in unison, as it jumps forward with the hind legs, lands on the paired forefeet, and brings the hind feet forward to plant them for another leap.

Scat: Dark-colored, brown or black. Long and slender, cylindrical, often unsegmented, averaging 2 to 4 inches long by 0.5 inch or less in diameter. Plant fibers and berry seeds are common in summer, but scats are predominantly covered with rodent fur wrapped around bones. Scats of the long-tailed weasel are often difficult to differentiate from those of other small weasels, and may be impossible to discern from those of the ermine or least weasel.

Coloration: Long-tailed weasels are interchangeable with short-tailed weasels, or ermine, in what exists of the fur market today because both have nearly identical fur, and both shed their summer coats each autumn to grow a silky white coat that is strikingly beautiful. The white tails of both species are tipped with black. Long-tailed weasels in southerly climes where winters are all or mostly snowless don't experience this photoperiodic response to the coming of winter and maintain their summer coloration the year-round.

The long-tail's summer coat consists of an upper and outer pelage of brown to cinnamon, with white fur inside the legs, under the belly, and below the chin. In this seasonal coat they are nearly identical to the ermine and least weasel except for their larger size and comparatively longer tails. Another difference is that long-tailed weasels in their summer coat have brown feet, whereas ermine have white feet.

Sign: Except for their scats and a faintly skunklike aroma at territorial boundaries and during mating season, long-tailed weasels leave little sign. Scraps of rodent skin or bone, broken eggshells under a bird's nest, and bird feathers scattered about, often with the feet left uneaten, are common clues left by the long-tail, but these may be tough to discriminate from other species of small carnivores.

Vocalizations: Long-tailed weasels are normally silent as they go about their business, but are known to be noisy when threatened. Voices include chattering, short alarm barks, and screeching.

Lifespan: No data available, but probably 4 to 6 years in the wild.

Diet

Like other terrestrial weasels, the long-tail is an efficient hunter of prey even larger than itself, and like those cousins, its main prey consistes of mice, voles, birds, and sometimes roosting bats. A long, stereotypically weasel body allows them to slip into almost any crevice a small rodent might hide, where a fast bite to the base of the skull from needle-like fangs insures a quick kill with little struggle.

Larger male ermine are known to take larger prey, as well, including adolescent cottontail rabbits more than twice their own mass, tree squirrels, and snakes. They've also been guilty of killing a chicken from time to time, and of eating eggs, but farmers generally like having weasels around because they keep mouse populations in check, and modern materials make it simple to weasel-proof a henhouse or rabbit hutch.

Like most weasels, the long-tail is a high-energy creature with a fast metabolism and high-energy requirements, all of which means that it takes advantage of the raw calories in fruits and berries whenever these seasonal fruits become available. Blueberries are a perennial favorite, with blackberries, grapes, and portions of apples favored as well. Scats will often show seeds and other evidence.

Mating Habits

Long-tailed weasels mate in midsummer, usually late June through August. Courtship and breeding lasts only a few days before these normally solitary hunters separate, and often find another mate. After mating, females experience delayed implantation, carrying the fertilized eggs of perhaps several males within her womb, but in a state of hibernation, neither growing nor dying. If the female survives the coming winter in good health, the eggs will implant to the uterine wall in late February or March. If she reaches spring malnourished or sickly, the eggs will abort without draining her resources.

If the eggs implant successfully, embryos develop quickly, and a litter of up to six pups is born about 30 days later, usually in April and May. Birthing dens are often those taken over from ground squirrels after their residents were killed and eaten, but may also be in hollow logs or rock crevices. Young are born blind and covered with white fuzz, but grow quickly under their mother's protection, nourished by her rich milk.

At about 35 days, the young weasels are weaned and learn to eat prey brought back to the den for them by the mother. At this point she also begins bringing her offspring wounded prey to give the pups valuable training in making kills (a trait seen with many carnivore mothers). After 2 months, the youngsters have grown enough and become skilled enough to hunt and kill rodents on their own, and the family unit begins to break up as male pups, then females, strike out to establish their own territories. Their mother may mate again after her brood leaves, and the females she gave birth to the previous spring are likely to birth their first litters the following spring. Males will probably not mate until their second spring.

Behavior

Like all weasels, long-tailed weasels are not social animals; the sexes live apart except for a brief interaction during the mating season, and same sexes never tolerate the presence of one another. A male's territory may overlap the territories of several females in an area, but there are defined boundaries separating his range from those of other males, and the two never socialize without fighting. Intruders are driven away aggressively, with females exhibiting at least the same amount of territorial defensiveness seen in males.

Although often active by day, long-tailed weasels are primarily nocturnal hunters, with acute night vision and binocular eyesight that permits them to accurately judge distance and depth when attacking prey. They possess olfactory senses keen enough to detect a bird roosting in a tall tree, the stealth needed to sneak up on it, and the natural weapons with which to dispatch it quickly and with as little fight as possible.

Although sometimes accused of being a chicken thief, a title the long-tailed weasel sometimes earned, farmers have always tended to favor having the species around because it's one of the best rat and mouse catchers in the animal world. Farmers, especially with today's materials, find it fairly simple to keep the proverbial weasel out of the henhouse, but weasels in the corn crib help to insure that rodents are not.

Long-tailed weasels in the north, where snowy winters cause them to grow a white coat of silky fur each December, are considered by trappers to be ermine, and there is still some demand for white weasel furs. The species has never been endangered, and populations are at least stable.

Ermine, or Short-tailed Weasel (*Mustela erminea*)

Often confused with the larger long-tailed weasel, especially in snow country where both species wear a beautiful silky white coat until spring, the ermine has long been coveted among both fur trappers and consumers, even in today's depressed fur market. In Europe, the black-tipped white tails of ermine were once used to trim or adorn the robes of royalty when they held court.

Ermine (Mustela erminea) *in white winter color phase.*

Despite its popularity as a pelt, the ermine has never been endangered. It has been accused of raiding a henhouse or two, but such accounts are typically overdramatized, because an average chicken is 5 times the size of an average weasel.

Geographic Range

Unlike the larger, but very similar, long-tailed weasel, ermine prefer an environment that offers snowy winters, and they range much farther north. This species has a circumpolar distribution, and can be found in the Northern Hemisphere around the globe, including Asia, Europe, and North America. Ermine live throughout Canada, except for its Great Plains Basin, throughout Alaska, and well above the Arctic Circle. To the south their range covers the northern east coast west to Minnesota, southward along the Rocky Mountain region from Canada to Utah, and westward to northern California.

Habitat

Ermine prefer northern mixed forests of coniferous and deciduous trees. The ideal habitat is riparian, or riverfront, with a year-round source of water, grasses and brush through which to hunt rodents, and higher terrain that allows ground squirrels and other burrowers—a group that includes the ermine—to dig deep dens. They appear to do well in cedar swamps and marshlands, but are never found in prairie or desert regions.

Physical Characteristics

Mass: 2 to 7 ounces.

Body: Typically weasel, with elongated, somewhat squirrel-like body, relatively short legs, long bushy tail. Muzzle short and pointed, horizontal whiskers extend from either side of nose, ears rounded and small, dark eyes face forward in the skull. Body length

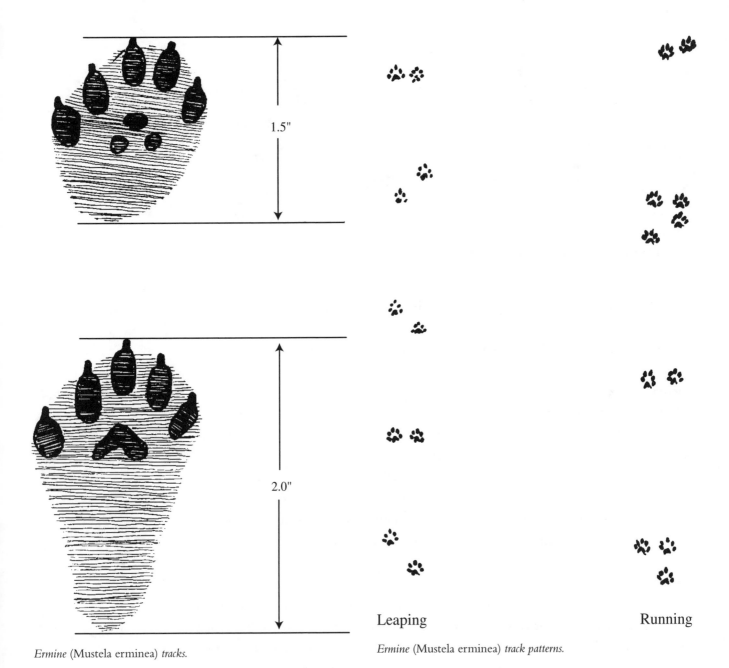

1.5"

2.0"

Leaping

Running

Ermine (Mustela erminea) *tracks.*

Ermine (Mustela erminea) *track patterns.*

7 to more than 13 inches. Males roughly twice as large as females. The ermine falls between the larger long-tailed weasel and the much smaller least weasel in size, but aside from a few minor physical and color differences, the three are nearly identical.

Tail: Typical length equals about 35% of total body length, measuring 2 to 3.5 inches. Tail is bushy, especially in its white winter phase, and always tipped in black, as are the tails of the least weasel and long-tailed weasel.

Tracks: Five toes on each foot, each toe tipped with claws that might be difficult to see even in snow or mud. Hind prints plantigrade, or elongated, usually less than 1 inch long, front prints about 0.5 inch long. Innermost toe may not print on firmer ground. Heel pad just rear of the toes on all four feet leave a forward-pointed chevron impression. Except in instances where size distinguishes them from one another, ermine tracks are very easy to confuse with those of the long-tailed weasel or least weasel, but differ from the more U-shaped impressions left by the heel pads of the mink's front and hind paws.

Typical track patterns are paired front and hind prints. At a casual gait with leaps of about 10 inches, the two front tracks print side-by-side ahead of the paired hind tracks. At a fast run with leaps of 2 feet or more, the hind feet come far forward, pivoting past the planted forefeet to land ahead of them on either side; the rocking-horse running gait common to nearly all four-legged animals.

Another feature of the casual, opportunistic gait is that it tends to meander back and forth in a kind of zigzag pattern, stopping at holes and dens to sniff out possible prey before moving forward and in the opposite direction. The advantage of this zigzag is that it allows a hunting weasel to search as much ground as possible within its territory.

Scat: Typical of the scats left by long-tailed and least weasels, and sometimes minks. Dark colored to black, 1 to 2 inches long, less than 0.5 inch in diameter, cylindrical, often segmented, tapered at one or both ends. Similar to the scat of a small domestic cat, except usually with a sheath of rodent fur.

Coloration: In its summer coat the ermine is light brown to reddish on its back, the back of its neck, to its black-tipped tail. The underparts from the throat to the tail, as well as the insides of the legs, are white, becoming more yellow in older animals. The feet are white, in contrast to the similar, but usually larger, long-tailed weasel, which has brown feet in its summer coat.

In winter the ermine's thick, silky fur is white and the tip of the tail is black, although populations in the southernmost part of the range, where winters are not snowy, may retain their summer colors all year.

Sign: Holes in fresh snow where an ermine dove in and burrowed below the surface for perhaps several yards before popping up again in an explosion of snow that spreads outward from the exit hole. Kills too large to be eaten at one sitting are cached under a loose spray of soil or snow, and scented with the ermine's skunklike perineal scent glands to discourage other predators from eating them.

Vocalizations: Generally solitary and silent, but vocal when faced with a threat. Agitated voices include screeches, hisses, and snarls. A quick barking chirp, similar to that of the red squirrel, and possibly used as a ruse for hunting them, indicates curiosity.

Lifespan: Average lifespan of an ermine in the wild has been estimated at 2 years or less, with females typically surviving longer than males. Maximum lifespan in captivity is around 7 years.

Diet

Ermine are almost strictly carnivorous, although it appears that they prefer some berries in their diets, as well as a few fibrous grasses to keep the excretory tract scrubbed clean. Most of the ermine's diet consists of mice, voles, chipmunks and an occasional red squirrel, pounced on by the fast and aggressive ermine as they pass an ambush point. Others are surprised inside their own burrows by this efficient hunter whose stream-lined body allows it to enter almost any place a mouse can. Small rabbits are taken op-portunistically, sometimes from nursing dens, but adult rabbits or hares are too large and strong to be taken.

Ermine are thought to be mostly nocturnal, but they might also be seen bound-ing about during daylight in wilder places. At a wilderness cabin I lived in for a year, there were numerous wild species that simply got used to my presence, and one of them was an ermine, probably drawn to the cabin after mice, who were themselves drawn to the odor of human food. Ermine are also attracted to rural barns and corn cribs for the mice and rats living there.

Typical of the weasel family, ermine are high-energy predators with a ferocious approach to hunting that gives them an ability to take down prey larger than them-selves. Long needlelike canines drive into the base of the victim's skull, piercing the spinal cord or brainstem, sometimes repeatedly, and killing it quickly in most cases.

Ermine are good swimmers, and may forage along the same shorelines as their larger cousin, the mink, for crayfish, small fish caught in shallows near shore, and small freshwater clams. Frogs and small watersnakes are on the menu as well, but larger snakes may make a meal of an unwary ermine, as will eagles, owls, and hawks.

Mating Habits

Ermine mate from June through July, when the normally solitary hunters are drawn to-gether by pheromonal scents emitted from receptive females. Pairs remain together for only a few days, and both sexes may mate with several partners over the course of the breeding period.

Mated female ermine carry the fertilized eggs inside them in stasis, where they neither grow nor die, until the following spring. After about 8 months, usually in

February or March, the fertilized eggs either implant onto the uterine wall and begin to develop, or, if the female is in poor health, spontaneously abort to conserve bodily resources for her own survival.

Once implanted, the eggs, which may have been fertilized by different fathers, develop quickly. After an active gestation period of roughly 35 days, females give birth in April or May to litters of up to eighteen pups, although seven is average. Females outnumber males at roughly 2 or 3 to 1, although that ratio may fluctuate in enviroments that are more or less than ideal. Birthing dens are similar to those of the long-tailed and least weasels, consisting of cracks in rocks, hollow logs or trees, or the burrows of past victims.

Young are born blind and covered with fine white fur broken by a mane of darker fur around their necks, the purpose of which has yet to be determined. Some researchers believe that the father helps by bringing food to a birthing female, but it appears that a male attending a denned female is most likely courting her, and the male may not always be the father. This may be a natural response by males to both insure themselves a healthy mate, or mates, as soon as the present litter is off on their own and the next breeding season about to begin.

Whether a male is present or not, ermine mothers nurse their young constantly until they're weaned at about 2 months. Females are able to mate about the same time they're weaned, sometimes even before, and will probably breed in their first summer of life. Male young are driven off soon after weaning to prevent inbreeding, and will probably not mate until their second summer, after establishing a territory for themselves.

Behavior

Mustela erminea is possessed of a constant, sometimes explosive physical energy, acute curiosity, and a short attention span, all of which combine to make it one of the most hyperactive creatures in nature. Although generally shy of humans, and especially pets, ermine have been known to scrutinize quiet humans in remote forests from close range, but are almost never seen in civilization, or rural areas where they might encounter a dog or house cat.

Being smaller than males, female ermine spend more time hunting in rodent tunnels and burrows, while larger males pursue chipmunks and red squirrels aboveground. This difference in preferred hunting environments probably explains why most of the ermine trapped are usually males. Both sexes can run in bounding leaps across the surface of snow to catch mice and voles, and either can lithely run up a vertical tree trunk after ground squirrels.

A typical ermine's range encompasses only about 5 acres, depending on the availability of good water and foliage, and whether or not an area supports a good prey base. With rodent numbers that can exceed 10,000 mice and voles per acre in an average habitat, there may be an ermine per acre, even though the rodent bounty is always shared with larger carnivores from foxes to bobcats.

Ermine are subject to a usually fatal disease in which a nematode (terrestrial parasitic worm) known as *Skrjabingylus nasicola* infects the ermine's nasal passages, causing excruciating pressure on the sinus cavities until the skull eventually cracks and the animal dies from a brain hemorrhage.

Striped Skunk (Mephitis mephitis)

Perhaps this weasel's most enduring and best-known image comes from the cartoon character Pepé Le Pew, whose moniker describes the intolerable stench emitted by this most odorous of North America's native weasels. All weasels have paired perineal scent glands that exude a musky scent used for marking territory and advertising for mates, but in the skunk these glands have been modified through evolution to actually shoot a stream of powerful smelling fluid from under the tail and into the face of an adversary.

An odor might not seem like much of a defense against large predators, but skunks generally go about their daily lives unmolested once they've achieved a size too large to be handled by eagles and owls. In one videotaped experiment, a rather silly researcher clad in a full-face grinder's shield and ankle-length rubber apron tormented a striped skunk until it pivoted around on its forefeet and sprayed him dead in the face. The aim was uncanny, and despite being protected from the spray's full force by his face shield, the volunteer victim immediately fell to his knees, vomiting and blinded by the fumes alone.

A skunk's spray can reach accurately to 15 feet, and a choking mist from it can drift more than 30 feet outward from the target on all sides. The odor can be smelled by humans from more than a half-mile for several days afterward, and a typical skunk can fire up to 5 times before exhausting its supply of scent. Field researchers are advised to keep a distance of at least 50 feet between themselves and subjects to avoid absorbing the scent into their clothing and equipment, should a skunk decide to spray a warning perimeter while being observed.

If you should be sprayed by a skunk, probably the most effective and available remedy for at least minimizing the stench is to wash body and clothing in bath of soap and tomato juice. Never wash affected clothing in a machine before handwashing it first, or the plastic tub found in many washing machines may take on the odor of skunk permanently.

Striped skunk. Illustration by Bob Hines, courtesy of U.S. Fish & Wildlife Service.

Geographic Range

Striped skunks occur throughout the United States, their range extending from the Pacific to the Atlantic, southward into Mexico from Texas and New Mexico, and northward through Canada's southern provinces. The species does not range as far north as Alaska.

Habitat

Mephitis mephitis prefers a mixed habitat of forest, sheltering brush, and open water. It can tolerate all but the coldest places, holing up for days at a time in excavated dens during blizzards, but is most abundant in regions that have mild winters.

Just as striped skunks have proved adaptable to most temperate habitats in the United States, so have they learned to view human habitation as a source of food. In rural areas they raid garbage cans, in subdivisions they go into garages in search of mice and pet foods, and even on the outskirts of major cities you might find skunks that make up a large part of their diets with food scraps scavenged from dumpsters.

Physical Characteristics

Mass: 6 to 14 pounds, with a few individuals in the far north exceeding 20 pounds.

Body: *M. mephitis* is normally about the size of a domestic cat, and a few of its unfortunate encounters with humans have resulted from mistaking a skunk for a cat in the dark. The body is less elongated than that of most smaller weasels, with a humped back and short legs. The head is proportionally small, with small rounded ears, a long pointed muzzle, and the forward-facing eyeballs of a predator. Body length 20 to more than 31 inches. The skull is easily distinguished from that of any other carnivore by having upper and lower canines, with just one squarish-shaped molar on either side of the upper jaw, and two molars on each side of the lower jaw.

Tail: Bushy, usually held erect or straight back, 7 to more than 15 inches long.

Tracks: Hind feet are plantigrade, almost human-shaped, 1.75 to more than 2 inches long, with five partially webbed toes, each tipped with a strong claw. Forefeet are

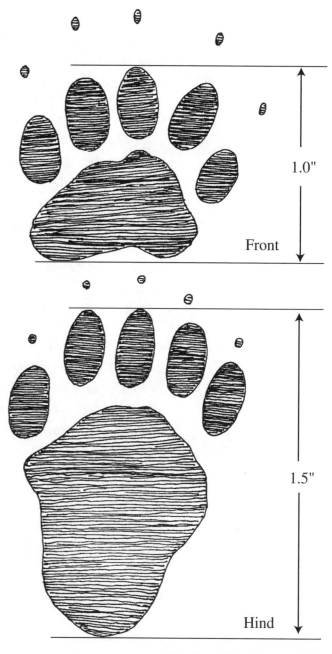

Striped skunk (Mephitis mephitis).

shorter, 1 to 1.5 inches long, with five toes and long, almost straight claws that extend 1 inch or more from the toe tips.

The striped skunk's walking track pattern reveals a waddling gait, illustrated by hind feet that print farther to the outside than forefeet, and a trail that may be lightly brushed by the skunk's bushy tail. Straddle 3 to 4 inches, walking stride 4 to 5 inches. At a run, all four feet print in an almost straight line, alternating with a hind print in front and a fore print at the rear, with short leaps of 5 to 6 inches between groups of tracks.

Scat: Cylindrical, segmented, tapered at one or both ends. Two to more than 4 inches long, about 0.5 inch in diameter. As individual sizes can vary greatly, so too can scat sizes, and skunk scat is easily mistaken for that of other mustelids.

Coloration: Striped skunks are easily recognized by their characteristic black and white color scheme, which is thought to be a day or night visual warning to tell potential enemies that they should keep their distance. The striped skunk is essentially black, with a distinctive triangle of white fur covering the top of the skull that extends in a thin white line downward along the top of the muzzle to the nose pad. At the rear of the skull the white cap separates at the neck into a pair of wide white stripes that extend to the tail along either side of the spine, then merge again atop the tail. In some individuals the stripe extends the top length of the tail, while in others the stripe may be shorter.

Sign: *M. mephitis* is a digger, its powerfully muscled back and long, strong front claws designed by nature to tear through the tough mass of roots in forest humus to catch rodents in their burrows, to excavate turtle eggs in spring, or to find grubs in a mostly rotted log. Each of these foraging activities leaves unearthed debris and a spray of soil around the excavation that might be mistaken for the diggings of other small animals, and getting a positive identification will probably require reading tracks left at the site. Note, however, that a skunk seems to be very precise about where it digs for food, often leaving neat little holes, as opposed to the necessarily wider holes made by foxes or badgers. Look also for stones and small logs that have been rolled over in search of insects or earthworms.

Vocalizations: Normally silent in daily life. Forceful exhalations appear to be an alarm, like the blow of a whitetail deer. Hissing, often accompanied by a partly open mouth to display the teeth, is an early warning to keep away. Snapping together of the jaws (a behavior seen in bears and numerous other species) is a sign that the animal is nervous and expecting a confrontation.

Lifespan: No established data, but pet skunks have lived more than 8 years in captivity, and it's likely that a striped skunk fortunate enough to reach maturity would live about the same number of years.

Diet

Striped skunks are the most omnivorous members of the weasel family, and probably most of their success as a species can be attributed to being able to subsist on a diet that can include grass roots, ants and grasshoppers, rodents, excavated turtle eggs, eggs of ground-nesting birds, snakes, frogs, berries, and carrion. Although not as skilled at fishing as the otter or mink, skunks frequent river and pond banks to drink, catch crayfish, and to harvest freshwater clams, which the powerful mustelid can pry open using its front claws. In winter, skunks feed on carrion, watercress, rodents, and sometimes appropriate kills from larger carnivores.

Striped skunks have also learned to regard humanity as a source of food, and in the twentieth century especially skunks began making a nuisance of themselves by digging through garbage cans and dumpsters for table scraps. Today striped skunks have become common nighttime scavengers in not just rural areas, but in suburbs, subdivisions, and within the outlying areas of major cities.

Mating Habits

Female striped skunks usually mate in their second year of life, after spending a year with their mothers to learn the skills of skunk survival. Males, which wander off to establish their own territories at the end of the first year, probably won't mate until their third year.

Female striped skunks are considered monoestrous, coming into heat only once each year between late January and March. It does appear, though, that receptive females that are not successfully impregnated during their first heat will experience a second heat within a week or two. No data has yet been established, but it seems likely that females undergo a period of delayed implantation, carrying the fertilized eggs alive but not growing until late March or April, when the eggs implant to the uterine wall or abort, depending on the mother's fitness.

Actual gestation is about 45 days, with most striped skunk cubs born in litters of up to six during May. Although born blind and helpless, the young emerge already patterned with the distinctive black and white markings that give them their common name, but their defensive scent glands don't begin to fully develop until after weaning at about 7 weeks. Males will have left soon after mating, probably to seek out another of the females whose territories overlap his own, and all parental care comes from the mother.

After weaning, young skunks begin to leave the den for short periods of play and exploration, always under their mother's very protective eye, and always prepared to rush back inside should a large hawk or eagle fly overhead.

Skunk kits remain with their mothers through their first winter, learning from her how to exist on their own. Prior to the coming spring, usually in January or February, the young strike out on their own, leaving the mother free to mate again at the height of breeding season.

Behavior

The striped skunk's defensive spray is known throughout the world, popularized in cartoons and caricatures, and always portrayed in a somewhat frightening light by movies in which it plays a character. In fact, this species is one of the easiest for humans to socialize with because adult skunks appear to be afraid of nothing. But neither are they aggressive without provocation—a mother is very protective of her brood, and a dog virtually guarantees that a skunk will spray—but there are numerous citings of people passing by wandering skunks, even on sidewalks, or surprising one in a garage, without being sprayed. Like a rattlesnake or porcupine, *M. mephitis* uses its defensive capabilities only when it feels mortally threatened.

And like the porcupine, skunks face danger with their rear ends. The first warning to an adversary may be a head-on chorus of hissing and snapping the jaws together, but if the skunk is pressed, as domestic dogs are wont to do, the skunk plants its front paws together and quickly pivots its rear 180 degrees to face the threat. A fully erect tail and arched back, usually accompanied by a short spurt of scent to help get the point across, are the final warning.

As a last resort, the skunk plants its forefeet in something of a handstand, and raises its rear end off the ground, tail raised and spraying organs pointed at the enemy's face. Twin streams issue from scent sacs just inside the skunk's anus, merging together a foot or so beyond to blend into a widening cloud of thick, visible mist. The ensuing fog of choking scent is usually directed with sufficient accuracy for most of it to hit its victim in the eyes from more than a car length away.

Even large animals that receive a faceful of skunk spray immediately lose their threat potential, typically panicking because the spray has blinded them temporarily, unable to smell because skunk scent literally overwhelms the olfactory centers and causes the nerves to shut down, and rolling almost convulsively on the ground in an effort to get the scent off their bodies. On human victims the spray causes temporary blindness, nausea, vomiting, dizziness, and physical collapse to at least the knees.

Skunk scent also serves more conventional purposes, warning intruders that a territory is already claimed, advertising for mates, and for making large caches of carrion unpalatable to other carnivores. Human manufacturers use skunk scent as a base for some perfumes because of its lingering qualities, and some human hunters use skunk scent to disguise their own odors when in pursuit of game.

Skunks are generally solitary creatures, with most of their activities taking place at night, and holing up to sleep the daylight away in an excavated den, a hollow log, or, increasingly, under the floors of barns and in the crawlspaces of houses. Because skunks are a carrier host of sylvatic rabies, and sometimes become infected with the disease themselves, because a resident skunk can be counted on to tear through any garbage left outside, and just because they smell bad, varmint removal has become a thriving business in many residential districts. Not surprisingly, most varmint removal professionals are fur trappers who have adapted their skills to this new industry.

Striped skunks are not hibernators, but neither are they well-adapted to very cold weather. In the northerly portions of this species' range, individuals of both sexes tend to become very lethargic during winter, particularly from late November through January, laying up in a sheltered den for a week or more at a time, especially during stormy weather. Like raccoons, striped skunks prepare for this contingency by eating almost gluttonously from late summer through autumn, accumulating a layer of insulating fat that equals 15% or more of its body weight. Females are especially reliant on body fats during the winter months, and may remain denned for longer periods than the males, which leave their dens periodically to forage.

Skunks have definitely been indicted as marauders of chicken coops, although their main objective, at least during the summer laying season, appears to be the eggs, not the chickens. Still, a single skunk can do a great deal of damage inside a henhouse, and leave it less than fragrant long after its departure. In a past era, farmers almost routinely trapped and killed marauders, but today an increasing number are opting to simply eliminate the problem by using modern, inexpensive materials, like sheet metal, steel mesh, and fiberglass panels, to predator-proof livestock enclosures.

Mink (Mustela vision)

At least as popular as ermine for making coats, stoles, and muffs, mink fur is silky and fine, and garments made from it are still considered a symbol of social status for ladies, although the trend toward wearing furs has diminished on the whole in recent years. Most minks that become fur are today raised on commercial mink ranches, and the musky skunklike scents produced by their perineal glands are collected for use as a lingering base in colognes and perfumes.

Mink (Mustela vision).

Geographic Range

Mink require a habitat of open and, preferably, flowing water, and the species can be found throughout the United States from the entire Atlantic coast to the northern, forested portions of the Pacific coast. Despite having been reported as living in every state except Arizona, mink are not commonly found in the arid southwestern states or the southern Great Plains Basin, and never far from a water source. To the north, mink are found south of the Brooks Range in Alaska, and eastward just south of the Arctic Circle, through Canada's Hudson Bay, on to the Atlantic coast, including an introduced population on Newfoundland.

American mink have also become established in Great Britain, where animals being raised on fur farms in the 1960s escaped their enclosures and successfully adapted to their new environment. Strong and aggressive, the mink has today become a fairly serious pest on the British Isles, where it has overpopulated and threatens to decimate native prey species that native predators rely on for food.

Habitat

Mink are never found far from a source of fresh water, most often a flowing stream or river that provides habitat for crayfish, minnows, frogs, snakes, rodents, and other small prey that makes up most of a mink's diet. Thick brush and tall grasses that typically line stream banks provide plenty of places to hunt or hide, and exposed riverbanks are good places to excavate or appropriate a den that allows for fast escape to the water. Mink are superb swimmers, able to dive underwater to forage for snails and crayfish like a river otter, but also patrolling local rodent habitat on nearby dry ground where long-tailed weasels hunt.

Physical Characteristics

Mass: 1.5 to 3.5 pounds.

Body: Typical of long-bodied weasels like the ermine, fisher, and otter: long and slender with short legs, long bushy tail, short round ears, forward-facing eyes, and a short pointed muzzle with long whiskers extending from either side. Body length averages 19 to more than 28 inches. Males often substantially larger than females.

Tail: Nearly as long as the mink's body, 15 to 20 inches, covered with long fine fur.

Tracks: Typically weasel, with five toes on each foot, multilobed heel pads that print in a U shape, and semi-retractable claws. The toes are partially webbed, revealing the mink's semi-aquatic nature, but webbing seldom shows in tracks except on wet snow or soft mud. Innermost, smallest, toe, which may fail to print on firm ground, is located farther to the rear and extended more to the inside, like a thumb, than it is in the tracks of other mustelid species.

Scat: Very similar to that of the river otter, but smaller, consisting of fish scales, small bones, and bits of crayfish carapace, sometimes wrapped inside rodent fur. Cylindrical, dark brown to black, tapered at one or both ends, segmented, sometimes more than 5 inches long.

Coloration: Chocolate brown with white patches on the chin, chest, and throat. The fur is soft and thick, with oily guard hairs that provide waterproofing, and doesn't change color with the seasons as with weasels and ermine.

Sign: Mink leave small scentposts of musky-smelling twisted grass stems along shorelines, smaller than those made by a river otter. Accumulations of crayfish carapaces, fish bones, and fins at favorite feeding spots.

Vocalizations: Normally silent. Chatters, squeals, and hisses if threatened.

Lifespan: Maximum lifespan for a mink has been estimated at about 10 years.

Diet

Mink are almost strictly carnivorous, and their semi-aquatic habitat provides a diversity of prey animals in every season. The diet changes slightly with the seasonal availability

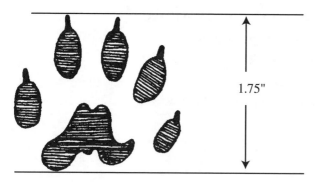

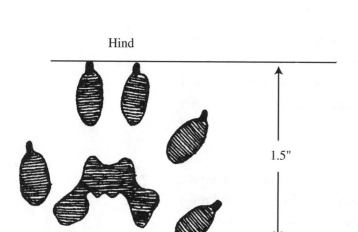

Front

1.75"

Hind

1.5"

Mink (Mustela vision) *tracks.*

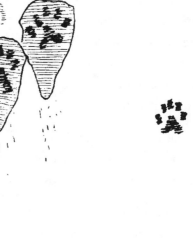

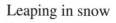

Leaping in snow   Running in mud

Mink (Mustela vision) *track patterns.*

of some prey species, but generally includes frogs, mice, crayfish, young muskrats, small rabbits, watersnakes, snails, and hatchling turtles. Other prey includes the eggs and young of waterfowl, including larger species like geese and mallards, although raids on the nests of large birds that are potentially dangerous to a mink are always conducted surreptitiously and with urgency.

Mating Habits

The mink breeding season coincides closely with that of most other Mustelids, peaking in February and March when females born the previous spring and males born the spring before that come together to mate. As with most species, females outnumber males, and a single male's territory may be overlapped by the ranges of several females.

Like most weasel species, both mink sexes are promiscuous, spending only a few days with one mate before going off to find another. It appears that at least some mink pairs remain together throughout the summer, but the male in a pair isn't always the sole father of the fertilized eggs carried in a state of delayed implantation within the female's womb. He takes no fatherly part in the relationship, but occasionally brings the female food when pregnancy or nursing duties restrict her ability to fend for herself.

Depending on the latitude, and counting the delayed implantation period before eggs begin to actually grow into fetuses, total time between mating and birth can number 40 to 75 days. True gestation time, from when the eggs implant to the time of birth, is more like 35 to 40 days. As with mated females of other species, this delay gives females in the northern range a buffer of time in which to become extra healthy to gestate and birth a litter of offspring, or, if she isn't, to conserve bodily resources for her own survival by spontaneously aborting the fertilized eggs.

Mink mothers typically give birth in April and May. Litters may number up to six blind and helpless pups, each weighing 8 to to 10 grams. The birthplace is usually a grass-, leaf-, and fur-lined den excavated into the side of a riverbank, and preferably opening onto a year-round access to open water. It seems probable that the dens of other species might also be used, but a den excavated by mink is identifiable as a round hole, about 4 inches in diameter, just above, and sometimes below, the water line. The hole marks a tunnel leading upward through the bank for a distance of 2 feet or more, finally opening onto a dry, enlarged maternal den deep within the earth.

After suckling for about 3 weeks, the fast-growing mink pups open their eyes and begin to move about the den and play. By 6 weeks the youngsters are weaned and can hunt for themselves. All are born with the swimming and hunting instincts of a mink, but the entire litter remains with its mother until November or December to learn about hazards like fast water and hungry owls. Both sexes reach puberty at 10 months. When the litter disperses in early winter, males are usually first to set off on their own, followed by their sisters, who may themselves give birth the following spring. The mother, too, will probably mate again after her offspring leave. Male pups probably won't mate in their first mating season, but those that successfully establish a territory of their own will mate in the second season.

Behavior

Like all weasels, mink are solitary animals, and this species is well-known for its aggressive behavior toward those of its own kind and, especially, sex. Males are extremely territorial and particularly intolerant of one another, fighting on sight in a screeching, chattering flurry of sharp teeth and claws. No real harm usually comes of territorial battles, which typically end as soon as it becomes apparent which is the strongest.

A tracker can use the mink's extreme territorial habits to advantage, because minks, like otters, leave scentposts of twisted grasses whose blades have been wiped with a strong, musky secretion from the weasel's perineal glands. These scentposts are much smaller than an otter's, consisting of only a few blades of grass spiraled together, and have an even more potent odor of skunk about them. Scentposts are often accompanied by scats nearby, which are not likely to be mistaken for those of an otter.

Although considered nocturnal, it isn't unusual to see mink going about their business in daylight, especially in winter when increased calorie needs and the mating season add motivation.

Apparently confident in their own ability to escape into the water, into a burrow, or by scrambling up a tree using their sharp semi-retractable claws, mink often make good subjects for photography. In every season and latitude the species tends to display more crepuscular tendencies, being most active during the twilight hours at dusk and dawn.

Among mustelids, the mink is second only to the otter in terms of aquatic agility. Its webbed toes provide the power to swim easily through river currents, to swim up to 100 feet underwater in pursuit of fish or crayfish, and to dive to depths of more than 10 feet in search of bottom-dwelling prey.

Mink pelts, although small, have historically been considered one of the most luxurious furs on Earth, and as such were once in demand, especially during the twentieth century. Trapping never put native populations in danger (largely because mink are wily and tough to catch), but it was deemed more financially expedient to meet the strong demand for mink garments with pelts taken from farm-raised animals. The first mink ranches were established in the 1950s, and a decade later there were more than 7,000 of them turning a profit throughout North America. By 1998 the number of mink ranches that had withstood the continuous campaigns from anti-fur organizations had dropped to 439. In 1999 the existing mink ranches produced nearly 3 million pelts, valued at $73 million in U.S. currency.

More than trapping, mink are in danger from loss of habitat. Most damaging is the tendency of humans to build along the natural river and stream fronts that a mink considers ideal habitat, and pets usually guarantee that existing mink populations will try to find new habitat. Some minks have learned to survive along developed riverbanks in municipal parks, which may be a heartening sign that humans and minks can coexist. One drawback is that more urban environments include waterways that are polluted by highway and other toxic runoff during rainstorms, sometimes by sewage overflow, and mink tend to birth smaller and less healthy litters in places where the water is less than clean.

THE BEAR FAMILY (FAMILY URSIDAE)

Bears are one of the most fascinating of nature's creatures. Some members of family Ursidae occur in northern Europe, Asia, and India, but the three species best known among them are native to North America. All are large and powerfully built, ranging in weight from up to 600 pounds for a mature black bear to more than 1,700 pounds for a large Kodiak brown bear. All have five toes on each foot, each toe tipped with a stout, functional claw. The hind feet of all species is elongated, almost humanlike, denoting the flat-footed (plantigrade) walk of a strong, but comparatively slow-running animal that has few natural enemies.

Until the latter part of the twentieth century it was commonly believed that bears hibernated, like ground squirrels, through the harsh months of winter. Today we know that bears don't enter the comalike torpor experienced by true hibernators, and sometimes leave their sleeping dens to wander during unseasonal midwinter warm spells.

Perhaps most interesting to humans are the bears' physiological attributes. Despite putting on about 25% of its body weight in fat each year, bears exhibit zero arterial blockage from cholesterol. Denned bears neither defecate nor urinate for months at a time, but they have a remarkable renal system that not only doesn't become toxified from a buildup of nitrogen urea, but converts this normally lethal waste product to usable amino acids, then recycles the water for use in bodily functions. If modern medicine could figure out how a bear can reprocess its own urine, the positive implications for humans suffering from kidney failure could be enormous. The National Aeronautics and Space Administration (NASA) is also keenly interested in how a bear can remain motionless in a deep sleep for several months without experiencing the progressive loss of calcium and bone strength suffered by human astronauts.

Black Bear (Ursus americanus)

Smallest of North America's three native bear species, the black bear is also the most abundant, and the most amenable to living in close proximity to civilization. Being a

Despite its frightening image, the American black bear is shy and retiring, and seldom seen even in places where its numbers are abundant.

natural prey of the much larger brown bear, which tops the food chain with no natural enemies, black bears are driven instinctively to withdraw from conflict with other large carnivores, including humans. This innate shyness means that people in the midst of black bear country seldom see one, and *U. americanus* never incurred the same wrath from people as the brown bear, whose instinct is to attack when surprised. The black bear was the original inspiration for the Teddy Bear, named after a young treed bear that outdoorsman-President Theodore Roosevelt refused to kill during a hunt. Smokey the Bear, fire prevention icon of the U.S. Forest Service, is also a black bear.

Geographic Range

Black bears were once common throughout North America. But the presence of such a powerful carnivore near human habitation is rarely tolerated, and in the twenty-first century the species' range is roughly half what it once was, restricted to woodland areas where bears can survive without coming into contact with people.

Today, black bears can be found south of the Arctic Circle throughout Canada and Alaska from the Pacific Ocean to the Atlantic coast. To the west populations are found from northern California east to the Rocky Mountains, and southward along the Rockies into central Mexico. To the east, black bears exist in healthy numbers from northern Minnesota to the north Atlantic states, with a few found along the Atlantic shoreline from New England to Florida. Black bears are not found in the Great Plains Basin of the United States or Canada.

Habitat

Black bear habitat is always wooded, always within close proximity to a source of fresh water, and usually contains thickets or swamps where an animal can doze the day away without being disturbed. Depending on geographic location, suitable forests and thickets can range from hickory woods in North Carolina to the Everglades of Florida to the alpine forests of the Rockies and the fringes of prickly pear and saguaro desert.

Physical Characteristics

Mass: 200 to more than 600 pounds, males about 20% larger than females. The largest black bear ever recorded was an individual named Tyson at Oswald's Bear Ranch in Newberry, Michigan, which weighed 880 pounds.

Body: Stout and powerfully muscled, covered by a thick coat of fur; looks especially large in late autumn, when the animal may be carrying up to 25% of its total weight in a layer of body fat. Total body length, from base of tail to nose, ranges from 4 to more than 6 feet, with males only slightly (about 5%) larger than females. Head large and round, with short rounded muzzle and small rounded ears standing erect on either side. Although some black bears have brown fur, especially in the western part of the species' range, they're distinguished from *Ursus arctos* by smaller size, lack of shoulder hump, and a rounded rather than upturned nose.

Tail: Short and heavily furred; no obvious purpose except covering the anus against insects; length 3 to 7 inches.

Tracks: Five forward-pointing toes on each foot, each toe tipped with a thick, curved claw that's surprisingly sharp, enabling the black bear to escape its only natural predator, the brown bear, by scaling even limbless trees. Claws always show in tracks.

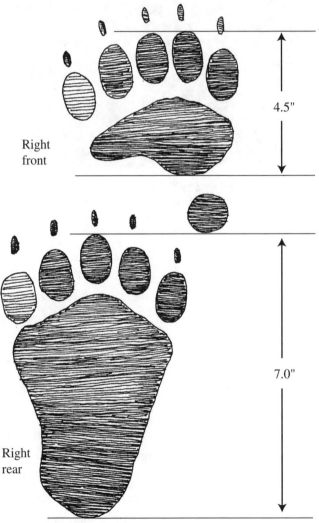

Right front

4.5"

Right rear

7.0"

Black bear (Ursus americanus). Foreclaws are sharper, more curved, and shorter than those of brown bears, giving the black bear an ability to climb trees.

Front tracks 4 to 5 inches long, 6 to 7 inches if rear of heel pad prints, usually as a round dot, to the rear of the print. Hind prints average 7 to 9 inches, 5 inches wide at the toes, and very much resemble the bare footprint of a human, except that the largest, most heavily impressed toe is to the outside, opposite our own, and usually obvious clawmarks extend 1 inch or more ahead of each toe. The normal walk is a shuffling gait, with a stride of about 1 foot, and a straddle of 10 to 12 inches, and hind feet printing on top of front tracks.

Running gait is the "rocking horse" pattern used to achieve maximum speed and agility by most four-legged species, where the forefeet are planted together as the hind feet come forward on either side. When the hind feet hit the ground, the forelegs and back are extended fully forward as the animal makes a powerful leap, coming down again on paired forefeet, and the gait repeats. As is common with this pattern, stride lengthens to 3 feet or more, and the pattern is paired forefeet planted side by side, bordered ahead of and to either side of the more elongated hind prints.

Black bear scats reflect the species' broad, omnivorous diet. This early-spring scat shows grass fibers and bits of rotting wood ingested when the bear foraged for grubs and insects.

Scat: Massive, reflecting the size of its maker. Usually cylindrical, dark brown to black when fresh. Smooth and unsegmented with flat, untapered ends when the animal has been feeding mostly on berries, vegetation, and insects; ant, beetle, and grasshopper legs often apparent in scat. Deposits become more like those of other predators when a bear has been feeding on deer-size kills or carrion, tapered at one or both ends, with small bones and fragments sheathed within a spiraled outer layer of fur. Length may range from segments of about 2 inches to scats as long as 8 inches; diameter from 1 to more than 2 inches, with larger diameters indicating larger bears.

Coloration: Black bears are usually coal-black in color, with long, shiny fur. In the normal color pattern, the only contrasting markings include brown patches covering either side of the muzzle, bordering a black stripe that extends from the brow along the top of the muzzle to the nose pad. Each brow will probably be marked by a single small brown spot above each eye, much the same as the markings seen in rottweiler and some other dog breeds. Young bears especially may have a spot of white fur on the chest.

There are several variations in the black bear's color pattern, nearly all of them seen around the Pacific coastline of North America. Black bears living west of the Great Lakes are often brown or cinnamon, and are occasionally misidentified as larger, humped brown bears. A blue-gray phase occurs near Alaska's Yukatat Peninsula, and those on Alaska's Gribble Island have a coat that may be almost completely white. Both of these color phases are found in Canada's British Columbia.

Sign: Older boar (male) black bears are usually well-established and can be very territorial toward intruder bears. Dominant males, usually 400 pounds or more, use regularly refreshed scat deposits to mark the intersections of trails that bound their territories, and often employ a nearby, usually smooth-barked tree as a scratching post. These trees are obvious to passersby who look upward, because they consist of five usually deep gouges extending downward along the trunk for a foot or so from a height of up to 7 feet, or as high as the individual could reach to leave a visual record of its physical size for intruders to see. Green trees, especially poplars, aspens, and cottonwoods, are often most obvious because their shredded fibrous bark tends to hang down in curled strips, but standing dead and barkless trees are also used as territorial markers, and sometimes seem to be preferred for their softer, decaying texture. Manmade, usually wooden, landmarks may also be used as scratching posts, including bridges, fenceposts, and power poles where a demonstration of height may not be possible, but a signature scent is applied through interdigital glands on the paws.

Sows (females) rearing cubs may also be territorial, although they appear to rely more on scent than visual markers of territory. Large boars have been known to kill cubs to bring a female into heat earlier than normal, although this is more rare among black bears than their larger cousin, the brown bear, so it behooves females with young cubs to be less blatantly territorial than bachelor males. Most of the obvious territorial sign a tracker finds will have been left there by males.

Other easily spotted black bear sign includes holes in meadows and knolls that almost appear to have been excavated by a shovel, but were actually dug in pursuit of rodents. Turned-up stones and rotting logs that have been rolled over and sometimes ripped apart are a common black bear sign, especially in spring when vegetation is scarce and fat-rich grubs are abundant. In late summer, fruiting wild cherry trees are often split apart at their crotches by bears trying to reach bunches in their upper branches, a foraging practice that has not endeared them to orchard farmers.

Vocalizations: Normally silent, but can use several voices that are similar to those of the brown and polar bears. A clacking or chomping of teeth, frequently accompanied by a white froth of saliva at the corners of the mouth, indicates anxiety, and a human close enough to witness this is well-advised to withdraw immediately. A loud huffing, usually issued from behind cover, is another warning against coming closer, and sometimes an invitation to leave the area. Low bawling sounds are used by mothers to communicate with cubs, while they tend to call back in louder, higher-toned bawls. Boars also bawl loudly during territorial fights, which are usually mostly bloodless wrestling matches.

Lifespan: Black bears can live as long as 30 years in captivity, but the average lifespan in the wild has been estimated at less than 15 years.

Diet

Black bears are the most omnivorous of North American bears. Grasses make up a large part of the bear diets throughout the species' range during its annual period of activity, and a black bear's digestive system can break down and assimilate the rough fibers with nearly the same efficiency as a deer. In early spring, when the forests are warming but edible vegetation has yet to sprout, much of the diet typically consists of the fat- and protein-rich larvae of moths and beetles that have wintered inside rotting logs and stumps. They sometimes dig through the top of a large anthill, deliberately agitating its occupants, then insert a forefoot into the mass of panicked insects, which attack the paw until its owner pulls it away to lick off the ants clinging to its fur. Exactly which foods constitute a typical black bear's diet can vary widely from season to season and from one region to another, and it's this omnivorous diet that allows black bears to be the most successful species in the family.

With a relatively slow running speed of about 30 miles per hour and a bulky body, bears are poorly designed as predators. They will appropriate deer and other kills from smaller, more skilled hunters if an opportunity presents itself, and are well-equipped for excavating rodents and ground squirrels, but can seldom chase down larger prey. One exception is in late spring, when black bears prowl the thickets in search of fawns still too small to outrun them.

The territorial range of a black bear may encompass more than 150 miles, but most travel less as they move from place to place following seasonal foods as they become available. However broad or narrow a territory, it must provide sufficient nutrition to enable its owner to put on a quarter of its body weight in fat for use in the coming winter denning period.

One dietary phenomenon that anyone researching black bears should be familiar with, especially in spring when the animals are emerging from winter dens, is the anal plug of mostly rough grasses that physically block the lower colon during the winter sleep. Just prior to denning, both black and brown bears eat a last meal of rough, mostly undigestible sedges, grasses, and sometimes pine needles, which then mass together and form a plug in the lower intestine. A similar intestinal blockage could be fatal for humans, but bears use a plug to insure that no excrement can foul their dens during sleep, especially not birthing dens. In spring, after having been awake a few days, the anal plugs are expelled, usually along territorial boundary trails. A tracker will find them easy to identify as nearly cylindrical, 2 to 3 inches long, and comprised almost completely of long grass blades and probably pine needles, coated with a mucouslike fluid when fresh. Since bears tend to stay close to their dens for the first week or so after waking, a freshly expelled anal plug is a good indication that a bear den, and probably its owner, are nearby.

Also note that black bears have a penchant for leaving the feet of squirrel-size and larger prey, biting them free of the carcass as it feeds, and leaving them where they fall. The purpose of this behavior is to remove the very sharp climbing claws of squirrels and other large rodents to prevent them from abrading the convoluted intestines of a bear's complex digestive system, which is unlike the straighter, less winding intestines of most carnivores.

Mating Habits

Like all bears, black bears are solitary except for the midsummer mating season. Males older than 3 years pair up briefly with females older than 2 years in June and July for roughly 2 weeks of courtship followed by mating, then go their separate ways, males to mate again should a receptive female become available. By this time females with grown cubs that have reached their second summer will have abandoned them, and will be ready to take another mate. Breeding sows will probably take just one mate.

After mating, both sexes resume almost identical habits, traveling sometimes long distances over well-worn bear trails that may be centuries old in some places to find the berries, nuts, and other high-carbohydrate foods needed to gain a layer of fat sufficient for denning. There's no animosity between mates, but a sow that senses she's pregnant will ward off further advances from a male with hard slaps and nips, because bears are designed by nature to fend for themselves.

Most black bears den in November and December, just before the permanent snows fall in the northern part of their range, and only then do the fertilized eggs a sow has been carrying in a state of dormancy within her womb implant to the uterine wall and begin to develop. If the sow is sickly or otherwise too unhealthy to gestate and nurse young, the eggs will involuntarily abort. Conversely, if a fertilized female is well-fed and strong, her litter size may increase from twins, which is the norm, to as many as five cubs. As with every species, large litter sizes are often a warning sign that bears are overpopulating, and that disease, famine, and other troubles are likely to follow.

Black bear dens are less conspicuous than would seem likely for such a large animal. Den sites are always located in a remote place where they won't be disturbed, especially by humans, but locations may range from excavations under the roots of a large tree to burrows in the side of a hill to large dry culverts under remote two-track roads. Den entrances are smaller than might be expected, just large enough for an occupant to squeeze through into a larger sleeping chamber. A small space is less drafty and loses less warmth than a more voluminous area, so den sizes are kept small and efficient.

Most black bear litters are born in January and February, after an actual gestation period of about 10 weeks. The naked 8-ounce cubs are usually born without waking the mother, and each of the blind, helpless newborns instinctively makes its way to a nipple. Once attached to a nipple, the cubs will remain there most of the time until spring, taking nourishment and growing rapidly. Not being a true hibernator, the mother's body temperature remains almost normal during the winter sleep period, keeping her offspring warm while she sleeps.

When mother and cubs emerge from the den in April or May, the youngsters will have grown to as much as 10 times their birth size, weighing from 2 to 5 pounds. Youngsters begin traveling with their mother on her annual migration to follow available foods, learning the foraging, hunting, and watering places that they may continue to visit throughout their own lives. By 8 months the cubs will have been weaned and will weigh 25 pounds or more. They can forage for insects and grasses, and catch an occasional rodent or frog, but are still too immature to survive on their own.

By the end of their first summer the cubs will have grown to as much as 75 pounds, and the white blaze that most carry on their chests will have faded to black. Typical of all bears, the cubs' mother will not mate in their first year of life, instead devoting all her time and energy to teaching and protecting her young. When she dens at the onset of winter, the cubs, which have also been putting on a thick layer of fat, will den with her. When mother and cubs awaken in spring, she will continue their educations until June, when the youngsters, which are now approximately 18 months old and weigh 100 pounds or more, are either abandoned or chased off to allow the mother to mate again.

Newly emancipated female cubs may breed in the coming mating season, but males will wander in search of their own territories, and will probably not mate until they've found one, usually at age 3 or 4. Females will continue to breed every other year until about age 9, while males may remain sexually active until 12 years old.

Behavior

Black bears are most active at dawn and dusk (crepuscular), although seasonal breeding and feeding activities may alter the normal pattern of sleeping through the day in secluded thickets. In places where they aren't disturbed by humans, bears may forage day or night.

Excepting the distractions of mating season, the overriding motivation in a bear's life is to eat, and they feed almost continuously from the time they awaken in spring until denning again in early winter. This seemingly gluttonous behavior is an evolved response to sleeping through the lean months of winter, when plant foods are scarce or nonexistent, and only the sleek and fast predators can catch enough prey to sustain them. A bear trying to forage or hunt in deep snows would have little chance of survival, but sleeping away the winter months requires taking enough nutrition into the den with them to live on until the return of warmer weather. A 200-pound bear requires 50 pounds of fat to remain healthy during the winter sleep period, so the summer months must provide enough food to not only keep an individual well-nourished, but to make it fat.

The solitary lifestyle of black (and brown) bears appears to depend largely on the amount of food available. Actually better equipped to catch fish with their sharply curved claws, black bears frequently come together along stream and river banks where suckers, trout, and salmon are spawning, and even nonrelated individuals tolerate the presence of one another. Similar congregations may be found in rich patches of ripening berries, in abandoned apple orchards, at landfills, and sometimes at campground dumpsters. During the latter half of the twentieth century it was an almost traditional pastime in the north to drive to municipal dumps in the evening to watch black bears, sometimes more than twenty of them, rummage through human refuse. The dump bears seemed to get along well enough once a hierarchy was established, but humans tended to get themselves into trouble, so today most city dumps and landfills are gated and locked after business hours.

Black bears have been known to kill small, easily caught livestock, like calves and sheep, for food, but their predations are rare and usually overdramatized. More real is the damage they inflict on corn crops, apple and cherry orchards, and bee yards. With their natural drive to feed bolstered by good intelligence, keen curiosity, and pound-for-pound physical strength roughly twice that of a strong man, black bears can do a great deal of damage to crops. Ripping down grape arbors, breaking the branches of fruit trees, and trampling sweet corn crops are some of the reasons farmers have for disliking them.

Black bears play an important role in the trophy hunting industry. Approximately 30,000 are killed by sport hunters in North America each year, but with little demand for fur, the species is in no danger from overharvesting. In fact, black bear numbers may prove to be too high as housing and other development projects occupy land that was previously black bear territory. Already there have been numerous cases of young black bears—nearly always recently emancipated cubs—who wandered onto the streets of rural towns in search of territory and attracted to odors emanating from restaurant dumpsters. In a few instances the trespassing animals have been shot dead, but public uproar has caused local authorities to adopt less lethal means of removing wandering bears.

Researching black bears in the field is less risky than it might sound; thirty-six humans were killed by black bears in all of the twentieth century (fewer than are killed each year by dogs), and biologists need have little fear of the animals. Unlike the larger and more aggressive brown bear, which instinctively charges toward a threat, black bears are generally quick to withdraw from the slightest chance of confrontation with humans. Mothers with small cubs are most likely to send them up a tree, then climb up after, until a potential enemy passes. Because of the species' keen sense of smell, few of the hikers detected by black bears will ever get a chance to see them.

In a few isolated cases, black bears, usually dominant males in excess of 300 pounds, have stood their ground, or even approached a human. The most unbending rule of such an encounter is never, ever run from the animal; no human can outrun the 30 miles per hour sprint of a black bear, and fleeing definitely identifies you as the weaker adversary. Running away excites the bear's predatory instincts, often causing it to give chase. Conversely, standing one's ground in the face of even a large bear typically reveals that aggressive behavior, including charges that sometimes stop within a few unnerving feet, are nearly always a bluff. A person who appears unafraid and strong is less likely to be bullied by a bear.

In rare instances where *Ursus americanus* can legitimately be accused of attacking a person, the motivation has usually been food. Few wild animals will eat human flesh, even when already dead, but an old or sickly bear that faces starvation because it can no longer make the sometimes long seasonal trek to follow its food supply might be tempted to prey on a small human.

Brown Bear (*Ursus arctos horribilis*)

Measured by weight, the brown bear is the largest land carnivore in the world, sometimes reaching twice the size of a black bear, and slightly heavier than the taller polar bear. Brown bears have no natural enemies except other brown bears and humans, so individuals are relatively fearless as they go about their business. Based on the accounts of field researchers like Doug Peacock, author of *Grizzly Years,* and the number of salmon fishermen who share river shorelines with brown bears each year at places like Alaska's Denali National Park, this species is neither afraid of nor hungry for humans. There have been instances where an old or sickly individual preyed on a human because it was starving, but in general, brown bears view humans much like

The brown, or grizzly, bear is the largest land carnivore on earth, and deserves respect.

skunks: repulsive and annoying but not particularly interesting. This may be one reason why modern scientists tend to drop the old suffix *horribilis* from the brown bear's Latin name.

Geographic Range

Brown bears are thought to have once roamed most of the globe, and probably all of North America from the Arctic Circle to Central America. Unfortunately, this largest of carnivores has always evoked fear in humans, the weapon-making species, and today brown bears are gone from most of their original range. An estimated population of 100,000 can still be found in northern Eurasia, with about 70,000 of those living in Russia. Isolated sightings have also been reported from the Atlas Mountains of northernmost Africa, and possibly on Japan's Hokkaido Island. Brown bears were extirpated from North America's Sierra Nevada Mountains, the southern Rocky Mountains, and from northern Mexico during the twentieth century, when populations in the lower 48 states of the United States fell from more than 100,000 animals at the turn of the century to a current low of 1,000. Brown bear populations in Alaska and western Canada remain fairly stable at an estimated 30,000 individuals.

Habitat

Brown bears are at home in a variety of habitats, but in North America the species seems partial to open areas like Arctic tundra, alpine meadows, and coastlines. Brown bears were a common sight on the Great Plains when the first European immigrants arrived. With a digestive system that can metabolize rough foliage and grasses nearly as well as a deer, the bears are at home on the plains, but never far from a thicket in which to sleep without being observed.

In Siberia, brown bears are more creatures of the deep forest, while European populations are confined to mountain woodlands. So long as a habitat provides vegetation, nuts, fruits, and rodents, fresh water, and a secluded place to rest, *Ursus arctos* can live there.

Physical Characteristics

Mass: 400 to more than 1,700 pounds, with the larger individuals in the north. Males approximately 10% larger than females.

Body: Very large and powerfully built. About twice the size of a typical black bear, with a distinctive large hump of muscle extending upward from the spine between the shoulders. Shoulder height 4 to 4.5 feet, body length 6 to more than 7 feet, standing height 10 feet or more. The head is large and broad, with small, round, furry ears at either side. Facial profile is almost concave, giving the impression of an upturned nose, and unlike the rounded muzzle and profile of a black bear.

Tail: About 3 inches long, well-furred, and the same color as the pelage.

Tracks: Similar to the black bear, but often much larger and with longer, more obvious clawmarks showing in tracks. Five toes on all four feet, with almost straight claws extending from the front toes to a length of 3 inches or more. Forefeet 5 to 6 inches long, discounting dot-shaped impression that may print 3 or 4 inches to the rear of the forefoot heel pad; forefoot width 8 to 10 inches. Hind feet 10 to 16 inches long, 7 to 8 inches wide, elongated and flat, almost human-shaped, and tipped with much shorter claws.

Scat: Similar to a black bear's but often much larger and with more mass. Shape is generally cylindrical, often segmented, and dark brown to black when fresh, with evidence of seeds, grasses, and berries in most samples. Diameter may exceed 2 inches. A single scat may be broken into several segments of 2 to 4 inches in length, or when feeding on rich meats, it might be coiled and in a single piece. Rodent and sometimes deer hair may be in evidence, wrapped spiral-fashion over bones and protruding objects, much the same as scats of other predatory species.

Coloration: Fur is usually dark brown, but varies from blond to nearly black in some individuals. The common name of grizzly bear stems from the white-frosted, or grizzled, appearance of the bear's shoulders and back. The brown bear's muzzle is the same color or darker than its pelage, but never lighter colored like the black bear's muzzle.

Sign: Large excavations in hillsides and meadows where ground squirrel burrows have been dug out in search of prey. Large rocks and down logs overturned. Bathtub-size depressions in the humus of brushy thickets where a bear slept.

Vocalizations: Grunts, growls, huffing, bawling. Clacking of teeth, often accompanied by a froth of saliva around the mouth, indicates anxiety, and researchers who witness such behavior should withdraw immediately but slowly, never turning their backs to the bear.

Lifespan: Up to 47 years in captivity, but normally less than 35 years in the wild. Some brown bears in Yellowstone National Park have been sexually active until 25 years of age. Potential lifespan has been estimated to be as long as 50 years.

Diet

Like the black bear, brown bears have a highly efficient digestive system that allows them to subsist mostly on vegetation. In spring, before many food plants have sprouted,

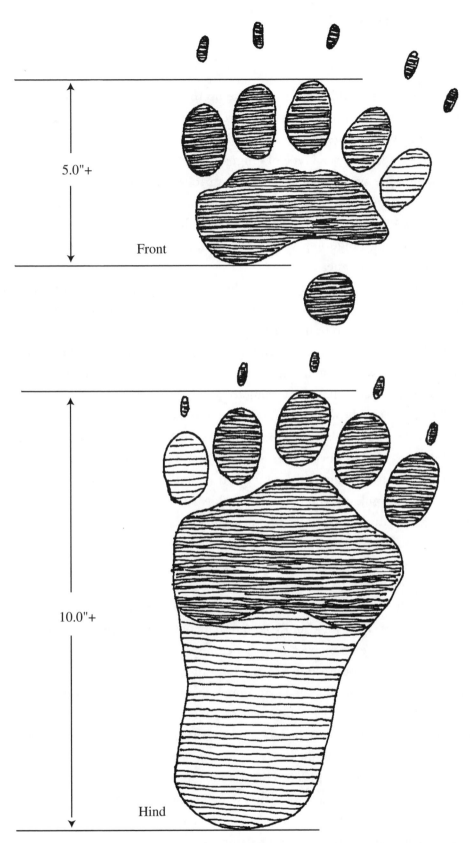

5.0"+

Front

Hind

10.0"+

Brown bear (Ursus arctos horribilis). *Heavier shading indicates portions of paw where greater weight is placed. Like all plantigrade (flat-footed) species, brown bears tend to walk with most body weight pressing downward on their outer soles, which leave a deeper imprint in tracks. The opposite of humans, bears have their largest toes on the outside, while the innermost toe registers faintly or not at all in tracks.*

grasses, sedges, roots, and lichens may make up the bulk of a newly awakened bear's diet. As the warm season progresses and more seasonal plants mature and fruit, a bear's diet and range will change to match available foods. Calorie-rich berries, nuts, and fruits are preferred, and several type of fungi are eaten as well.

When they're available, insects in their various stages of development are eaten, too. Rotting logs and stumps are home to beetle and other larvae whose grublike bodies are comprised mostly of fat. Spiders are eaten as they hang in their webs, and ants are gathered by sticking a big forepaw into their hill, then licking the clinging insects off with the bear's raspy tongue.

Brown bears will eat carrion when they can find or appropriate it from smaller carnivores. The seemingly instinctive hatred that exists between wolves and bears probably stems from the brown bear's practice of stealing carcasses brought down by hunting packs. Brown bears also prey on wolf pups if they can find a den of them guarded by only an Omega-wolf babysitter while the rest of the pack is away to hunt, but even a pair of wolves is usually sufficiently strong to deter a large brown bear.

Like black bears, brown bears are poorly equipped for hunting prey compared to more lithe and speedy predators. In the far north, big Alaskan brown bears frequent fur seal and walrus colonies during their summer mating seasons, seeking out newborn calves, males seriously wounded in mating battles, and individuals weak from advanced age. A brown's 35-mile-per-hour run is too slow to threaten healthy deer, but brown bears may follow caribou herds during their annual migrations, waiting for those most easily preyed on to reveal themselves by falling behind the herd.

In spring, right after the bears emerge from their winter dens, but before the summer growing season has gotten underway, most of the meat eaten by a brown bear consists of small rodents and ground squirrels dug out of their burrows by its massive, powerful forepaws. With mice and vole numbers typically numbering thousands per acre, rodents can make up most of a bear's diet in spring.

Marmots and ground squirrels are dug out of their dens and eaten, although many escape through one of several exit tunnels that typically branch outward from the burrows of subterranean rodents. Like badgers, brown bears digging after denned prey may be shadowed by a coyote, which is itself too fast and nimble for the bear too catch. The coyote is there to exploit the bear's excavating power by guarding the prey's escape route, snapping it up if it pops out. This system appears to be mutually beneficial for both carnivores, because a trapped rodent's sense of smell makes it aware that a coyote is waiting at the back door, and the prospect of certain death in both directions may cause it to flee in blind panic toward either predator.

Salmon fishing is probably the best-known of a brown bear's hunting skills, even to the point of becoming a tourist attraction in places like Alaska's Denali

National Park. During their spring and autumn mating seasons (depending on the species), mature salmon and trout (family Salmonidae) migrate upstream by the thousands in the same rivers where they were born to plant the next generation of their kind. Waiting to ambush the usually large fish at narrows, rapids, and shallows are brown bears of all ages and sizes, all of which learned to come to this particular place at this time of year from their mothers, who in turn learned to fish from their mothers, ad infinitum.

Spawning runs are perhaps the only time and place where normally solitary, anti-social, and extremely territorial brown bears are found in close proximity to one another. Fatty fish flesh has been a critical part of the bears' diet since before recorded history, and the animals have learned over many generations to tolerate the presence of one another so that all can share in an abundance of rich foods. Sows with cubs will keep their distance from adult boars, though, and even fight with one if it approaches too closely; boars have been known to kill, and sometimes eat, yearling cubs to induce their mother, who wouldn't normally breed until the cubs' second or third summer, into sexual readiness a year or two early. When the spawning run ends, the bears leave to resume a solitary and territorial lifestyle.

Mating Habits

The mating habits of brown bears are very similar to those of the smaller black bear. In the summer months between May and July, sexually mature sows at least 3 years old begin involuntarily and voluntarily advertising their receptivity through pheromonal scents and hormones contained in their urine. Boars 5 or 6 years of age are attracted to the prospect of sex, and seek out females in heat, advertising their own availablity through scat and urine deposits on trails that overlap a local female's territory. After roughly a week of courtship, depending on how quickly the female reaches a state of readiness, the pair copulate frequently for about 3 days, or until the sow realizes instinc-tively that she's been impregnated. Once her eggs are fertilized, the female will tolerate no further advances from the boar, and will drive him off (possibly to find another mate) with hard slaps and bites whenever he comes within reach. Females will probably take only one mate per mating season.

Mated sows carry the fertilized eggs alive but dormant within their wombs until October or November, just prior to the winter denning season. At this time the eggs will implant to the uterine wall if the female is healthy and has put on 25% of her own weight in a thick layer of body fat, or they will spontaneously abort to conserve bodily resources for her own needs. Implanted eggs grow rapidly, and in late January to early March, two, and occasionally as many as four, cubs are born inside a snug excavated den. Although bears are not true hibernators, based on the facts that their body temperatures drop only slightly and they can be awakened easily, the birthing mother may sleep through her offsprings' delivery. Weighing about 1 pound at birth, each of the blind and naked cubs will make its own way to a nipple and nestle into its mother's warm belly fur to nurse almost continuously until she awakens in April or May. At this point the cubs are fully furred, mobile, and able to travel with their mother as she begins the same annual foraging trek to seasonal food sources that they will make as adults, and teach to their own offspring.

At 5 months, in late June to early August, the cubs are weaned and begin to forage for themselves on grasses, forbs, and insects. Mothers share kills with the cubs, but they soon learn to catch rodents, frogs, and other small animals without help. At the end of their first summer, the cubs will weigh 50 pounds or more, and most smaller mammals will have become potential prey to them. Yearling cubs accompany their mothers to rivers where fishing bears congregate to feed on spawning fish but keep their distance from males that might kill them to drive their mother in an early estrus.

Cubs den with their mothers the first winter of their lives. When she emerges the following spring they remain with her until June or July, when she abandons them or drives them away. At this time the cubs weigh upwards of 150 pounds, and aren't easy prey for any carnivore. Mother brown bears are less likely to breed every other year than black bears, and some sows go unmated for up to 4 years between litters. Emancipated cubs establish their own territories, sometimes traveling more than 100 miles to find suitable habitat not already claimed, and continue to grow until they reach 10 or 11 years of age.

Behavior

With no enemies except man, and no fear of anything, *U. arctos* may be active at any time of the day, but the species' foraging habits are generally crepuscular. After feeding during the cool early morning hours, warm days are spent sleeping in dense thickets. Researchers should be exceptionally careful in such an occluded environment, and should always bear in mind that the instinct of a surprised grizzly is to charge, not retreat.

Carcasses of large animals are also to be avoided, observed only through binoculars, and never aproached more closely than 200 yards, preferably farther and from downwind. Brown bears, black bears, cougars, and wolverines make a habit of camouflaging carcasses too large to be eaten in a single sitting with a partial covering of leaves and debris. Each of these species is likely to defend that food source from any large competitor, including humans, and it's a sure bet that the owner of the carcass is nearby.

The overall territory of a brown bear may encompass more than 1,000 miles, but the average is usually less than 200 square miles, and territories will seldom cover more area than is required to meet the bear's needs. The territories of males average 7 times larger than those of females, and will normally overlap the territories of several females that are potential mates.

The concept of territory doesn't apply to bears in the same sense that it does to most territorial carnivores, because most of a bear's time is spent following ripening foods from one location to another. An individual might spend several weeks in a place where blueberries and other fruits are plentiful, but when available foods are gone from an area, so are the bears. This system works well because the bear's omnivorous diet and nature's own diversity insure that a number of food sources are available every month of its waking period.

Brown bear adults can't normally climb trees because their claws, which were more sharply curved to give them that ability when they were cubs, have grown out straight and long to make them more useful as digging tools. This adaptation reflects the brown bear's open habitat, as opposed to the heavily forested environment preferred by black bears, whose sharp, curved claws permit them to climb even smooth-sided trees. This does not mean that climbing a tree is always a good way to avoid a brown bear, though, because there have been instances in which a bear used the branches of a large pine as ladder rungs to clamber up after a treed human.

Brown bears have frequently been observed pushing against dead standing trees until they topple. This seemingly idle behavior has a real purpose, which is to stun prey animals that might be holed up inside. Once down, the trunk can be torn apart in search of grubs, ants, and sometimes the honey of a wild beehive.

Although this species is sometimes temperamental and often petulant, traits that do nothing to endear them to humans, accounts of brown bears preying on livestock or threatening rural Americans generally range from exaggerated to fabricated, most of them presented merely as justification for killing a bear.

Polar Bear (*Ursus maritimus*)

Polar bears are the most carnivorous of family Ursidae, largely because of the lack of vegetation in this species' Arctic habitat. Because this species regards virtually every other species as food, it has a definite predatory bent, and is one of the few terrestrial carnivores on earth that considers humans as prey under normal conditions. Norwegian fur hunters of the twentieth century have reported that some or most of the ten polar bears a hunter was permitted to harvest each year were not hunted, but shot in defense of themselves or their sled dogs.

Polar bear. Photo by Dave Olsen, courtesy of U.S. Fish & Wildlife Service.

Geographic Range

Polar bears have a circumpolar distribution, albeit only at the top of the globe. The species ranges throughout the Arctic region surrounding the North Pole, the limits of their range determined by the ice pack of the Arctic Ocean and of surrounding coastal areas. Polar bears have been reported as far south as the southern tips of Greenland and Iceland.

During the winter, polar bears range between the southern edge of the ice pack or the northern edge of ice formed off continental coastlines. In summer, bears will remain at the edge of the receding ice pack or on islands and coastal regions that remain ice-covered year round.

Six individual populations of polar bears are presently recognized: (1) Wrangel Island and western Alaska, (2) northern Alaska, (3) the Canadian Arctic archipelago, (4) Greenland, (5) Svalbard–Franz Josef Land, and (6) Central Siberia. Individual sightings have occurred as far south as Maine, in the United States.

Habitat

Because they spend their entire lives around and in the ocean, polar bears are categorized as marine mammals by some biologists, and the scientific name *Ursus maritimus*, or "seagoing bear," reflects this species' penchant for open water. Preferred habitat is the pack ice of the Arctic Ocean, where pressure ridges and buckled surfaces leave areas of open water in which foraging seals, a mainstay in the polar bear diet, find plenty of fishing opportunities.

When pack ice breaks up in spring, most polar bears migrate northward to stay with it, sometimes floating along on ice floes, and sometimes by swimming 20 miles or more to a colder, more suitable summer habitat. The spring break-up of pack ice leaves some polar bears stranded on solid ground in comparatively warm weather, unable to migrate north to permanent ice. In some of these places, like the little village of Churchill on Canada's Atlantic coast, polar bears have learned to feed at landfills, and a few of these appear to be voluntarily missing the annual migration northward in order to remain with a steady supply of people food.

Physical Characteristics

Mass: Adult males are typically much larger than females, with males weighing between 800 and 1,100 pounds, females 350 to 700 pounds. The largest polar bear reported was a male weighing 1,760 pounds.

Body: The body of a polar bear is large and stocky, but longer and sleeker than that of the more thickly built brown bear, with longer limbs that provide a longer and more efficient swimming stroke. Polar bears lack the large muscular shoulder hump of brown bears. Height at shoulder about 4 feet, body length 7 to 11 feet. The polar bear's head is proportionally small compared to other bears, with a slightly longer muzzle and an elongated neck.

Tail: Heavily furred, white to cream colored, 3 to more than 6 inches long.

Tracks: Polar bears have large feet designed for swimming long distances. Five widely splayed toes on all four feet. Heavily furred soles may obscure or blur print

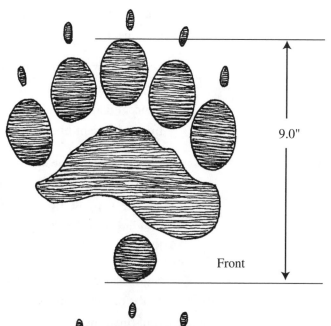

9.0"

Front

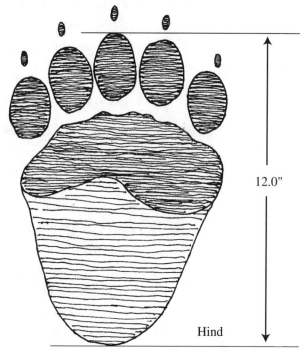

12.0"

Hind

Polar bear (Ursus maritimus). *Note that paws are exceptionally wide (averaging about nine inches), giving the polar bear snowshoelike flotation in deep snows.*

details. Foreprints 6 to 8 inches long, longer if measured from dotlike heel print; toes heavily clawed, but much shorter than the long, almost straight foreclaws of a brown bear. Hind prints 10 to more than 12 inches long, almost human-shaped, indicating a flat-footed (plantigrade) walk. Heel much narrower than that of a brown bear, tracks much larger than the black bear's. Bear tracks on pack ice or ice floes are always from a polar bear.

Scat: Similar to a brown bear; cylindrical, often segmented, 2 or more inches in diameter, often more than 6 inches long. Dark brown to black, often with seal fur in evidence. Polar bears also eat small amounts of vegetation, mostly lichens like reindeer moss, and plant fibers might also be apparent.

Coloration: The pelage is generally all white, contrasting against a black nose pad, and making the brown eyes appear to be black. In summer the coat may take on a yellowish hue, supposedly from oxidation in the warmer air, and polar bears that have been digging in soil or frequenting landfills might be a dirty gray. The polar bear's skin is black.

Sign: Seal carcasses from which all fat and larger pieces of meat have been chewed. Hides of these carcasses will be shredded from the bear's sharp claws. Regularly packed trails in snow around seasonal hunting grounds, marked at intervals, and especially at intersections, by scat and urine deposits.

Vocalizations: Normally silent. Huffing and grunting sounds are the most common noises made, but polar bears can growl and bawl like other bear species.

Lifespan: In the wild polar bears may live to be 30 years old. One captive female at the Detroit Zoo, in Detroit, Michigan, reached 45 years in 1999.

Diet

Polar bears are the most carnivorous species in family Ursidae, largely because their icy snow-covered habitat prohibits being a vegetarian. In this streamlined and fragile ecosystem, plankton eat algae, small fish eat plankton, large fish eat small fish, seals eat large fish, and polar bears eat seals. Nothing preys on a polar bear except man.

The polar bear's most common prey is the ringed seal *(Phoca hispida),* followed by the bearded seal *(Erignathus barbatus),* the harp seal *(Pagophilus groenlandicus),* the hooded seal *(Cystophora cristata),* and an occasional small walrus *(Odobenus rosmarus).* They will generally eat any animal they can catch, including sea birds, and often scavenge on carrion of dead whales and other large animals.

Polar bears are especially predatory of seals when the flippered mammals gather in large colonies along open shorelines to mate in January and February, and during their birthing periods in April and May. The usual technique is simply to stalk unseen as closely as possible to a crowded colony, then charge into their midst with sharp claws and teeth, hoping to mortally injure one or more seals before they can escape underwater.

In winter, polar bears also lie in wait on the pack ice at a seal's breathing hole, moving into position while the seal is underwater. When the seal resurfaces to take air, the bear slaps it with a powerful sharply clawed paw, killing or mortally wounding the animal, which is then dragged onto the ice and consumed.

Blubber (seal or whale fat) is the most preferred staple in a polar bear's diet, and well-fed bears will often eat only the blubber of their kills. More important than meat protein in the polar bear's frozen habitat is fat, which provides the necessary proteins and nutrients its body needs, as well as adding to its own layer of insulation. Arctic foxes have learned to make a practice of shadowing bears on the hunt to get the red meat they leave behind.

Polar bears aren't known to cache large kills that can't be eaten all at once, but partially consumed carcasses are always being guarded, and will be defended if approached too closely. As with other bears, never approach a carcass to less than 200 yards.

Mating Habits

Polar bears tend to mate earlier in the year than other bear species, with normally solitary males and females coming together to mate in April and May. After a brief period of courtship and mating that normally lasts about 3 days, the mates go their separate ways; both may mate again with another partner. Mating is terminated by the female, who seems to know when she's pregnant and wards off further advances from males with hard slaps and bites.

As with other bear species, mating fights between males of breeding age are rare, brief, and seldom injurious to either opponent. Physical size and body language are usually sufficient to determine which is the stronger animal, and when contentious males do battle, the contest is more of a wrestling match that ends as soon as it becomes apparent which is most powerful.

Polar bear females undergo a period of delayed implantation after mating successfully, carrying fertilized eggs dormant within their wombs until October or November, when the eggs implant or abort, depending on the female's state of health. At this time mated females migrate to ocean coastlines where banks and dunes provide places to excavate a birthing den, and nearby seal colonies allow for good hunting. Along Canada's Hudson Bay, the largest polar bear denning region on earth, dens may be excavated in dirt along the banks of both the ocean and rivers feeding into it. In other places dens are excavated into snowbanks.

While no species of bear truly hibernates, polar bears are the most active among them during the winter months. Mothers may lay up in their dens for several days at a time, but will remain active until they give birth in December or January. Twins are the norm, with each cub born blind, fully furred, and weighing about 2 pounds (twice the birth weight of a brown bear newborn). After giving birth, often in her sleep, the mother remains inside the den, sleeping and reserving bodily resources for her nursing offspring until April, when she emerges with her now 20- to 30-pound cubs to begin their education.

Cubs and mothers remain together for 2 to 3 years—up to a year longer than black or brown bears. Larger size at birth, a faster rate of growth, and longer period of maternal care all contribute to a young polar bear's chances of survival in the harshest environment on earth. Even with the best care, mortality for polar bear cubs is estimated to reach as high as 1 out of 3.

Male polar bears reach sexual maturity at 4 or 5 years, and will mate every year if they can. Females become sexually active at 3 or 4 years, but may not mate for up to 4 years between litters.

Behavior

Polar bears are solitary, carnivorous, and the most predatory of family Ursidae. Living in an environment where almost every meal means killing another animal has caused *U. maritimus* to regard all other creatures as potential prey, including humans. Unlike brown bears, polar bears that attack people normally perceive them as food, and *U. maritimus* can legitimately be considered a man-eater. Fortunately, humans are scarce or absent throughout most of the polar bear's range, so encounters are rare.

Polar bears may be active at any time of day or night, especially in the continuous daylight of the Arctic summer. To conserve energy, the animals spend an estimated 66% of their days either sleeping or lying in wait for a prey animal to present itself.

As its species name implies, the polar bear is an excellent swimmer. With a swimming stroke unique among mammals, the bear paddles with its forefeet only, letting the hind feet simply trail behind. Despite the seeming ungainliness of this stroke, polar bears can swim in excess of 6 miles per hour, and they've been observed swimming in open ocean more than 20 miles from pack ice.

Polar bear pelts were once an important commodity in the fur trade, with skins fetching as much as $3,000 apiece. The species has never been endangered, but fear that demand from the fur-buying public might change that prompted passage of the United States Marine Mammal Protection Act in 1972, which prohibited all sport hunting of polar bears. In 1973 those protections were also adopted by Canada, the Soviet Union, Norway, and Denmark. In 1993 the total world population of polar bears was estimated to be 28,370.

A real worry for not only polar bears but the world as a whole are earth's melting polar ice caps, which has caused sufficient concern for the usually silent National Aeronautics and Space Administration to issue a warning in 2003. Aside from the environmental catastrophe that has already begun from this phenomenon, loss of ice means loss of suitable habitat for polar bears, and that has placed the species in jeopardy more than the fur trade ever did.

THE SQUIRREL FAMILY (FAMILY SCIURIDAE)

Sciuridae is the family of squirrels, and is represented in North America by sixty-three species that include such diverse animals as marmots, chipmunks, and tree squirrels. The family name is Latin for "shade tail," an allusion to the long bushy tail of tree squirrels, but is actually a misnomer where short-tailed ground squirrels like prairie dogs and woodchucks are concerned.

Physical characteristics common to all squirrel species include having four toes on the forefeet, five toes on the hind feet. All are plantigrade, or flat-footed, with elongated hind paws that resemble human feet. All are rodents, with chisel-shaped upper and lower incisors that are adapted to gnawing and cutting wood or vegetation, but most will also dine on an occasional insect or small animal if the opportunity arises.

Gray Squirrel (Sciurus carolinensis)

Best known of the tree squirrels among human hunters, the gray squirrel has served as a food staple for as long as there have been people in the New World. In the days of colonial America it was common to refer to any long gun that was .45 caliber or smaller as a squirrel gun, which demonstrates how important a role this tree-dwelling rodent played in the lives of pioneers.

Although only the eastern gray squirrel has been selected to represent larger tree squirrels here, the species has several very close cousins throughout the forested areas of North America, and all of them share similar diets, mating, and behavioral traits. The

Gray squirrel (Sciurus carolinensis). *Squirrel shown is the black phase of the species, which is most common among oaks and maples. Gray-coated individuals tend to frequent beech and other gray-barked trees. Note the position of the "shade tail," from which the family name is derived.*

same can be said of the larger fox squirrel *(S. niger),* which shares almost exactly the same range as the gray squirrel.

Geographic Range

S. carolinensis occupies the eastern half of the United States to the Mississippi River, ranging as far south as Florida and eastern Texas, and north to the southernmost edge of Canada. Introduced populations also exist in Italy, Scotland, England, and Ireland, where the squirrels have thrived to the point of becoming a serious pest species.

Habitat

S. carolinensis requires trees in its habitat, and will not be found in prairie, desert, or rocky places that lack tall trees in which to forage, make dens, and to escape predators. The ideal habitat includes undergrowth and ground plants, and ready access to drinking water. Larger fox squirrels prefer a mixed habitat of conifers and hardwoods; smaller red squirrels are found in mostly coniferous forests.

Fox squirrel (Sciurus niger). *Largest of the North American tree squirrels, typically found in mixed coniferous and deciduous forest, where its grizzled, rust-colored coat serves as effective camouflage.*

Red squirrel (Tamiascurus hudsonicus).

Physical Characteristics

Mass: 1 to 1.5 pounds.

Body: Elongated and well-furred. Short legs, rounded head with short muzzle, small round ears. Body length 16 to 20 inches. No difference in body size between the sexes (dimorphism).

Some notable differences occur in skull size and fur color between gray squirrel populations in the northern and southern parts of the species' range. From north to south there exists a decreasing cline in skull size, although mandible sizes and dental arrangements remain unchanged. Also, individuals in the south tend more toward a gray coat, while populations in the north are more often black in color and better suited to life in a cold climate.

Tail: Well-furred, less rounded (more flat) along its top than in other tree squirrels. Length 8 to 10 inches, or about 50% of body length. Tail functions as an umbrella in rain and hot sun, and helps to keep its owner warm while sleeping in cold weather.

Tracks: Four toes on front feet, five toes hind. Tracks of front feet rounded, 1 to 1.5 inches long; tracks of hind feet elongated, 2 to 2.5 inches long. Track pattern much like that of a rabbit, but markedly smaller. Hind feet print ahead of forefeet, leaving a pattern like two side-by-side exclamation points (!!), indicating the hopping gait common

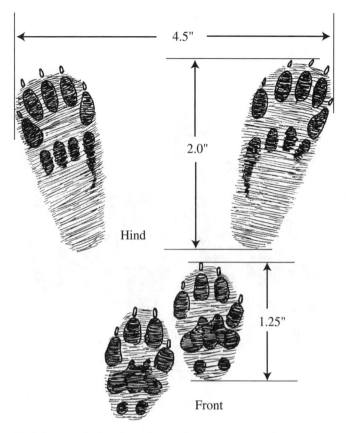

Hind

4.5"

2.0"

1.25"

Front

Typical tree squirrel tracks as they might appear on snow, damp sand, or mud.

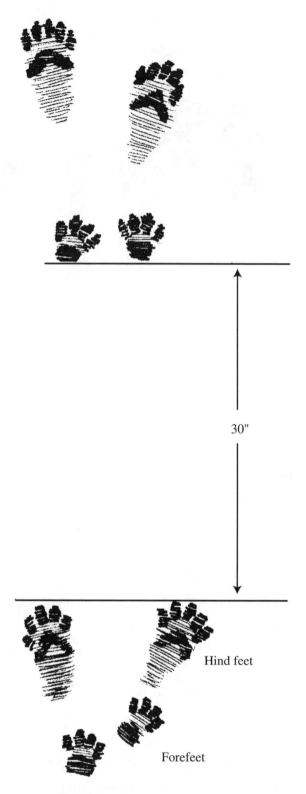

30"

Hind feet

Forefeet

Running gait

Typical tree squirrel running track pattern. Track pattern shown here is typical of all tree squirrel species, and denotes a hopping gait similar to that of rabbits and hares. Tracks are shown as they might appear on snow or in soft mud. On firmer ground, heels may not register.

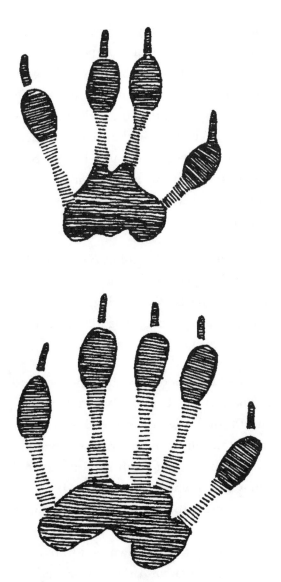

Red squirrel (Tamiasciurus hudsonicus) *track pattern on soft snow or mud.*

Red squirrel tracks as they might appear on firm snow or mud.

to all tree squirrels. Total length of track pattern 7 to 8 inches. Distance between track sets indicates gait: 10 inches for a casual hopping pace, 24 inches at an easy bounding run, 36 inches or more when the animal is fleeing danger.

Scat: Pellet-shaped, dark brown to black, 0.25 inch in diameter. Pellets often exhibit a thin "tail" of rough plant fibers on one end, indicating more fibrous browse. Roughly 1 dozen pellets per scat deposit, depending on the size of the squirrel.

Coloration: There are two distinct color phases in *S. carolinensis*. Populations that live in forests consisting all or mostly of beech trees tend to be gray, matching the smooth bark

Tree squirrel scats—typical of all species. Drier pellet form (top) is most common during winter. The form shown at bottom (note "tails" of plant fibers) is typical of a more succulent summer diet.

of the trees they inhabit. Those living among dark-barked trees like maples and oaks are mostly black, especially in the northern part of the range. Both color phases exhibit a grizzling of whitish guard hairs along the dorsal parts. Ears and underbelly are often lighter in color than the body. Albinism is uncommon, and doesn't occur at all in the colder northern latitudes, but albino colonies exist in southern Illinois, New Jersey, and South Carolina. Fox squirrel is larger with a reddish pelage; red squirrel is much smaller with a brown to orange coat and white underparts.

Helping to explain the variation in fur colors are studies that have shown black squirrels experience 18% less heat loss than gray squirrels in temperatures below freezing, along wth a 20% lower metabolic rate, and a nonshivering (thermogenesis) capacity that's 11% higher than in grey individuals.

Sign: Beechnut husks, opened acorn, walnut, hickory, and other nuts. In autumn, leafy nut-bearing twig ends are frequently found beneath food trees, the cut ends showing a neatly clipped, stepped bite left by the squirrel's sharp upper and lower incisors. Small patches of disturbed soil scattered atop the forest humus reveal where nuts have been buried in shallow holes for winter storage. In winter, hardpack snow will be pocked with holes, about 6 inches in diameter, where a squirrel burrowed diagonally downward to retrieve a buried nut, often leaving a spray of darker soil around the entrance.

Vocalizations: Chirping barks are frequently heard from territorial males, especially during the autumn and early spring breeding seasons. Alarm calls consist of short clucking barks that humans can usually imitate well by sucking one cheek repeatedly against the molars on one side of their mouths. The intensity of a squirrel's alarm is gauged by the frequency of the barks: a fast chattering denotes immediate danger, becoming less frequent as the source of alarm recedes.

Lifespan: Average lifespan in the wild is about 12.5 years, but one captive female lived to more than 20 years of age.

Diet

Gray squirrels feed mostly on nuts and seeds, with acorns, chestnuts, and other storable nuts being among the favorites. Tree buds make up a large part of the diet in winter and early spring, along with nuts that were cached in shallow holes the previous autumn. In summer the diet includes plants, grasses, and flowers. Pine and cedar nuts and buds are also eaten, but not as much as with other tree squirrel species, and mushrooms are sometimes nibbled on. Although mostly vegetarian, gray and other tree squirrels are also known to eat insects, tree frogs, and an occasional bird egg, with predatory habits being more common during times when nut crops are poor. Deer bones and antlers are gnawed on to wear down the constantly growing incisors, and to get the calcium and other minerals contained in them. Crops like wheat, and especially corn, are favored, making the squirrels a pest species in some agricultural areas.

Legend has it that gray (and fox) squirrels remember where they buried each nut, but in fact the squirrels possess an extremely acute sense of smell that can detect cached nuts by their odors, even under a foot of snow. Not all of these buried nuts are found, however, and during good years more nuts are buried than are needed to supply an animal's food requirements. In either case, a number of buried nuts go unretrieved each year, and many will take root to become new trees. In this way squirrels contribute to the expansion and health of their own habitats by carrying off nuts to germinate in places where they couldn't otherwise be spread.

Mating Habits

Gray squirrels, like all tree squirrel species, typically have two mating seasons per year, one in May through June, and a second in December through February, with populations in the northernmost parts of the range occurring as much as 1 month later. Males older than 11 months are drawn to pre-estrus females by the scent of sexual pheromones about a week prior to mating, and may come from as far away as half a mile. The testes of mating males become greatly enlarged prior to mating, increasing in mass from their nonbreeding weight of approximately 1 gram to as much as 7 grams at the peak of their heat.

Females may breed as young as 6 months, especially where population densities are low, but most mate at 15 months, and remain fertile for about 8 years. Estrus is indicated in the female by an enlarged pink vulva that makes it easier to identify the sexes, which are nearly identical during nonbreeding months. The vulva is typically swollen for just 8 hours, and vaginal cavities are closed except during estrus.

Territorial battles between males are common and noisy during the mating seasons, with contenders battling sometimes furiously on the ground and in the trees.

Embattled males are often so preoccupied that they become easy prey for carnivores. In areas where populations are high or females are scarce, the males of gray and other tree squirrel species have been observed actually biting off the testicles of competing males.

Once paired, copulation is short, generally lasting less than than thirty seconds, after which mates go their separate ways. Males will attempt to breed again with as many partners as possible, but mated females will breed with other partners only until they become pregnant, which they appear to realize instinctively. After being impregnated, females form a mucous plug within their vaginal cavities that blocks further entry by sperm, and reject further sexual advances.

Gestation lasts an average 44 days, with two to four kits born in an elevated leaf-lined nest in a hollow tree. Young are born naked (altricial) but whiskered (vibrissal), each weighing about 4 ounces. Newborns nurse almost constantly for the first 7 weeks, and their mothers remain with them in the nest except for short outings to eat, drink, and relieve themselves. During these brief periods the young are left alone and may fall prey to raccoons, weasels, and predatory birds (especially small owls) that are capable of entering the den opening, but nursing female squirrels will fight viciously in defense of their offspring, and predation is usually minimal. Still, a mother never wanders far from her young, and her territory may shrink as much as 50% while the young are suckling.

During the nursing period, mother squirrels may move their young to different nesting locations as the situation demands. In cold months the nests are always in an enclosed den, but in warm weather young may be nursed in an open dish-shaped nest of sticks and leaves located in the crotch of a high tree limb. By 10 weeks of age the young will have become identical to adults, and are weaned, after which the family separates and mothers provide no more maternal care. Adult size and mass are reached at 9 months.

Behavior

With the exception of flying squirrels, which are nocturnal, all tree squirrels are active during daylight (diurnal), with peak activity occurring about 2 hours after sunrise, and 2 to 5 hours prior to sunset, depending on the season. They avoid activity during the heat of the day in summer, resting in loafing platforms made from sticks and leaves and located in overhead branches. Unlike maternal nests, loafing platforms are flatter and less concave because they don't have to contain youngsters that might fall out of a nest with lower sides. Loafing platforms are often indicative of their builder's age, with those that are more haphazardly constructed usually being made by younger, less experienced animals.

Male and female gray squirrels are virtually identical in color and size, but the activities of an individual can provide clues to its sex. Generally, males are more active in autumn and winter, when food, territory, and mates motivate them to be alert for competitors and more defensive. Females tend to be more active during the summer months, when they must work to regain the energy lost while rearing the previous spring's litter, and to put on fat needed for the coming autumn mating season.

While a number of sometimes widely differing estimates have been made of how much acreage is required to support a healthy population of gray squirrels, how large or small a territory must be is ultimately determined by the availability of resources. A single city block can be home to a half-dozen of the animals so long as sufficient food, water, and trees are available, and in urban parks, where they receive regular handouts from humans, population densities may be even higher.

In fact, urban and residential areas have proved to be so attractive to gray squirrels that a small pest removal industry has sprung up in response to their invasion of attics, ventilation ducts, and other places where their presence brings them into conflict with the human population. The problem has become severe among transplanted populations in Great Britain, where gray squirrels are ranked second only to the Norway rat (*Rattus norvegicus*) in terms of property destruction.

Despite their status as pests in some areas, gray and other squirrels have a strong following among wildlife enthusiasts, and squirrel-watching has become nearly as popular as bird-watching. Gray and fox squirrels are also very popular with small game hunters, and represent millions of dollars in revenue to state governments and the sport hunting industry each year.

Woodchuck (*Marmota monax*)

Largest of the squirrel family, the woodchuck and its close relatives, the yellow-bellied marmot, hoary marmot, and Olympic marmot, are ground-dwelling burrowers that lack the bushy tail associated with tree squirrels. This species gets its common name from the Cree Indian word *woochuk,* which that tribe used to describe all marmots, but the woodchuck retained it because its burrows are most often found near forests.

Probably best known as the "groundhog" that emerges from hibernation each year on February 2 to predict when winter will end, the woodchuck is the most populous marmot species in North America. Because nearly all its habits and characteristics are shared by other marmots, the information given here about woodchucks is generally applicable to all species.

Woodchuck (Marmota monax).

Geographic Range

The range of *M. monax* extends from the Atlantic to the Pacific coast across North America, extending in a line to the north from New Brunswick, across the southern shore of Hudson Bay, through the Yukon Territory and into central Alaska. The southern boundaries extend from Virginia to Arkansas, and northwest to British Columbia. Being burrowers, they will not be found above the Arctic Circle where permafrost prevents digging, although more than a decade of study has shown that

Scat: Elongated and irregular in diameter, usually tapered at one or both ends, with plant fibers in evidence. Dark brown to black in color, lightening with age. Length 2 to more than 4 inches.

Coloration: Dark brown to nearly black along the dorsal region and sides, interspersed with coarser guard hairs that are banded with alternating red and yellow, tipped with white. Underbelly paler. Head and feet much darker. Tail dark-colored, much shorter in comparison to tree squirrels.

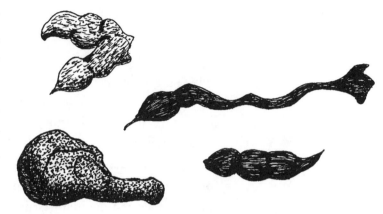

Marmot scat.

There is one annual molt from late May to September, which begins at the tail and progresses forward. The feet are black and plantigrade. The woodchuck's long incisors are white or nearly white, lacking the dark yellow pigmentation of other large rodents like porcupines or beavers.

Sign: Burrow entrances 10 to 14 inches in diameter dug into knolls and hillsides, sometimes beneath the roots of standing trees, and occasionally into and under a hole in the trunk of a standing hollow tree. The woodchuck also possesses three nipple-like anal (perineal) scent glands that secrete a musky odor, and trees, stumps, or other prominent objects around den entrances will often be scented.

Vocalizations: Woodchucks are often vocal, particularly when alarmed, which explains its nickname, "whistle-pig." The alarm cry is a single loud, shrill whistle, often preceded by a squirrel-like bark. The call used to attract mates, to warn intruders impinging on its territory, or from mothers calling young to the safety of the burrow, is a loud whistle followed by a less piercing call, and ending with a series of softer whistles that cannot be heard except at close range. Teeth grinding, chattering, and even doglike growls are common when woodchucks are cornered by a predator.

Lifespan: Young woodchucks are preyed on by most carnivores and predatory birds, but those that reach adulthood may live up to 6 years in the wild, or up to 10 years in captivity.

Diet

Woodchucks are mostly herbivorous grazers, preferring clovers, alfalfa, plantains, grasses, and most succulent ground plants during the summer months, but subsisting for short periods on the bark and buds of wild cherry, sumac, and other shrubs in early spring, before favored food plants are available. Poplar, cottonwood, and aspens are of particular importance because they provide food in the form of bark, buds, and leaves throughout the woodchuck's active time of year.

Like most sciurids, woodchucks and other marmots will also eat an occasional bird egg, grasshopper, snail, or small tree frog, and probably the young of most small rodents. These minor predations appear to be opportunistic in nature. Marmots aren't known to eat carrion, but they will gnaw shed antlers and bones for the nutrients contained in them.

Because the geographic range and habitat of the woodchuck encompasses most of the richest farming areas in North America, this species more than any other marmot has incurred the ire of farmers. Lands cleared for planting provide good habitat, and crops like alfalfa, clover, wheat, and especially corn are relished by woodchucks that can eat in excess of 1.5 pounds per animal per day, breaking down and killing plants while they feed.

In late summer, the woodchucks begin to feed more urgently. Each animal needs to gain about 25% of its body weight in a layer of fat that will insulate and sustain its body through the coming winter. During this period before winter snows send it into its burrow, a woodchuck becomes especially territorial and protective of the food resources it contains. Trespassers, especially yearlings wandering in search of their own territories, will be decisively driven off as green food plants become more scarce with shortening and cooling days.

Mating Habits

Breeding takes place in early spring, usually within 2 weeks after the woodchucks emerge from hibernation in late March or April. Adults are normally solitary, but the territories of adult males will typically overlap those of several females whose territories surround their own. This arrangement, which is seen in most animals, permits established males to make contact with receptive females without trespassing onto the territories of other males. When two males do compete, the battles consist of boxing and matches in which both contenders stand erect on their hind feet, slapping and biting one another until the weaker animal withdraws.

Females are believed to be monoestrous, and take only one mate per breeding season. Males stay in their mates' dens for about 1 week—the only time these normally solitary animals are social—before leaving to seek out another female. After a gestation period of approximately 32 days, females give birth to litters of one to nine naked and blind young, with five being the average litter size, in April or May. Newborns weigh about 26 grams, and measure about 4 inches long.

Females have four pairs of teats and nurse their young from a standing position, staying with them almost constantly for their first 2 weeks. At 3 weeks, the young begin crawling about inside the den, and at 4 weeks they open their eyes. By 5 weeks, the young woodchucks are fully active and begin exploring for short distances around the den entrance, scurrying back inside if the mother issues an alarm whistle.

Young woodchucks are weaned at 6 weeks, but may remain with their mother until July or August, when she forces them to disperse. Yearlings must find or excavate their own burrows after leaving their mothers, and will hibernate alone in their first winter. Females will probably mate on emerging from their dens the following spring, but competition may force young males to wait until the next spring, after they've established their own territories.

Behavior

Woodchucks are the most solitary marmot species, and both sexes are generally hostile toward one another on meeting (agonistic). Battles are usually of short duration and relatively bloodless, but established adults will not tolerate trespassers. Reports of several individuals sharing a den stem from observations made during the short mating period when males occupy the dens of their mates, or of nearly grown offspring denning with their mother.

Being diurnal, woodchucks are most often observed during the day, although some have been known to become partly nocturnal if harassed by humans. The stereotypical image of this species is that of an animal standing erect, forelimbs held tightly to the front of its body, as it surveys the surrounding area. While that posture is common with animals that have been alerted, woodchucks prefer to spend most of their time on all fours, foraging and feeding. When not feeding, the animals are fond of sunbathing and cleaning their fur in the open, but never far from the den entrance.

If alarmed, a woodchuck will quickly retreat into its den, turning to face outward once inside. This is a defensive position from which the marmot can bite and claw with surprising ferocity should a predator attempt to dig it out. The sharp incisors and viciousness of a large woodchuck defending itself is adequate to convince most predators, including badgers and coyotes, to seek easier prey, but black and brown bears are often successful in digging them free.

Like most burrowing animals, a woodchuck's den always has at least one, sometimes as many as five, escape exits several yards from its main entrance, but that may be of limited value when the animal digging inward to get it is a large bear. Bears, like badgers, are often accompanied by a coyote when digging after marmots; the coyote stands guard over these escape holes while the bear digs, waiting to snap up the den's occupant if it pops out. That cooperative tactic is effective when the prey is a smaller ground squirrel, but a large marmot may prove to be more than a coyote can handle, and if a woodchuck can fight its way to a nearby tree, it will probably escape both enemies. None of the marmot species are as agile at climbing as their tree squirrel cousins, but all can climb trees well enough to escape most predators, if they get a head start.

Like other marmots and ground squirrels, the woodchuck is a true hibernator, spending the cold winter months in a comalike slumber within a grass-lined sleeping chamber deep inside its den. The animals enter the den to stay prior to the first permanent snowfall, usually in late November in the north, in December in the southern part of the species' range. Once inside and asleep, the marmot's body undergoes remarkable physiological changes; its body temperature falls from a normal 97°F to 40°F, and its heart rate slows from about 100 beats per minute to just 4 beats per minute. It remains in this state until warming days cause it to emerge in April, although its deep slumber appears to become lighter as spring approaches.

The animals do not ritually step out of their dens to see if they cast a shadow on February 2, but large gatherings of humans, like the annual Groundhog Day festival held in Punxsutawney, Pennsylvania, usually create enough commotion to awaken a hibernating woodchuck. This bit of American folklore, which coincides with Candlemas Day, probably has its roots in an Old World belief that sunny skies which allowed the European badger (*meles meles*) to see its shadow heralded another 6 weeks of wintry weather.

THE HARE AND RABBIT FAMILY (FAMILY LEPORIDAE)

Rabbits (genus *Sylvilagus*) are sometimes confused with hares (genus *Lepus*), but there are a number of physical traits that distinguish the two: Rabbits are generally smaller, with shorter ears and less powerful hind legs; hares are more at home in open areas, where they escape predators by outrunning them, while rabbits prefer brushy habitats where they can hide; hares give birth to fully furred young in relatively open places, while rabbit newborns are born naked in a sheltering burrow or nest, and require a more prolonged period of maternal care. Both are prolific breeders, with reproductive rates adapted to counter heavy predation from numerous carnivores.

Despite some physical similarities, these animals are not rodents, as once thought, but members of the order Lagomorpha, a group that also includes the even more rodentlike pikas. One defining difference between lagomorphs and true rodents is a second smaller and shorter pair of incisor teeth directly in back of the chisel-like upper incisors, which serve as a kind of cutting board when the jaw is closed. (See illustration page 27.) This dental arrangement gives the animals a very sharp scissorlike cutting action when nibbling fibrous sedges, permitting them to chop tough cellulose into very fine pieces that digest more easily.

Lagomorphs are also remarkable in that males carry their scrotum ahead of the penis, instead of behind it, a characteristic seen in no other mammals except marsupials.

Currently, there are eighty species of lagomorphs worldwide, all of them categorized in thirteen genera belonging to two families, family Leporidae (rabbits and hares) and family Ochotonidae (pikas). Native populations of lagomorphs are found on all continents except Antarctica, southern South America, and Australia, although introduced populations of rabbits in Australia have thrived and have long been part of that continent's ecosystem.

Snowshoe Hare (*Lepus americanus*)

Also known as the varying hare because individuals in the northern parts of its range grow a white coat in winter, the snowshoe hare gets its common name from oversized hind feet that give it the greater weight displacement in deep snows and the muddy marshes that are this species' preferred habitat. One of the smallest hares, the snowshoe "jackrabbit" is a vital prey species for many carnivores, especially the lynx and bobcat.

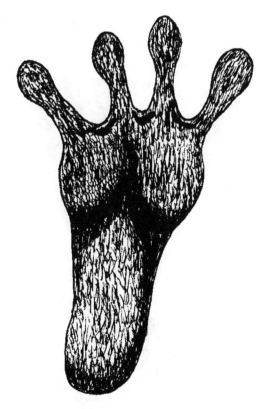

Snowshoe hare (Lepus americanus). *Snowshoe, or Varying, hare in its all-white winter coat. Snowshoe hares in southern latitudes may remain brown all year.*

Snowshoe hare left hind foot. Long, well-furred feet and widely splayed toes give the snowshoe hare an unexcelled ability to run atop snow.

Geographic Range

Snowshoe hares inhabit the northern United States from New England through New York, Michigan, northern Wisconsin, northern Minnesota, and northern North Dakota. To the south, their range extends only along mountain ranges that are snow-covered in winter, to northern California along the Cascade mountains, to Colorado along the Rockies, through West Virginia and Virginia along the Allegheny and Appalachian mountain ranges. To the north, snowshoes inhabit nearly all of Canada and Alaska south of the Arctic Circle. Perhaps notably, the snowshoe hare's northern range butts up to, but rarely overlaps, that of the Arctic hare (*Lepus arcticus*), with a precise demarcation line between the ranges of either species.

Habitat

Unlike rabbits, which tend toward thickets and prefer to hide from danger, snowshoe hares prefer more open areas where they can rely on powerful hindquarters and large feet to speed them out of reach of predators at speeds in excess of 25 miles per hour. Relatively open bogs, marshes, and swamps are preferred during daylight hours, but at night the hares venture out to feed in more open areas, like fields and meadows, river and lake shorelines, aging clearcuts, and roadside ditches.

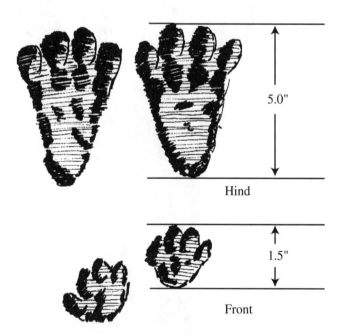

5.0"

Hind

1.5"

Front

Snowshoe hare tracks. Tracks and patterns similar to those of other rabbit and hare species, except hind paws are especially wide and well furred, making L. americanus *exceptionally well adapted to life in snowy habitats.*

Physical Characteristics

Mass: 2 to more than 4 pounds, less than half the weight of larger hare species; about the same weight as an eastern cottontail rabbit, with which the snowshoe shares much of its range.

Body: Rabbitlike, humped back, long powerful hind legs, disproportionately long and wide hind feet. Body length 15 to 20.5 inches. Head round, muzzle blunt, large eyes at either side of the head. Ears shorter than those of most other hares to lessen loss of heat from them in cold temperatures, ear length roughly 3 inches. Males, called "bucks," are slightly smaller than females, or "does," which is unusual among most mammals, but typical among leporids.

Tail: Dark gray to black on top, whitish below, 1 to 2 inches long.

Tracks: Four toes on front and hind feet. Forefeet comparatively round, 1.5 to 2 inches long; hind feet very large, with widely spread toes, 3 to 4.5 inches long. In winter, tracks may be obscured by a heavy coat of fur on the underside. Hind feet print ahead of forefeet at a casual hop, leaving a track pattern that looks like paired exclamation points (!!), similar to those of a fox squirrel, but much larger. A set of all four tracks measures 10 to more than 16 inches. Distance between track sets may be more than 15 feet, with longer leaps denoting a faster pace.

Scat: Typical of all rabbits and hares; generally marble- or egg-shaped, occasionally acorn-shaped, with spherical forms usually indicating a diet of drier, less succulent vegetation. Diameter about 0.5 inch. Color usually dark brown when fresh, becoming lighter colored and more sawdustlike with age. Scat pellets are generally found in groups of a half-dozen or more.

Coloration: Brown in summer, slightly grizzled, with a darker dorsal line, and longer fur than the cottontail. Underside whitish, face brown, ear tips black. Often with a white patch on top of head. At the start of winter in snow country the animal's coat turns entirely white except for black tips on the ears. Snowshoes in Washington and Oregon normally don't exhibit this photoperiodic color change, remaining brown all year, and in the Adirondack mountains there is a population that remains black (melanistic) all year.

14.0"

11.0"

40.0" - 70.0"

24.0"

Slow Hop

Fast Run

Hare and rabbit track patterns.

Under normal conditions, snowshoe hares are known for their seasonal molts. The winter molt usually begins in November as a patchy, mottled coat of white spots that become larger until the animal is completely white, a process that takes about 70 days to complete. It's interesting to note that snowshoes possess two separate sets of hair follicles, one of which grows only white hairs, and the other set growing the brown and

Scat pellets typical of rabbits and hares. Pellets are fibrous, usually round, and deposited randomly in groups of six to more than twelve pellets.

gray hairs of the summer coat. Color phases are regulated by daylight, not temperature, which during abnormally warm winters can result in white hares when there is no camouflaging snow on the ground.

Sign: Typical of all rabbits and hares: stripped, barkless shrubs like sumac, dogwood, and willow during the winter months. Neatly clipped grasses and ground plants in summer. Trails are often regularly used and well-packed; trails in snow may be packed to a depth of more than 1 foot, permitting high-speed travel in troughs too narrow for predators to use.

Vocalizations: Normally silent. Mothers purr to young while nursing. Newborns whimper and whine. Most remarkable is the high-pitched alarm cry, a prolonged squeal that is normally heard only when the hare has fallen into the grip of a predator. In all cases the calls of a hare is generally lower toned than those of a rabbit. When battling over territory, two hares may growl and hiss. Also heard occasionally is the thumping of a hind foot being pounded repeatedly against the earth, especially when the animal suspects danger, but can't locate its source; an attempt to entice a predator into revealing itself.

Lifespan: Few snowshoe hares die of old age, but become prey to a host of predators as soon as their reflexes slow, and many don't reach adulthood. Average lifespan 3 or 4 years.

Diet

The snowshoe hare's diet is more broadly varied than other leporids, but normally vegetarian. The animals graze on green grasses, vetches, asters, jewelweed, wild strawberry, pussy-toes, dandelions, clovers, and horsetails, as well as the buds of aspen, poplar, birch, and willow. In winter, snowshoe hares forage on buds, twigs, bark, and the tips of evergreen twigs. If plant foods are scarce, they may eat carrion, and have been known to raid traps baited for carnivores to get the meat in them.

A notable trait among leporids is their need to re-ingest feces to thoroughly digest them. Because much of the vegetation a hare or rabbit eats is comprised of tough cellulose, and because most of the animals' digestion processes are contained in the lower gut, foods must be eaten and digested twice to extract all the nutrients from them. As with cud-chewing ruminants, this practice, known as "cecal fermentation," permits the animals to quickly ingest food plants from a place where feeding may be hazardous, then retire to a safer location where foods can be completely digested at their leisure.

Despite being considered food by so many carnivorous species, snowshoes are among nature's best survivors, a fact that can be seen in the lack of fat on their bodies. With a broad diet that encompasses almost every type of vegetation, as well as carrion when times get hard, the hares have little need to carry food reserves on their bodies, but they do need to maintain a body that's as lean and muscular as possible to escape fleet-footed predators like the coyote. Mountain men of old, for whom hares and rabbits were a staple winter food, often found themselves suffering from "rabbit starvation" by winter's end, a sometimes serious form of malnutrition that forced their bodies to consume muscle mass in lieu of fats.

Mating Habits

Breeding season of the snowshoe hare runs throughout the summer months, beginning in March, when the males' testicles descend, and extending through August, when the testicles again retract and become dormant. Males pursue females by their pheromonal scents, frequently congregating around receptive does in groups.

Mating contests between breeding males resemble boxing matches in which both contenders rise on hind legs and bat at the muzzles of one another with sharp-clawed forefeet. If one of the combatants is knocked onto its back, the powerful, clawed hind feet are used to kick and scratch against an adversary's underside. Despite the apparent ferocity of these battles, they usually end quickly, when the weaker animal withdraws, and are seldom seriously injurious to either party.

Snowshoe does are polyestrous, coming into heat whenever they aren't pregnant throughout the summer months, and both genders engage in sex with different mates almost indiscriminately (polygynandrous). This seemingly lascivious behavior helps to insure that these prolific breeders have a strong, widely varied gene pool.

Gestation takes about 35 days, with litters of two to eight fully furred precocial young being birthed in a makeshift nest atop the ground, but sometimes in the recently abandoned burrow of a fox or coyote. The young hares are able to run within 2 hours of birth, and begin feeding on vegetation their first day. Mothers nurse their litters for about 30 days, but will probably become pregnant again before they're weaned. Adult does may birth as many as four litters per summer, and newborn females may begin mating almost as soon as they've been weaned. The species' rapid reproduction rate makes it resistant to heavy predation from the many meat-eaters that hunt it, and makes it unlikely that snowshoe hares will become a major concern for conservationists.

Behavior

Snowshoe hares are solitary animals, but population densities are often high enough to force them to live together. Under ideal conditions, an adult's territory may encompass as much as 18 acres, but when populations peak, the amount of land an individual can claim may shrink to a fraction of that size.

Actual population densities may range from 1 to as many as 10,000 individuals per square mile, with numbers typically increasing steadily for a period of about 9 years, then drastically falling off in the following year. Direct causes for this sudden decline, which appears to be a normal phenomenon with this species, include sudden epidemics of pneumonia, severe fungal infections, salmonella, and tularemia. The root cause of these plaguelike illnesses is most likely malnutrition brought on by depletion of food resources. A secondary effect of the snowshoe's cyclic decline is a sudden decline in populations of the lynx, which relies heavily on hares in its own diet, about 1 year later.

Notably, the greatest fluctuations in snowshoe hare populations occur in north-western Canada, and the least in Colorado's Rocky Mountains. Explanations for this phenomenon include greater diversity among predator and prey species in the warmer regions, while colder climates tend to less varied, with relationships between hunter and hunted being more critically symbiotic.

Lepus americanus isn't classified as nocturnal, but the hares do show a reluctance to be active in sunlight. In clear summer weather the animals are most likely to feed and breed during the hours between dusk and dawn, but may also be seen foraging at mid-day when skies are overcast or rainy.

Snowshoes have very good directional hearing, a keen sense of smell, and large protruding eyeballs positioned at either side of the head that permit them to detect ap-proaching danger, but they tend to freeze, relying on their natural camouflage, unless a predator's body language reveals that it has seen them. When a hare does run from dan-ger, it zigzags through underbrush at high speed, changing direction instantly to make itself hard to follow visually, as well as physically. Like whitetail deer and rabbits, the hares rely on a maze of trails, each scented with frequent scat deposits, to confuse the most acute sense of smell.

Although they can run fast and erratically enough to outmaneuver predators in thick cover, snowshoe hares must escape quickly, because they tire after a few hundred yards, while their main enemies can maintain top running speed for a mile or more. When it begins to slow from exhaustion, a hare will freeze and remain motionless, hop-ing to go undetected by its pursuer. At this point the hare is in real danger if the pursuit continues, and is likely to be caught. If open water is nearby, a hare in imminent danger will probably try to swim away from a predator.

On warm summer evenings, snowshoe hares, like rabbits, are frequently seen rolling about on the gravel shoulders of rural roads. These dust baths are taken to loosen shedding fur and to help dislodge fleas and mites. The animals sometimes engage in this behavior in early morning, but most dust baths are taken in the evening because more parasites are contracted while sleeping during the daylight hours.

Eastern Cottontail Rabbit *(Sylvilagus floridanus)*

Immortalized by nursery school fables and songs like "Here Comes Peter Cottontail," this is the most common and most recognized member of *Sylvilagus*, the genus of rabbits. Like all rabbits, it differs from its close cousins, the hares, by having shorter, more rounded ears, a generally smaller body, and shorter, less muscular hind legs. Also like other rabbits, and unlike hares, the cottontail is a fast but short-distance runner that prefers to elude its enemies in thick cover, rather than outrunning them across open terrain.

Because the cottontail is so common, and because its physical traits, behaviors, and diet are generally representative of every rabbit species, it has been selected to represent all members of genus *Sylvilagus*.

Geographic Range

Cottontails have the widest distribution of any rabbit in North America. To the north, the species ranges to the Canadian border, ranging northward across it only a few miles in southern Manitoba and Quebec. Except for Maine, its range covers all of the eastern

Eastern cottontail rabbit (Sylvilagus floridanus).

United States from the Atlantic coast to North Dakota, and south to Texas, extending through Mexico into Central America and northwestern South America. To the west, cottontail populations are found along the Rocky Mountains from Mexico through eastern Arizona and into Nevada.

Habitat

Perhaps the most adaptable of all lagomorphs, the eastern cottontail seems to be at home in almost any brushy or forested environment that provides a source of drinking water and plenty of cover in which to hide. Historically, the eastern cottontail has inhabited deserts, swamps, coniferous and deciduous forests, and rainforests. Currently, the eastern cottontail seems to prefer edge environments between woods and open terrain, including meadows, orchards and farmlands, hedgerows, and clearcut forests with young trees and brush. The eastern cottontail's range extends into that of six other rabbits, and six species of hares, although, like all rabbits, it prefers less open terrain than hares.

Physical Characteristics

Mass: 2 to more than 4 pounds.

Body: Typically rabbitlike, with high rounded back, elongated ears 2 to 3 inches long, muscular hindquarters, and long hind feet. Head rounded, with short muzzle, flat face, and large dark eyes located at either side. Body length 14 to 18 inches.

Tail: Brown on top, fluffy cotton-white below. Length 1.5 to 2.5 inches.

Tracks: Four toes on all four feet. Forefeet nearly round, 1 to 1.5 inches long. Hind feet elongated, 3 to 4 inches long. Claws generally show prominently in tracks.

Scat: Pelletlike, usually spherical or egg-shaped, sometimes flattened discs, usually less than 0.5 inch in diameter. Color usually dark brown, becoming lighter and more fibrous looking with age. Pellets often deposited in groups of six or more.

Coloration: Brown, grizzled coat interspersed with gray and black hairs, generally uniform over back, sides, top of tail, and head, except for a reddish patch on the nape of the neck. Bottom of tail white and cottonlike. Ears black-tipped. Underside lighter, buff-colored. Cottontails undergo two molts per year: the spring molt occurs from mid-April to mid-July, and leaves a short summer coat that's predominantly brown; from mid-September through October, the brown coat is shed for a longer and warmer grayish winter coat.

Sign: Neatly nipped-off flower and plant stems. Smooth-barked shrubs stripped of bark down to the cambium layer show where rabbits browsed in winter. Oblong "forms" of

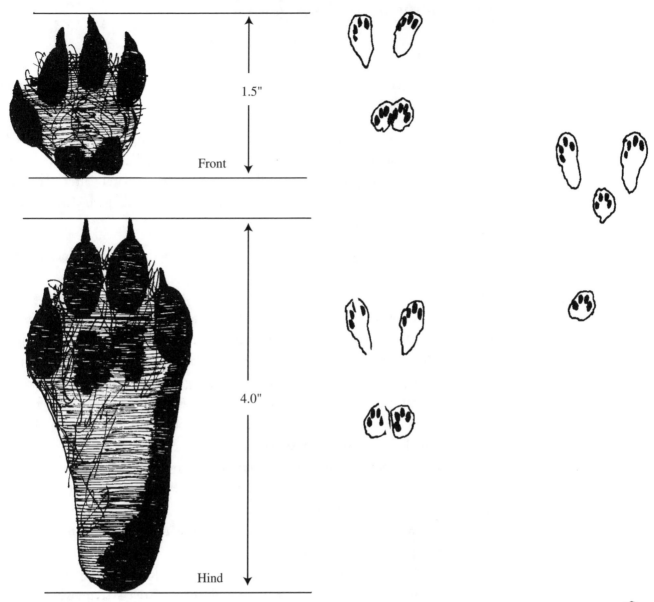

1.5"

Front

4.0"

Hind

Cottontail rabbit tracks.

Hopping

Running

Eastern cottontail (Sylvilagus floridanus) *track patterns.*

pressed-down grasses, snow, and sand where a rabbit lay for an extended period while resting or sleeping.

Vocalizations: Normally silent. Vocalizations include a bleating distress call intended to startle a predator into hesitating briefly and giving a surprised rabbit the chance to flee. Bucks (males) chatter and squeal loudly during and immediately after copulation. Nursing does purr while suckling young, and sometimes emit a sharp alarm bark if an intruder approaches too closely to their litters.

Lifespan: Up to 5 years, generally no more than 2 years because of heavy predation.

Diet

The eastern cottontail is believed to be strictly vegetarian, with roughly 50% of its summer diet consisting of green grasses, and the balance comprised of wild strawberry plants, clovers, alfalfa, and a broad variety of other ground plants. Its double row of upper incisors allows for chopping tough cellulose fibers into fine clippings that are easier to digest.

In habitats where winter snows make ground plants unavailable, the cottontail diet turns to more woody browse, especially the smooth bark of saplings and shrubs, like red osier dogwood, staghorn sumac, rose, lilac, and young polar, birch, and aspen. They also eat the buds and tender twig ends of most trees, including pines and cedars. Deepening snows actually work for the rabbits by allowing them to reach higher up to get bark and twigs that were previously inaccessible.

Like other rabbits and hares, digestion of these tough plant materials is made possible by a process called cecal fermentation, a natural variation of the cud-chewing process seen in ruminant species. Except that with cecal fermentation the mass of ingested plant material passes completely through the digestive system, where it's partially broken down, and is expelled through the anus as green pellets. The predigested pellets are then re-eaten and passed through the digestive system a second time, where the cellulose is completely broken down and nutrients extracted for use by the rabbit's body. Although repulsive to humans, cecal fermentation, like cud-chewing, permits rabbits and hares to quickly eat plant foods in places that are inherently dangerous for them to stay, then retire to a more secure location to complete the digestive process.

Although generally considered nocturnal, cottontails may be seen foraging at any time of day in places where they feel safe. In summer, they tend to sleep away the heat of the day in cool underground burrows, sometimes in shaded brushy thickets, but the colder temperatures and increased energy needs of winter often force them to forage throughout the day. In every season, feeding activities are somewhat crepuscular, peaking in the first 3 hours after sunrise, and again in the first 2 hours after sunset.

Mating Habits

Like all rabbits and hares, cottontails exhibit remarkable reproductive powers—an indication of their status as food for so many species of meat-eaters.

As with other lagomorphs, cottontails reach sexual maturity at 2 to 3 months of age, and many of those born during the summer-long mating season are likely to mate before the coming autumn. In fact, an estimated 25% of the rabbits born in a summer will be the offspring of juveniles who are themselves less than 6 months old.

The start of mating season coincides with the spring molt, when adults begin shedding their grayish winter coats for the brown summer coats. The onset of breeding is also influenced by lengthening days (photoperiodic), warming temperatures, and the availability of green foods.

Bucks, whose testicles are retracted and inert during the winter months, become sexually ready in mid-February, although does aren't normally ready to breed until mid-March. This interval gives adult males a period in which to seek out prospective mates. Both genders remain sexually active until late August or September, with mating season ending earlier for individuals in places where winters come earlier.

Like other rabbits and hares, cottontail does are polyestrous, accepting a number of mates throughout the summer mating period, and birthing as many as four litters in a single season. There is no lasting bond between mates, and each go their separate ways after breeding. This seemingly promiscuous breeding habit helps to insure a varied gene pool within a species possessed of such prolific reproductive abilities.

Prior to mating, cottontails perform a curious courtship ritual in which the buck chases a doe until she tires, and eventually turns to face him. The pair then rise on hind legs and spar briefly with the forepaws, after which both crouch on all fours, nose to nose, and the male jumps straight upward to a height of about 2 feet. The female replies by jumping upward herself, and both rabbits may repeat the action several times. The exact purpose of this jumping behavior is uncertain, but is probably used as an indication of the fitness of either animal to mate.

After being impregnated, does spurn further advances from males. Gestation lasts an average 30 days, at the end of which the mother-to-be retires to a sheltered burrow or hutch, which may be an abandoned fox den, a natural enclosure under the branches of a fallen tree, or sometimes under the floor of an outbuilding. There, in a grass-lined nest that has been further insulated with fur nipped from the mother's underbelly and from around her four pairs of nipples, she gives birth to four or five—sometimes as many as eight—naked and blind (altricial) young. Newborns weigh about 1 ounce (25 to 35 grams), and require almost constant care. The young grow fast, gaining more than 2 grams per day, and by 5 days have opened their eyes.

By 2 weeks of age, the young are fully furred and have begun to venture outside the nest to feed on vegetation. At this point the mother is nursing them only about twice a day, and may have already become pregnant with her next litter. Weaning oc-curs at about 20 days, and the young rabbits, who may have become intolerant of one another, disperse. Those born in spring or early summer are likely to sire or birth their own litter, perhaps two litters, before summer's end.

Behavior

Eastern cottontails are popular with sport hunters who typically use dogs to flush and pursue them into shotgun range, and rabbit meat is very palatable. Although not a long-distance runner, an adult cottontail can exceed 18 miles per hour through thick brush, leaping 12 feet or more, and instantly changing direction by as much as 90 degrees. The flaw in their escape habits, which are often effective against predators, is that the animals tend to run in a circle, coming back to cross their own trails and thereby confuse the noses of wild carnivores. Human hunters have learned to exploit this by using dogs to chase rabbits back to where they stand waiting to shoot them.

Cottontails are also a staple of the fur trade. The pelt is silky and thick, and tanned plews are often sold in backcountry gift shops. Other uses include the trim around boot tops, parka hoods, and mittens, and sometimes as an entire fur coat. Rabbit fur isn't water-repellent or as long-lived as beaver, ermine, or mink, but it is plentiful, inex-pensive, and nice to the touch, and there is a market for skins.

Cottontails are not well-liked by farmers, gardeners, or landscapers. Their sum-mer feeding habits and reproductive capacity can result in tremendous damage to crops, while winter-browsing of shrubs and fruit trees makes them a pest to golf courses and orchards. The problem is often exacerbated, or even caused, by a historical reluc-tance to permit the cottontail's natural enemies to live near human habitation.

Except for brief mating encounters during the summer mating season, eastern cottontails are solitary animals that tend to be intolerant of one another. Territorial sizes are dependent on food and other resources, but generally encompass between 5 and 8 acres. Males, which normally claim larger territories than females, tend to extend their claims to include the territories of local does during the summer.

Nearly every predator large enough to kill a rabbit considers the cottontail to be prey. Hawks, owls, and eagles hunt them from the air, skunks and other weasels prey on the young in their burrows, bobcats pounce on them from hiding, and the speedy coyote chases them through the underbrush. The rabbits' best defense is freezing against or under camouflaging foliage, where a predator can't see its body, and a maze of seemingly random trails can make finding it by scent very difficult at best. Nevertheless, most cottontails won't survive into their third year, but reproduc-tive rates are high enough to insure that this species is unlikely to be threatened by overpredation.

OTHER PAWED ANIMALS

Raccoon (Procyon lotor)

Raccoons are members of the Procyonid family, which also includes the ringtail and coati of the southwestern United States and Mexico, as well as the lesser pandas of Asia. All procyonids have five toes on each foot, all are excellent climbers, and all are omnivores.

Few animals are better recognized than the raccoon, with its distinctive bandit-masked face and striped tail. Cartoons and caricatures of the raccoon usually depict it as a thief, an allusion to both the animal's bold penchant for stealing from humans, and to its masked face. Although considered prey by raptors and larger carnivores when they're young, an adult coon is ferocious when cornered, and only the largest predators are willing to tackle one. This game and aggressive nature, which is also seen in the wolverine and badger, is a good defense against larger predators whose objective is to kill their food with as little effort or danger to themselves as possible. Unfortunately, that nature also makes raccoons willing to invade rural and residential areas to raid gardens, knock over garbage cans, and steal an occasional chicken.

Aside from causing property damage, raccoons are harmless to people unless cornered. One danger they do pose is rabies, a disease which some of them contract and die from each spring, especially when local populations are too high. Raccoons can also be hazardous to pets, inflicting sometimes serious wounds to dogs, and the species is well-known for drawing hunting dogs into deep water, where the coon then climbs onto the dog's head and drowns it.

Raccoon (Procyon lotor).

Geographic Range

Excepting the treeless Great Plains Basin and the desert southwest, raccoons are found throughout the United States from the Pacific to the Atlantic. To the north their range extends only a little north of Canada's southern border. To the south raccoons range far into Mexico.

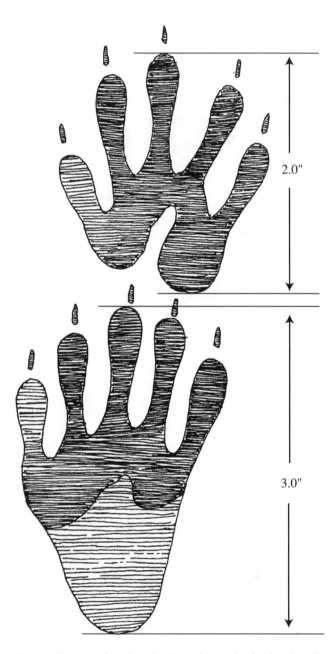

2.0"

3.0"

Raccoon (Procyon lotor) *tracks. Note plantigrade (flat-footed) walk, typical of powerful species not designed to run fast.*

Habitat

Raccoons are among the most intelligent and adaptable of mammals, but their preferred habitat will always include trees large enough to climb in search of a good observation point or to escape predators—especially domestic dogs, which are more likely to attack a raccoon than are wild carnivores like coyotes or bobcats.

Raccoon habitat will also always have a source of open water. The animals are superb swimmers, able to easily outdistance most enemies across lakes or rivers, but more importantly they require a water source that provides small prey like crayfish, clams, small fish, and frogs.

Physical Characteristics

Mass: 12 to 48 pounds, with an occasional individual reaching 60 pounds or more in the far north.

Body: Built much like a bear, stocky, muscular, with a humped spine and thickly furred over a layer of insulating fat. Males are generally larger than females, but the largest individuals reported have been old females. Body length 23 to more than 38 inches, arched back 8 to more than 12 inches high. Head proportionally small with short pointed muzzle tipped by a black nose. Ears erect, large, and rounded at the tips.

Tail: Striped with alternating bands of darker fur, 7 to more than 14 inches long, roughly half as long as the animal's body.

Tracks: Easy to identify; five toes on all four feet, each toe tipped with an elongated fingernail-like claw. Toes are long and fingerlike, with four pointing forward, and a shorter thumblike toe extending to the inside, making it look very much like a human hand. Tips of the toes leave a bulbous impression just rearward of the claws. Forefoot length 2 to 3 inches.

Hind feet are flat-soled and elongated, indicating the plantigrade walk of a slow runner that has little to fear in its daily life. The general outline is somewhat human-shaped, like all plantigrade mammals, but has uniquely raccoon features that include four fingerlike toes pointing forward, each terminating in a bulbous tip and fingernail claw, and one shorter thumblike toe well to the rear of the others and pointing inward. Length 3 to 4 inches.

Procyon lotor's normal gait is a shuffling walk, much like a bear, in which soles of especially the hind feet tend to scrape the earth as they're brought forward, leaving scuff marks to the rear of the hind track. Hind prints generally register separately and beside front tracks at a relaxed walk. The bushy tail may brush over

Raccoon tracks in the damp sand of a streambank. Note different sizes.

tracks on sandy or dusty soils. Stride up to 2 feet between paired sets of front and hind prints, depending on terrain and an individual's size. Straddle 3 to 4 inches, but can reach 6 inches in large old animals, indicating the species' wide, powerfully built physique.

At a fast run that can reach 15 miles per hour on flat ground, the raccoon gait changes to the almost universal "rocking horse" pattern, in which forefeet are planted side-by-side to act as a pivot while the hind feet are brought forward on either side. When the hind feet make contact with earth, the coon springs forward, forefeet extended, and the gait repeats anew. At a fast run, the distance between sets of all four tracks may reach 3 feet.

Scat: Distinctive and easy to identify. Cylindrical and usually unsegmented, the same diameter throughout its length. Ends usually untapered and flat. Two to 3 inches long by up to 0.5 inch in diameter.

Coloration: The most obvious charateristics of the raccoon are its black mask around the eyes, and a bushy tail with up to ten black rings running circumferentially along its length. The pelage is grizzled, with fur color that varies from gray to reddish.

Sign: Shells of turtle eggs that have been excavated from buried nests along sandy lakeshores and eaten. Crayfish carapaces and emptied clamshells along the banks of rivers and ponds.

Vocalizations: Most common is a chirring sound, sometimes described as cooing, made when the animal is curious or generally relaxed. Territorial and mating sounds include screeches, snarls, and growls.

Lifespan: Raccoons have lived up to 16 years in captivity, but in the wild most don't make it past 4 years because of predation from birds of prey, land predators, and automobiles.

Diet

Like bears, raccoons are omnivorous and opportunistic, able to subsist on a broad variety of vegetation, insects, and other small animals. Most foods are obtained along or near shorelines, where the majority of scat and sign are found. As with bears, raccoons are particularly fond of calorie-rich berries, nuts, and fruits of all types, and in many habitats and seasons vegetation might make up most of the foods a raccoon eats.

To the consternation of gardeners and farmers, raccoons are very fond of corn, and the normally solitary animals are known to descend on cornfields in force, sometimes decimating an entire field when they break down stalks to get at ripening ears. The animals can also damage fruit trees and grape arbors by climbing to get at hanging fruit and knocking it to the ground.

Although poorly designed for chasing down prey, raccoons consume animal flesh whenever they can get it. The carnivorous portion of their diets typically include more invertebrates than vertebrates. Crayfish, grasshoppers and other insects, small rodents, frogs, birds and hatchling turtles are components of the raccoon's diet. Essentially, any small animal that can be taken with little effort or danger is prey. Carrion may also be eaten, but not with the same regularity or in the same volume as coyotes or other scavenging species.

Raccoons are also known for their habit of washing foods at the edges of waterways, a practice alluded to by its species name, *lotor,* which translates to "the washer." The purpose behind this practice was once a mystery, but is now known to be a sorting process in which the animal uses its extraordinarily sensitive fingerlike toes to separate inedible matter from its foods. Whereas many animals must simply swallow small prey bones and all, the raccoon can pick out and remove the parts it doesn't want to eat.

Mating Habits

Raccoons become sexually mature at 1 year, but males will probably not breed until 2 years because they need to first establish their own territories.

Mating season begins in late January and extends through early March, peaking in February. Populations in the far south may begin mating as early as December. Males travel to females from as far as 3 miles, attracted to them by pheromonal scents. Mating doesn't normally occur immediately, but is preceded by several days of courtship, during which males den with females.

Once impregnated, females reject further sexual overtures, and males go on their way, often to find another receptive female. Female raccoons are believed to take only one mate per breeding season.

After a gestation period of 60 to 70 days, females retire to a secluded leaf-lined den in a large hollow tree, under its roots, or sometimes in dry culverts and other manmade shelters. There the mother will give birth to litters of four to eight cubs in April or May, with larger litter sizes indicating healthy, well-fed females. Cubs weigh about 2 ounces at birth, and come into the world blind, deaf, and almost naked (altricial). Young open their eyes at 3 weeks and begin to move about the den. At 2 months they leave the den to explore, but remain close to the safety of its entrance because raccoon cubs are prey for most carnivores and predatory birds. During this delicate stage in their development the mother may move her cubs to an alternate den, carrying them one at a time by the nape of the neck. If a larger predator threatens, she will push her young up a tree, then follow them, much like a black bear. If caught by surprise or cornered, the female will defend her litter viciously enough to discourage most carnivores.

By 3 months the cubs will have been weaned, and begin foraging on their own for insects and other small food animals. The family remains together throughout the summer and following winter, but separate before the next spring mating season, when the mother will probably mate again. Males typically leave first, setting off to find their own territories, followed by female siblings who will likely take mates of their own in the coming breeding season.

Behavior

Except for mating and rearing young, raccoons are solitary creatures. The species is generally thought to be nocturnal, but in wild places where there are no humans or, especially, dogs, the animals may be seen foraging and hunting along shorelines at any time of day.

Raccoons are not true hibernators, but during periods of extreme cold or snow the animals may lay up in a den for a week or more until the weather breaks, living off a normally thick layer of body fat while conserving energy. Denned raccoons are normally alone, but mothers and cubs from the previous spring will den together, and courting pairs may stay together for up to 1 month prior to actually breeding.

Raccoons have highly developed tactile senses, and some researchers believe the sense of feel in their forepaws may be several times more acute than our own. What is known for sure is that raccoons possess the tactility needed to locate and catch snails, crayfish, and other underwater foods by feel alone. Along with that extraordinary sense of feel, a raccoon's handlike forepaws can grasp, pull, and tear with strength sufficient to pry open clams and remove the carapaces of crayfish, or even hatchling turtles.

An ability to grasp also makes the raccoon a good climber. Large smooth-barked trees like beech and sycamore can sometimes resist the animal's relatively dull claws, but rough-barked trees like maple and oak, or white pine are easy for it to climb. Raccoons lack the agility to pursue prey through treetops the way a fisher or pine marten can, and generally climb only to escape enemies. On rare occasions the animals have lost their grip and fallen, but are able to survive long falls of 30 feet or more with little or no injury to themselves.

P. lotor is also an adept swimmer, and frequently takes to the water to escape, especially when pursued by hunting dogs. They rarely swim unless motivated by danger, however, because coon fur lacks the repellent oils contained in the fur of aquatic mammals, and their coat becomes heavy when saturated. If a hunting dog should pursue a raccoon into water, the raccoon is notorious for turning and climbing onto its head, holding it underwater with its own weight, and sometimes drowning the dog.

Beaver (Castor canadensis)

This uniquely American aquatic rodent has played an important role in the development of North America. Its luxurious water repellent fur was in great demand by Old World society for more than 200 years, until overtrapping exterminated the species over much of its original range. The original tophat, known colloquially as a "beaver," was a symbol of prosperity among gentlemen in Europe and Great Britain before silk supplanted beaver skin as the construction material of choice.

The demand for beaver pelts was also responsible for building a number of financial empires, some of which still exist. The Hudson's Bay Company, the British East India Trading Company, and Sears-Roebuck all owe their beginnings to trade in beaver pelts.

Geographic Range

Nearly exterminated by overtrapping throughout most of its original range in the 1800s, the beaver is one of North America's greatest wildlfe success stories. Today, thanks in large part to lack of demand for their furs, beavers are found throughout North America except for the desert southwest. To the north, *C. canadensis* ranges across Canada from the Atlantic to the Pacific coast south of Hudson Bay and into Alaska

Beaver (Castor canadensis). *Large, social, aquatic rodent, noted for building dams and sturdy lodges. Flat, scaly tail serves as a rudder, and is slapped hard against the water as an alarm to others in its colony when a swimming beaver is startled.*

south of the Arctic Circle. The species' southern range extends into the northeastern border of Mexico.

Habitat

Beavers can live in almost any habitat that provides fresh water to a depth of at least 5 feet (deeper is preferred) the year-round, with sufficient trees and shrubs to provide food and building materials for lodges and dams. Small rivers and streams are dammed to create ponds that can be metered to remain at a constant level suitable for beaver habitation, and these ponds also provide habitat for many other species, including fish, reptiles, amphibians, waterfowl, and other aquatic mammals. Larger streams and lakes also make good beaver habitat, but if their waters are deep enough, resident beavers will forgo building dams or lodges, instead excavating dens into the shoreline, where they're known as bank beavers.

Physical Characteristics

Mass: 45 to more than 60 pounds, with the largest beaver recorded weighing 109 pounds.

Body: Rodentlike, with a stout body, short legs, and humped back. Comparatively small round head with short round muzzle and small round ears. Beavers have the ability to voluntarily seal their noses and ears while swimmimg underwater, and they have a clear eyelid to protect their eyes from debris. Like all rodents, beavers have large central incisors that are always growing, and must be worn down constantly through gnawing to prevent malocclusion.

Tail: Tails are unfurred, broad, and flat, covered with large, black scales. No other animal possesses this uniquely paddle-shaped tail, which has evolved to serve as a rudder while the animal is swimming. Length 11 to 18 inches. Muskrat and nutria are similar in body shape, but are much smaller and have slender, more ratlike tails.

Tracks: Five toes on all four feet, although the innermost small toes may print lightly or not at all. Forefeet about 2.5 inches long. Hind feet about 6 inches long, elongated and black, with widely spread toes connected by webbing. Front and hind feet normally print side-by-side in pairs, with forefeet usually printing to the outside of hind prints, sometimes overlapping slightly. Distance between paired front and hind tracks averages about 4 inches. Webbing of hind feet may not be visible in tracks on ground harder than wet mud.

Scat: Cylindrical, of uniform diameter, usually 1.5 to 2.5 inches long. Always found along shorelines. Beaver scat is distinctive and easily identified because it contains chips of wood and bark. Color is dark brown to black when fresh, becoming gray and sawdustlike, crumbling easily, after only a few days.

Coloration: Body and head covered with thick brown fur. Webbed feet on all 4 limbs are black, flat paddle-shaped tail is black. Long gnawing incisors are amber to orange color due to pigmentation in enamel.

Sign: Most obvious are beaver dams and lodges. Dams are made of intertwined sticks and mud, usually 2 to 3 feet wide, that span the width of rivers and streams. Lodges are tepee-shaped (conical), also constructed of sticks and mud, rising to a height of 5 feet or more at the top, and are always sited in water. Entrances to lodges are always below the water's surface. Bank

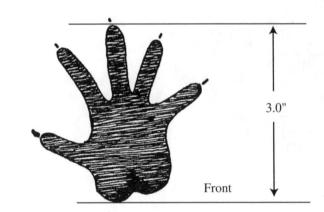

3.0"

Front

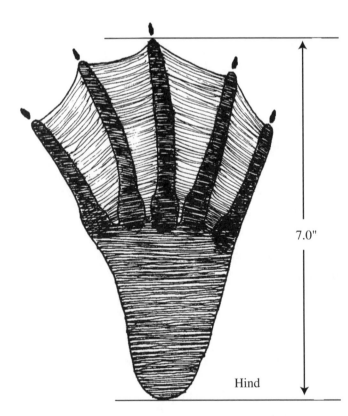

7.0"

Hind

Beaver tracks. Webbing of hind feet seldom prints except in very soft mud. Nimble fingers of front paws give beavers very good dexterity.

beavers, those living in larger rivers and lakes, may not build lodges or dams, and the entrances to their excavated burrows will also be underwater.

Another obvious beaver sign is its "cuttings," trees that have been toppled by gnawing through their trunks in a V-shaped cut, leaving stumps that are conical, like a sharpened pencil. Most trees are smaller softwoods, especially poplar, aspen, and birch saplings 4 to 6 inches in diameter, but trees more than 2 feet across have been felled. From a distance these felled trees appear to have been cut with an axe, but closer observation reveals twin gouges made by the rodent's incisors. Felled trees will never be far from water, usually within 100 yards.

A generations-old beaver lodge that has been added to with each passing year can reach impressive proportions.

Beaver sign on the ground includes obvious, well-used slide troughs at shorelines, where tree branches used for construction and as food are dragged into the water. Near these slides there are often territorial scentposts made from twisted tufts of long grasses that carry a strong musky odor deposited from the beaver's perineal (anal) glands.

Vocalizations: Normally silent, but beavers are capable of making a number of typically rodentlike sounds that include a variety of chirps and chattering. When threatened, the feisty beaver may screech, chitter, and hiss. Perhaps the most notable call that I've heard personally is a high-pitched cry used between a pair of new mates to keep tabs of the other's whereabouts; this call is probably best described as a monotonic treble "beeeeeeeee," that is prolonged for 2 to 4 seconds.

Although not a vocalization, the most commonly heard noise made by beavers is the tail slap made when a swimming animal is alarmed. This smacking noise is made by raising the flat tail above the water's surface, then bringing it down hard to make a resounding noise that warns other colony members to submerge. The individual making the alarm may also submerge, but an alpha beaver might remain on the surface to further scrutinize the source of its alarm.

Lifespan: About 8 years.

Diet

Beavers are strict vegetarians, and there is no record of them eating any type of animal matter. At all times of year, most of the diet consists of young, tender bark from saplings and shrubs. Felled trees are stripped of their branches by the beavers' powerful incisors, then the bark is gnawed off and eaten before the cleaned sticks are transported for use in construction of dams or lodges. Smaller diameter sections are gripped in the beaver's handlike forepaws and rotated as parts of it are stripped free of bark, much like a human eating corn on the cob. Large branches are gnawed as they lie on the ground.

Summer foods also include ground plants like plantains, young sedges, and the sprouts of most shoreline (riparian) plants. The thick rootstocks of pond lilies are also favored, although the crisp flesh is bitter to a human palate. Some leaves, especially those of deciduous softwoods are eaten as well, along with buds and tender twig ends.

In autumn, when ground plants begin to die off, beavers begin storing food for the coming winter by pulling branches underwater and anchoring their gnawed ends in the mud, where they remain refrigerated and fresh through the frozen months. During the long months of winter, when the surface of ponds are likely to be covered by a nearly inpenetrable shell of thick ice, the animals may not surface at all, retrieving food from the underwater larder as needed and swimming back into the lodge with branches clenched firmly between their incisors. Inside the lodge, the limbs are eaten free of bark and the woody cores discarded by pushing them back into the water.

Most mammals lack the digestive system needed to reduce tough plant cellulose to a form from which usable nutrients can be extracted as food, but beavers have a digestive sac, called a cecum (pronounced "see-come"), located between the upper and lower intestines whose purpose is to do just that. Inside the cecum are colonies of microorganisms that break down plant tissues so that nutrients from them can be absorbed and assimilated as the mass passes through the lower intestine. Chips of wood and fibers that cannot be digested are passed into the colon, where they scrape clean that organ and help to maintain the animal's rectal health.

Mating Habits

Beavers of either sex reach puberty at about 18 months, but, like most social or pack animals, only the alpha, or parent, pair are permitted to mate within a colony; grown offspring must leave to establish their own territories before breeding. Parent pairs typically mate for life unless one of them is killed, and will occupy the same territory throughout their lifespans. When the founding pair is gone, their lodge and pond are taken over by another pair, usually their own offspring, and the cycle continues.

Mating takes place within the lodge from late January through February, often with young from the previous year present. Gestation averages 14 weeks, with litters of one to eight kits (usually five) being born during a period between late April and June, the earlier births occurring in more southern parts of the species' range. Kits weigh about 1 pound at birth, and enter the world fully furred, with eyes open and incisors already erupted. Newborns can swim immediately after birth, and usually take to the water in their birth lodge's exit hole less than an hour after birth.

By the time newborns are a week old, they will have begun exploring the waters around their lodge, always under the watchful eye of at least 1 adult. Mothers continue to nurse their young inside the lodge for about 30 days, but as they grow and spend more time outside, both parents provide attention and care. Older offspring, which remain with their parents for 2 years before striking out to find their own mates and territories, also provide care and protection for their younger siblings, and all adults serve as rafts for young beavers when they become too tired to swim.

Despite receiving some of the best parental care in the animal world, a few beaver kits end up as food for a variety of predators. The speedy river otter is especially skilled at preying on beaver young, which helps to explain why otters are nearly always found where there are beavers, but ospreys, large pike, and even alligators will take a small kit if the opportunity presents itself.

By the end of their first summer, the yearling kits may weigh in excess of 15 pounds. The older siblings that helped to raise them, now 19 months old, will probably leave the parental lodge in late July or August to find their own mates and territories, but females may remain with the parents for another winter.

Beavers remain active for as long as winter weather permits, and in the southern parts of their range they may continue to forage and work throughout the winter. In the north, where snow and sometimes bitterly cold temperatures make swimming above water an impossibility, resident beavers might not be seen until spring thaw. If the ice is thin enough to be broken from below, the animals might be seen feeding on shore, or occasionally even playing on the frozen surface, but the dead of winter in snow country is a poor time to observe beavers.

Behavior

Beavers are nature's own construction engineers, second only to humans in their ability to change an environment to meet their needs. On seeing a beaver habitat for the first time, it's common for human researchers to comment that the animals' felling of nearby trees has wrecked that area, but the reverse is actually true. In damming a stream to create the deep water needed to insure that the entrance to their lodges or bank dens will always be underwater, inaccessible to most predators, the beavers inadvertently turn a stream into a pond that benefits nearly every other animal in the area. Deer, elk, and moose feed on on the abundance of water plants growing along that pond's shores, fish that wouldn't otherwise live in a smaller flowing stream find ideal habitat in the pond's deeper waters, and waterfowl of all kinds nest in the cattail forests at the pond's edge. Nearly every species in any given habitat gains from the richness a beaver colony brings to the environment.

Unfortunately, as both *Homo sapiens* and *C. canadensis* continue to expand their numbers and range, the two species run afoul of one another with increasing frequency. Owners of resort cabins and investment properties do indeed suffer financial loss from the beaver's cutting of white birch trees along riverfront tracts, as well as loss of real estate that is flooded by the damming of streams. Timber companies dislike beavers because their ponds flood, and subsequently kill, sometimes large numbers of commercially valuable lumber trees, everyone complains when roadways are flooded, and submerging electric or gas lines can have a negative impact on the municipalities those utilities serve. With fur prices too low to entice trappers into performing the hard labors required to operate a trapline, civil authorities find themselves in the unenviable position of controlling beaver numbers by trapping, poisoning, shooting them, and destroying dams.

Muskrat (*Ondatra zibethicus*)

This New World aquatic rodent is often identified with more destructive terrestrial rodents, especially the Old World Norway rat *(Rattus norvegicus),* which has plagued human populations since biblical times. In fact, the muskrat is not parasitic of humans the way Norway rats are known to be, nor is it a vector of the numerous rat-borne diseases that have historically plagued humans. Confusion between the two species stems from a tendency for both rodents to inhabit urban waterfronts, where the harmless 4-pound muskrat is often mistaken as a gigantic specimen of the 1-pound Norway rat, or the even smaller black rat *(R. rattus).*

Historically, the muskrat has played an important role in the commercial development of North America. Its soft water-repellent fur is still in such demand that approximately 10 million of the animals are trapped each year, and its very tasty flesh was once sold under the name "marsh rabbit."

Geographic Range

Nearctic: The muskrat is found in swamps, marshes, and wetlands from northern North America south of the Arctic Circle to the Gulf coast and the Mexican border. Early in the twentieth century, muskrats were introduced to northern Eurasia, where populations appear to be thriving.

Muskrat (Ondatra zibethicus). *Mid-sized aquatic rodent. Note the round, scaly tail, unlike the flat tail of the larger beaver.*

Habitat

Muskrats are found only in wet environments, particularly places having at least 4 feet of water the year round. Preferred locations are marshes, where water levels remain steady and most of the species' favorite foods are found in abundance. The animals shelter in excavated bank burrows whose entrances are generally underwater and may extend inshore at an upward slant for several feet, terminating in an enlarged chamber.

Physical Characteristics

Mass: 1.5 to more than 4 pounds, sometimes larger in the north.

Body: Ratlike, with a humped back, short legs, and a long unfurred tail. Body length 16 to 24 inches. Head larger than true rats, with blunt, squarish muzzle, and small round ears.

Tail: Triangular, flat on bottom and sides, ridged on top. Unfurred, black, and covered with small scales. Length 7 to 12 inches, or about 50% of body length.

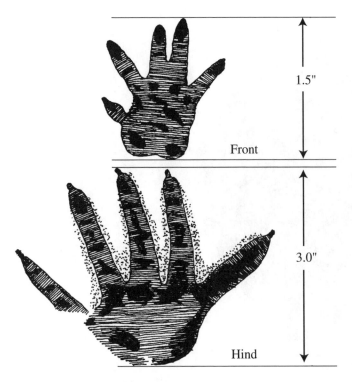

Muskrat (Ondatra zibethicus) *tracks.*

Walking in snow   Running in mud

Muskrat track patterns.

Tracks: Five long and widely spread toes on all four feet. Innermost toe of front and hind feet offset from the other four, almost thumblike. Webbed hind feet elongated and plantigrade, similar to a human foot, but heel portion may not print, resulting in tracks that can range from 2 to 3 inches long. Foreprint 1 to 1.5 inches long. Straddle about 3.5 inches, stride about 3 inches. Hind tracks usually print behind, and sometimes overlap, foreprints. Long tail may leave serpentine drag marks between tracks, sometimes broken where the animal raised its tail.

Scat: Distinctive and easy to identify. Deposits typically consist of curved pellets that are connected in side-by-side fashion, and usually left on logs, flat rocks, or other prominent places where they serve as obvious territorial markings. Color is brown, with a fine sawdustlike texture. Individual pellets 0.5 to 1 inch long.

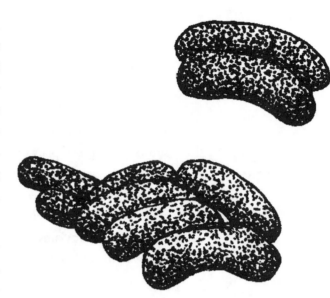

Muskrat scats. Fibrous, brownish pellets, each about half an inch long. Deposited on logs and other territorial landmarks, where it serves as a scentpost. Note parallel arrangement of pellets, unique to muskrats.

Coloration: Dark brown dorsal area, lighter brown on sides, with grayish underbelly; underbelly darker in winter than in summer. There will often be a small dark patch on the chin. Tail black.

Sign: Most obvious are the muskrat's feeding platforms, sometimes called nests or rafts. These flat, irregularly round platforms are comprised of reeds, horsetails, and cattail stalks placed atop stumps and logs at the water's edge, sometimes in the water. Platforms are often flattened, indicating that they've been used frequently, and may be covered with clipped grasses and other edible vegetation, small opened clamshells, and crayfish carapaces. Freshly cut grass blades and reeds floating near the platform indicate recent use.

Smaller platforms of cut grass stems, usually mixed with mud, found on shorelines are territorial scentposts, marked with musky secretions from the muskrat's perineal (anal) glands. These scentposts are nearly always made by territorial males, seldom by females.

Vocalizations: Normally silent. When threatened or alarmed, the muskrat can squeak, chatter, or emit a high-pitched bark.

Lifespan: About 4 years.

Diet

Muskrats are primarily vegetarian, with an efficient digestive system that can break down coarse cellulose into usable nutrients. Webbed hind feet propel them forward and backward with equal ease when swimming on or below the surface, and one individual was reported to have spent 17 minutes underwater. Voluntary skin flaps close the nostrils and seal the mouth behind their chisel-like incisors, allowing the animals to bite off submerged plants without taking water into their mouths or noses.

In summer the animals feed on grasses, sedges, plantains, cattail shoots, wapato, wild rice, and a wide variety of other aquatic and shoreline vegetation. When winter snows make green plants unavailable, muskrats forage underwater for watercress, cattail roots, and wapato tubers, bringing foods onto the ice through body-size plunge holes that are smaller than those made by river otters.

Despite a preference for vegetables, muskrats routinely eat the flesh of other animals. Freshwater clams are a common component of their diet in any season, but frogs, earthworms, dragonflies, waterfowl eggs, and young snakes are among the prey eaten by this opportunistic rodent.

Whatever the diet consists of, a muskrat normally consumes a daily volume of food equal to about 33% of its body weight. This high metabolic rate keeps the rodents busy finding food through most of their active day, and occasionally causes them to run afoul of farmers when they enter planted fields through irrigation ditches to feed on crops.

Mating Habits

Muskrat populations in the southern part of the species' range can breed year round, with females giving birth to as many as five litters per year. Northern populations mate only in the summer months between March and August, birthing two to three litters per year, depending on latitiude and the availability of warm weather.

Males are more territorial than females, but unless overpopulation forces them to be protective of mates and habitat resources, there are seldom fights between them. When there are territorial disputes, they're usually limited to brief wrestling matches and nips from the combatants' sharp incisors, ending as soon as the weaker animal withdraws.

Males are drawn to females by pheromonal scents, leaving their own territories, which typically overlap the territories of several females. Males remain with mates for 2 to 3 days, denning with them until the female becomes pregnant and spurns further advances, then leaving to find another mate if there is one nearby.

After a gestation period of about 30 days, females give birth to an average of six young, although litter sizes may be as high as eleven if mothers have been particularly well-fed and healthy; larger litter sizes have been observed more often among northern populations. Young are born in a grass-lined birthing chamber at the end of the mother's tunnel-like burrow, where few predators can detect or reach them. Muskrat kits enter the world covered with fine dark fur, but blind and helpless, weighing about 22 grams each.

Mothers nurse their litters almost constantly for the first 8 days of their lives. The muskrat kits grow quickly, and by 10 days they begin leaving their mother's burrow to swim and dive around its underwater entrance. After 30 days the young are weaned and driven away by the mother, who may have already become pregnant again while she was nursing them.

Emancipated offspring may not travel far to establish their own territories, depending on population densities and availability of resources, giving rise to the belief that muskrats sometimes live in colonies. In reality, each of the animals exists individually, without cooperation from the others. Adult size is reached between 6 and 7 months of age, with females reaching puberty first, and male yearlings will probably leave to establish their own territories, although inbreeding is probably common.

Behavior

Because muskrats are prolific breeders during warmer months, they often live relatively harmoniously in large groups, each with its own small territory. Territorial size is determined by the abundance of food and other resources, and when populations become large enough to burden these resources, territorial disputes increase both in frequency and ferocity. Adolescents are forcibly driven off, and there have been instances of cannibalism.

Muskrats may be active at any time of day or night, with peaks occurring at dusk and dawn. Adolescents are sometimes seen traveling far from water as they search for new territories, but most sightings are near or in water. With poor hearing and weak nearsighted vision, the animals are often easy to approach and observe, so long as the observer remains downwind and moves slowly, utilizing cover whenever possible.

On land, muskrats move slowly, with a running speed of about 8 miles per hour. This causes them to remain close to the water's edge, and to be especially alert when feeding atop their waterborne rafts. Major aerial predators include ospreys, owls, and hawks, while bobcats, coyotes, and otters take many as well. Mink are known to invade maternal chambers from their underwater entrances to prey on newborns, but only surreptitiously, because a mother muskrat defending her young is too dangerous an opponent for the small weasel. Young raccoons will sometimes attempt to dig downward into nesting chambers from above if they can detect them by scent, but most learn to abandon this practice because their labors usually net only an evacuated burrow.

Despite having a naked tail and lightly furred feet, muskrats are able to withstand subfreezing temperatures and long periods in cold water because of a physical adaptation knwn as "regional heterothermia," which allows these extremeties to remain just above freezing without suffering cell damage. The animals' warm, fine fur retains most body heat even underwater, and a layer of fat beneath the skin further insures that loss of warmth is minimal. In especially cold weather, the muskrats retreat inside their underground burrows, sometimes laying up there for as long as a week, until warmer temperatures return. The burrow's underwater entrance remains unfrozen during these periods, permitting residents access to underwater foods, and giving them an exit through which to relieve themselves without fouling the fastidiously clean den.

Muskrats, usually youngsters, sometimes incur the wrath of farmers by denning inside drainpipes and irrigation tiles, plugging them with their nests of grasses and reeds. The problem isn't generally widespread or serious, and is easily prevented by covering pipe openings with steel mesh fine enough to prevent entry.

Porcupine (Erethizon dorsatum)

The single species of North American porcupine has similar counterparts throughout the world, demonstrating the viability of its defense mechanism. All are lumbering, heavily built rodents that have adapted to ward off faster and stronger predators with a covering of highly modified hairs interspersed in the fur on their backs and tails. These modified hairs, or quills, have evolved to become stiff, sharply pointed needles whose ends are covered with minute barbs. The porcupine's genus name, *Erethizon*, is Latin for "He who rises in anger," an allusion to this species' natural defense.

Because predators are almost universally evolved to kill food animals through hard physical contact using teeth and claws, these quills provide the porcupine and its relatives with a shield that few can penetrate without suffering serious, sometimes fatal injuries to themselves. A carnivore with a mouthful of firmly embedded quills can no longer eat, nor does it have the means to extract them, and most will suffer a serious infection. A few predators, most notably the fisher, have learned to flip porcupines onto their backs, exposing the unquilled underbelly, but even the fisher suffers an occasional injury.

Porcupine (Erethizon dorsatum).

Geographic Range

The common porcupine is native to boreal North America from Alaska and across Canada south of the Arctic Circle to Labrador. Its range covers the western half of the United States, southward from Montana through New Mexico, and into northern Mexico. In the eastern half of the United States, porcupines are found only in the northernmost regions, covering most of New England, northern Michigan, northern Wisconsin, and northeast Minnesota.

Habitat

Porcupines are found primarily in coniferous forests, but may spend part of the year in deciduous woods while seasonal foods are available. Preferred habitat is mixed forest consisting of pine, hardwoods, softwoods, and a variety of ground plants, but nearly every environment in which porcupines are found will include tall trees and a source of fresh water nearby. There have been reports of porcupines frequenting riparian (riverfront) areas in mountainous regions, and even denning in rock crevices, but never far from woodlands that serve as food, shelter, and refuge from enemies.

Physical Characteristics

Mass: 8 to 40 pounds, with the largest specimens occurring in the north.

Body: Rodentlike, with humped back and short legs. Dorsal region and, especially, tail covered with coarse hairs and approximately 30,000 hollow, barbed quills that can be voluntarily detached on contact, but not thrown. The longest quills occur on the rump and tail, the shortest on the neck; there are no quills on the underbelly. Body length 25 to 37 inches. Head small in proportion to body, and round, with short muzzle, flat face, and small round ears. Prominent yellow-orange incisors are ever-growing and must be kept from growing past one another (malocclusion) through constant gnawing.

Tail: Large, round, and clublike, heavily covered with quills. Length 6 to 12 inches.

Tracks: Four toes on forefeet, five toes on hind feet. Toes are long and articulated, each tipped with a heavy, slightly curved claw 0.5 to nearly 1 inch long. Front track 2 to 3 inches long, including claws; hind track 3 to 4.5 inches long, including claws. Tracks elongated and plantigrade (flat-footed), with thick, distinctive pebble-textured soles. At a walk, the porcupine's usual gait, hind prints register ahead of foreprints, occasionally overlapping. In snow the porky's wide, low-slung belly often drags, leaving a trough that can obscure tracks. In sand, tracks may also be obscured by the heavy tail, which typically swings back and forth, leaving striated broomlike markings.

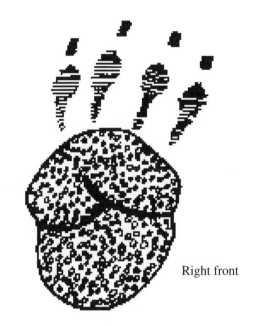

Right front

Left hind

Porcupine (Erethizon dorsatum) *tracks.*

Spring
Segments connected by grass fibers

Autumn
Fibrous, indicating a diet
of rough cellulose

Spring
Soft form indicative
of a succulent diet

Autumn
Soft, but more fibrous
than summer scats

Summer
Steady diet of green plants

Winter
Fibrous from a woody
diet of bark and twigs

Porcupine (Erethizon dorsatum) *scat forms.*

Scat: In winter, curved pellets with a sawdustlike texture, much like the muskrat's, but not connected. Pellets are dark brown, each about 1 inch long, and distinguishable by a small groove running lengthwise along the inside radius.

In spring, when the diet changes from woody fare to green plants, pellets are often shorter, with more squared ends, and connected together by grass fibers like a string of beads. Other forms seen from spring through autumn include formless, misshapen segments, still usually deposited as individual pellets, and showing evidence of plant fibers.

Coloration: Most porcupines are covered with coarse gray hairs, but some may be brown, or even black. Unquilled belly is lighter in color than back and sides. Hollow quills are black-tipped with whitish shafts.

Sign: Most obvious at all times of year are the porcupine's winter gnawing of smooth-barked pines, especially near the trees' tops, that leave irregular patches of

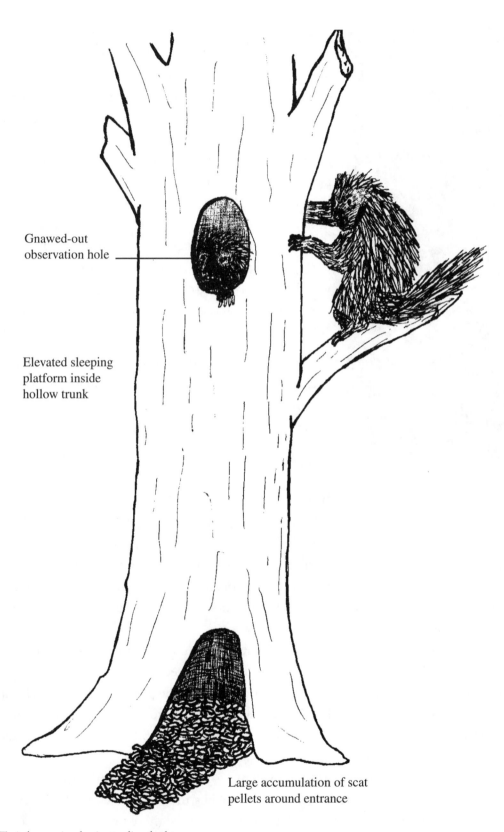

Gnawed-out
observation hole

Elevated sleeping
platform inside
hollow trunk

Large accumulation of scat
pellets around entrance

Typical porcupine den in standing dead tree.

Old porcupine denning tree made from a standing hollow white pine. Note large accumulation of scat pellets around entrance.

exposed wood. In winter, when porcupines feed almost exclusively on pine bark and buds, there are usually scatterings of needle-bearing twig ends lying about the snow under trees that serve as food sources (red squirrels also nip off cone-bearing twigs from spruces and hemlocks). Den openings at the base of hollow trees generally have large accumulations of winter scat pellets about their entrances. Bones and antlers of large animals, especially deer, are often gnawed to obtain the minerals in them, leaving gouges much larger than those made by smaller squirrels that do the same. Too, look for gnawings in processed lumber, especially wood that has been treated with varnish, which the porcupine may actually eat in quantity because of its salt content.

Vocalizations: Usually silent, even when cornered. Most vocalizations are heard during the autumn mating season, when males may grunt, squeak, and sometimes snort while in pursuit of mates.

Lifespan: Up to 8 years.

Diet

Like beavers, and unlike most rodents, the porcupine is entirely vegetarian. In early spring, before most ground plants are sprouted, the animals climb high into poplar, aspen, and cottonwood trees to feed on their sticky, fleshy buds. During this brief lean period, buds of willow, staghorn sumac, beech, and most other trees and shrubs are eaten as well, but those in the poplar family seem to be favored.

From spring through summer, the porcupine's tastes turn toward more succulent green plants. Young grasses and sedges, plantains, sprouted beechnuts, cresses, mustard, chickory, dandelions, and other greens are only a few of the plants that help to make up *E. dorsatum*'s varied summer diet. As summer progresses into autumn, the diet expands or changes to match ripening fruits like serviceberries, blueberries, wild cherries, and other nuts or fruits.

When winter snows return and again make ground plants unavailable, porcupines begin looking to the trees for sustenance. Like rabbits, they will sometimes feed on bark stripped from sumac, cherries, and dogwoods, but unlike those terrestrial bark-eaters, porcupines can climb with ease into the tallest trees to reach the tenderest bark and twig ends.

Most preferred in winter are pines, especially white pines, and a single large tree may be occupied by a porcupine for several weeks at a time. Preferred portions include the smooth green bark at the top and ends of branches, bud ends, and young twig ends. Unfortunately, these feeding habits have made the timber industry look unfavorably on porcupines, whose winter gnawings can kill commercially valuable trees by "girdling" them with a belt of stripped bark that encircles the trunk.

Another feeding habit that causes friction between porcupines and humans is the animal's tendency to eat any wood that has traces of salt in it, including perspiration-soaked tool handles, plywood boats, decks, and the wooden siding or shingles on rural houses. In one instance, legendary tracker Olas J. Murie described an outing in which he was forced to leash a half dozen pocupines that persisted in gnawing his canoe by looping cord around their necks and tying them to a tree until morning. The salt-loving rodents can cause considerable damage and expense, but are dissuaded easily enough by metal siding and concrete foundations.

Mating Habits

Female porcupines may mate as young as 6 months of age, but competition will likely prevent males from breeding until 18 months. The testes of male porcupines descend into scrotal pouches between late August and early September, and spermatogenesis peaks during October. Mating occurs in October through November, and during the approximately 60 days of breeding that follows, males may travel from several miles distant to court prospective mates. It's during this time that the normally silent porcupines are likely to be vocal, especially when several eligible bachelors pursue a single female into a large tree while squabbling with one another over which of them should breed her. Male porcupines are seldom violent toward one another, and never use their quills on their own kind, but these arboreal pursuits can be especially dangerous if a shoving match among the upper branches should cause one of the contestants to fall to the ground from a great height. Males that are pushed from a tree branch and survive the fall will withdraw to seek out a mate elsewhere.

Females are generally passive in the mating ritual, waiting for males attracted by their pheromonal scents to come to them. Courtship is mostly the male's domain, and consists of much squeaking and grunting, an odd hopping dance, climbing trees together, and marking the female with urine. Females remain in estrus for just 12 hours, so time spent between mates is brief. If a female fails to become pregnant within that period, she will come into heat again (polyestrous) in another 25 to 30 days.

A longstanding jocular answer to the question of how spiny porcupines engage in sex has been, "carefully." But in fact mating occurs in the same manner as other animals. When the female is ready, she voluntarily brings the quills along her back downward and holds them flat against her body, then raises her tail over her back, exposing the un-quilled underside, as well as her genitalia. The male then mounts her from behind in conventional fashion.

After mating, a mucouslike plug forms in the female porcupine's vaginal cavity to prevent further entry by sperm, and she loses interest in mating again. Her mate, who might have come from several miles distant, will set out to find another receptive fe-male before the breeding period ends, and takes no part in the rearing of offspring.

The porcupine's gestation period lasts approximately 30 weeks, which is very long for a small mammal, and probably includes a period of delayed implantation, al-though no data has been established yet. Pregnant females give birth to a single pup (twins are rare) in April or May within a den that's usually located inside a standing hol-low tree, but sometimes in a rock crevice. Young are precocial, born fully quilled and with eyes open, but the quills are soft and do not harm the mother. After being exposed to open air for about 1 hour, the newborn's quills harden, and the youngster becomes a smaller duplicate of its mother.

In captivity, mother porcupines have been observed to suckle their young for pe-riods spanning several months, but youngsters in the wild are able to subsist on vegeta-tion within 2 weeks, so nursing in a natural environment is probably much shorter. My own encounters with young porcupines found living alone in the wild has convinced me that adolescents as young as 1 month are fully capable of caring for themselves.

Under normal conditions, young porcupines may accompany their mothers for 5 months or more, and females may mate with the same male their mothers breed with in the coming autumn. Males tend to wander off in search of their own territories dur-ing their first summer of life.

Porcupine populations rise and fall in cycles of roughly 12 years. The typical cy-cles consists of decline that extends for a period of 2 years, followed by a rise in num-bers over the next 10 years.

Behavior

Porcupines are normally solitary, but, except for the autumn mating season, rarely show territorial aggression toward one another. In particularly harsh weather, several adults may take shelter in the same cave, roadway culvert, or outbuilding crawlspace to wait out a storm, with no apparent animosity between them. When fair weather returns, the animals separate and resume their solitary lifestyles.

Porcupines do not hibernate, but during the winter months, pregnant females es-pecially seek out a den in which to give birth or take shelter from bad weather. These dens, which may be vital to an animal's survival, are used regularly throughout the winter, and are defended against usurpers, although ownership is rarely challenged and battles over possession are never violent.

Unlike other animals, which keep their dens and nests fastidiously clean, the entrance to a porcupine den is always marked with scat pellets, sometimes a small mountain of them if the den has been used repeatedly for several winters. When the den is inside a hollow standing tree, there will usually be a ledge inside, 10 feet or more above its base, where the animal sleeps, and this platform is often partially or entirely constructed of scat pellets compressed to a hard surface under the resident porcupine's weight. Just above this elevated platform there will be a small observation hole gnawed through the tree's shell, and a sharp-eyed hiker can often spot a porcupine who lives there peering out to watch him pass by.

In summer, porcupines rarely shelter in dens, but escape biting insects and the heat of day on a thick branch high up in a tree, where they can be spotted from afar as an uncharacteristic large bump. They don't build nests the way squirrels do, preferring to rest in the open, the heavily quilled tail and rump pointed toward the tree's trunk, in the direction from which predators must approach. This simple strategy is proof against bobcats, raccoons, and most other climbing carnivores, but the fisher is able to clamber past the porcupine along the underside of the branch to emerge in front of it, thereby gaining access to its unprotected head.

Many species that are thought to be nocturnal adopt that habit to avoid contact with humans, but porcupines prefer to forage at night even in places where there are no people. Just before sunset they emerge from dens or elevated resting places to forage for food plants on the ground.

Only the most hungry or inexperienced predators chance tackling a foraging porky, but if one does, the porcupine points its tail end toward the enemy, turning as the predator circles to keep its most potent armament toward the adversary. Given an opportunity, the porcupine will escape by climbing out of reach, but a predator foolish enough to press its attack will be rewarded with a slap from the heavily barbed tail.

Along with timber companies that dislike *E. dorsatum* for its winter foraging of pine trees, farmers consider it a destructive nuisance of corn crops and orchard trees, homeowners resent its gnawing of wooden structures, and many dog owners learn to hate them for the injuries their quills inflict on pets. To others, the porcupine is almost revered; it's one of the few, and sometimes the only, species that a lost and hungry woodsman can catch on foot, and humans are the only predator that can kill the spiny animal with impunity—a sharp blow across its nose from a club does the job. Native Americans use the animals' quills to adorn ornamental birch bark boxes, which today fetch a good price in gift and souvenir shops.

Armadillo. Photo by John and Karen Hollingsworth, courtesy of U.S. Fish & Wildlife.

Nine-Banded Armadillo (*Dasypus novemcinctus*)

One of North America's most interesting mammals, as well as being its most armored, the nine-banded armadillo is one-of-a-kind. Instead of developing quills, powerful scents, or other defensive weapons to discourage predators, the armadillo took a more passive evolutionary path, growing an armor of hard, bony (ossified) plates that few predators can penetrate.

The common name was first ascribed to this species by Spanish conquistadors in the early sixteenth century, who called it *armadillo,* or "little armored man." The Aztec Indians knew it as *azotochtli,* or "turtle rabbit." Both names are descriptive, but reflective of the frame of reference possessed by either group.

Dasypus novemcinctus is the only mammal besides humans that suffers from lepromatid leprosy, and there is cause to believe that it might be a vector for that disease. Human researchers should exercise caution when handling the animals, or when working around their scats and dens, to avoid any possibility of contracting this disease.

Geographic Range

The first confirmation of armadillos in the United States occurred in 1854 along the Rio Grande river, and the species has been slowly migrating northward since that time. Theories to explain this migration include global warming, human-induced modification of habitats by livestock overgrazing, and extermination of major predators within the armadillo's range.

Today armadillos are found from Mexico to Peru and northern Argentina in the south, and on the islands of Grenada, Tobago, and Trinidad. In the United States, armadillos are found in Texas, Louisiana, Missouri, Florida, extending northward into most of Oklahoma and Arkansas, and eastward across the southern portions of Mississippi, Alabama, and Georgia. Environmental scientists have predicted that by 2050 armadillos will have migrated as far north as Virginia. A cousin, the Hairy Armadillo (*Chaetophractus vellerosus*) is found only in Bolivia and Argentina.

Habitat

Armadillos have proved remarkably adaptable to a variety of habitats, from the sand and sagebrush of Texas to the bayous of Louisiana to the Florida Everglades. So long as an environment provides fresh water and the insects that make up the bulk of its diet, the species seems capable of living in any type of environment that isn't subject to extended periods of subfreezing weather.

Physical Characteristics

Mass: 6 to 17 pounds. Males about 10% larger than females.

Body: Stocky with short, powerful legs adapted to digging. The most notable physical characteristic of nine-banded and other armadillos are their leathery pebbled skin and ossified dermal plates on the back, sides, tail and top of the head that form a turtle-like carapace. This carapace consists of three distinct sections: a scapular (shoulder) plate, a pelvic (hip) plate, and a series of hinged telescoping bands around the abdominal section. The bands are connected by flexible, hairless skin, and the anterior edge of each abdominal band overlaps the next band to form an unbroken shield. The underbelly is covered with tough, leathery skin, but not armored. Body length 24 to 32 inches.

Despite its common name, the nine-banded armadillo can have from seven to as many as eleven abdominal plates, with the greater number of plates occurring in specimens in the northern parts of the species' range (where individuals tend to grow larger), and the lesser number occurring in the southern range; only in the central part of the armadillo's range does it normally live up to its common name.

The armadillo's head is almost cone-shaped, ending in a piglike snout designed for rooting through soil. There are no incisor or canine teeth in frontal jaw, and the peglike molars are primitive, with single roots and no enamel on the adult teeth. The ears are thick-skinned, pointed, and piglike, 3 to 4 inches long.

Tail: 9 to 15 inches long, covered by 12 to 15 overlapping segmented rings.

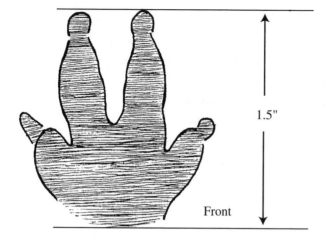

1.5"

Front

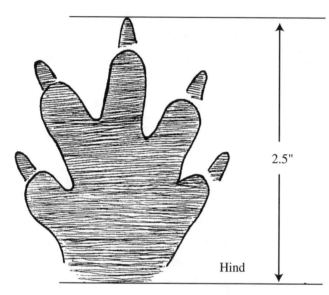

2.5"

Hind

Nine-banded armadillo (Dasypus novemcinctus) tracks. Thick, strongly built feet with long, curved claws that are well adapted for digging food in rocky soil. Partial tracks in dry sand may look similar to deer tracks.

Tracks: Armadillo forefeet have four digits, the hindfeet five, each with center toes much longer than outermost toes. Innermost toes of front and hind feet much smaller and more offset than the others, helping to identify left and right tracks. Thick, strong digging claws are evident in tracks, which in dry sand can be mistaken for deer tracks. Forefeet about 1.5 inches long, hind feet about 2.5 inches long.

Scat: Irregular, sometimes elongated, but often round and marblelike, consisting largely of clay and sand ingested as the animal feeds on insects; 1 to 1.5 inches long.

Coloration: Gray, yellowish, or brown. Lightly furred with long grayish hairs, especially on hind legs. Scapular and pelvic plates slightly darker than abdominal rings, with raised pebbled surface appearing as whitish dots against a darker background.

Sign: Rooted-up soil, rotting logs clawed apart, excavated anthills.

Vocalizations: Nine-banded armadillos are very vocal, grunting almost constantly as they forage.

Lifespan: About 8 years.

Diet

The nine-banded armadillo primarily eats animal matter, including ants, beetles, grasshoppers, small reptiles and amphibians, hatchling birds, eggs, mice, and sometimes carrion. Some plant matter, principally roots and berries, are also eaten. The foraging technique consists of rooting through soil and rotting wood, much like the peccaries with whom the species shares much of its range, and digging for insects and grubs with the powerful foreclaws. Foods appear to be located mostly through use of the animal's acute sense of smell.

Being mostly insectivorous, armadillos are an important part of their habitat, as well as being beneficial to humans, because their feeding habits help to control populations of many species of potentially harmful insects. An armadillo can consume more than 40,000 ants in a single meal, and each adult eats an estimated 200 pounds of insects per year.

Mating Habits

Nine-banded armadillos mate during a period between July and August. Little is known about this species' mating habits, but males are doubtless attracted to receptive females through pheromonal scents contained in their urine, perhaps in their scats. Like most mammals, the home range of established males probably overlaps the territories of several females in an area.

After mating, the normally solitary males and females go their separate ways, with males probably seeking out as many mates as they can before the breeding season ends. Females do not immediately become pregnant, but undergo a period of delayed implantation that typically lasts between 3 and 4 months. This phenomenon insures that females are healthy enough to withstand the drain on bodily resources that gestating a litter will require. But unlike most female mammals, armadillos don't always spontaneously abort a fertilized egg they cannot physically afford to gestate, and there have been incidents in which a mated female carried her single egg in stasis for 2 years before actually becoming pregnant.

If all is well, a female armadillo's fertilized egg will attach to her uterine wall and begin to develop in November. Although there is just one egg, it will divide into quarters and begin growing four separate but genetically identical embryos, all of them of the same sex. This unique reproductive phenomenon has made armadillos a preferred lab animal for medical research requiring identical subjects as an experimental constant.

After a gestation of 17 weeks, expectant mothers retire to a maternal den excavated in the side of a knoll or riverbank, sometimes under the roots of a large tree, but always close to a source of food and drinking water. Den openings average about 8 inches in diameter, and may extend inward for a distance of 15 feet, terminating in an enlarged grass- and leaf-lined nursing chamber. Inside the den chamber, safe from most predators that would eat their young, female armadillos give birth to their quadruplets in March or April. The young are born fully formed, with eyes open, and within a few hours can walk about inside the den. Their armor is soft, however, and will not be sufficiently hard to provide them protection against enemies until they're weaned, 3 to 4 weeks after birth.

After weaning, the mother leaves the den with her litter to teach them the skills of foraging. Looking much like piglets, the young armadillos follow behind her at a trot as she searches for food, eating almost constantly in an effort to replace the fats and other precious resources lost during the previous 6 months of pregnancy and nursing. Offspring remain with their mother until July, when she abandons the fully armored and self-sufficient youngsters to mate again. Armadillos reach sexual maturity at about 1 year, and will mate at 18 months.

Behavior

Nine-banded armadillos generally exhibit nocturnal or crepuscular habits, but temperature, not light, appears to be the factor that most dictates when their active times will occur. Being almost entirely unfurred, and unable to hibernate, armadillos cannot tolerate long exposure to freezing temperatures, and will lie up in a warm underground den during periods of cold until warmer weather returns. Like all mammals, the animals have an ability to regulate their body temperatures, but they have very little insulation. More than any other reason, this inability to survive cold weather limits how far north the species will migrate.

Likewise, armadillos are poorly suited to extreme heat. In open desert, where their dermal plates can become unbearably hot under a noonday sun, the animals will shelter in earthen burrows, emerging only in the cooler hours of morning and evening. In forest habitats, especially those containing streams or ponds, armadillos may be active at any time of day.

One of the armadillo's more remarkable behavioral traits is that species' almost complete lack of territoriality. The animals have never been observed fighting over territory, or even mates, but there are reports of several of them, usually individuals of the same sex, denning together. There have even been incidents where armadillos share dens with animals of different species. Such behavior is unheard of with other mammals. Typical territories span 10 to 25 acres, but are never defended, even when they overlap with the territories of other armadillos of the same sex.

Legend has it armadillos curl into a tightly armored ball when threatened, but even though this behavior has been observed, it doesn't appear to be a habit. Humans who hunt armadillos for sport and for meat (the flesh is similar to pork) report that pursued animals tend to run from them at surprisingly fast speeds approaching 15 miles an hour. If cornered, armadillos can quickly dig out of sight, much like the badger, then curl up inside the tunnel they've excavated, wedging their bodies against the walls so tightly that they can't be pulled free.

Although nine-banded armadillos are poorly suited to swimming, the animals frequently cross rivers and streams. If a stream is shallow and narrow, the animals simply walk across to the opposite side along the stream's bottom, remaining submerged for as long as 5 minutes. If a river is too wide or deep to permit that approach, the animals can swim slowly by inflating their intestines with air sufficient to make them float for a short period, and swim across.

Virginia Opossum (*Didelphis virginiana*)

The opossum is North America's only marsupial, or pouched mammal, although several marsupial species occur in South America. The opossum is something of a

Virginia opossum (Didelphis virginiana).

dichotomy. With fifty sharp teeth (more than any other land animal on the continent) and a diet that consists mostly of animal flesh, it might be classified as a carnivore, while a prehensile tail, lemur-like eyes, and semi-opposable thumbs might seem to make it a primate.

Geographic Range

Opossums are found throughout most of North America, from Central America and Mexico in the south, throughout the United States east of the Rocky Mountains into southwestern Ontario, and in California. As noted by Olas J. Murie in 1954, opossums are highly adaptable, spreading to the west coast of North America in the late 1800s, and into northern Michigan in the 1980s. When North America was first colonized by Europeans, opossums didn't occur north of Pennsylvania.

Habitat

Opossums are found in a variety of environments, but prefer swamp and marshes. They frequent roadsides in this type of habitat to feed on car-killed animals, and often visit dumpsters at campgrounds.

The opossum is poorly suited to cold climates because its nearly hairless tail, nose, and ears are subject to frostbite. Nonetheless, opossums now live in regions that experience sometimes bitterly cold winters, and in these places they've learned to take shelter in abandoned burrows or other relatively warm places for days at a time.

Physical Characteristics

Mass: 4 to more than 14 pounds at maturity, with the largest animals occuring in northern latitudes.

Body: 12 to 20 inches from nose to rump. Shoulder height 4 to 8 inches. Stocky build, about the size of a house cat, for which it's sometimes mistaken. Strikingly pink nose with long whiskers. Small rounded ears. Eyes large and close-set, denoting excellent night vision and good depth perception.

Tail: 10 to 20 inches, nearly naked and ratlike, responsible for the common but mistaken belief that opossums are members of the rodent family. The tail is prehensile, meaning that it can function as a working limb, allowing its owner to curl it around objects and hang from it, and may be important for helping to subdue prey animals.

Tracks: Front: About 1.5 inches long. Five toes, usually splayed, with bulbous tips, claws showing in tracks. Hind: 2 inches long, four toes pointing forward with bulbous tips, claws showing. Fifth toe is distinctively long and thumblike, pointing inward at the perpendicular or to the rear. Straddle about 4 inches, walking stride about 7 inches. Tail drag leaves a serpentine pattern in soft soil or snow.

Scat: Segmented, 1 to 2 inches long and about 0.5 inch in diameter. Segments often connected by fur or plant fibers, black to brown in color, often with berry seeds in evidence.

Coloration: Body fur ranges from grizzled black to gray to nearly white in the northernmost part of its range. Face nearly white. Ears darker than face, tipped with white. Tail pinkish gray. Nose pink.

Sign: Seldom seen because opossums aren't territorial, but nomadic. Usually consists of debris from scavenged garbage, or carcasses that have been fed on, and easily mistaken for sign from other small carnivores.

Vocalizations: Mostly silent. Hisses and squeals when threatened, or when engaged in mating battles.

Lifespan: 7 to 8 years in the wild, depending very much on predators and human hunters.

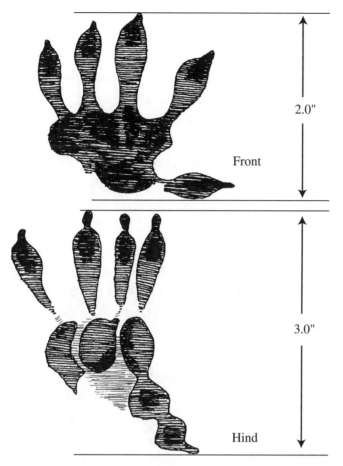

2.0"

Front

3.0"

Hind

Opossum (Didelphis virginiana) *tracks.*

Opossum walking track pattern.

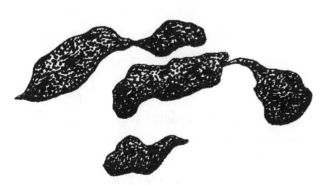

Opossum scat. Scats segmented, each segment 1″ to 1.5″ long. Scat contents reflect an omnivorous diet, and may contain fur, bone, seeds, and undigested plant fibers.

273

Diet

Although best known as carrion eaters, opossum diets encompass virtually anything that can be metabolized as food. They do indeed consume road-killed deer and other animals, sometimes even living inside a large carcass for days at a time, but opossums are also adept hunters, able to prey on snakes, mice, frogs, tadpoles, and a variety of insects.

Fruits and vegetation also make up a large portion of the opossum diet when these are in season. Wild berries, especially blueberries, are preferred foods, but the animals are fond of farm crops like sweet corn, apples, and pears. In winter when plant foods become hard to find, opossums may take up residence in rural barns, where they not only feed on stored grains, but also prey on rats and mice.

Mating Habits

The mating season for opossums lasts from January to July, occuring earlier in southern latitudes than in the north, and in warmer climes females may have two, sometimes three, litters per year. Mating is typically initiated by the males, which are attracted to females by pheromonal scents. Fights between males are common during this period, marked by screeches, hissing, and sometimes violent battles.

Because male opossums have a uniquely forked penis, there exists an old myth about them copulating through the females' noses. In fact, mating is performed in the same way as it is in most other species, with males mounting females from behind.

After copulation, the pregnant female rejects any further solicitations, and the male moves on to find another receptive mate, while the female retires to make a nest in a suitably secure crevice or abandoned burrow. After a brief gestation of 12 to 13 days a litter of about eight blind and hairless young are born, each the size of a small bean, and immediately make their way to the mother's fur-lined marsupial pouch where each fixes itself to one of her eleven to thirteen nipples. The young remain fixed to the nipple for the next 60 days, after which they leave the pouch and travel about with the mother by clinging to her tail and back. By 100 days the youngsters are no longer dependent on their mother, and leave to find their own ways in the world. Females typically mate in their first year.

Behavior

Opossums are primarily nocturnal, sleeping away the daylight hours in a variety of secluded places that can range from abandoned animal dens and outbuildings to house crawlspaces and derelict automobiles. At dusk they emerge to forage and hunt for food, returning to a secure bedding spot at sunrise, but not necessarily in the same place they spent the previous day. They are not social animals, with males being especially aggressive toward one another, and it's rare to see two or more adults together. When opossums are seen in a group, the animals are virtually always newly emancipated littermates that are finding their bearings before going separate ways.

Opossums have adapted well to humans, raiding garbage cans and dumpsters, living in barns and outbuildings, and even invading occupied homes from time to time. Both sexes can act very aggressive when cornered, hissing loudly and showing their pointed teeth, but only the largest of them will consider an actual confrontation with animals of equal or larger size. If a show of ferocity fails to discourage an enemy, the animal will live up to its name by "playing possum," falling onto its side, eyes tightly closed, and pretending to be dead, often urinating and defecating to help enhance the image. The pretense is so strong that opossums in this state have been petted without breaking it, although this is never recommended.

Opossums differ from other species by being true nomads, traveling from one food source to another, but never claiming a territory. Because of that, and because much of the opossum diet is comprised of carrion, they are potential vectors of many diseases like rabies and tularemia, and are prime suspects in the rampant spread of bovine tuberculosis among whitetail deer.

Despite their scavenging habits and human prejudice, opossums have historically been of value to people. The flesh is edible and usually considered quite good by those who can overcome their bias, while pelts have served as garment trim, and the fur as paintbrush bristles. Opossums have also served as lab animals for scientific research, in part because they're relatively intelligent, and because they don't evoke the same sympathetic response from animal rights advocates as rabbits and other more socially accepted species.

CHAPTER 5

BIRDS

TERRESTRIAL BIRDS

American Wild Turkey *(Meleagris gallopavo)*

When the Founding Fathers of the then fledgling United States of America put their heads together to decide which native bird was best suited to represent their young nation, it was Benjamin Franklin who suggested that they choose the wild turkey. He reasoned that the wild turkey, more than any other bird, had contributed to the strength and growth of the country by serving as a food staple for whole families of pioneers who had forged civilization from its vast wilderness. In the end, Franklin's nomination was rejected in favor of the more fierce image of the bald eagle, but not because anyone disputed the turkey's importance.

The wild turkey represents one of North America's most successful exercises in game recovery and management. By 1920, unrestricted hunting had completely eliminated the birds from eighteen of the thirty-nine states in their historical range, and fewer than 100,000 individuals still remained in the United States. Game laws and relocation efforts implemented after WWII focused on increasing turkey numbers even beyond their original range, and by 1959 populations had increased to almost 500,000. By 1990, the estimated population had risen to more than 3 million, and wild turkeys were found in all 48 of the continental United States. Today, populations of wild turkeys continue to grow, but the Department of the Interior's prognosis is that further expansion will be limited by continuing loss of habitat through deforestation and residential development.

American wild turkey (western). Photo by Gary M. Stolz, courtesy of U.S. Fish & Wildlife Service.

American wild turkey (eastern).

Geographic Range

Once nearly decimated over most of its range by overhunting, today the wild turkey has been reestablished and has one of the widest ranges of any game bird of North America. The species is found from the western and southern United States to the Atlantic seaboard and New England. Throughout this range there are six recognized subspecies, with one additional subspecies, the ocellated turkey, found in Central America.

In the continental United States the two most common and easily recognized subspecies of wild turkey, *Meleagris gallopavo silvestris*, which is found predominantly in the East, and *M. gallopavo merriami* in the western states. The eastern subspecies is distinguished by brown-tipped tail, rump, and back feathers, whereas those feathers are tipped with tan, or sometimes almost white, on western birds.

Habitat

Wild turkey habitats are as varied as their broad geographic range, and include mixed coniferous and deciduous forests, grasslands, agricultural areas, orchards, and freshwater shorelines. Overgrown brushlands where the bird's broad wingspan prohibits quick escape from danger are usually avoided, as are swamps where fast, stealthy predators like the bobcat and fisher find the big birds easy prey. Because the birds roost in high overhead branches through the night, suitable habitats will always include tall, usually deciduous, trees with widely spaced branches.

Physical Characteristics

Mass: 7 to more than 22 pounds. Weight varies considerably depending on the time of year and resource availability, with larger specimens generally occurring in the northern parts of the species' range.

Body: Large, stocky bird. Males, known as toms or gobblers, have a dark, iridescent body, a reddish naked head, a "wattle" consisting of fleshy lobes hanging down from the chin, and a "caruncle" consisting of a wartlike fleshy projection on the forehead. Thick reddish legs have dark-colored spurs projecting from their rears, about halfway up; adult males, and an occasional female, have a tail-like breast tuft, or beard, extending outward from the breast, typically growing longer as the bird ages. These beards are comprised of hairlike feathers called mesofilophumes, and are prized by sport hunters who consider them trophies. Standing height for males averages about 48 inches.

Adult females (hens) and adolescents (jennys and jakes), are smaller and duller than adult males, lack a breast beard, have a grayish head, lack leg spurs, and the back of the neck is feathered. Standing height for adult females averages about 36 inches.

Tail: Long, extending nearly to the ground when walking. Most distinctive is the gobbler's habit of raising its tail upright and fanning it widely during the spring mating season. Tips of the tail feathers are light brown, followed by a black band, with narrow alternating black and brown bands extending to their bases.

Tracks: Three-toed, with the longer center toe extending straight forward, flanked on either side by shorter toes that are symmetrically angled outward and forward. Claws normally evident in tracks. Thick segments of toes usually obvious, typically with four segments in the outer toes, five segments in the center toe. Rear toe generally prints as a round dot behind center toe, between outer toes, but on snow or mud the entire rear toe may print. Track length about 4 inches. Tracks similar to those of the sandhill crane, except that the crane's digits are narrower, outside toes are asymmetrically angled, and segments are not so obvious.

Scat: In winter, when foods are drier and succulents are unavailable, scats tend to be cylindrical, unsegmented, and

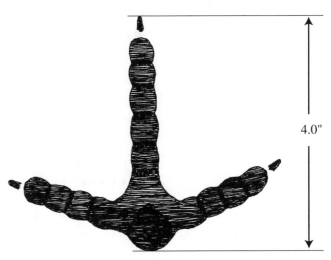

4.0"

American turkey (Meleagris gallopavo) track. Note lack of rear toe in track.

slightly curved, with one end rounded, the opposite flat. Dark brown, greenish, or black in color. Length up to 3 inches, diameter usually less than 0.5 inch.

During the warmer months, when much of the turkey's diet consists of green plants, scats become softer and more variable in shape. Typical forms range from nearly spherical to flattened discs that are sometimes layered, similar to a cowpie, but about 1 inch in diameter.

Coloration: The wild turkey is a colorful bird, with unfeathered legs and feet that are usually pink, sometimes pink and gray. The head of the adult hen is grayish, but the head of the gobbler ranges from red to blue to nearly white, depending on the bird's hormonal status and on the season.

Flight feathers are black with brown stripes and narrower bars of white. The wattles and caruncle are pink to red, becoming more brightly colored during the mating season. The tail-like breast beard, usually absent in females, is black.

Like many birds, turkeys have sharp eyesight and good color vision, and much of the communication between them is visual. The brilliant head and wattle of a dominant male in spring serves to attract females, while at the same time warning competitors that a territory has already been claimed. Fortunately, most of the turkey's most dangerous predators are color-blind, while even large birds of prey, which can see colors, find the big bird too massive to be considered as prey.

Sign: Most obvious in the woods are the invariably numerous scats spattered on the forest floor under large, usually deciduous, trees. Trees that have been used as regular roosting places by several birds will have scats of varying ages beneath them, with the oldest and whitest scats being visible from a distance. Scats are usually accompanied by a scattering of feathers that fell to earth when the roosted birds preened themselves.

Too, look for scratchings and disturbances in forest humus and in grassy areas where the birds feed. Because turkeys tend to travel in flocks that may number more than a dozen birds, their foraging habits tend to leave obvious sign of their passing. Loosened soil, flattened and disturbed grasses, and displaced leaves are all signs that turkeys have been there.

Vocalizations: Varied, ranging from hollow clucking sounds to low chirping to the distinctive gobble of mating adult males.

Lifespan: 5 to 12 years. Mortality rate of young can be as high as 50% in their first year.

Diet

Varied and omnivorous. Turkeys generally forage in groups, scratching the earth underfoot with their clawed toes to expose edible plants, seeds, grubs, and insects. The species also eats blueberries and other fruits in season, and may occasionally crack the husks of acorns with their strong beaks to reach the fleshy nut inside.

Wild turkeys usually forage during daylight hours, and are especially active in the early morning, after descending from their arboreal roosting places. They may also be seen feeding in open areas during the day, but are more likely to remain behind concealing cover during daylight, or in the shade of a forest on hot summer days. In the early evening, flocks will often forage in open places on the way to nightly roosting trees.

Turkeys are not migratory, but, like most animals, they change habitats out of necessity when winter makes summer foods unavailable. Winter feeding places often include evergreen woods consisting, especially, of cedars, whose seeds make up a large portion of the species' diet during the cold months.

Mating Habits

Wild turkeys reach sexual maturity at 10 to 11 months. Females will probably mate in their second spring, but young toms may be forced by competition from larger, older males to wait until their third year. Mating takes place from February through April, sometimes extending into May in the nothernmost parts of the species' range.

Just prior to the spring mating season, the naked heads, wattles, and caruncles of mature toms take on brilliant hues of mostly red, interspersed with patches of blue, to indicate that they've reached sexual readiness. During this period, males become especially bold, frequenting open areas, from roadside meadows to hayfields, where they fan out their tails, strut, and gobble loudly enough to be heard from more than a mile distant.

The purpose of this ostentatious display is to attract females, which may come from as far as 2 miles and form harems as large as one-hundred individuals, although most mating flocks number about twenty. Dominant gobblers will gather and hold as many hens as competition from other males will allow, herding them from behind, often with tail fanned, wings held slightly away from the body, and with a strutting walk intended to make the gobbler look as large as possible. Harems may include adolescents, and even young males are tolerated so long as they don't try to usurp the dominant tom's authority. Only a single male will mate within each flock, however, and that alpha male will at least attempt to breed with every receptive hen in his harem.

If a dominant male is challenged, the toms square off with fanned tails and outspread wings, and stalk around one another in a display of body language. If neither contender is discouraged, the contest becomes more physical, with both toms flying at one another, feet extended and spurs raking. The spurs, which are similar to those seen on domestic roosters, are the toms' main weapons, and may reach lengths of more than

1 inch. Spurs are primarily stabbing instruments, used for jabbing with a downward motion when their owners fly upward and descend on top of an opponent. As natural weapons go, they aren't very effective, and probably most of a gobbler's real power lies in the bludgeoning force of its powerful wings. As with most wild species, mating battles are seldom more than mildly injurious to either party.

After copulation, hens gestate for roughly 18 days before leaving the flock to lay an average of eight eggs (clutches as high as fifteen eggs have been reported) in a leafy depression on the ground, usually under a concealing shrub, low evergreen bough, or within the thicket of branches formed by wind-felled trees. Wild turkey eggs are about 50% larger than chicken eggs, with most measuring more than 3 inches long, and have shells that are beige in color.

Despite being on the ground and seemingly vulnerable, few large predators can reach most turkey nests, and smaller egg-eaters, like raccoons, skunks, and ermine, are unwilling to risk the wrath of a protective mother hen, so predation on eggs is minimal. Nesting hens leave their clutches periodically to feed during the warmth of the day, but never for long periods. After an incubation period of about 28 days, the eggs hatch. Hatchlings are precocious, and within days are able to follow their mothers, who rejoin the flock, where the entire family enjoys the protection of a group.

Behavior

Turkeys are active only during daylight hours, roosting at night in tall trees. The turkey is a wary bird with keen eyesight and good hearing, able to detect most predators at a distance in their open feeding areas. Adults can run in excess of 10 miles per hour, and when pressed can fly at remarkable speeds up to 55 miles per hour for several hundred yards, or until reaching the safety of tall trees.

In autumn, usually September or October, turkeys gather in wintering flocks of several males and sometimes more than twenty females. There appears to be no animosity between adult males at this time, with none of the strutting displays seen during the spring mating period, and members are generally silent unless the flock gets separated. The goal at this time is to feed and put on fat reserves against the coming winter, and the turkeys concentrate on eating to the exclusion of all else.

Since their comeback, turkeys have become perhaps the most popular game bird in the United States, bringing in revenue that numbers in the millions of dollars each year to states that allow them to be hunted. Turkey hunting actually helps conservation efforts by prompting governmental and sporting organizations to preserve or create habitat where turkeys and numerous other species can thrive. Although hunting seasons are strictly regulated, *M. gallopavo* is not endangered, and thanks to good conservation efforts, it can today be found in habitats where it historically didn't exist.

Ruffed Grouse, or Partridge *(Bonasa umbellus)*

Ruffed grouse are the most widespread of the grouse family, which includes sage hens, prairie chickens, and ptarmigans. All of the grouse prefer a four-season environment where winters include snow, and none are migratory. The scientific name Bonasa means "like a bison," which probably alludes to this bird's stout physique, and the manelike collar of feathers that both sexes can voluntarily "ruff" outward to make themselves look larger to an adversary.

Ruffed grouse. Illustration by Bob Hines, courtesy of U.S. Fish & Wildlife Service.

Geographic Range

Ruffed Grouse are a northern species, found from Newfoundland on the Atlantic seaboard, across Canada on the southern shores of Hudson Bay, and extending northward into central Alaska. To the south, their range covers New York to Michigan, Wisconsin, and northeastern Minnesota, with populations extending southward through the Allegheny and Appalachian Mountains into Tennessee, Virginia, and northern Georgia. Their range also includes the Rocky Mountains south into northeastern Nevada, and the Cascades down to northern California. All of the places where ruffed grouse are found will be places where winters are snow covered, but south of the Arctic Circle.

Habitat

Ruffed grouse prefer mostly coniferous forests in the rugged north woods, especially thick swamplands of red and white cedars, which provide most of its winter foods. These birds are rarely seen in deciduous forests, and then only when passing through to coniferous woods. They also avoid fields and other open areas, unlike their cousins, the prairie chickens. The ideal ruffed grouse habitat is overgrown, sheltered from wind, and canopied enough to be shaded at all times of day. The species generally avoids human habitation.

Physical Characteristics

Mass: 2 to 3 pounds.

Body: The ruffed grouse is a stoutly built bird that stands approximately 18 inches tall. The ankle (tarsus) is partially feathered on both legs. A ruff of feathers around the neck, larger on males, can be erected when the bird is excited or agitated to make it appear to be larger than it is. A white stripe extends from the base of the beak, around

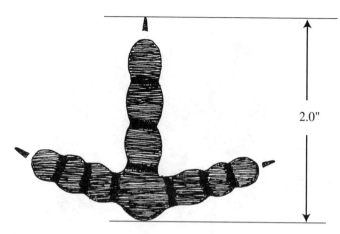

2.0"

Ruffed grouse (Bonasa umbellus) *track. Track similar to that of a wild turkey, except much smaller, and almost never found in the open areas frequented by turkey flocks. Also, hind toe may print faintly to the rear of tracks on soft sand or snow.*

the eyes, to the rear of the head. Top of the head is partially crested with about three short, upright feathers that angle backward.

Tail: Wedge-shaped in the resting positon, wider at the end, tapering inward toward the body, consisting of roughly twenty wide feathers that have wide black bands at their outer ends, and are tipped with gray. Males fan their tails widely, much like a tom turkey, to help attract females during the mating season.

Tracks: Usually three-toed, with longest center toe extending straight forward, flanked on either side by shorter toes extending forward and outward at symmetrical angles. On softer soils and in snow, the rear, grasping, toe will print lightly and partially behind the three forward toes; on firmer soil the rearmost toe might not print. Forward toes exhibit three obvious segments per toe. Tracks about 2 inches long (discounting rear toe), similar to but much shorter than those of a wild turkey. Aside from the usually obvious size difference, there's little danger of confusing tracks from a large partridge with those of a small turkey because turkeys tend to travel in flocks and prefer open areas, while ruffed grouse are solitary and keep to canopied woods.

Scat: Winter scats are usually brownish and elongated, of even diameter throughout their lengths, and crescent-shaped. One end will normally be flat, the opposite end rounded. Like its tracks, ruffed grouse scat is very similar to that of a wild turkey, but usually less than half the size at about 1 inch long, and nearly always found in deep woods that turkeys tend to avoid.

Summer scats tend to be softer, less pelletlike, revealing a more succulent diet of greens and insects. Color is generally black or dark brown, usually with a chalky white (calcareous) substance at one end, sometimes throughout. In any season, scats become lighter and more crumbled with age, deteriorating more quickly than the scats of mammals.

Coloration: Although considered to be the same species, ruffed grouse exhibit two distinctive regional color phases: A red morph (color phase) occurs in the Appalachian range and in the Pacific northwest, while the gray morph is predominant in the northern range east of the Pacific. Both color phases wear the same black collar (the ruff), with a wide black band at the end of the tail, a light colored breast speckled with darker horizontal crescent shapes, and an almost scaled appearance on wings and back.

Sign: Scats beneath cedar, hemlock, and spruce trees. Collections of scats of varying ages on a large downed observation log. Green pine needles, pieces of poplar buds or catkins, cedar nut husks on the ground beneath trees a partridge has fed from.

Vocalizations: Clucks and chirps, difficult to distinguish from the sounds made by other birds. Most distinctive is the trademark drumming sound made by territorial males during the spring mating season. This drumming sound is made by beating the wings rapidly against the breast while standing atop a wide downed log. The sound has been likened to that of a two-stroke engine that sputters but refuses to start, and many have mistaken it as the noise made by a poorly tuned chainsaw.

Lifespan: About 3 years in the wild.

Diet

More than a quarter of the adult ruffed grouse's diet is made up of seasonal fruits, including strawberries, serviceberries, blueberries, and wild cherries. Prior to fruiting, the sugar-rich blossoms of these shrubs and trees are also eaten, as are grass sprouts.

Insects are also eaten opportunistically, from moths that cling to tree trunks during the daylight hours to grasshoppers, crickets, grubs, and ants found in the forests where partridge forage. Young chicks too small to fly and forage in the trees make insects most of their diets, using these protein-rich foods to grow quickly.

When winter snows make most food plants and fruits unavailable, grouse continue to feed on withered berries so long as they're available, but also find good sustenance in the winter buds. Many shrubs and trees produce pre-leaf sprouts by midwinter, leaving the grouse with a normally plentiful diet of tender buds from river willow, cedar, beech, and other shrubs or trees.

Mating Habits

Ruffed grouse breed throughout April and May, although a warm spring might cause males to advertise for mates as early as mid-March, and chicks born the previous spring may take part in their first mating season, at about 10 months of age. The mating season appears to be initiated mostly by a photoperiodic response to lengthening days, although warming weather undoubtedly plays a part as well.

Male ruffed grouse play the most active part in mating, advertising their availability by standing atop an elevated position, usually a down log or large stump, and "drumming," beating their wings rapidly against the breast to produce a sound similar to that of a small piston engine. Drumming posts are above ground to make the sound audible from more than a mile distant, as well as to permit males a good view of the surrounding terrain, but are rarely higher than 4 feet above ground. Receptive

Ruffed grouse nest with eggs.

females respond to the sound and come to where the male has stationed itself. Copulation normally takes place on the ground within a few yards of the male's drumming post.

Adult male partridges (roosters) frequently compete for prime drumming stations, particularly in areas where there are numerous females. Battles between them consist mainly of shoving matches in which contenders fly at one another atop the drumming site, attempting to push one another off. A few dislodged feathers mark the ground where these contests took place, but battles are usually bloodless, and the weaker male withdraws to find another drumming spot.

After mating, male and female ruffed grouse separate, the male to find another mate, if one is available. The eggs grow quickly inside the female, and after a gestation period of 1 to 2 weeks, she begins laying them, one per day, in a bowl-shaped ground nest constructed of grasses, twigs, and pine needles. Clutches average about eleven eggs, and when all have been laid, the female sits on them almost constantly until they hatch, about 24 days later.

Not all eggs hatch. Cold spring weather, especially combined with rain or late snows, can kill embryos within the eggs, and also new, unfeathered hatchlings. Many small predators prey on both eggs and hatchlings, even though mothers attempt to locate their nests in places that are inaccessible to raccoons and larger egg-eaters. Smaller predators, such as ermine and mink, will dine on eggs if the opportunity arises, but they prefer to avoid the flailing wings of a protective mother grouse if more easily obtainable foods are available.

Chicks are fed a diet of mostly insects by their mothers for the first month, after which they begin foraging near the nest site on their own, but always under their mother's watchful eye. A high-protein diet of bugs causes the young birds to grow quickly, and by 10 weeks all surviving chicks can forage on their own, and fly away from danger. At this point the family separates, and no more maternal care is given.

Behavior

The most memorable, and probably the first, encounter a typical hiker has with ruffed grouse is a startled reaction to the birds' explosive and noisy eruption from cover. Partridge have an instinctive tendency to sit tight until a potential enemy has approached to within just a few feet, then burst into flight with a sudden loud flapping of wings. This defense uses the bird's very good camouflage to conceal it from sharp-eyed predators, then, if a predator approaches too closely, the grouse's almost violent blast from cover nearly always guarantees a short head start while the enemy recoils involuntarily.

Except for the spring mating season, ruffed grouse are solitary birds. Males especially seem to claim terrritories, but there are almost no disputes beyond mating season, and territorial boundaries are respected. Drumming from territorial males helps to reinforce the peace, and may continue well past the mating season, through the month of June.

Despite its popularity as a game bird, the ruffed grouse is not endangered, although populations in some areas dipped noticeably in the late 1990s. More dangerous to ruffed grouse populations than hunting is deforestation of the species' natural habitat. Cutting timber from large tracts of forest insures that grouse will neither mate nor live there.

American Woodcock, or Timberdoodle *(Scolopax minor)*

This member of the sandpiper family (family Scolopacidae) is perhaps best known as a migratory game bird to sport hunters. Often confused with the common snipe, with which it shares most of its range, this shorebird actually prefers wet, overgrown woodlands and mostly-dry swamps, while true snipes tend toward shorelines.

Geographic Range

The American woodcock is native only to North America, where its range covers all of the eastern states to a rough line extending from Minnesota south to eastern Texas. To

American woodcock (Scolopax minor).

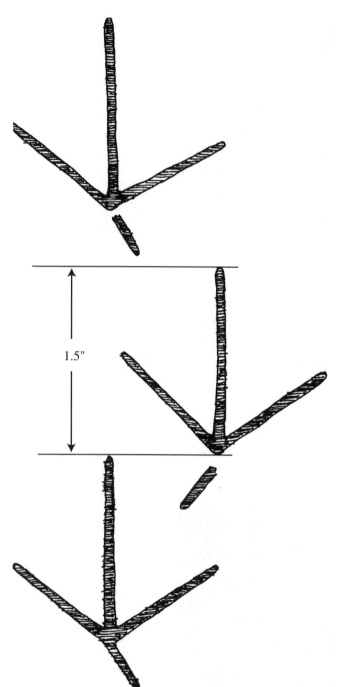

1.5"

American woodcock (Scolopax minor) tracks.

the north, woodcocks are found in southeast Manitoba, eastward along the southern borders of Ontario and Quebec. A few individuals are reported to winter on islands in the Caribbean Ocean.

Habitat

Woodcock habitat is primarily in damp, mostly deciduous woods and overgrown thickets, where moist soil with moderate to low acidity provides an abundance of earthworms. Small meadows and glades surrounded by forest are its preferred mating grounds in spring, while the leaf-covered floors of deciduous forests are best for foraging. Nesting areas include coniferous and mixed forests that provide good cover, as well as older clearcuts. Despite being classed as a sandpiper, this shorebird always tends toward woodlands, although never more than a mile from a source of open water.

Physical Characteristics

Mass: 4 to 10 ounces, adult females about 10% larger than males.

Body: The American woodcock is short and stout compared to the closely related snipes, with a thick body, comparatively large rounded head, and very short neck. Also distinguished from other sandpipers by three large blackish bands that run across the top of the head, instead of the lengthwise stripes found on snipes. Large brown eyes are set far back on the skull to provide good rearward vision. The slender, sharply pointed bill is specialized for probing into soil, and measures 2 to 3 inches long. Body length 10 to 12 inches from tip of beak to end of tail. The wings are broad and rounded, spanning 17 to 19 inches when spread.

Tail: Very short and wedge-shaped, 2 to 2.5 inches long, and comprised of twelve narrow feathers that taper to rounded ends.

Tracks: Three forward-pointing toes, one rearward-pointing grasping toe that angles to the inside, enabling the bird to grasp small branches when perched. Rear toe prints lightly in soft soil, sometimes not at all. Track length 1.5 inches, discounting rear toe.

Scat: Seldom seen, but most likely to be found on the ground beneath low shrubs. Typical form is cylindrical, rounded at one end, slightly crescent-shaped. Dark brown to nearly black in color. Diameter about 0.125 inch, length up to 1 inch. Scats usually lack seeds and vegetable matter.

Coloration: Plumage is patterned with brown, buff, and black, which camouflages the bird extremely well in its woodland habitat. Wing feathers give the appearance of black scales when folded against the sides. A narrow dark band extends from the front of the eyes forward to the base of the beak. Legs tan to gray. Both sexes exhibit the same patterns and colors (monomorphic).

Sign: Woodcocks leave little sign of their presence. Most often found, especially during the summer molt, are feathers that have been discarded under low-lying shrubs and bushes. Leaf litter below these bushes will often show evidence of having been disturbed when the bird probed for earthworms, but this sign is easily missed and difficult to discern from sign left by other small local animals.

Vocalizations: The most commonly heard vocalization, especially in spring and early summer, is a nasal beeping sound that has been described as an unmelodious "peent" that lasts for about 1 second. This call is usually heard from males that are attempting to attract females during the spring mating season, but apparently serves as a territorial claim in summer, as well.

Also commonly heard is the tremolo whistling of the woodcock's wings in flight. With each downbeat of the wings, the flight feathers make a high pitched whistle that is especially apparent to hikers who approach a quietly sitting bird closely enough to cause it to burst into flight. A variation of this sound is heard from adults during the spring mating season, when males fly upward 200 to 300 feet, their wings issuing a rapidly repeated "woo-woo-woo" sound, then fall earthward a hundred feet or so, and repeat the process.

Lifespan: 3 to 4 years, average.

Diet

An estimated 50% to 90% of the woodcock's daily diet consists of earthworms, but numerous other insects are eaten as well, including beetles, moths, flies, centipedes, and the larvae of most insects. Because the woodcock is a ground forager, nearly all of the insects it eats are on the ground or under leafy humus; it doesn't pursue flying insects or snap them out of the air the way flycatchers and some other birds are adept at doing.

Woodcocks are extraordinary earthworm hunters, able to sense minute movements under the ground. Most sensitive is the long beak, which is kept in contact with the earth almost constantly. An earthworm moving within several inches of the woodcock creates minute vibrations that are detected through the bird's beak, and it makes an unerring stab beneath the forest duff to grasp the worm before it can escape underground. If no movement is detected, a woodcock may stamp the ground with one foot to incite lethargic worms into motion, all the while keeping the tip of its sensitive beak in contact with the earth. And although there's no data to confirm this, it seems apparent that woodcocks also possess an acute sense of smell, and are able to narrow their searches for worms through odors.

Woodcocks also eat some vegetation, particularly seeds, grass sprouts, and buds in early spring when they migrate northward. Earthworms and insects are preferred in any season, but if spring weather arrives late in the woodcock's summer habitat, causing these small animals to remain dormant for an extended period, vegetation is made to suffice until temperatures rise.

Mating Habits

Both genders of woodcock reach sexual maturity at 10 to 12 months. Courtship and nesting span the warm weather months, from spring to early fall, beginning as early as late February in southern latitudes, as late as May in the northernmost regions. Mating is preceded by a northerly migration of sometimes large flocks of these normally solitary birds. Males may begin courting during that migratory flight, but breeding takes place only after the birds have reached the forests in which they were born.

Woodcocks are territorial, with males and females staking out territories in their winter and summer ranges that they'll continue to use throughout their lifespans. The species is also among the most nonviolent of animals, and there's no record of either sex battling over territory. Females seem content to nest within as little as 50 yards of one another, and can sometimes be seen foraging for worms in such close proximity that it makes them appear friendly to one another. Males who find themselves in competition for the same territory resolve their disagreements with puffed-up displays and excited chirps, but never fight.

Male woodcocks assume the most active role in mating, and their advertisement for mates is one of the most obvious in the bird world, even though most courting is done during the hours of darkness. On reaching their summer range, males find a clearing, sometimes referred to as a "singing site," where they can fly upward and descend freely, with no interference from an overhead canopy. There, the male begins displaying by flying 200 to 300 feet upward on wings that make a high-pitched twittering sound when flapped rapidly against the air. On reaching the apex of its flight, the woodcock falls or glides earthward to a height of about 100 feet, then rises again on twittering wings. Between aerial displays, males rest on the ground and utter their distinctive "peent" cries.

Receptive females are drawn to the male's courting display from a mile or more distant, initially by the distinctive whistling of its wings, then, as the female draws closer, by its silhouette against the sky. On meeting, the pair engages in a brief courtship in which the male again plays the most active role, peenting and occasionally flying upward for several yards on twittering wings. Copulation generally occurs within an hour, then the female leaves, and the male returns to advertising for mates. There is no lasting bond between mates, and both will likely breed with several partners over the course of the summer.

Impregnated female woodcocks withdraw to their own, usually heavily wooded, territories almost immediately after mating. Those not fertilized by their previous matings will probably respond to the calls of another male and mate again, but those whose eggs have begun to develop will seek out a suitable nesting site.

Like turkeys and grouse, female woodcocks are ground-layers, making rough nests of available leaves and debris directly atop the forest floor, always behind or under covering foliage, and usually in a place that's difficult for most predators to access. A few, usually inexperienced, mothers may lay their eggs directly atop the forest floor if the weather is warm.

Eggs are laid within a week or so of mating, and the usual clutch size is four gray-orange eggs that measure about 1.5 inches long. Incubation lasts about 21 days. Newborn woodcocks are precocious, walking around the nest within hours after hatching, but they cannot feed themselves for the first 3 to 4 days, and must be fed earthworms by the mother. By 4 days the hatchlings will have begun feeding themselves with small insects and plant sprouts, and will begin probing for earthworms with their long beaks. By 30 days the young are nearly fully grown, and disperse to find their own territories.

Behavior

The American woodcock is a normally solitary bird that avoids bright daylight. Most active at dusk and dawn (crepuscular), woodcocks spend the sunlight hours sleeping in shaded undergrowth, usually on the ground, where its mottled camouflage makes it virtually invisible. When darkness falls, the birds leave their seclusion to probe the forest floor for earthworms and nightcrawlers, which are also most active at night.

The woodcock's large eyeballs give it exceptional night vision, while their placement near the rear of the head provide a field of view that permits them to see movement from behind, a valuable ability for birds that spend much of their time facing downward. Being primarily nocturnal, the woodcock's greatest danger comes from above, usually in the form of hunting owls. Terrestrial predators, especially foxes and bobcats, also prey on woodcocks, but it appears that relatively few birds are taken by these carnivores.

Like ruffed grouse, most of a woodcock's defense against predators lies in the mottled camouflage pattern of its feathers, and an instinctive reluctance to reveal itself. When approached by a potentially dangerous animal (including humans) the birds remain almost stubbornly motionless under shading foliage, virtually invisible to even the sharpest eye, until the predator is mere feet from their hiding spot. Then, the woodcock bursts from cover in a flurry of twittering wings that startles the enemy into hesitating for the brief second it needs to become airborne.

Escape flights seldom cover more than 100 yards before the woodcock again settles into an obscure hiding place, a habit also seen in ruffed grouse. This method of escape is effective against animal predators, but human researchers and sport hunters can exploit it by noting in which direction a woodcock flew, then very slowly following, knowing that the bird has gone to ground again within a few dozen yards.

Woodcocks have been referred to as timberdoodles by hunting magazine writers, but this moniker rightfully belongs to the closely related common snipe *(Gallinago gallinago)*, whose marshland habitat frequently overlaps that of the true woodcock. The name alludes to the corkscrewing flight pattern used by flushed snipes, whose spiraling escape over relatively open marshes is designed to make them a difficult target for hawks that are adept at plucking prey birds out of the air. The woodcock's forested habitat doesn't require such evasive maneuvering, and in fact often prohibits such aerobatics. A woodcock often flutters while flying away from an enemy, but isn't known to employ the corkscrew flight used by snipes.

Common Raven (*Corvus corax*)

Largest of the family Corvidae, which also includes crows, magpies, and jays, the raven may be the smartest bird species in the world, arguably second to the smaller American crow *(Corvus brachyrhynchos)* in terms of social structure and a rudimentary language. This innate intelligence has made both crows and ravens popular in zoos and as pets, where some individuals have even been trained to speak simple words, like "hello." Some cultures have revered these birds enough to incorporate them into their heritage—a spread-wing raven was once the icon painted on the sails of ships belonging to the Scottish clan MacDougall.

The raven's historical range was once broader than it is today, but for centuries the big, bold birds were easy targets for farmers who blamed them for crop damage, and for varmint hunters who eradicated them for sport. Today ravens enjoy legal protection in many states, and the species appears to be rebounding.

Geographic Range

Ravens are common throughout most of the world, and especially in the northern hemisphere, where they range well above the Arctic Circle. Around the globe, ravens

Common raven. Photo by Lee Karney, courtesy of U.S. Fish & Wildlife Service.

are native to northwest Europe, Great Britain, the shorelines of Greenland, Iceland, northern Scandinavia, central Asia and the Himalayas, northwest India, Iran, northwest Africa, the Canary Islands, and Central America South to Nicaragua.

In North America the species is found throughout Canada and Alaska, throughout the western states, along the Rocky Mountains southward into Mexico. Absent throughout all but the northernmost eastern states, except along the Appalachian Mountains, where it extends southward to Georgia.

Habitat

Ravens are adaptable to almost any environment, but are partial to cooler climes where winters include at least some snowfall. The birds are capable of withstanding extreme cold, and it might not be coincidental that the rugged, cold habitats that ravens seem to prefer are places where humans are sparsely populated.

All suitable raven habitats will include elevated places where females can nest well above ground, out of reach of most predators. In mountainous terrain, rocky crags and cliff faces are used for nesting, but it appears that most prefer to nest in the tops of standing trees, particularly conifers.

Physical Characteristics:

Mass: 1.5 to 3.5 pounds, with heavier individuals occurring in the north.

Body: The raven is the largest of all-black birds, standing 24 inches or more, or roughly 50% larger than the closely related common crow. Wingspan about 46 inches. All-black bill is comparatively larger than the crow's, with the upper side covered with

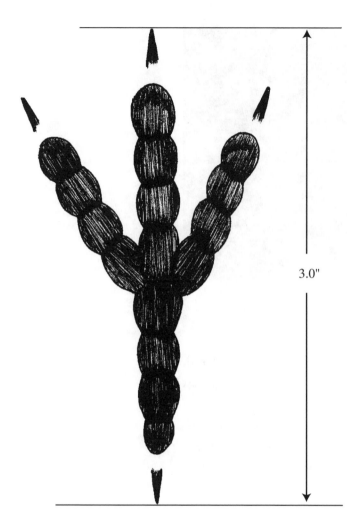

3.0"

Raven (Corvus corax) track as it might appear in wet sand or fresh snow. Note thickly muscled toes and long, sharp claws, larger than the two inch long track of the crow. Known primarily as a scavenger, the raven is a capable hunter of rodents, frogs, and other prey up to the size of a small muskrat. May eat eggs of other bird species.

short black nasal feathers about halfway out from the head. Neck, and especially the throat, is more thickly feathered than the crow's. The sexes are nearly identical, except that females tend to be roughly 10% smaller than males.

Tail: Wedge-shaped and much longer than that of the crow, extending nearly to the ground, sometimes dragging when the bird is walking.

Tracks: Three thick, segmented toes facing forward, center toe longer than outer toes; one toe facing rearward, used for grasping. Forward facing toes less splayed than in some species (like the turkey) with less of an angle between outer toes and center toe. Rear toe usually in line with center toe, not offset as in crows and many other species. Claws exceptionally long in comparison to most non-predatory species, measuring up to 0.5 inch, and normally showing in tracks. Track length (excluding claws), about 3.5 inches from tip of rearward toe to tip of center forward toe.

Although very strong fliers, ravens tend to walk from one place to another with a strutting gait that might be described as almost cocky in nature. The typical pattern is a staggered line of left and right tracks, evenly spaced, and all pointing forward—as opposed to the pigeon-toed (inward pointing) or duck-footed (outward pointing) tracks of many other species. Distance between left and right tracks averages about 6 inches, with a narrow straddle of about 2 inches between left center toe and right center toe. Note that rear toes tend to drag as the bird steps forward, leaving scrape marks behind them, and revealing its habit of angling the forward toes upward as it walks.

When taking flight, ravens, like most birds, prefer to get a running start that consists of a series of hops in which paired left and right tracks print closely together, but have a space of 2 to 3 feet between pairs. Tracks tend to point forward, not angled, and rear toes seldom leave scrape marks.

Scat: Varied, sometimes solid, but most often watery and formless. Solid scats are typically dark, brown or blackish, unsegmented, evenly cylindrical in shape, and curved. Diameter less than 0.5 inch, length ranges from less than 1 inch to more than 2 inches.

Solid scats are often indicative of a poor diet that lacks good nutrition and moisture. Scats turn white as they become drier with age.

A more succulent diet of fresh carrion and other animal flesh results in a semi-liquid scat form that's most often found beneath trees and other elevated perches. These splattered scats may be up to 2 inches across, and usually have a mucouslike consistency, with traces of yellow or white. Occasionally there will be more solid segments included, as well as insect legs and carapaces in summer.

Coloration: All-black feathers and bill. Legs and feet unfeathered and black. Feathers have an iridescent quality because of oils, making the bird shiny in sunlight, and causing it to have a purplish cast under bright conditions.

Sign: Accumulations of scat under roosting trees, especially obvious atop snow. Discarded all-black feathers under roosting trees, especially in summer. In winter, wingtips often brush against snow when the bird is taking flight, leaving imprints of flight feathers, as well as a good indication of wingspan; the same phenomenon may be seen on dusty roads and sandy shorelines.

Vocalizations: Classified as a songbird by ornithologists, ravens are among the loudest and most vocal of birds, which makes them easy subjects for study. Less easy is deciphering the precise meaning of the species' numerous calls, which range from the familiar croaks and caws to short whistles and clucks. It's commonly accepted among ornithologists that both ravens and crows have a rudimentary language, but the process of defining them is a work in progress.

The most often heard call is a croaking "awwk" that keeps members in touch with others of the same flock. A call used to alert others to the presence of food is a higher-pitched and less hoarse "ock."

A less commonly heard raven voice consists of a repeated clucking sound that has sometimes been mistaken for the mating call of a male grouse. This sound, which humans can imitate by placing the flat of the tongue against their upper palates, then sucking it abruptly downward, is a hollow cluck, almost a popping noise. The call is usually in two stages, a lower toned cluck followed by a slightly higher pitched one, but different combinations are sometimes used. The call is apparently a communication, but is often issued from lone ravens perched on a low branch, and its exact meaning has yet to be determined.

Another raven call that often goes unidentified or misidentified is a hollow whistle that sounds much like the noise humans make by blowing across the mouth of a glass sodapop bottle. The exact meaning of this call has yet to be determined, but it seems to be uttered mostly in the early morning, and from lone individuals perched overhead.

Lifespan: About 6 years in the wild.

Diet

Ravens, like the related crows, jays, and magpies, are best known as scavengers of carcasses, but the species' diet is actually broadly omnivorous. Carrion, especially the carcasses of larger animals like deer, represent a large, easily obtained source of food, but ravens, like most of the birds in their taxonomic family, are versatile feeders that can subsist on nearly any digestible organic material.

Being scavengers that rely on vision, ravens possess extraordinary eyesight and good color discrimination, which allows them to see dead or dying animals from great distances. A very long beak filled with olfactory receptors gives the birds an ability to detect the spoor of blood from several miles distant; among birds, only the turkey vulture (*Cathartes aura*) has a more acute sense of smell.

Much of the reason ravens are known primarily as carrion eaters has to do with the birds' habit of frequenting roadways where large numbers of animals are killed by motorists. Smaller road kills, like squirrels, are simply carried off in the birds' talons to be eaten in a less hazardous location. Deer and other animals too large for transport draw sometimes large congregations of ravens and crows, although rarely both at the same time, because ravens are loath to share a bounty with their smaller cousins.

Ravens do share large carcasses with coyotes and wolves, and in fact intentionally advertise the presence of large dead animals to these more powerful carnivores by giving a raucous display in which a flock of them, sometimes ten or more, circle above the carcass with a cacophony of croaking calls. Before the larger carrion eaters respond, attendant ravens busy themselves eating a carcass's soft parts—eyeballs, nose pad, and around the anal cavity—but the birds lack the strength necessary to tear through tough hide to reach fleshier, more preferred portions. Coyotes and wolves have learned to recognize the ravens' display as a sign of easily obtained food. After the larger carnivores have eaten their fill, the ravens descend to peck the remaining flesh from nooks and crannies inaccessible to teeth.

Large dead animals that are in places too open to attract carnivores may remain inaccessible to ravens, although they have learned that carcasses at the roadside are often split open from impact, but the birds also frequent carcasses after they've begun to decay. Rotted flesh isn't generally eaten, but fly and insect larvae, beetles, and other invertebrates that feed on decayed organic matter can make up a large portion of the roadway raven's diet.

Although not known for their hunting prowess, ravens also have a predatory side. Raids on the eggs and newborns of smaller nesting birds, especially those that nest on the ground, are fairly common, and ravens frequently make meals of hatchling turtles in early summer, as well as snakes, frogs, mice, and voles. The birds can often be seen foraging in meadows for grasshoppers and mice, and in freshly plowed fields for earthworms. Few small animals are excluded from the diet of this opportunistic hunter. In some areas, predation of ravens on the young of endangered species, like desert tortoises and least terns, has caused them to be considered pests.

Ravens are also fond of fruits and seeds. Raspberries, blueberries, and most other berries are eaten in season, but the birds dislike having their vision hampered by the dense foliage of a berry thicket, and will fly up into nearby trees often to survey the surrounding area for danger. More favored are fruiting trees, like crabapple, service-berry, and wild cherries, which allow ravens an unrestricted view while they feed. Cornfields are sometimes plundered, and cobs carried off in the birds' feet to a safer, more open feeding spot. Ravens and crows also incur the wrath of farmers by eating seeds from freshly planted fields.

Like most species in family Corvidae, ravens are known to carry off and to store foods in elevated larders that range from cracks in cliff faces to holes in standing trees, and even church belltowers. It doesn't appear that foods are cached for long-term storage, but rather to provide a safe place for them to be retrieved and eaten within a few days.

The tendency to cache items also extends to nonfood objects. Ravens and, to a lesser extent, crows are known for stealing small shiny objects, like watches, marbles, and even coins, then flying off with them clutched in their feet to stash the objects in an elevated cache, which might also be used for storing food. The purpose behind this behavior isn't known, but the thievery of ravens has been well-documented.

Mating Habits

Ravens reach sexual maturity at 11 to 12 months. Mating takes place from late February through early March, later in the north than in the south. It appears that breeding season is initiated by several factors, including lengthening days, warming temperatures, and probably pheromonal scents emitted by receptive females.

Both males and females become territorial at the start of breeding season, driving off other ravens of the same sex, and becoming generally intolerant of all larger birds within their claimed domains. Males tend to pursue females, and their territories are generally sited to overlap those of several females, even though both sexes are typically monogamous, accepting only one mate per breeding season.

Courtship between prospective mates is a ritualized affair of elaborate displays and dances. The female indicates her readiness to breed to an attendant male by crouching low to the ground and extending her wings, their tips drooping to the ground, in a posture of submission. The male struts around her, breast and neck feathers ruffled to make himself look as large as possible. If the male is an acceptable mate, the crouched female raises her tail, exposing her genitalia, and shakes it rapidly. The male then mounts her from behind in typical bird fashion, pressing her to the ground and holding her in a submissive position by covering her outspread wings with his own. Copulation lasts less than a minute, and may be repeated several times before the pair flies off together.

Mated pairs are highly territorial, remaining together and defending their clutching area from intruders throughout the summer, and often longer. Both mates participate in building a broad dish-shaped nest, about 3 feet in diameter, of large sticks encasing a more densely intertwined wall of smaller sticks, and lined with feathers, fur, grass, and other soft materials. The raven's larcenous nature and innate intelligence sometimes results in nests that are lined with socks and small articles of clothing stolen from clotheslines, while the nest walls may include wire, plastic drinking straws, string, or other suitable man-made objects.

The raven's best-known nesting places are rocky ledges on high cliff faces, out of the wind, but other equally elevated and sheltered locations are also used. Nesting ravens have been sighted atop power poles, farm silos, microwave towers, and once even on the roof of an abandoned car. In forested country, the birds often nest at the tops of tall pines, especially those standing in open marshes.

Pregnant females begin laying their eggs almost immediately after their nests are completed, within about 10 days of mating. Clutch sizes average four to five blue-green, brown-spotted eggs, each about 3 inches long. Eggs are incubated by the female, although some reports claim that males may sit on the eggs for short periods while their mates leave to drink and feed. Males also bring their nesting mates food.

Raven eggs hatch after an incubation period of about 18 days, in late March to early April. Similar in size to chicks of the domestic chicken, hatchlings are born naked in the south, covered with a fine fuzz in the north. Both parents care for the young, bringing them insects and scraps of meat.

Young ravens learn to fly at about 8 weeks, and leave the nest with their parents. Adolescents can be differentiated from their parents by being slightly smaller, and because they lack the blue-black iridescence of an adult, especially around the head and shoulders. Parents and young remain loosely together throughout the summer and following winter, with the family growing progressively less cohesive as the young ravens approach maturity. Yearling ravens leave their parents to establish their own territories and to find their own mates in the following spring.

Behavior

Ravens are complex birds, which historically led to some disagreement about their habits and behaviors among ornithologists and laymen alike. Adult birds are indeed solitary, but only until they find mates. Mated pairs probably remain together for life, yet widowed mates will rarely remain alone past the next spring mating season, and widowed parents of immature nestbound young will probably find a new mate to help raise the offspring soon after losing the parental mate.

Although described by some authorities as being solitary in nature, ravens are most often seen in flocks that can number fifteen birds or more. The explanation behind this seeming contradiction is that only unmated adults in search of their own territories are solitary. Mated adults tend to remain together throughout the year, probably until one of them dies, and the bond between parents, offspring, and siblings seems to diminish very little as the birds age.

The primary reason that related ravens flock around a carcass is to create an intimidating show of force to discourage other ravens, and even eagles, from attempting to appropriate a good source of food. Bald eagles and other large raptors have little to fear from individual ravens, and in fact consider them prey, but a half-dozen or more ravens gathered at a deer carcass is more trouble than even a pair of eagles can contend with. Too intelligent to engage a larger, better-armed eagle in individual combat, the ravens persist in harassing the raptor by jumping from all sides to peck at it. Unable to enjoy its spoils, the eagle eventually abandons the carcass to find a less annoying meal elsewhere. That same tactic works against smaller carnivores, like foxes and opossums, but not coyotes or wolves, which ravens rely on to tear through tough hide that their own beaks can't penetrate.

Historically, ravens have been persecuted by humans for superstitious reasons, which themselves spawned erroneous, but persistent, beliefs that ravens were somehow bad birds. Edgar Allan Poe's immortal poem, "The Raven," refers to the bird with the words "devil" and "demon," and even the legendary John James Audubon incorrectly accused the raven of preying on lambs. Prompted by these and other myths, and perhaps intimidated by the raven's bold curiosity and obvious intelligence, farmers in the New World made a point of shooting the birds on sight for centuries. By the first quarter of the twentieth century, this once common species had all but disappeared from much of its historical range in the eastern United States. Today raven numbers are rebounding, especially in the western states, but many eastern states still classify them as endangered or threatened.

Black-Capped Chickadee (Poecile atricapilla)

This tiny but endearing bird has long been a favorite among birdwatchers. Chickadees have been described as the toughest birds in the forest, because when eagles, hawks, and other species known for their fierceness have fled south to warmer climes, the little chickadee remains, energetic and seemingly cheerful in the coldest, most hostile weather.

Geographic Range

Black-capped chickadees are native only to North America, where they range from central and western Alaska, and throughout Canada. In the west, the species

Black-capped chickadee. Photo by Lee Karney, courtesy of U.S. Fish & Wildlife Service.

ranges south to northern California and Nevada, and through the Rocky Mountains as far south as New Mexico. In the eastern and central United States, chickadees are found as far south as Indiana and New Jersey.

Habitat

Black-capped chickadees prefer open deciduous woodlands, but are not uncommon in mixed or mostly coniferous forests, cedar swamps, or among willow and dogwood thickets along river and lakeshores. Many sources list them as being most common at the edges of forest and field, but this may be due more to the number of observers in those places than to the actual number of chickadees living there.

Physical Characteristics

Mass: About 3 ounces.

Body: Black-capped chickadees are easily recognized by their short, plump body, solid black cap and bib, and white cheeks. Standing height 5 to 6 inches; wing span 6 to 8 inches. Bill proportionally short, about 0.25 inch long. Sexes alike in color and size. Difficult to differentiate from the Carolina chickadee, whose range slightly overlaps that of the black-capped in the southeastern edge of the latter's range, except that the true black-capped chickadee's breast bib is more irregular along its lower edge.

Tail: Proportionally long, dark gray.

Tracks: Small and very faint, even on snow or mud. Three toes pointing forward, center toe slightly longer than outer toes; outer toes arrayed at outward-pointing angles to either side. Rear toe typically points straight backward, used for grasping. Track length about 0.5 inch, discounting rear toe. Black-capped chickadees hop rather than walk, leaving paired side-by-side tracks with 3 to 4 inches between pairs.

Scat: Difficult to find, but usually on the ground below branches where the birds perch. Solid form is cylindrical and blackish when fresh, rapidly becoming white as it ages; length about 0.125 inch, diameter about equivalent to a No. 2 pencil lead.

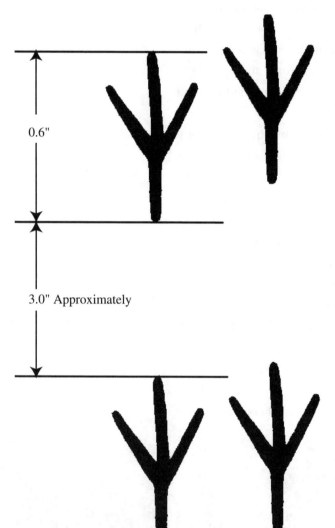

0.6"

3.0" Approximately

Black-capped chickadee (Poecile atricapilla). Chickadees are tiny birds, weighing only about 3 ounces. Their tracks are always faint, and sometimes undetectable except on the softest media.

Coloration: Black skull cap, black bib, white cheeks, back greenish-gray, with streaks of white and black. Wings and tail dark grayish, flanks buffy. Upper wing feathers have white edging.

Sign: Seed husks, sometimes discarded feathers on the ground below perches. Chickadees leave little evidence of having been in a place, but the birds' energetic activities and vocal nature usually make their presence obvious.

Vocalizations: Black-capped chickadees have a range of vocalizations that are used to communicate not only among themselves, but apparently with grosbeaks and other small bird species commonly seen feeding with chickadees. The simple-sounding calls have been found to be surprisingly complex and language-like, encoded with information on identity and recognition of other birds, as well as predator alarms and gathering calls. The call for which chickadees are best known suggests its common name: "dee-dee-dee-dee." Its song consists of two or three whistled notes, the first higher in pitch, described as "fee-bee-ee."

Lifespan: Chickadees live an average of 2.5 years in the wild, although birds up to 5 years aren't uncommon. The oldest wild black-capped chickadee on record lived 12 years and 5 months.

Diet

Black-capped chickadees are omnivorous, feeding on most forest-dwelling insects, their larvae, and spiders, many of which are snapped up as the birds hop about on the trunks of rough-barked trees, like oak, ash, and white pine. Fat-rich grubs and caterpillars are especially preferred during the birds' mating season. Chickadees are an important species in terms of mosquito control, with insects making up roughly 70% of their diets during the summer months. Because chickadee communities tend to be large in the habitats where they live, this species' impact on the numbers of parasitic and agricultural insect pests can be significant.

During the growing season, flowers, fruits, and seeds make up the other 30% of a chickadee's diet. Summer plant foods include nectar-rich flowers, numerous seeds, and many types of berries, including serviceberry, blackberry, goldthread, rose hips, and blueberries. Chickadees have also been observed eating waxy berries like soapberry and the autumn fruits of poison ivy. It's believed that chickadees play an important role in dispersing undigested scat-borne seeds throughout their habitats, thereby helping many plants to propagate.

In winter, chickadees eat seeds of cattails, cedars, and dogwoods, as well as the tender bud-ends of river willow, pines, and most other trees, sometimes hanging upside-down from twigs as they feed. Hibernating spiders and insects are plucked from recesses in the bark of trees, where they've taken refuge until spring.

Chickadees also eat carrion when they can get it, especially in winter. Many hunters have noted that their skinned and hanging deer are a major attraction for chickadees, which focus most of their attention on fats, rather than meat. They also help to clean the bones of larger prey animals brought down by carnivores.

Mating Habits

Black-capped chickadees generally reach sexual maturity at about 12 months, although it appears that some females born in early spring may mate later in the same breeding season in which they were hatched. Mating extends from April to early July, earlier in the south than in the north, and adults mate only once each year. Chickadees probably do not possess a keen sense of smell, so mating is most likely triggered by warming and lengthening days, less by pheromonal scents.

Male and female chickadees are typically already paired from the previous autumn. Unpaired males and females are drawn to one another through vocalizations, which studies suggest are complex enough to be considered a form of rudimentary language. Courtship appears to have no ritual, but consists of much flitting around one another. Mating competitions between breeding males is usually brief and limited to shoving matches in which contenders vie for possession of a perch. Breeding season is the only period of the year in which these social birds exhibit territorial behavior.

Once paired, mates retire from the rest of the flock to find a nesting site, usually inside a standing hollow tree or a knothole in a large dead branch. Females do all of the nest building, while their mates bring them gifts of food. Nests are constructed of grasses, animal fur and feathers, and pine needles.

Fertilized females begin laying as soon as the nest is completed, with clutch sizes ranging from five to ten roundish marble-size eggs with white shells and red-brown spots, especially around their larger ends. Both mates watch over the nest, but only the female sits on the eggs, leaving for brief periods that seldom exceed 5 minutes to drink and relieve herself. After a short incubation of about 12 days, the eggs hatch.

Chickadees are born blind and naked (altricial), but they grow quickly on a diet of mostly insects that are brought to them by both parents. By 9 days the chicks will have grown feathers, and by 16 days they'll have learned to fly. Both parents continue to feed them a high-protein diet of insects until the young are 3 to 4 weeks old, at which time they'll have matured sufficiently to fend for themselves.

Behavior

The black-capped chickadee is a social bird, but with two extremes. During the spring-summer mating season, pairs withdraw from their flocks to incubate and rear young, joining them again between May and August, typically later in the north than in the south.

Before and after their mating season, black-capped chickadees exhibit some of the most social behavior in the animal world, gathering together in flocks that may number in the dozens. Further adding to the size of a chickadee flock are numerous similar-size but unrelated bird species that fly, feed, and often roost—but are not known to interbreed—with the chickadees. These friends of the chickadee include grosbeaks, nuthatches, warblers, vireos, and small woodpeckers. Aside from an occasional squabble at birdfeeders, there seems to be no animosity between the different species, and it's thought that this communal behavior, like schooling fish, provides safety from predators by making it difficult to isolate a single individual from the confusion of a large flock.

Probably due in large part to its social flocking behavior, the chickadee suffers relatively few losses from predation. Bird predators include small forest-dwelling owls and hawks, red squirrels and arboreal snakes that prey on eggs and hatchlings, and occasionally a pine marten or fisher that catches one roosting in the darkness of night. Being active by day, chickadees have relatively poor night vision, but their habit of sleeping on small-diameter end twigs, where vibrations from an approaching arboreal predator can be felt, insure that the tiny birds aren't easy prey at any time of day.

Black-capped chickadees are not migratory, and although they possess the ability to fly from an unsuitable environment to another, better habitat, the species prefers to remain within as small an area as possible, sometimes living their entire lives within just a few acres. This quality has helped to endear them to bird lovers, because chickadees remain in the same territory throughout the coldest winters, and are regular visitors to bird feeders.

To help them resist cold, chickadees' metabolisms slow while sleeping in cold weather, and their body temperatures drop slightly, much the same as a hibernating mammal. This phenomenon doesn't appear to have an effect on the birds' ability to react to danger, but it does serve to conserve energy in very cold weather. Despite this ability, subzero weather is said to be the greatest killer of chickadees, which frequently die of hypothermia while roosting.

Chickadees are not threatened, and their numbers are at healthy levels throughout the species' range. Continued logging of forested habitat, with subsequent loss of nesting sites, is the biggest threat to populations of *P. atricapilla*. A positive note is that chickadees have shown themselves willing to use man-made nesting boxes in lieu of natural sites.

SHORE AND WATER BIRDS

This section deals with bird species whose lives are spent mostly or entirely around water. These include geese, swans, and ducks, herons, cranes, and bitterns, and many species of hawks and eagles. The water birds selected for coverage here represent only a

Great blue heron. Photo by John Cossick, courtesy of U.S. Fish & Wildlife Service.

small number of the species that fall into this category, but they are some of the most important, from an ecological standpoint, and many of the characterics of each are applicable to other members of the same family.

Great Blue Heron (*Ardea herodias*)

One of our most magnificent shorebirds, the great blue heron is an icon of marshlands throughout North and Central America. The great blue heron is a seasonally migratory species, wintering and breeding during the summer months in northerly climes, then migrating to warmer regions with their young before snowfall. A less migratory all-white subspecies, the great white heron, is found almost exclusively in shallow shoreline habitats around the Florida Keys. In places where both white and blue heron populations meet, another intermediate subspecies, the Wurdemann's heron, can also be found.

Geographic Range

The great blue heron breeds throughout North America, Central America, the Caribbean, and the Galapagos Islands. A migratory species that avoids snow, the great blue heron moves northward in spring to mate and live in more northerly climes that range from the Pacific coast of southern Alaska, throughout the southern half of Canada, across all of the lower 48 United States, most of Mexico, and into Central America.

In late autumn, usually November and December in the northernmost parts of its range, blue herons and their now-grown young fly southward to winter in warmer regions that extend from the coastal Canada up to Nova Scotia, through the southern half of the United States, Mexico, and into South America. In winter, the more northern populations are concentrated around the Pacific and Atlantic coastlines, where temperatures are kept warmer by latent heat from the oceans.

Habitat

The great blue heron's habitat will always be at the edge of a body of water, including rivers, lakes, beaver ponds, marshes, saltwater, and Great Lakes shorelines. Smaller streams are sometimes frequented, but these will nearly always be tributaries of a larger body of water nearby.

Herons, like most large stilt-legged shorebirds, take flight more slowly than smaller birds, and they prefer a running start of several steps. They tend to avoid overgrown

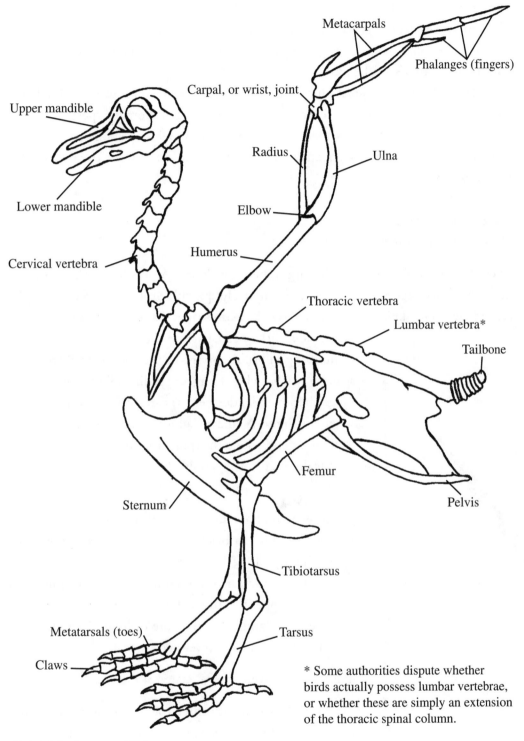

Metacarpals

Phalanges (fingers)

Carpal, or wrist, joint

Upper mandible

Radius

Ulna

Lower mandible

Elbow

Cervical vertebra

Humerus

Thoracic vertebra

Lumbar vertebra*

Tailbone

Femur

Sternum

Pelvis

Tibiotarsus

Metatarsals (toes)

Tarsus

Claws

* Some authorities dispute whether
birds actually possess lumbar vertebrae,
or whether these are simply an extension
of the thoracic spinal column.

Typical skeletal structure of birds.

shorelines where willows, dogwoods, and other tall shrubs inhibit freely spreading their wings to a span that can exceed 6.5 feet. For these reasons, most herons can be found in relatively open shallows, where cattails and reeds provide cover, and most of the heron's favorite prey animals can be found.

The habitat of the great blue heron can usually be relied on to reward field researchers and naturalists with a diversity of other stilt-legged shoreline species, like bitterns, egrets, and cranes. The same habitat nearly always yields an abundance of other species that have a part in the aquatic food chain, from ducks and geese to mink and otters to fish and frogs.

Physical Characteristics

Mass: 4.5 to more than 5.5 pounds.

Body: The great blue heron is the largest heron in North America, standing 38 to 54 inches from its large feet and long, comparatively spindly legs to the top of its black-crested head. The skull crest consists of two blackish stripes that extend from the eyes at either side of the head, back to the nape of the neck, and terminating in black, upward-curling plume feathers. Wing span 66 to 79 inches. Long, daggerlike bill, about 8 inches long. The long, slender neck is carried in an S shape, even when in flight. A line of almost shaggy-looking plume feathers extends along the spine from neck to tail. Sexes are identical, except males are likely to be slightly larger than females.

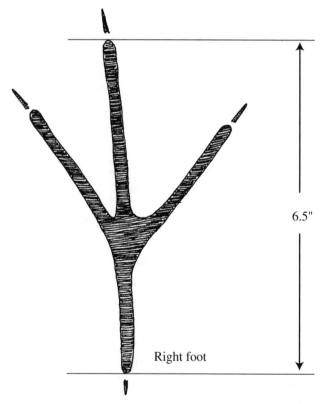

6.5"

Right foot

Great blue heron (Ardea herodias). Sandhill crane track is similar, except that the sandhill lacks a rear toe. Placement of toes indicates which foot left a track because the outermost toe is extended farther to the side to help increase the heron's balance.

Juveniles resemble adults, but lack the crest, and instead have a dark gray to black cap extending from the nape, across the top of the head, around the yellow eyes, to the top of the characteristically rapierlike bill. Juveniles also have a dark upper bill, rust-colored edging on the back and wing feathers, and lack the mane of long plume feathers that encircle the adults' lower necks.

Tail: Comparatively short, squared at the end, blackish tip.

Tracks: Four-toed, with three toes pointing forward, and one gripping toe pointed rearward. Total length, from tip of rear toe to tip of center front toe, about 6.5 inches. Note that the outermost front toes of either foot are widely splayed from the inner two toes, which are themselves held nearly parallel to one another. A track with a splayed outer toe that points left was made by the left foot, and vice-versa.

Scat: Sometimes cylindrical, dark brown when fresh, 0.5 inch in diameter, about 1 inch long. More often, scats are semi-liquid, mucouslike spatters among shoreline grasses, sometimes with evidence of fish scales, but often indistinguishable from those of other large shorebirds.

Coloration: White crown stripe extending front to back across the skull, bordered at either side by a black plume extending from behind eye to off the back of the neck. Blue-gray back, wings, and breast, often appearing all-gray from a distance. Brownish patch under the leading edge of both wings, black patch at elbow wing joint. Flight feathers black-tipped, contrasting against wing centers, and against a spinal tuft of gray-blue plume feathers when the wings are folded. Long, gray neck, sometimes marked with rusty brown, especially in younger birds. Breast streaked with white, black, and red-brown. Bill yellowish. Legs brown, sometimes dyed green from wading through algae, thighs may be marked with brown. Eyes yellow, round, and obvious.

Sign: Cattail and other reeds pushed aside to leave a trail of foliage displaced by the bird's large body. These trails are often marked by blue-gray feathers pulled free as the heron pushed through foliage.

Vocalizations: The great blue heron is less vocal than most members of its family, usually going about its business in silence. The most common call between mates is a hoarse, low-toned, and relatively quiet croak, not greatly different than that of a raven. A gutter "rawk" sound is made when the bird is distraught, and sometimes while it's in flight. When disturbed near its nesting site, a parent of either sex may utter a nasal "rawnk" that sounds similar to the call of a Canada goose.

Lifespan: About 7 years.

Diet

Although generally thought of as daylight operators, blue herons also frequent shorelines at night, especially warm, moonlit nights, when many of the birds' prey remain active through the night and lunar glow makes hunting by night easier. A typical heron spends about 90% of its day hunting for food in the shallows.

The great blue heron's hunting technique is effective and relatively simple. Able to wade shallows more than a foot deep without getting its feathers wet, the heron spends most of its waking hours standing motionless inside the concealment of a reed marsh. If no prey wanders within the bird's reach, it may move to a new location with slow, stealthy steps, placing each foot softly to avoid disturbing food animals and fine silt that can swirl up in clouds and obscure the bottom. Perhaps because of their shapes, neither movement of the heron's legs or the silhouette of its body against the sky seem to disturb smaller animals that make up most of this species' diet.

Edible animals in the great blue heron's diet include small fish of about 4 ounces, crayfish, snails, small clams, frogs, snakes, and small rodents. Because most of these creatures are crepuscular in their habits, herons and other shoreline birds tend to be most active in the twilight hours of predawn and dusk.

Larger prey is captured by the heron's long, sharply pointed bill, which shoots forward, propelled by unwinding the springlike S shape of its neck, and impaling the target with sometimes unerring accuracy. The prey, which is now actually holding the heron's bill from opening, is then thrown straight upward into the air with a toss of the bird's head, where it slides free of the tapered bill and is caught in the heron's wide-open mouth on the way down. Maybe most impressive is that prey animals tossed into the air are caught by their heads nearly every time, which generally disposes of their biting ends first, and orients small fish so that their spiny fins will lie back and down as they slide into the bird's gullet. In a few rare, and usually well-heralded, instances, herons have choked to death when fish became lodged in their throats, but the vast majority of great blue herons become superbly skilled at skewering and flipping prey into their own mouths.

Smaller prey, like snails and small clams, are held down with one of the heron's large, strong feet, and pecked or pried at with its bill until the shell's occupant has been consumed. Besides being an effective stabbing weapon and a good prybar, the heron's long, pointed bill can serve as a needlenose plier, reaching through chinks in natural armor—including the carapaces of turtles small enough to be gripped and held by one foot. Crayfish are sometimes pecked apart to get at the meat beneath their carapaces; other times, especially when their shells are softest, right after molting, they're simply swallowed whole. Snakes are pecked on and around the head until they die, then swallowed whole like a string of spaghetti.

While few small animals are beyond a great blue heron's dietary bounds, the birds also eat seeds and tender sprouts found around their shoreline habitats. Like most meat eaters, herons appear to require at least some of the nutrients and vitamins that can be obtained only by eating plants.

Like otters, blue herons and their cousins are popular culprits whenever a favorite fishing hole becomes depleted of game fish. In reality, overfishing by sport anglers and death from parasites or disease are the most common reasons for diminished fish populations. As in every predator-prey relationship, fish taken by herons are almost exclusively small, weak, and slow, often sickly, individuals that are, by nature's standards, genetically deficient.

Mating Habits

Solitary by nature, blue herons gather to breed at different times, depending on the latitude in which they live. Some adults, including chicks born the previous spring, may remain in southern latitudes year-round, and these populations begin mating early, from November through April. In the northern parts of the species' range, where herons and other shore birds don't live during the winter months, breeding is delayed until after the birds arrive at their summer habitats, with most mating occurring from March through May in the coldest climes. The instinct appears to be triggered mostly by warming, lengthening days in the north, but the heron's long bill probably endows it with an acute sense of smell that permits locating responsive mates by pheromonal scents, too.

Blue heron mating territories vary in size with the environment—wooded lakes, for example, have smaller areas of open shoreline—but a strong male heron tries to claim as much open space as it can hold from competitors, including claim to females whose own territories overlap those boundaries. Even so, claimed territories seldom exceed more than 3 or 4 acres.

Disputes between breeding males are resolved by a display of stalking one another, stiff-legged and with feathers fluffed outward to make themselves appear larger. If one of the contenders doesn't concede to being overmatched, the two may fly at one another, feet extended for clawing, and sometimes stabbing with their beaks. Territorial battles are seldom more than mildly injurious to either party, and less able males move on to find less well-defended territory.

Females are often regaled with dances that consist of a male leaping straight upward to a height of 3 or 4 feet, wings outspread, then fluttering back to earth. These mating displays aren't as ritualized as those of the whooping crane, but they're no less spectacular to watch.

Mated pairs of herons often stay together throughout the breeding months, but more polygamous behavior may be seen in areas where there are fewer males than females. Males aren't remarkably paternal, but they do sometimes sit on the eggs while their mates take a break, and they defend nesting sites from small predators.

Great blue heron nests are large, dish-shaped platforms of intertwined reeds, lined with softer pine needles, cattail fluff, grasses, and feathers. Overall diameter may exceed 6 feet. Nesting places are often difficult to find, as nests are often constructed atop dry grass hummocks above standing water, and concealed by a forest of bulrushes and cattails.

Great blue herons have also been observed nesting within the branches of standing trees near water. These nests appear as a bowl-shaped rough outer wall of sticks, cushioned on the inside with an insulating layer of softer materials. Some tree nests may be constructed atop existing raven or other large nests, but the prevalence of tree-nesting is probably limited by the presence of raptors, like ospreys and bald eagles.

As the size of their nest indicates, great blue heron eggs are roughly 50% larger than a chicken egg. Females begin laying eggs in batches every 2 to 3 days until reaching an average clutch size of three to seven pale blue eggs, with the larger clutch sizes occurring more frequently in the north; a natural adaptation to counter increased mortality from predation and cold. Both parents, but especially the mother, incubate the eggs and defend the nest site.

After an average incubation of 28 days, the eggs hatch. Heron chicks are semi-altricial, born eyes-open and covered with pale gray down, but are easy prey for their first 7 weeks, when they learn to take refuge by hopping into overhead branches. By 9 weeks, the chicks will usually have gained sufficient strength and feathers to fly short distances.

Both parents provide meals for their chicks, with voles and mice making up most of the hatchlings' diet in many cases, followed by fish, insects, and snakes. Parents also provide aggressive protection against predators until the young reach 10 weeks of age and about 2 feet of height, when the rapidly growing herons can fly and feed themselves. By summer's end, the young will have mostly or entirely dispersed to seek out their own territories.

Behavior

While great blue herons are solitary by nature, except for the breeding months, neither are they especially intolerant of one another. In habitats where food and other resources are abundant, adult males may forage the same shoreline with a few yards between them. In some especially good habitats, heron populations can increase to a point where some biologists consider them colonies.

Places where great blue herons can make a nuisance of themselves include fish hatcheries and rearing ponds, where fry and small tank-raised fish are easy prey. Commercial and governmental fish hatcheries generally defeat the birds by covering their stock tanks with a roof to lessen the amount of sunlight striking the water in them, or by adding a roof of light fencing. Pond owners have had good luck with discouraging herons by placing heron decoys, flags, and other scarecrows around their shorelines.

Unlike most large herons and cranes, the great blue heron was saved from plume hunters who once harvested large numbers of long fluffy feathers to adorn hats and clothing worn by refined society. Its drab feathers didn't hold the appeal of brightly colored plumes taken from flamingos and great white egrets, which kept the blue heron from being subjected to the overhunting that endangered those and other prettier species. Today, great blue herons in the United States are protected under the United States Migratory Bird Treaty Act.

Great blue herons are the most widespread and commonly seen large shorebirds in North America, and they have never been endangered. Despite that, the species faces danger from loss of marshland habitat, which is even today being filled and developed. A number are also killed by collisions with power lines during migratory flights, prompting some communities to install orange basketball-size spheres over the wires at intervals to make them more apparent to flying birds.

Sandhill Crane (*Grus canadensis*)

Sandhill cranes are the second best known of North America's large shorebirds. Standing as large or larger (depending on subspecies) than the great blue heron, sandhills are also migratory, flying hundreds of miles north each spring to summer breeding grounds, then flying with their grown young south to warmer regions before winter snows set in. Adults wear a distinctive cap of short reddish feathers that make them unlikely to be confused with any other species.

Sandhill cranes. Courtesy of U.S. Fish & Wildlife Service.

Sandhills are closely related to the whooping crane (*Grus americana*), which has long been an endangered species. Both birds wear a red skullcap, but the adult whooping crane is marked by a black trangular stripe extending rearward from its eyes, and by all-white plumage.

Geographic Range

During the summer months, sandhill cranes range as far north as Alaska's northern coastline, throughout the northern half of Canada, into Michigan, Wisconsin, and northeastern Minnesota. To the west, their range extends southward along the Rocky Mountains, and west to Oregon. Perhaps notably, the Pacific coast is devoid of sandhill cranes to a distance of at least 100 miles inland.

In winter, sandhills and their grown young return to their winter habitats along the southern border of the United States from Florida to California, southward into western Mexico. Populations have been reported as far south as Cuba, and as far north as Russian Siberia. In spring, before the full heat of summer sets into their southern wintering grounds, the cranes fly hundreds of miles north to mate, incubate, and rear the next generation in a cooler climate.

Habitat

Sandhill cranes are always within walking distance of a freshwater shoreline. Active by day, they're most often seen frequenting fields and meadows in search of insects and rodents. By night, the cranes retire to a nearby shoreline, often the same marsh where they nest, to sleep and keep eggs or young warm through the chill of darkness. Sandhill cranes tend to avoid dense forests where trees and vegetation inhibit spreading their wings, and they prefer to live well away from human habitation.

Physical Characteristics

Mass: 8 to 9 pounds, with larger individuals occurring in the south.

Body: Sandhill cranes are heavy-bodied with long necks and legs, and a long rapierlike bill typical of herons and cranes. Body length from tip of bill to claws averages between 4 and 5 feet. Wings about 22 inches long; total wingspan 5.5 to more than 6 feet. Males and females indistinguishable, except that males are normally slightly larger.

Tail: Long, drooping grayish feathers about 1 foot long that hang downward with an almost ragged appearance when the bird is standing erect, sometimes referred to as a bustle.

Tracks: Three forward-pointing toes, each tipped with a claw that measures about 0.5 inch long. Middle toe is longest, 2.5 to 3 inches, and points straight forward. Outer flanking toes point forward at outward angles from the center toe. The single rearward-

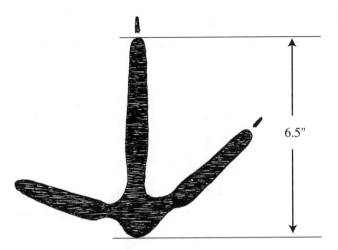

Sandhill crane (Grus canadensis). Note that the outside toe extends outward at a greater angle than the other two toes to give the bird better balance, indicating that this track is from the left foot.

6.5"

Sandhill crane track in wet sand.

pointing toe is about 1 inch long, is located higher up on the ankle, and doesn't print in tracks; this short toe also prevents sandhills from roosting in trees like blue herons. Tracks may be mistaken for those of a wild turkey in meadows where both species forage, except that wild turkey tracks tend to be slightly longer and more robust, with obvious segmentation, whereas the crane's toes are more slender and lack obvious segments.

Scat: Easily mistaken for that of other large birds with similar diets, especially great blue herons, except that sandhills tend to forage in dry meadows and fields, while most shorebirds remain near water. In solid form, scats are cylindrical, dark brown when fresh, roughly 0.5 inch in diameter, about 1 inch long. Scats are often semiliquid spatters among meadow grasses where the cranes hunt, sometimes with evidence of insect parts, but often indistinguishable from those of other large shorebirds.

Coloration: Sandhill cranes are easily identifiable by their bright red skullcaps, which cover the tops of their heads from the base of the long bill, around the eyes, and halfway to the rear of the skull. Directly below the red cap are cheek patches of near-white that contrast with the gray feathers covering the rest of the body. Wing and tail feathers are edged with darker gray to nearly black. Older adults also tend to become stained with a brown color on their wings and back, the result of algae and minerals in shoreline waters where they nest and sleep.

Juvenile sandhills have wing feathers tipped with brown, and all-brown head and neck, but lack the red skullcap of the adults. By their second year, most juveniles will have grown their full adult plumage. Researchers should note that sandhill cranes in juvenile plumage are virtually indistinguishable from juvenile whooping cranes.

Sign: Depressions in tall grasses where the cranes have sat down, football-size or larger. Discarded large grayish feathers in grassy areas are a reliable indication of sandhill cranes.

Vocalizations: Most identifiable is a high-pitched staccato cooing sound, heard most often from marshy shorelines, and especially in early spring, when groups of migrating birds are establishing territories and advertising for mates. Other voices in the same timbre include a short "awwk" that serves as an alarm, and a more prolonged version that indicates greater fear or agitation.

Lifespan: 20 years or more in the wild.

Diet

Like other herons and cranes, sandhill cranes eat an omnivorous diet that consists of mostly animal matter, but also seeds and young vegetation. Like the much smaller woodcock, sandhills use their long bills as probes to unearth and find worms and insects, but also as a spear for impaling small rodents, snakes, and frogs. The sandhill is a capable fisher, but prefers to spend its daylight foraging hours in open fields, rather than along shorelines where it might need to compete with great blue herons.

In northern latitudes especially, sandhill cranes make vegetation and berries a large part of their diets. Their long bills are used to winnow seeds, to nip off young grass and other shoots, and to pluck sugar-rich berries. During the spring migration, when flocks of cranes travel northward to summer mating grounds, their arrival often coincides with the spring planting season, and many farmers complain that sandhills eat the seeds from their freshly planted fields.

Mating Habits

Sandhill cranes are sexually mature in their second year, but some individuals, especially males, may be forced by competition to wait longer before breeding. The most active breeding ages span between 2 and 7 years of age.

Most sandhill cranes are migratory, leaving wintering grounds in warmer latitudes in spring, before the heat of summer, and flying several hundred to more than 1,000 miles to reach the northerly latitudes where they were born. Mating season begins immediately after the birds arrive in their summer habitat, preceded by a brief period in which males in particular engage in relatively nonviolent territorial battles that consist primarily of flying at one another with flailing wings and outstretched feet. Although cranes spend most of their active days on dry land, preferred nesting territories are always at the edges of or near marshy shorelines.

After territories have been established, usually between mid-March and early June, depending on latitude, the rituals of mating begin. Most spectacular of these rituals are the mating dances that are performed to some degree by all large cranes and herons. Much like the whooping crane, which it closely resembles, the sandhill male woos a prospective mate by jumping high into the air, wings outstretched to make his size appear more impressive, and fluttering to the earth. These leaps are accompanied by the birds' staccato cooing, and dances may continue for an hour or more, until the female becomes enamored enough to accept the male, or leaves to find a more suitable mate. Frequently the female will dance, as well, but most displaying is done by the male.

After mating, crane pairs set to work constructing a nest. A few incidents of sandhills nesting on dry land have been reported, but nearly all nesting sites are along remote shorelines with standing water and emergent (surface-growing) vegetation that includes bulrushes, cattails, and hummocks of rough grasses. Large grass hummocks, or "deadheads," that stand well above water are favored nesting spots not only for cranes, but for most waterfowl. Nests are constructed from sticks, reeds, and grasses taken from the surrounding area, and consist of a walled platform, up to 6 feet across, in the center of which is a smaller egg cup that has been lined with softer grasses, cattail fluff, and down feathers. Time from start to completion is about 7 days. It should be noted that sandhills sleep in nests at all times of year, but those used by males, or outside of the brooding period are flat, with only a residual egg depression in their centers.

Expectant female cranes begin laying a clutch of one to three eggs, usually one per day, as soon as the nest is completed. Eggs are long and oval, about 4 inches in length, with dull brown shells that are irregularly spotted with rust-colored markings. Incubation begins as soon as the first egg is laid, and both parents assume responsibility for sitting on them, and for defending the nest against raccoons and other egg-eating predators. Note, however, that males sit on the nests only during daylight; from dusk to dawn, all incubation is done only by the female.

After an incubation of about 30 days, the young hatch, one every 2 or 3 days. Chicks begin wandering from the nest as young as 6 hours after hatching, sometimes swimming for short distances, but never far from the watchful eyes of at least one parent. The first hatchling is dominant and frequently bullying of its younger siblings, so parents use their own bodies to keep chicks from fighting. Chicks are fed a diet of mostly insects for their first 30 days, after which the mother feeds them bits of their own broken eggshells, probably for the nutrients they contain. At this point the parents begin leading their offspring away from the nesting site to teach them the hunting skills they'll need in coming years. The family returns to the nesting site each evening, often calling loudly to one another as they settle in to sleep in relative safety among the marshes. By their fifth week, chicks will have become strong fliers, but both parents continue to look after their brood for about 9 months, separating just prior to the migratory flight south.

Although sandhill cranes are perenially monogamous, it appears likely that established pairs reunite each breeding season for several consecutive years. The strong family bond shown during the summer months dissipates once the birds have migrated to their southerly wintering grounds. Yearling chicks may remain with their mothers for a month or more, but will normally have become independent before the spring flight north.

Behavior

While sandhill cranes are essentially solitary, adults 2 years and older spend three-quarters of each year with mates and offspring, separating only for the roughly 3-month period spent in their winter habitats. Although considered a migratory species, distances traveled between warm wintering grounds and cooler summer habitats may vary considerably; some cranes might fly many hundreds of miles, while other populations merely migrate from lowlands to mountaintop lakes. Most individuals tend to return to the places where they were hatched.

During annual migrations, sandhills flock together in survival groups, relying on numbers to discourage predators that might prey on the young especially. These groups are not cohesive, and there's little social stability among their members. On reaching the places where they'll spend the summer or winter seasons, the birds break away from their flocks to establish individual territories.

Like most heron and crane species, sandhills are diurnal by nature, sleeping through the night on large, dry nests concealed within marshes. The birds are most active during the twilight hours of dusk and dawn (crepuscular), when small rodents are traveling to or from foraging places, and when most cold-blooded reptiles, amphibians, and insects are sluggish. On hot summer days, the birds may retreat from the open places where they hunt to the cooler breezes of their nesting marshes, standing silently for hours, often on one leg in typical crane fashion, and feeding on an occasional frog or snake.

Unlike the related whooping crane, sandhill cranes aren't considered to be threatened, and are in fact considered pests by farmers who complain that flocks of migrating birds can pick clean newly seeded crops. Because of real or supposed damage to crops, and despite the species' diet of insects and rodents that are harmful to agriculture, sandhill cranes are legally hunted in Texas, Kansas, and seven other states along the birds' migratory flyway. At the time of this writing, Wisconsin authorities are debating whether to open a hunting season for sandhill cranes.

Hunting sandhill and other cranes isn't a recent development; by the beginning of the twentieth century, private and commercial hunters who killed the birds for the roughly 3 pounds of rich, red meat contained in their breasts had reduced sandhill populations to the point of causing concern. In 1918 the practice was banned under federal law, but continued lobbying from the agricultural community caused those protections to be relaxed. In the early 1960s crane hunting was again made legal in New Mexico when that state staged a "depredation hunt," and a precedent was set for the states that followed. Today, hunting sandhill cranes is becoming increasingly popular among sport hunters, even spawning a market for crane calls, crane decoys, and guided crane hunts.

Canada Goose (*Branta canadensis*)

The Canada goose is one of the most easily recognized birds on the continent. There are four recognized subspecies, *B. canadensis occidentalis*, *B.c. hutchensii*, *B.c. minima*, and

Canada goose. Photo by Claire Dobert, courtesy of U.S. Fish & Wildlife Service.

B.c. leucopareia, all of which are smaller than the true Canada goose, but share its distinctive markings. In general, individuals are larger in southern populations, and breasts are darker in western populations.

Geographic Range

Canada geese are found throughout their native North America, with specific subspecies being more regional. The larger pale-breasted *B.c. canadensis* is found mostly along the eastern portions of North America, while the equally large brown-breasted *B.c. occidentalis* inhabits the west. The smaller pale-breasted *B.c. hutchensii* is found in central and western Canada. *B.c. minima,* as its name implies, is the smallest of Canada geese, and is found in western Alaska. *B.c. leucopareia* of the Aleutian Islands is threatened, and is distinguished from *B.c. minima* by its larger size, paler breast, and, often, a wider white neck ring. All subspecies tend to winter in the southern parts of North America, then fly north in spring to mate and raise the next generation. This migratory habit has been artificially changed in many locales by humans who feed waterfowl throughout the winter months, making it unnecessary for flocks to travel south in search of food.

Habitat

Every goose habitat (as well as those of their duck cousins) will include a relatively large body of open freshwater—usually a lake or pond, but sometimes large, slow moving rivers—where the birds can escape or avoid terrestrial predators by swimming into deep water. In midsummer and in their southerly wintering grounds, Canada geese are often seen swimming along the shorelines of larger bodies of water, including the Great Lakes, but nesting areas will always be along marshy shorelines of, usually, smaller lakes and beaver ponds, where cattails and reeds provide cover, grassy hummocks provide dry nesting sites, and calm shallows hold an abundance of edible aquatic vegetation.

Like most large birds, including herons and turkeys, the terrestrial portion of a Canada goose habitat will always be in open places where spreading their large wings won't be inhibited by trees or undergrowth. Grassy, open meadows along shorelines are especially preferred.

Physical Characteristics

Mass: Slightly more than 2 pounds for *B.c. minima,* smallest of the subspecies, to more than 19 pounds for *B.c. canadensis.*

Body: Large, heavy body with massive breast muscles, long comparatively thin neck. Females tend to be slightly smaller than males, although both sexes share the same colors and patterns. Short, stout legs positioned close together under the bird's body cause it to waddle as it walks. Feet large and webbed. The flat bill is lined around its outer edges with teethlike projections, called "lamellae," that are used for cutting grass and other stems that serve as food. Wings long and very strong, spanning 50 to more than 65 inches when spread.

Tail: Short, black-tipped, terminating in a blunt point. Seen from above while the bird is in flight, the tail exhibits a white semicircle just forward of its black tip.

Tracks: Three-toed, with thick webbing extending from the tip of one toe in a semicircle to the tip of the next. Webbing normally shows in tracks, with the heaviest impressions being made by the longest center toe, which points straight forward, and the outer flanking toes, which also point forward, but at outward angles from the center toe. Track length about 4 inches, width from end of outermost to tip of innermost toe about 4 inches. Walking track pattern exhibits an extreme toe-in (duck-footed) stride in which all toes point inward. Stride length from one track to that made by the opposite foot is about 6 inches.

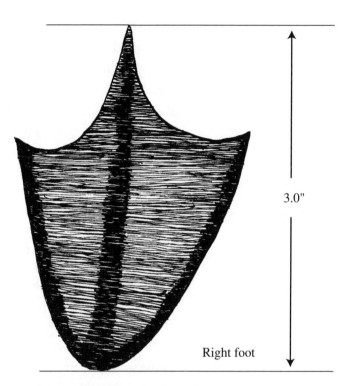

3.0"

Right foot

Canada goose (Branta canadensis) *Three forward-pointing toes print most heavily on soft ground, but webbing between them will print more faintly, often not at all.*

Note that Canada goose tracks are very similar to those of the smaller ducks and the larger swans, with the only obvious difference being one of size and stride length. A typical large (i.e., mallard) duck leaves a track roughly 3 inches in length, with a stride of about 4 inches. A mute or trumpeter swan has a very large track that can exceed 6 inches, with a much longer stride of 9 inches or more.

Scat: Cylindrical, with a consistent diameter from one squared (flat) end to the other, occasionally with a larger bulbous form at the end that was excreted first. Diameter about 0.5 inch, length up to 3 inches, but often shorter. Color typically olive-brown when fresh, becoming darker with age. Grass and other plant fibers, clipped short by the goose's toothed bill, are usually obvious in fresh deposits. Dimensions given are for *B.c. canadensis*, largest of the Canada geese, and vary downward in size for the smaller subspecies.

Coloration: *B. canadensis* have a black neck, bill, head, legs, and feet. A white patch, sometimes called a chinstrap, extends from behind the eye, under the chin just rearward of the bill, to the rear of the opposite eye. The upper body and back are brownish-gray, with whitish breast and underbelly (breast is brown in the western subspecies *B.c. occidentalis*). The smaller subspecies *B.c. leucopareia* and *B.c. hutchensii* have a distinctive white ring around the base of the neck, just above the breast. Wings are brown, with darker tips. These color patterns are unique to the Canada goose and its subspecies, making it unlikely to be confused with any other bird.

Sign: Flocks of geese often gather in open, grassy areas, especially during migratory flights, and the grasses in these places can be clipped nearly to ground level when large numbers of birds feed on them. Such places may exhibit a trampled look from the flattening effect of having been walked over by many flat, heavy feet. These places are usually well-marked with scats.

Vocalizations: Historically described as a honk, only the high-pitched call of migrating Canada geese in flight accurately matches that definition. When nesting, the call between mates might be described as a high-pitched "rrawwnk." The call of an agitated or threatened goose is a rapidly repeated "awnk-awnk-awnk," which becomes quieter as the source of agitation withdraws. Like swans and ducks, geese can also make a loud hissing sound, heard especially when the birds are attempting to drive off intruders during the mating and nesting seasons.

Calls of the Canada goose (also ducks) are normally heard only during daylight hours. An exception occurs during the spring hatching season, when the nested birds, eggs, and hatchlings are preyed on at night by bobcats, coyotes, and an occasional large otter.

Lifespan: The reported maximum lifespan in captivity is 28 years, although typical lifespan in the wild is about 8 years.

Diet

Canada geese are believed to be entirely herbivorous, although there have been accounts of the birds eating grasshoppers and other small insects. On land, the birds eat a variety of plants, including most grasses, plantains, dandelion shoots and flowers, and wild strawberry plants and fruits. Most types of nontoxic berries are eaten when in season and when in proximity to the birds' feeding areas—they will never venture into woods or brushy places where opening their wings in escape might be impeded.

Despite having no true teeth, Canada geese are able to snip free small, more easily digestible sections from rough grasses and other stems using the serrated teethlike lamellae that border the outer edges of their bills. By pinching leaves and stems in their bills, then pulling with a quick jerk of the head, geese are able to cut free small mulchlike snips of rough vegetation, which digest more easily than would longer blades of grass or stems.

Aquatic plants also make up a large part of the Canada goose diet, especially during the nesting season when parents prefer to remain close to their eggs. Pondweeds, pondlily, and waterlily leaves are eaten, along with tender cattail sprouts, wapato, and freshwater seaweeds. As the summer progresses and plants begin to mature, most types of seeds are eaten, including wild rice and grass seeds of all types.

A notable characteristic displayed by geese and ducks while feeding on aquatic vegetation is the tail-up posture assumed by them while plucking food plants from the bottom of shoreline shallows. By tipping their bodies 90 degrees, with tails pointing skyward and heads underwater, the birds are able to extend their long necks to reach food plants growing in the muddy bottom. Sometimes this feeding method will be observed with lone geese or ducks, but most often there will be a pair or more, which take turns foraging underwater while companions remain upright to watch for potential danger.

Mating Habits

Canada geese, like ducks, swans, and other migratory waterfowl, breed in the spring, returning to the same waterways where they were born. Mating begins as early as March in southern latitudes, but as late as June in the northernmost parts of the species' range. Individuals born the previous spring are sexually mature, but may not mate until 2 years old if competition is strong. Fortunately for the geese, there exists an almost even ratio between geese (females) and ganders (males), and adults of either sex take only one mate per season, so breeding rivalries are less common than with some waterfowl species.

Canada geese mating rituals are unremarkable in comparison to those of many other waterfowl species. When two males do compete for a female, the contest consists mostly of hissing and flying at one another with outspread wings that are used as bludgeons. Battles are of short duration and neither contender is likely to be injured. When the vanquished suitor withdraws, the winning male approaches the female with head down, neck outstretched and undulating from side to side.

Most older geese will arrive at their breeding habitats already paired with a mate. Sometimes the pairs will have joined during the flight north, but the majority of adults will be with the same mate they had the year before, and perhaps for several years prior to that. Some biologists believe that Canada geese mate for life, but an adult whose mate is killed by hunters or predation will find another mate prior to or during the following breeding season.

Copulation between Canada geese is unusual in that it takes place on the water, and the female may be partially or wholly submerged during the act, held underwater by weight of the male when he mounts her from the rear and covers her body with his own. However, coitus is quick, lasting only a few seconds, so there is no danger of the female being drowned during mating.

Choice of a nesting site is at the female's discretion; her mate simply follows where she leads. Likewise, the male takes little part in actually building the nest, and his role is generally limited to offering bits of reeds and grasses to his mate. Preferred nesting sites are on a raised point surrounded by water, especially grassy hummocks, snags of wind-felled trees, and occasionally atop a muskrat house. Nests tend to be quickly made, simple affairs, usually little more than a rounded depression in the grass, formed by the female's large feet and heavy body. (In one unusual instance, a particularly inexperienced goose tried nesting atop a raised platform that had been constructed for ospreys, 15 feet above the surface of a beaver pond; none of her eggs escaped predation from the ospreys.)

Females begin laying eggs within a day or so of mating, laying one egg about every 36 hours until a clutch of two to as many as nine eggs have been deposited in the nest's center. Eggs are slightly larger than a Large chicken egg, measuring almost 4 inches long, and are cream-colored. Mothers partially cover their clutches with an insulating layer of down feathers plucked from their own breasts, which help to keep the ova from becoming too cool or too warm, and are turned regularly to insure even exposure all around.

Ganders remain close-by during the nesting period, but don't take part in incubating the eggs. When the sitting goose leaves to feed or relieve herself, the gander's job is to guard the nest against predators. Smaller egg eaters, like foxes, skunks, and crows, are chased away by loud honking and the male's bludgeoning wings. Larger carnivores like coyotes are led away on a "wild goose chase" when the gander pretends to be injured, enticing predators to follow by flopping pathetically and giving the impression of being easy prey.

After an incubation period of 25 to 28 days, the eggs begin hatching. Despite having been laid as many as 3 days apart, all eggs begin hatching within 24 hours. Hatchlings break free of the shell using their single egg tooth, and by the end of 48 hours, all goslings will have freed themselves. Hatchlings are born covered with downy yellow coats that are marked with patches of green-gray atop the back and neck. Their legs, feet, and bills are blue-gray, but grow darker as the birds mature.

Goslings are able to swim within hours after hatching, and leave the nest with their parents immediately, usually on the same day they were hatched. The young are imprinted on their mother, and follow her wherever she leads, while the father generally follows behind. The goslings grow quickly, and by summer's end have become slightly smaller replicas of their parents. In autumn, the entire family joins with other groups of migrating geese to form the sometimes large flocks that we see flying southward each year. When the flocks return to their northern summering grounds the following spring, goslings will have reached full adulthood and seek out their own mates.

Behavior

The best-known characteristic of the Canada goose is the distinctive V-shaped formation of a migrating flock. These flocks, which may number more than thirty birds, are made up mostly of families that have been joining the same flock to make annual migratory flights to the same places for many generations. By flying together in large groups over long distances that may span more than 1,000 miles, the geese find safety in numbers when they land in a strange place to spend the night each evening.

A benefit of flying in the trademark V formation is that it creates a slipstream behind each bird, beginning with the foremost—and generally the strongest—gander who leads the flock. This arrangement permits every bird following the leader to "draft" behind the goose immediately in front of itself, much the same as race car drivers employ the vacuum generated by the vehicle in front of them to lessen the amount of fuel their own cars expend while maintaining an equal speed. Drafting behind one another permits adolescents and other less strong geese to keep pace with the most powerful individuals, while at the same time insuring that the long flight is much less taxing to flock members than it would be if the big birds were making the same trek alone.

Although Canada geese flock only during annual migratory flights, individuals are seldom seen alone. The birds aren't social in the same way that turkeys tend to live their lives as members of large groups, but mated pairs typically remain together throughout each year until one of them dies, and parents look after their broods throughout most of the youngsters' first year of life.

Canada geese, particularly those of the smaller subspecies, are frequently preyed on by carnivorous mammals, large raptors, and an occasional alligator in their southern winter habitats. Large fish of the pike family have been observed eating goslings, as will most types of hawks and owls. Raccoons, skunks, oppossums, and ravens are known for preying on unhatched eggs—but always with respect for the bludgeoning power of an irate parent's wings—while bobcats especially make a habit of patrolling spring nesting grounds at night, when the geese are effectively blind.

Nested geese are seldom preyed on during the day, when their keen hearing, eyesight, and the panoramic field of vision provided by placement of eyeballs at either side of the head permit them to see approaching danger from the air or ground. In most nesting habitats, Canada geese are too large and strong to be considered prey by daytime predators, and the birds' aggressive defense of nests and hatchlings is sufficient to discourage carnivores even as large as a coyote. An interesting behavior exhibited by nested mothers is their tendency to lie flat, neck outstretched atop their eggs, when they spy an approaching enemy, thus lowering their conspicuous head and neck below the predator's line of sight while their mates lead it away on the proverbial wild goose chase.

Another threat to nesting populations of Canada geese comes from swans, particularly the much larger and notoriously aggressive Asian mute swan (*Cygnus olor*). Introduced to the United States as a replacement for dwindling populations of native trumpeter swans (*C. buccinator*) the mute swan's powerful physique places it beyond the abilities of most wild predators, allowing it to become firmly established around the Great Lakes region and along the northern Atlantic seaboard. An unforeseen result of this aggressively territorial species' success has been the displacement of native ducks and geese from their historical nesting areas. The presence of mute swans also inhibits the return of native swans, which has caused wildlife authorities to consider eradicating them from the Great Lakes region.

Although protected from spring hunting under the 1918 Migratory Bird Treaty, and again by the imposition of autumn bag limits in 1960, the Canada goose in general has never been threatened. The smaller Aleutian subspecies was once listed as endangered by the U.S. Fish and Wildlife Service after populations were reduced to just 800 birds by the introduction of a non-native fox in 1967, but good recovery efforts and steadily increasing numbers caused them to be downlisted to threatened in 1990, and the danger appears to have passed. In 1999, populations of the Aleutian Canada goose were estimated at 15,000 individuals nesting on eight islands.

In fact, Canada geese populations in general have increased to the point of making them a serious pest along many urban and suburban waterways. In some places, flocks that can number in the hundreds leave large volumes of scats sufficient to create bacterial infestation of land and water, including the fungal infection known as "swimmer's itch." Adding to the problem are goose populations that have become year-round residents in areas where they should migrate. In both these instances the troubles are caused, or at least exacerbated, by human populations, because Canada geese inhabiting remote northern waterways are not overpopulated, nor do they remain through the winter. Canada geese, like deer, squirrels, and numerous other species, have learned to occupy territories close to human habitation because those places are shunned by wild predators, and many well-meaning people contribute to these problems by feeding wild species.

PREDATORY BIRDS

While most species of birds can be considered predatory, some are exclusively so. Eagles, ospreys, hawks, and owls make up this large group of hunting birds whose diets consist almost entirely of the flesh of other animals. All are strong, fast fliers with very keen eyesight, powerful feet with sharp talons evolved for gripping prey, and hooked beaks designed to tear flesh from bone. Most are active during daylight, but the owls are possessed of extremely good night vision that allows them to be uncannily accurate night hunters. Some, like the bald eagle and the osprey, are famed for their ability to snatch fish from water, while others are skilled at catching other birds in flight. All prey on rodents and, depending on their own size, rabbits, and all have an indispensible role in controlling populations of prolific animals that would otherwise multiply beyond the capacity of their environment.

Bald Eagle *(Haliaeetus leucocephalus)*

Best-known of the predatory birds, the bald eagle has become a symbol of fierce independence and strength, and has been the national bird of the United States since 1782. Benjamin Franklin had argued that the national bird should be the uniquely American wild turkey, stating that the bald eagle was a bird of poor moral character because of its habit of stealing food from other predatory birds. Certainly Franklin was right in his assertion that the turkey had played a much more important role in the forging of a new nation by feeding early pioneers, but the poor homely turkey just didn't evoke the same image of strength and pride as the eagle.

Despite being the emblem of the United States, the bald eagle was nearly extirpated by the widespread use of the insecticide DDT (dichlorodiphenyltrichlorethane) in the mid-twentieth century. DDT spread through the food chain to bald eagles and other accipiters, where it caused females to lay eggs that had weak shells, or sometimes no shells at all, cutting reproduction to almost zero. By the time the United States banned DDT in 1972, the bald eagle's numbers had fallen from an estimated 50,000 individuals to about 800 breeding pairs in the lower 48 states. Enactment of the Endangered Species Act in 1973 prompted a concerted, and ultimately successful, recovery effort. By 1995, bald eagle numbers had risen to

The bald eagle is an example of how good wildlife research and management can bring a species back from the edge.

about 3,000 breeding pairs, hatchling rates were up, and the species was downlisted from endangered to threatened. By the beginning of the new millennium, some biologists were suggesting that it was safe to remove bald eagles from the Endangered Species List altogether.

Geographic Range

The bald eagle is native to North America and was once common from central Alaska, throughout Canada and the United States, southward to the Mexican border and the Gulf of Mexico. Today bald eagles may still be found over much of that original range, but there are fewer of them, especially in the southern United States, than there once were.

Habitat

Bald eagles are able to live anywhere on the North American continent where there are adequate nest trees, roosts, and feeding grounds. Suitable habitats include temperate forest, rainforest, prairies, desert, and mountains. Being especially capable fishers, open water is a necessity in every bald eagle habitat, and this may include large rivers, lakes, or ocean.

Physical Characteristics

Mass: 6.5 to 14 pounds; females typically larger than males.

Body: Large bird; females typically larger. Males 30 to 35 inches long, females 34 to 43 inches long. Legs are feathered halfway down the tarsus. Wing span may exceed 7.5 feet. Sexes are identical in plumage.

Tail: Moderately long, 6 to 8 inches, slightly wedge-shaped.

Tracks: Bald eagles have massive tarsi (feet), short and powerful grasping toes, and long talons. The talon of the hind toe is used to pierce vital areas while the prey is held immobile by the front toes, and is powerful and highly developed in all eagle species.

9.0"

6.0"

Bald eagle (Haliaeetus leucocephalus) tracks. The heavy, muscular toes tipped with sharp, curved claws that grip and pierce prey animals are especially well adapted for catching fish swimming near the surface.

Scat: Typically birdlike, but larger than that of most birds. Solid form is irregularly cylindrical, dark brown in color, usually white at one end, sometimes bulbous at one end, about 3 inches long and less than 0.5 inch in diameter. Alternately, scat form may be massed, sometimes nearly liquid. Look for undigested fish scales, fur, or feathers.

Coloration: Bald eagles aren't truly bald; the term is an abbreviation of the word "piebald," which describes a spotted or patchy color pattern, especially in black and white. The adult bald eagle's dark brown body—which can look black against the sky—stands in stark contrast to the white feathers of its head, neck, and tail. Long, hooked bill is yellow, the cere (the fleshy swelling at the base of the upper beak) is yellow. Eyes and feet are yellow; legs are yellow and unfeathered.

Immature eagles are irregularly mottled with brown and white until 4 or 5 years of age, but, like adults, their feet and legs are bright yellow. Eyes darker yellow or brown, bill and cere dark gray.

Sign: Large, brushy nests at the tops of usually dead standing trees. The ground around these nesting trees is typically scattered with a variety of feathers, fish fins and scales, and small bones and fur.

Vocalizations: Probably best described as a screeching whistle that's often heard while the bird is in flight. Eagles can also croak or squawk much like a crow.

Lifespan: Approximately 15 years in the wild; up to 50 years in captivity.

Diet

Bald eagles are strict carnivores. Best known as fishers, eagles swoop down onto the waters of a lake or large river to snatch shallow-swimming fish in their powerful, hooked talons, then fly off with the prize to feed at leisure on some lofty perch. Although not so skilled at catching fish as its slightly smaller cousin, the Osprey (*Pandion haliaetus*), the eagle is larger and stronger, able to carry away fish and other prey weighing in excess of 8 pounds.

In fact, the eagle's large size can work against it while fishing. Ospreys and smaller hawks who share the waterways found in every bald eagle habitat are better suited to catching bluegills, perch, and young bass that aren't easy targets for an eagle's large feet. This has led to the larcenous behaviors that Benjamin Franklin found so objectionable, in which an eagle waits for its smaller, more nimble cousin to capture a fish, then steals that fish for itself—or as the Odawa Indians say, "The osprey catches the fish that an eagle eats."

Despite being most commonly known as a fisher, the bald eagle is an efficient hunter of other prey, as well. With the "eye of an eagle," this raptor can spot a foraging rabbit from more than a mile distant, then swoop down onto the unsuspecting prey at a diving speed of nearly 200 miles per hour—or about the same speed as a WWII fighter plane. When just a few yards above the target, the eagle applies brakes by spreading its wings wide to catch air like a parachute, and, with a bit of luck, lands directly atop its next meal with sharp-clawed talons that pierce its body with a viselike grip. In fact, not every strike results in a kill, but with the power to take hares, muskrats, young beavers, and most other small animals, the eagle usually finds sufficient opportunity to keep itself and its young well-fed.

Other birds also serve as eagle prey. Smaller species, like blue jays and redwinged blackbirds, are too undersized and quick, but ducks, immature geese, swan cygnets, and an occasional young heron or crane are taken if an opportunity presents itself. Often these prey birds are taken with the swooping attack while on the water or ground, but bald eagles are agile enough on the wing to take most shore and water birds out of the air, too. Crows and ravens are also preyed on, and these birds will often alert a tracker to the presence of hunting eagles by gathering in a tree whose branches prevent the wide-winged raptor from diving, then cawing loudly.

Other eagle prey includes large snakes, especially watersnakes and cottonmouths, small alligators, and large bullfrogs. Carrion is sometimes eaten, especially in winter, and eagles are occasionally seen feeding on road-killed deer, but the birds generally prefer to hunt or steal fresh meat.

Mating Habits

Bald eagles become sexually mature at 4 years, but may not mate until age 5. In the northern part of the species' range, mating takes place between mid-February and mid-March, but in the south eagles may mate until August. Mating appears to be initiated by the female, who typically approaches a suitable male with ducking gestures of her head. Both eagles then take to the air, flying up to an altitude of several hundred feet, usually over water, then turning toward one another and locking their talons together. With feet locked in this manner, both birds free-fall nearly to earth before relinquishing their grip and flying upward again to repeat this behavior. The precise reason behind this activity is unknown, but it appears to be a test of strength and agility to determine if a male is physically strong enough to be a candidate for mating. The male must be able to keep up with the female as she flies upward, and his eligibility to mate—as well as his personal safety—demands that he have strength enough to recover from the free fall.

If a male is deemed acceptable, the receptive female repeats the head-down gesture, raising her tail and presenting her cloaca (genital cavity) to the male. The male then mounts her from behind with his talons instinctively closed into fists to protect her from being harmed by his claws. The male maintains his position atop her by pressing his closed fists firmly against her sides, gripping her body tightly between his feet during copulation. As with most bird species, intercourse is completed within a few seconds.

Historically, bald eagles have been thought to mate for life, although it appears that may not be true in all cases. What is certain is that mated pairs will remain together for at least as long as it takes to rear the next generation. Immediately after mating, the pair seek out a suitable nesting site high in a large tree (usually a conifer), or sometimes on a cliff ledge, and always near open water. Nests consist of a rough outer shell of interwoven sticks, with a softer interior lining of grasses, moss, fur, and feathers. Newly constucted nests measure about 6 feet in diameter by about 1 foot deep.

Pairs that have mated in previous years will probably use the same nest for many years, building onto it with each passing year, so the size of a nest is indicative of the number of generations that have been reared there. Some very old nests have reached huge dimensions, measuring more than 20 feet across, 10 feet deep, and weighing in excess of 1 ton. Providing a nest isn't toppled by wind, or doesn't crush the tree onto which it's built, it will continue to be used year after year, sometimes by succeeding generations who were themselves hatched there.

Impregnated females occupy the nest as soon as it's finished, laying their first creamy white 5-inch-long egg within about 3 days, usually in late March or early April. They will lay another every 1 to 3 days thereafter until a clutch of usually two, but sometimes three, eggs have been deposited.

Incubation of the eggs is performed mostly by the female, and exclusively by her at night, while her mate sleeps in a nearby tree. After an incubation period of 35 to 42 days, the eggs begin to hatch, with the oldest hatching first, and its siblings hatching every 2 or 3 days thereafter in the same order in which they were laid. By mid- to late June, all eggs will have hatched.

Sibling rivalry is fierce, and sometimes violent, between eagle chicks. The eldest hatchling is typically the largest, and will try to steal food from its younger and smaller nestmates. Parents will not intervene, leaving the younger chick to fend for itself in a real example of survival of the fittest. In a clutch of two, both eagle chicks will probably survive to the fledgling stage, but a third chick's odds of survival are greatly decreased.

Feeding duties are performed by both parents, and one will always be nearby when the other is away hunting. Hawks, and especially ravens, that might prey on the chicks are driven off vigorously, and predation on eaglets is virtually nil. By 60 days of age, the chicks will have grown to become fledglings, and will fly short distances with their parents. Parents will continue to hunt for and feed their brood for an additional 30 days, when the eaglets will have become educated and strong enough to fend for themselves. The family remains together until autumn, when the offspring strike out to establish their own territories.

Behavior

Native only to North America, the bald eagle is as big or slightly smaller than the golden eagle (*Aquila chrysaetos*) of Eurasia, North Africa, and North America, but it is no less a predator. Stories of eagles carrying off small children and lambs are groundless, but the big raptors have often incurred the wrath of farmers—and a few pet owners— by occasionally snatching up small dogs, cats, chickens, and rabbits.

Bald eagles are migratory only by necessity; if they possess access to open water, they will remain near their summer nesting sites the year around. Those in the north that don't have access to open water in winter fly to southern latitudes, or to coastlines where waters remain unfrozen enough to permit fishing. In northern latitudes where small mammals and other prey remain plentiful, adults have been known to remain all winter, even though lakes and rivers are frozen.

An exception is yearling eagles that have been recently emancipated from their parents. Juveniles in search of their own territories have been known to migrate more than 1,000 miles in search of mates or habitat. These youngsters may remain nomadic for as long as 5 years, or until they find a mate and settle down to raise their own offspring.

Eagles rarely fly at night, but the reason has less to do with lack of night vision than with air currents. Like vultures and other long-winged raptors, bald eagles prefer to glide rather than fly because gliding requires less expenditure of energy. Thermal updrafts, which these birds rely on to hold them aloft for hours at a time, are normally present only during the daylight hours, when a warming sun causes heated air to rise. For that reason, most eagles are seen on the wing between the hours of 8:00 A.M. and 6:00 P.M.

An unusual behavior among eagle mates is their occasional tendency to copulate outside of the mating season. Except for humans, sexual intercourse for the pleasure of it is virtually unheard of in the animal kingdom, and some biologists believe that this behavior might be related to the strong bond that exists between eagle mates.

Today, the bald eagle remains a symbol of strength and courage. It's the main icon of the Presidential Seal of the United States, and among most Indian tribes it's the messenger that carries prayers to the Creator. So strong is the image of power conveyed by this most striking of raptors that many states have found it necessary to protect the species by making it illegal to possess their feathers.

CHAPTER 6

AMPHIBIANS

FROGS

Frogs are a critically important species because they serve the human interest on numerous levels. Few high school biology students have not dissected, or at least studied the internal organs of, a frog. The number and arrangement of a frog's working parts, as well as its general body structure, is sufficiently similar to those of the human anatomy to make it the species of choice for introducing medical students to the basics of animal physiology.

Perhaps more importantly, frogs in the wild have proved to be an accurate and sensitive early warning of environmental problems. The presence of toxic chemicals in groundwater are indicated by increased mortality, tumors, and mutations in frogs of all species. So, too, is the increase in levels of harmful ultraviolet light that penetrates earth's apparently thinning atmosphere made evident by increased frog mortality. While the controversy over whether or not humans are harming this planet rages on, governmental and university studies of the impact environmental changes are having on frog populations are being monitored with concern.

All true frogs spend their lives in or around water. All are born from eggs laid in water, all undergo a tadpole phase in which they live and breathe underwater like fish, and all require a source of fresh water in their habitats. Some species have adapted to survive long periods of drought by burying themselves in mud and entering a dormant state until the rains return, but they too must have at least a seasonal source of open water in which to procreate and live.

The presence of some species of frog in every freshwater habitat around the world is a tribute to their design. Despite their seeming fragility, frogs are one of nature's most successful members of the animal kingdom.

Bullfrog *(Rana catesbeiana)*

North American bullfrogs are the largest frogs found in North America. Source of the frog legs that "taste just like chicken," they're considered a delicacy in some regions, a pest in others, and commercial livestock in several countries around the world. Like all "true" frogs of the family Ranidae, bullfrogs require a permanent source of unpolluted freshwater, they begin life underwater as gilled fishlike tadpoles, the adults are predatory, and those in the north hibernate in muddy pond bottoms during winter.

Geographic Range

The original, natural geographic range of *Rana catesbeiana* can never be be known. Originally a native frog of the eastern United States and southeastern Canada, the bullfrog gained such fame for its batter-fried legs that a number of entrepreneurial types transported them to "frog farms" outside their natural range to be reared as livestock of sorts. There are records of bullfrogs being transported to California and Colorado for that purpose as early as 1896, but most bullfrog relocations were not recorded.

Today, bullfrogs are still found throughout the eastern half of the continental United States, ranging from Nova Scotia on Canada's Atlantic seaboard, south to central Florida, and eastward to a rough line extending from Minnesota southward to eastern Texas. The species is also found along the Pacific coast of the United States, ranging

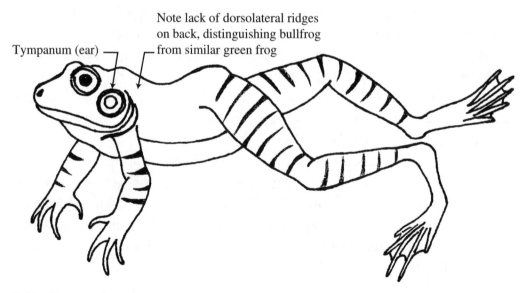

Note lack of dorsolateral ridges on back, distinguishing bullfrog from similar green frog

Tympanum (ear)

Bullfrog (Rana catesbeiana).

southward from Washington, through Oregon and California, into northern Mexico. Isolated populations occur in many inland western states as well, including Colorado, Arizona, Kansas, and Nebraska.

Bullfrogs have also been transplanted to other continents. In Argentina, Brazil, and Uruguay the rearing of bullfrogs for commercial use by restaurants (many of them in the United States) is an important growth industry. Bullfrogs are being raised in Hiroshima, Japan, for the same purpose. Wild transplanted populations are also established in Hawaii and Puerto Rico.

Habitat

Although bullfrogs have been observed traveling distances of more than a mile to find new territory, established frogs are almost never found more than a few yards from fresh water. The preferred habitat is shallow, marshy shorelines where cattails and bulrushes provide both shade and concealment from predators, while pondlily and waterlily leaves—which bullfrogs are generally too heavy to sit on—provide good hunting grounds for insects and smaller frogs.

Like all true, or ranid, frogs (and unlike the more terrestrial toads), a bullfrog's skin is thin and offers no protection against dessication. The animals must wet their bodies frequently to prevent loss of critical moisture, and they cannot tolerate saltwater. Being porous and evolved to absorb liquids, the skin of a frog makes it especially susceptible to the poisoning effects of toxic chemicals. Similar to the proverbial canary in a coal mine, frogs serve as an important early warning against water pollution.

Bullfrogs differ from other true frogs by having a much higher tolerance for heat and ultraviolet radiation. Shallow ponds that are warmed by sunlight beyond temperatures that other frogs can withstand are suitable habitats for bullfrogs, and in some cases bullfrogs may be the only species of frog present in these ponds.

Physical Characteristics

Mass: About 1 pound, occasionally larger.

Body: Largest of all frogs in North America; body length 3.5 to 8 inches, large sacral hump on back. The sex of an adult bullfrog can be determined by the size of the dark bull's-eye circle, or tympanum, located just behind the eye. In males, the tympanum, which covers the inner ear, is much larger than the eye, while females have a tympanum that's equal to or smaller in diameter than the eye. Mature males also have yellow underchins, and a swelling at the base of the inside front toes, neither of which are seen in females. The green frog is very similar, especially in the north, but has a pair of skin folds, called dorsolateral ridges that extend down either side of the back from the tympanum to the pelvis; the bullfrog lacks dorsolateral ridges.

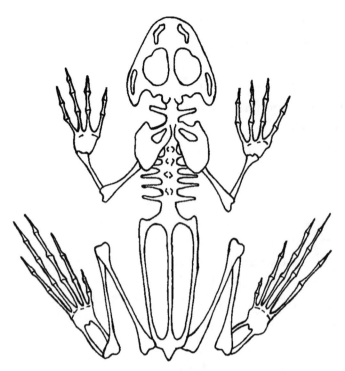

Skeletal structure of a typical pond frog (family Ranidae). Note four toes on forefeet, five toes on hind feet, smallest toes innermost.

Tail: Present only in the tadpole and immature stage. Like all frogs, the tail is absorbed as the frog matures, leaving only a rounded point where the hind legs meet in adults.

Tracks: Four toes on the forefeet, five toes on the hind feet. The hind feet are fully webbed, with the second toe from the outside being especially elongated. The outermost toe of the hind foot is much shorter, while the remaining three toes to the inside run in descending order of length, with the innermost toe being shortest. Hind foot length varies with animal size, but can exceed 2 inches.

Toes on forefeet are much shorter, with a natural downward curve that gives them the appearance of claws, although frogs have no claws. The outermost toe is shortest; the second toe from the outside is longest. The innermost toe is short, but typically thicker and thumblike.

Scat: Rarely seen because most frogs deposit their scats in the water. Scat deposits left on vegetation range from dark-colored pellets, a quarter-inch long or shorter (similar to those of a mouse) to small mucouslike smears that can be mistaken for the droppings of a small bird.

Coloration: Usually uniform over the upper body, but can vary from dark green to brown, with the latter being more common among southern populations. Black spots over the back are more opaque than in other species, and contrast less against the skin. Upper portions of the hind legs are marked with usually distinctive rows of black stripes that extend around them. The tympanum circle located to the rear of each eye is dark brown with a darker circle in its center. The underbelly and throat are normally white, but during the breeding season will become a dull yellow on mature males only. The outer perimeter of each eyeball is ringed with a gold-colored border.

The coloration and pattern of the bullfrog is similar to those of all North American frog species that contend with numerous predators. Green or brown skin blotched with darker spots on the upper body make a motionless frog more difficult to see from above by herons and cranes. The white underside causes it to contrast less against a bright sky when seen from below by a large bass or pike.

Sign: Muddy furrows through the mat of thick-growing aquatic weeds at shorelines. Too, look for "holes" where floating plants have been displaced by the impact of a jumping frog's body. All frogs leave these disturbances, but those of the bullfrog are typically much larger than those of other species.

Vocalizations: The mating call has been described as a baritone "jug-o-rum." The territorial voice is a deep croaking. The alarm call is a barklike squawk uttered as the frog jumps into the safety of water. Bullfrogs are heard mostly during the hours between dusk and dawn, especially when nights are warm; seldom heard during the heat of the day.

Lifespan: Bullfrogs are known to have a lifespan of 7 to 9 years.

Diet

All frogs are predators, but the greater size of the bullfrog makes it remarkable among them. Like its smaller cousins, the bullfrog feeds on most types of insects, including flies, dragonflies, bees, and other larger insects that come into range. The method of capture is typically froglike, with the bullfrog waiting motionless, moving only its eyes while the prey comes within striking distance of a long, sticky tongue that can shoot out from its mouth to a distance nearly equal to the frog's own body length. Momentarily stunned and stuck to the tongue's sticky end, the prey is swiftly recoiled into the frog's open mouth and swallowed whole. The whole process happens faster than the human eye can follow.

Bullfrogs capitalize on their greater size by preying on animals too large for their smaller cousins to handle, which gives them a more diverse diet with more prey options. Hatchling snakes, tadpoles, young fish, small mice, and other frogs—including smaller bullfrogs—are included in the bullfrog diet. There have even been incidents of bullfrogs eating bats and hatchling birds. Non-native bullfrog populations in western states have been directly blamed for the extirpation, or near extirpation, of several types of native frogs, as well as the endangered Mexican garter snake (*Thamnophis eques*).

Bullfrogs and other frogs have an unusual method of subduing larger prey animals. Sometimes, the prey is first stunned by striking it with the tongue, but often the bullfrog simply pounces onto the prey's back, gripping it tightly with handlike forefeet, then wrestles and pummels the hapless creature to death.

In several regions, particularly those western states where bullfrogs were introduced by humans, *R. catesbeiana* is considered a threat to native populations of frogs and, especially, fish. Bullfrogs have been blamed for depleting fish hatcheries of fry and minnows, especially trout, and they sometimes invade commercial and private fish ponds where they do the same. No one has been willing to assign (or accept) blame, but it appears that Colorado's Wildlife Division may have contributed to the problem by accidentally stocking trout streams with minnows that had been infiltrated with bullfrog tadpoles.

Masses of frog eggs in water.

Mating Habits

The bullfrog mating season varies with latitude; in the north, where warm weather comes later in the year, bullfrogs typically mate from late May through July. In the southern latitudes, mating may occur as early as February and continue until October. This species' breeding season is longer than that of any other frog species on the continent, which contributes to its unparalleled survivability.

Fertilization of bullfrog eggs is external, performed without conventional copulation. The female deposits her dark round eggs, 6,000 to more than 20,000 of them, in a foamy gelatinous string in shallow water, usually among a growth of aquatic vegetation that helps to hold them in place. The male accompanying her then positions himself above the egg mass and releases his sperm. In most cases, the eggs are fertilized by a single male, but occasionally the egg string will be fertilized by two or more males.

About 4 days after fertilization, the eggs begin to hatch into tiny spotted tadpoles, fishlike larvae that have both a tail and gills. The predatory tadpoles begin feeding immediately, first on microscopic organisms, then on larger aquatic insects and other creatures as they grow. Field studies of westernized bullfrogs has also shown that in the absence of animal prey, their tadpoles can subsist solely on aquatic vegetation.

Unlike those of other frog species, bullfrog tadpoles exhibit an inordinately high survival rate in the western United States because most native fish and other aquatic predators appear to find them unpalatable. Having a bad taste contributes to the tadpoles' longevity, and to the ultimate success of bullfrog populations that can grow to pest status. Studies among Japanese bullfrog populations indicate that bullfrog tadpole numbers may be successfully controlled through the introduction of largemouth bass (*Micropterus salmoides*), which seem not to mind eating them.

Bullfrog tadpoles mature slowly, relative to other frog species whose tadpoles reach maturity at about 4 months. Bullfrog hatchlings spend their first winters (and sometimes a second) as tadpoles, before finally absorbing their tails, growing legs, and learning to breathe air as adult frogs. Even after their metamorphosis into adults, bullfrogs will not reach sexual maturity for another 2 years.

Behavior

Like all freshwater amphibians, North American bullfrogs are so-called cold-blooded creatures that remain active only during temperatures above freezing, which, probably not coincidentally, is when nearly all of its prey are active. During winter in the north, where open waters freeze, bullfrogs and other ranids hibernate by burying themselves in the muddy bottoms of lakes and ponds, where they remain without breathing until the return of warm weather.

Adult male bullfrogs are especially aggressive, and will defend the approximately 10 to 50 feet of shoreline (depending on population densities) that they claim as their own from other male bullfrogs. Female bullfrogs are usually tolerated, but males fight one another for territory in brawling battles that are a combination of wrestling, kicking, and pummeling one another with blows from the forelimbs.

The same aggressive nature has made bullfrogs that were transplanted to the western United States a real threat to native frogs and other prey species. Being adapted to life in eastern forest lakes and beaver ponds, the bullfrog's tenacity and high reproductive rate is necessary to insure holding its own against large numbers of predators that range from raccoons, hawks, and snakes to herons, foxes, and opossums.

In the west, where predators that can successfully prey on bullfrogs are fewer, *R. catesbeiana* has proved to be a serious predator in its own right. Being the top predator in isolated ponds in Arizona and California, especially, has made the tenacious bullfrog a threat to native populations of smaller leopard frogs, trout minnows, and small snakes. In a few recorded instances, bullfrogs have completely wiped out native species, prompting authorities to initiate capture and removal programs that have proved marginally successful.

Ironically, the problem of bullfrog predation may be controlled best by a recently discovered fungal infection known as Cutaneous Chytridiomycosis. According to the American Center for Disease Control (CDC), chytridiomycosis is caused by a zoosporic fungus called Batrachochytrium dendrobatidis, which develops solely within keratinized cells and causes extensive hyperkeratosis, characterized by necrosis of skin on the backs of frogs. Death occurs by an as yet unknown mechanism, but it is known that epidemics of chytridiomycosis has decimated entire populations in Australia and Uruguay, and there are fears that this infection could do the same to frog species in North America.

Spring Peeper (*Pseudacris crucifer*)

One of thirteen species of North American tree frogs, few of which grow in excess of 2 inches, the tiny spring peeper is one of the most commonly heard springtime frogs in any forest where they live, even though many people who hear them attribute their sometimes raucous peeping to other frog species. So loud is the chorus of peepers from

Sucker pads at ends of toes

Blackish X-shape on back

Spring peeper (Pseudacris crucifer) *tree frog.*

early spring to early summer that campers sometimes complain about the din.

Spring peepers live up to their common name by being good climbers not only of trees but even surfaces as smooth as a kayak's hull. Their long toes are equipped with the small suction discs that are a trademark of tree frogs, giving them an ability to climb that equals many of the insects they hunt. Like all tree frogs, their habitat will always be canopied forest, where an ability to climb trees provides access to a larger number of food insects, as well as a means of evading most predators.

Spring peepers may be confused with cricket frogs, which have similar size, color, and markings, except that cricket frogs are water frogs, and lack the suction disks at the ends of their toes that identify tree frogs.

Geographic Range

Spring peeper frogs are native to most of eastern North America. Their range covers the southern halves of Quebec, Ontario, and the southeastern quadrant of Manitoba in Canada, extending southward from eastern Minnesota to east Texas. The species is rare in Georgia, and absent from most of central Florida.

At present two subspecies of spring peeper are recognized: most common is the Northern Spring Peeper (*Pseudacris crucifer crucifer*). Less known is the Southern Spring Peeper (*P.c. bartramiana*), which is found only in southern Georgia, northern Florida, and the southernmost tip of Florida. The two are easily distinguished from one another by their bellies, which are unmarked on *P.c.crucifer*, and marked with dark stripes on *P.c. bartramiana*.

Habitat

Like all frogs, spring peepers need standing water to breed, but their reliance on ponds is substantially less than that of the Ranid frogs, like bullfrogs, leopard frogs, and pickerel frogs. But like all tree frogs, and unlike ranids, peepers require acre-size or larger ponds of standing water only to mate and lay eggs. For most of the summer months they rely less on standing water than pond frogs, but keep to the shade of canopied forest, where they can elect to warm themselves in direct sunlight on cool mornings, or withdraw into shadow to prevent their skin from drying during the heat of the day. The ideal habitat provides both water and forest, making cedar swamps a preferred habitat, but oak, maple, and other hardwood forests with spring-fed streams are also likely to yield good populations of peeper and other tree frogs.

Physical Characteristics

Mass: 1 ounce or less.

Body: Very small frog; body length about 1 inch. Marked with some semblance of a black X shape across the back. Females typically much larger than males.

Tail: Only during the aquatic tadpole stage, absorbed by the body as the frog matures, and absent in the mature stage.

Tracks: *P. crucifer* has webbing only on the hind feet. There are obvious disks at the tips of its four fingerlike front toes, and on its five hind toes. Except for the occasional faint impression made by jumping against soft mud at the shoreline, this frog leaves no visible tracks. Its weight is so miniscule that it disturbs very little it touches. One exception is that wet frogs may leave a damp silhouette of their bodies and, sometimes, feet on the dry, flattened leaves of deciduous forest floor.

Scat: Tiny, usually cylindrical pellets smaller in diameter than a No. 2 pencil lead. Deposited randomly, and not likely to be found unless the frog is actually witnessed defecating.

Coloration: Like other tree frogs, spring peepers have a limited chameleonlike ability to change their skin colors to match the surrounding environment, so peepers in marshy swamp may be olive, those in rocky country tend to be gray, and peepers living among the leaf litter of a deciduous or coniferous forest may range from brown to rust-colored. The belly is a lighter shade of the back color. The best identifier is a roughly X-shaped cross on the frog's back. Black stripes run longitudinally along either side of the body, extending to under the lower rims of the eyes, and terminating at the end of the nose. There are dark bars running circumferentially around the hind legs, and another connecting the eyes atop the head.

Sign: Peepers leave almost no visible sign, and those that do leave are difficult to find. In dry, undisturbed pine needles, the early morning passage of a tree frog may be seen as a dotted line of sometimes wet, occasionally mucous-smeared, depressions of displaced needles, usually with 5 to 6 inches between them.

Vocalizations: Spring peepers are easily recognized by the piping whistlelike call of the mating male. True to its name the call is a high-pitched "peep-peep-peep" that is often mistaken for the chirping of a bird, except that it's heard only at night. The call is repeated at intervals that become more frequent with a male's rising excitement over a mate or a competitor. There appears to be tendency for mating males to sing together in small groups, usually trios, in which the most dominant member begins the chorus with a deeper toned peep before being joined by the others in higher pitched calls.

By midsummer, when seasonal water holes have dried up, and the mating season is ended in most places, the peepers whose combined calls had been deafening only weeks before will go nearly silent. Exceptions include occasional peeping on warm, rainy nights, and frequent territorial calls in September and October, prior to hibernating in northern populations.

Lifespan: 3 to 4 years.

Diet

Peepers are most active after dark, even—and perhaps especially—on cool evenings when most snakes, toads, and larger frogs that might prey on them have gone dormant. The peeper's ability to tolerate even freezing temperatures gives it a distinct advantage over predator and prey alike, because many of the insects it relies on as food also become lethargic in the cool of night. Until the first permanent snows of winter cover the ground in northern climes, spring peepers are easy to locate at night by the tiny thumping sounds they make while hopping atop leaf litter, and cool nights are when flashlight-armed field researchers are likely to find them in abundance.

Like all frogs, spring peepers are predatory, but their tiny size limits prey to mostly insects, spiders, grubs, and worms. Some believe that peepers favor their prey by its availibility rather than actual preference as food, but the ability to hunt both at ground level and among the trees insures that a wide variety of insect prey is available to them. Despite having a good ability to climb, the little frogs are seldom found more than 15 feet above the earth, possibly because nearly all flying insects travel close to the ground.

Typical of frogs, peepers possess a long, sticky recoiling tongue that they can shoot forward with sufficient accuracy to stun and then pluck insects from arboreal perches. Probably most prey is taken on or near the ground, however, including spiders, ants, and beetles. Insects too large to simply catch and draw into their open mouths are pounced on, then pummeled into submission before being eaten alive, and always head-first.

By day, when warming sunlight brings forth snakes, toads, and even large spiders that might prey on them, the tiny peepers retreat to secluded hollows that are usually at ground level to sleep away the day. Preferred hiding places include damp rotting logs or stumps, hollows under rocks, and sometimes just by burrowing beneath leafy forest debris. In nearly every instance these sleeping places will be damp and small, helping to prevent loss of moisture from the frog's skin.

In deep, moist swamps, where an overhead canopy and damp sphagnum or other mosses retain sufficient moisture to keep these terrestrial frogs from drying out, peepers may be active at all times of day. This is especially true in spring, when days are cooler and hatches of mosquitoes and other insects is at their annual high.

Mating Habits

Spring peepers reach sexual maturity at 3 years of age. Breeding begins earlier than with frogs of the ranid family, starting in late March or early April, and extending through May. This early mating season is probably an evolutionary trait developed to give the tiny tree frog a head start at procreation before larger, more cold-blooded predators become fully active. Because peepers, like all frogs and toads, must lay their eggs in water, having a greater tolerance for cold than frogs that would willingly eat them on emerging from their own hibernation is a necessary advantage.

The peeping mating and territorial call that gives this frog its name is uttered only by males from elevated perches atop large blades of grass, cattails, or shrubs growing at the shorelines of permanent or ephemeral (seasonal) freshwater ponds. The sound is made by inflating an air sac beneath the lower jaw, then forcefully expelling the captured air. Calls become more frequent on warm nights, when rising temperatures make the frogs more active and larger diurnal frogs have gone sedentary. The louder and faster a male sings, the more likely it will be to attract a mate, and at the height of mating, the individual peeps of this smallest of "chorus" frogs can combine to create a din that can be heard from a mile distant, being especially loud during warm, rainy evenings.

Males are territorial during the mating season, driving away competitors by leaping onto them and engaging in a pummeling wrestling match similar to that used to subdue larger insect prey. Territories are typically quite small, sometimes encompassing no more than a square foot of shoreline, and battles over these spaces may be frequent, especially during periods of high population densities. Neither frog will be injured, and the contest ends when the stronger animal is able to turn its opponent onto its back.

Male peepers are polygynous, and will mate with as many females as possible throughout the breeding period. Mating takes place in shallow water, where a male jumps atop the larger female's back, spurring her to expel a gelatinous string of eggs into the water, where they're attached to submerged vegetation. The eggs, which may number between 750 and 1,200, are then fertilized by an expulsion of spermatazoa from the male.

If temperatures are warm, the eggs may hatch into tiny tadpoles in as little as 4 days, but may take as long as 2 weeks in colder climates. The hatchlings feed on plankton and vegetation for the next 2 months, slowly growing legs and absorbing their tails before emerging from the water as fully developed frogs in June or July. The newborn frogs resemble adults, complete with the darker brown X shape on their tan colored backs, although this marking may be irregular or incomplete on some individuals.

The young frogs immediately leave the water, or are eaten by larger frogs and other predators, retreating to the safety of nearby forest. There they feed on spiders, mites, ticks, ants, and other insect life, growing rapidly until they've reached full adult size at the end of summer. In late October or early December, depending on latitude, the young frogs find small holes in mud or rotting wood to hibernate until the coming of spring. During unseasonably warm autumn evenings, the adults seem to be confused, and will often begin peeping as though it were the spring mating season.

Behavior

Like other frogs, spring peepers are territorial, even beyong the mating period, but their territories tend to be small, ranging from 4 to 18 square feet. Excepting for spring migrations to nearby breeding ponds, the frogs remain close to their claimed territories, traveling less than 150 feet from them—mostly at night—throughout their entire lives.

Spring peepers are perhaps most notable for their ability to be active in temperatures cold enough to send other amphibians and reptiles into a lethargic stupor. In most northern habitats where they live, peepers are the first cold-blooded creatures to emerge from hibernation in spring, the first to mate, and the last to hibernate prior to the onset of winter. The little treefrogs are even active in temperatures below 32°F.

Equally remarkable is the peeper's ability to withstand extreme winter cold. Ranid frogs hibernate through winter by burying themselves in soft mud at the bottoms of ponds, where surrounding water prevents them from freezing solid. But spring peepers hibernate in small hollows on land, where their bodies are subjected to ambient temperatures that may fall well below 0°F in northern latitudes. During the hibernation period, water in the little frog's body can actually freeze solid without killing the animal, so long as an antifreeze solution of converted glucose continues to flow through internal organs to prevent ice crystals from forming within them. In North America, only the gray treefrog (*Hyla versicolor*) shares this ability to freeze without dying.

Despite being common and plentiful throughout eastern North America at the time of this writing, biologists warn that existing populations of spring peepers require protection from human encroachment. This species is especially susceptible to poisoning by water runoff containing herbicides, pesticides, and silt from farmlands and golf courses, all of which can kill eggs, tadpoles, and adults.

TOADS

There are more than a dozen species of toads in North America, ranging from the inch-long oak toad *(Bufo quercicus)* of the southeastern United States to colorful species like the red-spotted toad *(B. punctatus)* of the desert southwest to a giant 9-inch immigrant known as the marine toad *(B. marinus),* which has become well-established in Florida and Texas.

The most terrestrial of froglike amphibians, true toads begin their lives as a string of eggs deposited in water, where they hatch into plant-eating tadpoles, much the same as frogs. But unlike frogs, which remain in or near open water throughout their lives, toads spend their adult lives on land, returning to water only to mate, and are often found far from water. The thicker, bump-covered skin common to toads is more efficient at retaining body moisture than that of their thinner-skinned frog cousins, permitting them to range farther and occupy more diverse habitats.

Although no toads cause warts to humans who handle them, all toad species share a wartlike texture on the skin of their backs. The purpose of these warts is twofold; they provide a three-dimensional surface the makes the animal more difficult to see against a natural background, and, should that camouflage fail to escape the notice of a sharp-eyed predator, the warts exude an irritating toxin that few enemies can overcome. Most toxic of these warts are a pair of enlarged parotid glands located just behind the eyes, where the poison they secrete can be most effective against predators that try to swallow them head-first.

American Toad (Bufo americanus)

The American toad covered here is the most widespread of New World toads, and is typical of all toads in most respects. Its defining characteristics and habits are applicable to the majority of toad species in North America, and, indeed, the world.

Geographic Range

American toads are native only to North America. The species is commonly found throughout the eastern half of the continent, from Hudson Bay in northern Canada to Chihuahua in northern Mexico, extending eastward to cover nearly all of the eastern United States. The species becomes less populous about 200 miles inland, and is absent

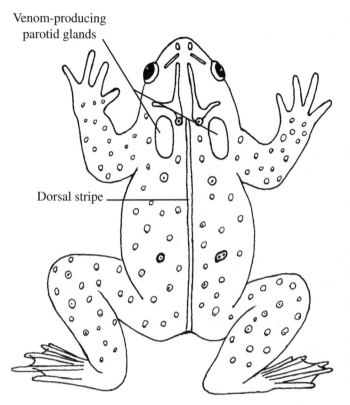

Venom-producing
parotid glands

Dorsal stripe

American toad (Bufo americanus). *Thick, warty skin retains moisture better than the thin, smooth skin of true frogs, allowing toads to live terrestrial lives. Note the thicker legs and stout body, uncharacteristic of more trimly built frogs.*

from most of the Atlantic sea to a range of more than 200 miles in the south, including all of Florida.

Although *B. americanus* is found only in eastern North America, it has very close cousins to the west. The Great Plains toad *(B. cognatus)* is found along the Rocky Mountains from Canada to most of northern Mexico. The even more similar Western toad inhabits most of the Pacific coast from southern Alaska to southern California, inland to a range of roughly 500 miles. The Woodhouse's toad, or common toad *(B. woodhouses)* occupies roughly the southern half of the United States, where its range overlaps that of those already mentioned, but it too is absent from peninsular Florida. Florida's peninsula is home to the Southern toad *(B. terrestris),* which is present nowhere else. Although visually distinguishable from one another, these species are quite similar in size and appearance and in the role they play in nature.

Habitat

American toads and their close cousins have demonstrated an ability to adapt to a broad variety of environments and habitats, so long as there's an at least semipermanent source of fresh water in which to mate and lay eggs within 1, perhaps as far as 2, miles. Like frogs, toads require unpolluted pools of standing water that will remain at least 6 inches deep from spring to midsummer, but toads are far less reliant on water than the thinner-skinned frogs, and often inhabit places too dry to support even tree frogs.

Being able to range inland because their thick-skinned bodies lose moisture more slowly than frogs has enabled toads to become commonplace nearly anywhere it can find edible insects in sufficient numbers. At least one species can be found in nearly every suburb, and even rural communities where there are drainage ditches or runoff ponds, and they provide a real service to gardeners by eating large numbers of insects.

Seldom seen except during the hours of dusk and dawn, or sometimes during warm rainy days, toads sleep away the heat of day by backing into shaded hollows in building foundations, under the flooring of outbuildings, or in drainpipes and culverts. The animals always shelter facing outward, where they can detect and meet approaching enemies head-on, where the toxin-producing parotid glands located to the rear of either eye can be employed to good effect.

Physical Characteristics

Mass: About 6 ounces at maturity, females larger than males.

Body: Length 2 to slightly more than 4 inches. Unlike the more slender and athletic pond frogs, American toads have short legs, stout bodies, and thick skins that are covered with obvious bumps. These wartlike protrusions contain poison glands that produce a noxious milky fluid which all mammals and most other predators find intolerable. These toxins are also found in the skins of larvae during the tadpole stage.

A toad's sex can be determined by examining the underside of its throat, which is darker brown or gray than the white throat of the female. Too, female toads are generally about 20% larger than males, and females are typically of a lighter color overall than males.

Tail: Evident only during the tadpole stage, and, like frogs, absorbed as the toad matures into its adult morph.

Tracks: Froglike, but stouter and better suited to travel on land. There are four toes on the front legs, five webbed toes on the hind feet. Toads can walk in a rather ungainly fashion by extending the forelegs and raising their heavy bodies, but they can also hop in a manner similar to frogs by bunching their hind legs and then pushing forward. Toad hops are shorter than those of the more lithely built frogs, but the track pattern is the same, with forefeet printing close together between hind tracks.

Scat: Tiny pellets, often crescent-shaped, about 0.075 inch in diameter by 0.125 inch long. Dark brown or black, similar to those left by mice.

Coloration: The skin color of American toads can be a variety of brown-gray hues. Some are rust-colored with light patches of olive or gray, many are mostly gray, but always with darker colored warts prominent against the lighter colored skin. Slight color changes have been noted in response to stress, temperature, and humidity, but toads are generally not chameleonlike. *B. americanus* is most easily distinguished from other toad species by several dark spots on the back, sometimes bordered by white or yellow, that contain only one or two warts each. The underbelly is white, becoming yellowed as the animal ages, and adult males have grayish throats. The eyeball pupils are oval and black with a perimeter of gold.

Sign: Very little. Look for scrape marks left by the animal's body and toes at the entrance of enclosed daytime hiding places, made as it backed into them.

Vocalizations: American toads have a prolonged high-pitched trilling call with a duration of 4 to 20 seconds, made by inflating the elastic sac beneath their chins, then expelling the trapped air forcefully. The trilling becomes louder and more constant during the spring breeding season, but young males especially continue to call throughout the summer.

Lifespan: Although most American toads don't live to maturity because of predation, especially by snakes, adults may live up to 10 years. The longest recorded lifespan in captivity is reported to be 36 years.

Diet

American toad tadpoles, like those of most froglike amphibians, graze on aquatic vegetation and microscopic organisms during their development in the aquatic stage. In the adult morph, the terrestrial toads become almost strictly carnivorous, feeding on insects, worms, and smaller vertebrates, like snake hatchlings.

Despite a human tendency to regard toads with some disgust, referenced by colloquialisms that use the word "toad" as a metaphor for anything small and ugly, toads are among the most beneficial of creatures. Depending on the size of the toad, and the size and availability of insects, an adult toad may eat between 100 and 1,000 insects per day, which makes them a valuable resource for the control of mosquitoes and other biting insects. Gardeners consider toads a valuable ally for controlling pests like potato beetles and larvae harmful to vegetable crops.

American toads are most active at dusk and dawn (crepuscular), and during warm, especially rainy, summer nights. They might also be seen foraging during warm, overcast days. Rain and heavy dewfall causes most insects to become lethargic and stationary, making them easier prey.

Smaller flies and mosquitoes are simply swallowed, but larger insects, like dragonflies and locusts, are engulfed head first in the toad's jaws, then shoved completely into its mouth by using the forefeet.

Unlike many toads, which pounce onto their prey to stun it prior to eating the animal, American toads possess a sticky recoiling tongue that can shoot out to a distance of several inches to capture both flying and crawling insects. American toads may also pounce on larger prey, but the ability to capture prey perched beyond reach of toads that do not have a recoiling tongue helps to make *B. americanus* perhaps the most successful of toads.

Mating Habits

American toads reach sexual maturity at 2 years, although males especially may not breed until 3 years in places where the species is populous and there exists strong competition for territory. The mating season is roughly 30 days, and, depending on latitude, may begin as early as March, extending into April, and sometimes as late as July. Trigger mechanisms include warming temperatures and lengthening days, but unseasonable cold spells are likely to delay or interrupt normal mating periods.

Like all frogs and toads, *B. americanus* must have open, shallow water in which to mate, and these ponds, marshes, or stream eddies must be permanent or semipermanent to give their aquatic tadpole young sufficient time to develop. Males arrive at breeding places about 1 week in advance of the females' arrival, and immediately begin calling for receptive mates with their unique trilling call. Male toads are territorial, occupying small tracts of shoreline that may encompass several yards, and chasing away competitors through wrestling matches that result in no injury to either contestant.

Female toads drawn to the males' mating calls appear to select their mates through idiosyncrasies within the calls, although exactly how that is done has yet to be discovered. Once a mate has been chosen, the female hops into shallow water within that male's territory, and is mounted by the male without ceremony. Adult male toads possess dark, horny pads, called amplexicaul pads, on the first and second two toes of their forelegs that help them to maintain a firm grip atop the larger female's back. The male uses his amplexicaul pads to remain firmly in place as the female carries him with her to a place suitable to lay her eggs.

When the female toad determines where to lay her eggs, she expels them from an orifice between her legs in a long, gelatinous string that has measured from 20 to as many as 66 feet when laid out. The round eggs, each with a diameter of about 1.5mm, are countershaded, being almost black on top and lighter below to help camouflage them against predators. The ova are contained in two parallel rows within the string, and may number from 2,000 to as many as 20,000. As she expels her eggs, the male perched atop her back fertilizes them externally by expelling his own sperm onto the string.

After mating, the female leaves, while the male resumes calling for another mate. There is no parental care for the eggs, which begin to hatch after a period of 3 to 12 days, with shorter gestation times being indicative of warmer water temperatures. The all-black hatchling tadpoles begin feeding on plant life immediately, quickly growing to a length of 0.5 inch. Like adults, toad tadpoles secrete a toxin from their skins that deters most predators, and they tend to remain in water too shallow for larger fish to negotiate, but in many habitats fewer than half will survive to maturity.

Fifty to 65 days after hatching, usually in June or July, the tadpoles will have absorbed their tails, grown legs, and will leave the water to live on land as young adults. The emergent toadlets are lighter-hued versions of adults, measuring about 0.5 inch long, and they become predatory immediately. Their first meals will consist of mosquitoes, gnats, and small ants, with larger insects being preyed on as the toads grow to a full adult length of more than 3 inches over the next 3 years.

Behavior

Except for the spring mating season, American toads are solitary. By day the animals take shelter in small, enclosed places to escape the heat, backing into holes and hollows where they're protected against danger from any direction except head-on. Thus situated, a toad can see and face approaching predators, and because most predators swallow prey headfirst, the toad's toxin-producing parotid glands can be used to good advantage.

American toads are generally considered to be nocturnal, but it might be more accurate to say that they avoid sunlight. In shaded woodlands, under heavily overcast skies, and particularly during warm rains, they may hunt at all times of day. In fact, rainy days are favored by toads because they seldom drink, but take in most of the water their bodies need through absorption from rain, dew, or by swimming.

Despite being well-protected from most predators by the toxins its skin produces, the American toad is considered food by at least some snake species. Most garter snakes (*Thamnophis sirtalis*) seem to be oblivious to the toxins produced by a toad's glands, and one, the Hognose Snake (*Heterodon simus*), is especially adapted to prey on toads of all species. Not only is the hognose snake immune to the toad's poison, it possesses a pair of sharp venom producing teeth in the rear of the upper jaw that serve to not only poison prey as it's being swallowed, but to puncture and deflate toads that inflate their bodies with air to make it more difficult for predators to swallow them.

Much like snakes, toads shed their skins several times each year to accommodate their growing bodies. Shedding is especially frequent during the first year of adult life, when skins are replaced as frequently as every 2 weeks. Replacement of skin becomes less frequent as the toad matures, until at adulthood—3 years—the shedding process occurs about every 3 months. At all ages, toads loosen and pull their own dead skins off in a usually single piece using their jaws, then eat it, presumably for the proteins it contains.

Toads living in northern latitudes where winter snows send insects into hibernation will also hibernate until spring, while those in warmer regions go dormant only during cold spells, again following the example of their insect prey. Much as they do during the heat or cold of summer, toads back themselves into a burrow or hollow, where, like spring peeper tree frogs, they allow the outer surfaces of their bodies to freeze, maintaining life only in their internal organs with a flow of converted glucose that acts as an anti-freeze of sorts.

The toxins produced by toads are of interest to the medical community. Although there exists some variation in concentration and content from one species to another, toad venoms in general have been found to contain cardioactive agents, vasoconstrictors, and anasthetic properties. Drug users who smoke the dried skins report hallucinogenic effects, but licking a toad's skin with the tongue, which some sources have recommended as a means of inducing euphoria, will cause severe irritation of mucous membranes, and may induce seizures, or even a heart attack.

CHAPTER 7

REPTILES

SNAKES

Easily the most widely feared reptiles in the world, snakes are also some of the most ecologically important animals in nature. Despite being cast in a negative, and often demonic, light in song and story throughout human history, snakes of all species play a keystone role in every environment in which they're found. All are carnivorous; many are constrictors that kill their prey by grasping it in their jaws and coiling their bodies around the victim to squeeze the animal until it dies of suffocation. Some are venomous, equipped with sharp teeth or fangs that pierce a victim's skin and inject a usually fatal dose of poison. A few are nonvenomous, but possess teeth that can inflict serious wounds on small prey animals.

All snakes are hairless, legless crawling animals, accomplishing forward locomotion by using numerous muscles in their scaled undersides to push backward against the earth in succession, propelling their bodies in a smooth slithering motion. None can crawl backward, but their long, extremely flexible spines permit them to change direction, and even double-back on themselves.

A few species spend much time above ground in the branches of trees, safe from other predators, but most of these cold-blooded creatures can be found warming themselves in open places under a morning sun.

No snake harbors animosity toward humans, and even the most venomous will withdraw from conflict if allowed to do so. Myths aside, humans are not prey for snakes of any size, and most are too small to eat animals larger than a rat. Even at that,

Brown snake (Suzanne L. Collins, The Center for North American Herpetology).

E. Ribbon Snake (Suzanne L. Collins, The Center for North American Herpetology).

most eat seldom in comparison to most animals, subsisting on one meal for sometimes weeks.

Common Garter Snake (*Thamnophis sirtalis*)

The genus includes: *Thamnophis sirtalis parietalis* (red-sided garter snake), *T. sirtalis similes* (blue-stripe garter snake), *T. s. pallidulus* (maritime garter snake), *T. s. semifasciatus* (Chicago garter snake), *T. s. dorsalis* (New Mexico garter snake), *T. s. annectens* (Texas garter snake), *T. s. fitchi* (valley garter snake), *T. s. infernalis* (California red-sided garter snake), and *T. s. tetrataenia* (San Francisco garter snake).

Geographic Range

This is the most common of the many species of garter snakes that live in North America, and it's the only species of wild snake found in Alaska, ranging farther north than any other North American reptile. Absent only from the arid southwest, the common garter snake is native from Texas and Florida to Canada.

Habitat

The common garter snake is highly adaptable and can survive cold better than any other North American snake, and perhaps better than any other species in the world. Although never very far from water, this snake is common to a wide variety of habitats, including hardwood and pine forests, marshes, drainage ditches, and even suburbia. Its importance in controlling rapidly reproducing populations of mice, rats, and larger insects can be noted by the protection afforded resident snakes on military bases.

Physical Characteristics

Mass: Usually less than 1 pound, but very old individuals may reach more than 3 pounds.

Body: May reach 4 feet or more, but usually around 1 foot.

Tail: Tapered to a thin point, unadorned by rattles or by markings different than those on the body.

Tracks: Undulating grooves left in loose sand, forest debris.

Scat: Seldom seen, but watery with varying mixes of black, white, and brown. The snake often excretes feces when handled to make itself less attractive as food to predators.

Coloration: Like all garter snakes, *T. sirtalis* has lateral stripes, sometimes spotted, of white, yellow, green, blue, orange, or red against a darker background that ranges from black, dark green, or brown. Despite this wide variation within the species, it can be distinguished from other *Thamnophis* species by the location of the lateral stripe, which is always limited to the second and third rows of scales up from the ventral scales. There is usually a double-row of black spots between the lateral stripes. Distinguishing between the many subspecies of *Thamnophis* requires a detailed field guide.

Sign: Shed skins during the summer months.

Vocalization: Generally silent. The common garter snake can make a low hissing sound when threatened, but even this is rare.

Lifespan: Little data exists for establishing a mean lifespan for the common garter snake, but several sometimes contradictory studies have concluded that an average lifespan in

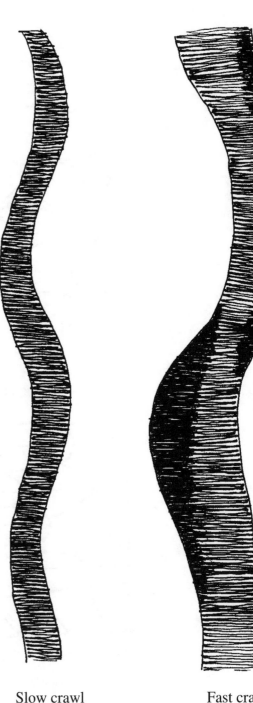

Slow crawl   Fast crawl

Typical snake track patterns.

Flat scales

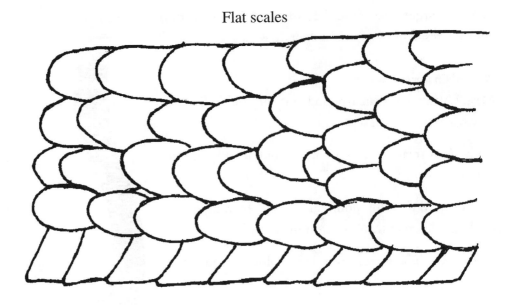

"Keeled" scales with longitudinal ridges

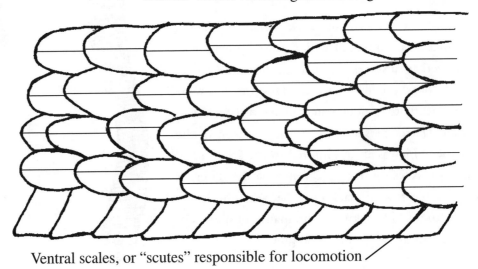

Ventral scales, or "scutes" responsible for locomotion

Types of scales on a snake's body.

the wild is probably 2 years, depending very much on whether or not the snake is killed as prey. Maximum lifespan in captivity has been 14 years.

Diet

The diet of a common garter snake varies with the habitat in which it lives. These snakes can subsist on earthworms and grasshoppers, frogs, toads, birds, and rodents that are small enough to be swallowed, and an occasional fish or tadpole. Having no fangs or venom, *T. sirtalis* uses stealth to ambush prey, usually snatching it by the head with a very fast and accurate strike. With its head engulfed, the prey animal struggles less as it's held in place by small, serrated teeth that line the snake's jaws. Constriction is also used to immobilize prey as it is slowly swallowed whole. Digestion may take several days.

Mating Habits

Common garter snakes are ovoviviparous, meaning that they bear live young which are incubated from fertilized eggs carried in the mother's lower abdomen. Sexual maturity is reached at 1.5 years in males, 2 years in females. Mating occurs in spring just after the snakes emerge from hibernation in April or May, depending on climate. Males emerge first, and immediately begin to congregate around the den entrances of females, where the males emit pheromonal scents to advertise their willingness to breed. Male snakes are polygynandrous, or promiscuous, and will seek out another mate as soon as they've finished breeding a female. Female snakes have the ability to store a partner's sperm, ejecting it if a more suitable mate comes along. After mating, females retire to a safe birthing den, continuing to hunt and feed themselves over a gestation period of 2 or 3 months before finally bearing a clutch of about fifteen young, sometimes as many as fifty, depending on the mother's size and health. After birth, baby garter snakes are abandoned by the mother and must find food on their own.

Behavior

Like most snakes, garter snakes tend to be most active during the day, and sometimes on especially warm summer nights. When the evening chill sets in they take refuge under logs and debris, or even in garages, to await the returning warmth of morning. In the morning garter and other snakes move to open places, including roads, railroad grades, and hiking trails, where the sun's warming rays help them to regain a normal body temperature of about 86°F. As the sun rises and makes the ground at these basking places too hot for comfort, the snakes once again seek more shaded spots, taking refuge in the same types of enclosed places that serve as sleeping quarters.

Common garter snakes are very sociable, although they also tend to spend much of their time alone during summer. When two snakes meet they communicate with one another through a system of chemical scents, called lipids, that are exuded through their skins. These pheromonal scents are used by breeding snakes to advertise both their availability and their sex, although it appears that a number of male snakes are sometimes endowed with female lipids that cause other males to court them by mistake. Lipid-borne pheromones also help garter snakes to track one another when they gather together prior to hibernation in the fall.

Being social, garter snakes tend to congregate in a single large burrow below the frost line where the small amount of body heat generated by their numbers helps to keep all of them safe from freezing until spring returns. It appears that the trails used by garter snakes are well-established and permanent around mating and denning places, because the same routes are followed by newborn snakes when they leave the den, and used by them to return prior to hibernation. Like most snakes, garters are both predator and prey in their ecosystem. Newly born snakes may be eaten by frogs, toads, turtles, and even some insects. Larger snakes are prey to hawks, foxes, raccoons, opossums, and larger snakes.

With a top speed of about 3 miles per hour, garter snakes are easily caught in the wild. When cornered they coil into striking position like a viper and may hiss. When handled they often bite, but the bite is a bluff intended to frighten their captor into dropping them, because the snake's tiny teeth are incapable of penetrating human skin. Perhaps most effective against humans is the garter's ability to exude foul-smelling chemicals through its skin.

Garter snakes are popular as pets, and some biologists warn that over-collection of them for that market has caused a decline in their numbers that could one day become serious for this environmentally important predator. That problem seems especially likely to occur in the north, where denning snakes gather together in larger numbers, and are more easily collected. One subspecies, the San Francisco garter snake (*T. s. tetrataenia*), was placed on the Endangered Species list in 1967.

Corn Snake (*Elaphe guttata*)

This member of the rat snake genus (*Elaphe*) is also known as the red rat snake. Often mistaken for vipers because of the blotched markings on their backs, these snakes are nonvenomous, but larger individuals are capable of inflicting a painful bite when handled. The orange-colored eastern race is sometimes mistaken for a copperhead (*Agkistrodon contortrix*). The darker brown-on-gray western, or Great Plains, race resembles a rattlesnake (genus *Crotalus*), with the most obvious identifier being that it has no rattles. Even the true rat snake *(E. obsoleta)* exhibits considerable color variation, or race, within its own species, with some individuals being black, some yellow, and others gray.

Geographic Range

Eastern corn snakes are found in the eastern United States from southern New Jersey south through Florida, west into Louisiana and parts of Kentucky. The species appears to be most abundant in Florida and the southeastern United States.

Habitat

Corn snakes may be found in woodlands, on rocky sunlit hillsides, and in meadows, usually in search of warmth or rodents. They also tend to occupy the crawlspaces under barns and outbuildings. Preferred habitats will include a stream or pond, but they are frequently found far from water.

Physical Characteristics

Mass: Usually less than a pound, occasionally in excess of 4 pounds.

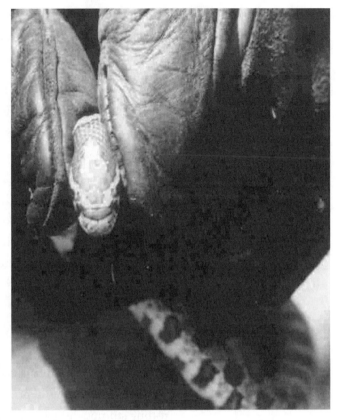

Corn snake.

Body: Corn snakes are typically slender with a length of 2 to 6 feet.

Tail: Slender and without rattles.

Tracks: Undulating grooves left in the surface of loose sand on dirt roads and trails.

Scat: Seldom seen; but small, elongated blobs that are black and white with varying shades of brown or gray.

Coloration: Corn snakes are non-venomous, but mimic venomous species like the copperhead, ranging in color from orange to brownish-yellow, with large black-edged red blotches down the middle of the back. On the belly there are alternating rows of black and white marks that make it resemble an ear of Indian corn, and these are believed to have been the origin of this species' common name. Considerable variation occurs in the coloration and patterns of individual snakes, depending on age and region. Hatchlings are more subdued, lacking the brighter coloration and contrasts found on adults.

Sign: Shed skins during the summer months. Skins retain the snake's markings, but without coloration.

Vocalizations: Generally silent, but may hiss if cornered. Corn snakes are among several species that will vibrate their tails in dried grass and dead foliage to create a rattling sound that mimics the noise made by a coiled rattlesnake.

Lifespan: Corn snakes have lived up to 23 years in captivity, but their lifespan is generally much less in the wild due to predation.

Diet

Like most snakes, corn snakes don't normally feed every day because their digestive systems work slowly. Hatchlings tend to feed on small lizards and tree frogs, while adults feed on larger prey like mice, nesting birds, and roosting bats. Their small inward-pointing teeth are incapable of killing prey directly, so corn snakes are constrictors, using their coils to suffocate food animals before swallowing them whole and usually head-first. If the prey is small and relatively harmless, the snake may swallow it alive.

Mating Habits

Corn snakes breed from March to May, earlier in southern climes than in the north. Impregnated females deposit a clutch of roughly twenty eggs from late May to July in rotting stumps, decaying vegetation, and other moist locations that will remain at about 80°F until the eggs hatch in about 60 days. Eggs are not cared for by the mother, and will be abandoned soon after they're laid. Corn snake eggs hatch from July through September, earlier in the north than in the south. Hatchlings are about 3 inches long at birth and mature at about 2 years. Being relatively uncommon and shy, little hard data has been established about the reproductive behaviors of corn snakes.

Three mice regurgitated by a captured corn snake.

Behavior

Corn snakes are active both day and night so long as temperatures are neither too hot nor cold, and are more nocturnal than many North American species. They're good climbers, ascending trees to capture birds, and may steal eggs that are small enough to swallow. Although secretive and seldom seen, they may also enter barns and outbuildings in search of rodents that live in them. In nature they spend much of their time slithering through rodent burrows, especially to find litters of young mice and voles, which makes gathering field data about them more difficult than with most snake species.

In the heat of a summer day, during cool nights, or if the snake has a full belly, it will secrete itself under fallen trees, under farm outbuildings, or in rock cracks until hunger or environmental conditions prompt it to hunt or mate. Corn snakes are not an endangered species, but they are listed by the state of Florida as a Species of Special Concern because they face habitat loss in the lower Florida Keys.

Eastern Hognose Snake *(Heterodon platyrhinos)*

The family of hognose snakes, so called because of their distinctive upturned snouts, is comprised of twenty species that may be found in both North and South America, with at least one of them being present from southern Canada to Patagonia. Although only the eastern hognose snake has been showcased here, all members of this unique group share the colloquial name "puff adder," which alludes to their ability to rise up and spread their necks, very much like a cobra, and hiss loudly in a display of feigned ferocity. Despite their apparent aggressiveness, hognose snakes are among the most harmless to humans, and the eastern hognose especially is known for its habit of playing dead when confronted with danger.

Eastern Hognose Snake. Photo by Ed McCrea, courtesy of U.S. Fish & Wildlife Service.

Geographic Range

The genus *Heterodon* is endemic to North America, and includes the eastern hognose snake, as well as five other species. As its common name suggests, the eastern hognose is found throughout the eastern United States, ranging from southeastern South Dakota to Texas, eastward to the Atlantic seaboard from southern New York to Florida.

Habitat

The eastern hognose, like most of its cousins, prefers to live in a woodland environment, especially deciduous or mixed deciduous and coniferous forests, although the species is sometimes found in brushlands and overgrown clearcuts. Preferred habitats include plenty of sticks, leaves, and other forest debris under which the snakes can root with their upturned noses in search of prey. A temperate species, *H. platyrhinos* can tolerate four-season environments where winter temperatures fall below 20°F.

Physical Characteristics

Mass: Stout, sometimes in excess of 4 pounds.

Body: Up to 3 feet, occasionally larger. The eastern hognose is a short, thickly built snake with a pointed upturned snout and wide neck. The anal scale plate is divided into halves. Although considered non-venomous where humans are concerned, the hognose possesses a pair of enlarged teeth at the rear of the upper jaw that do inject venom into prey as it's being swallowed. These teeth are designed to puncture toads that inflate themselves as protection against being swallowed, and they give the genus its name, *Heterodon*, which translates to "different tooth." They also mean that a human must have part of his anatomy fully inserted into the back of the snake's mouth to receive a venomous bite.

Tail: Blunt, no rattles.

Tracks: Serpentine grooves in dry sand, unusually wide in comparison to other snakes of similar length.

Scat: Seldom seen, but mucouslike elongated blobs of black, white, and varying shades of gray and brown.

Coloration: The colors range from yellow, to light brown, or grayish, and are often tinted with rust. The eastern hognose exhibits considerable variation in body color and markings; some herpetologists believe that this variation is because the species is a relatively new member of the hognose genus, and hasn't yet evolved a permanent camouflage color scheme.

Sign: Shed skins with keeled (ridged) scales that are usually arranged in rows of 25 scales per row.

Vocalizations: Generally silent. Loud hissing when cornered, much more vocal than most snakes. Vibrates tail against dry leaves and debris to imitate the buzzing of a rattlesnake.

Lifespan: 10 to 15 years, although many are killed as prey in their first year.

Diet

The forest-dwelling hognose snake's diet reflects its habitat. Its senses of smell and heat detection are keen enough to detect prey animals hidden beneath leaf litter, which it then unearths by rooting with its namesake hognose.

Predominant in the hognose's diet are toads, frogs, mice, salamanders, and small lizards. This snake is especially immune to the toxins excreted through the skin of toads, and is in fact one of the few species that makes toads a large part of its diet. After unearthing denned toads from their daytime burrows with its snout, the hognose swallows them headfirst. The toad's natural defense is to inflate its body by gulping in air to prevent itself from being swallowed, but a pair of venom-producing teeth located at the rear of the snake's upper jaw are adapted to circumvent that defense by puncturing the toad and deflating it. Once deflated and paralyzed by venom, the toad becomes relaxed and easy to ingest. Enlarged adrenaline glands in the snake's body also help it to resist the bufotoxins secreted from parotid glands and warts.

Mating Habits

Little data has been established about the hognose snake's mating habits or reproduction, making it an ideal candidate for field research.

Eastern hognose snakes generally mate between May and June, depending on temperature and latitude, but those living in southern regions where temperatures remain warm year-round may mate again in August or September. There is no bond between mates, and both go their own way after breeding. Females seek out natural depressions or secluded holes in soft sandy or loamy soil, depositing a clutch of whitish, thin-shelled eggs that are ovoid in shape and measure about 1.25 inches long in late June or July. Clutch sizes appear to relate to the mother's physical size and state of health, and may vary widely in number from four to as many as sixty eggs. After laying her eggs, the mother abandons them.

Kept warm by sun-warmed earth, the eggs hatch after a gestation of 50 to 65 days, most of them in August or September. Unusually, incubating eggs actually grow during the gestation period, resulting in relatively large hatchlings that may be from

6 to 10 inches long. Although generally lighter in color than adults, the hatchlings are duplicates of their parents.

Young hognose snakes spend much of their time in hiding, feeding on small insects and growing quickly for their first year. Garter and other snakes prey on the hatchlings, as do opossums, skunks, ravens, and numerous predatory birds. Ironically, toads that are eaten by adult hognose snakes will also prey on hatchlings. If a hatchling survives until it reaches adulthood at 3 years, it has little to fear from most predators except large owls or hawks.

Behavior

Hognose snakes are best known for the unique way in which they react when threatened. Like all snakes, the hognose first tries to withdraw from confrontation, but if cornered it coils its body like a rattlesnake, raises its head, and spreads its neck like a cobra to make itself look larger. The image of formidability is enhanced by loud hissing as the coiled snake undulates, waving its head back and forth and constantly writhing. These behaviors have earned this species monikers like "puff adder," "blowsnake," and "American cobra."

If an enemy persists, the snake secretes foul-smelling lipids from glands in its skin and defecates, smearing the unpleasant odors over its body as it writhes. The snake may actually strike at its assailant, but this too is a feint, and although its nose might butt against the enemy, its mouth remains closed.

Finally, if the attacker hasn't been dissuaded by these feigned threats, the snake simply falls to the earth, rolls onto its back with tongue lolling out, and plays dead. If the snake is rolled upright onto its belly, it immediately turns over onto its back again. Presumably, the belly-up position is intended to keep the snake's most distasteful side presented to an enemy. If this last-ditch effort succeeds, the hognose waits until the enemy has withdrawn, then rights itself and moves off.

Researchers should be aware that the scenario just described, though typical, isn't an absolute. Large, old snakes that have become accustomed to being near the top of the food chain may persist in a show of aggression and refuse to play dead. Conversely, a younger and less confident hognose may simply fall over at the sight of a human.

Like garter snakes, the eastern hognose is active in temperatures cold enough to send most of its serpent brethren into hiding. This resistance to cold makes it one of the first snakes out of hibernation in spring, and one of the last to retreat into a den in autumn, which gives the hognose a real advantage over other snakes when it comes to feeding.

Eastern hognose snake populations are stable and healthy throughout their range, but there is some concern about the closely related southern hognose (*H. simus*), which is thought to have already gone extinct in some places. Development of the woodlands which the snake depends on as habitat is blamed in part, but so is the spread of fire ants, which are an aggressive predator of hognose hatchlings. At the time of this writing *H. simus* is being considered for federal listing as an endangered species.

Eastern Diamondback Rattlesnake *(Crotalus adamanteus)*

Considered by many to be the most dangerous rattlesnake in North America, the eastern diamondback has earned that reputation by proving fatal to 40% of people unlucky enough to be bitten by this species. Unlike its close cousin, the western diamondback *(Crotalus atrox)*, which inhabits open areas in the desert southwest, this rattlesnake occupies more junglelike terrain, where close-range surprise encounters between itself and humans are more likely.

Only slightly larger than its desert-dwelling relative, the eastern diamondback is disproportionately more dangerous because its venom contains not only the tissue-dissolving hemotoxin common to all rattlesnakes, but also a fast-acting neurotoxin like that found in cobras. Working in tandem, these poisons insure that prey will be overcome swiftly, before escaping into the thick country where eastern diamondbacks hunt.

Because humans are likely to be close to an eastern diamondback before detecting its presence, researchers should exercise extra caution in places where this species lives. In most cases, the snake will advertise itself by buzzing the rattles on its tail, but, like the deadly fer-de-lance *(Bothrops atrox)* snake of South America, eastern diamondbacks are known to remain quiet under concealing foliage in hope that an enemy will pass by without notice. With either species, hikers are well-served by carrying a long (5 feet or longer) walking stick with which to poke inside shadowed places where a snake might hide, thereby forcing it to reveal itself or to retreat.

Geographic Range

The eastern diamondback inhabits coastal lowlands from southeast North Carolina, throughout Florida and its Keys, and westward to eastern Louisiana. (Western diamondbacks are found from central Texas through southern New Mexico, Arizona, and California, extending southward into central Mexico.)

Habitat

Eastern diamondbacks prefer well-foliated environments, including dry swamps, palmetto groves, and pine forests. The species is seldom found in wet swamps or marshes, but may inhabit dry shorelines. Despite having an apparent aversion to water, these snakes have been reported swimming in shallow waters of the Atlantic as they travel between islands off the Florida coast.

Physical Characteristics

Mass: Usually about 6 pounds, but may reach weights of more than 14 pounds.

Body: Up to 8 feet long, but usually about 4 feet at maturity. Broad, triangular head with large sensory pits located below and between eyes and nostrils in the upper jaw. Long, tubular fangs normally folded backward to lie flat against the upper palate.

Tail: White with black peripheral rings, and tipped with rounded, segmented rattles that are stacked atop one another in a roughly cone shape. Each rattle is a remnant of the last scale, left when the snake molted. End rattles may be broken on older individuals.

Tracks: Serpentine undulations in sand and loose earth.

Scat: Seldom seen but typically snakelike, with an elongated mass of white, black, and brown.

Coloration: It has a row of large dark diamonds with brown centers and cream borders down its back. The ground color of the body ranges from olive, to brown, to almost black. The tail is usually a different shade, brownish or gray, and banded with dark rings. The head has a light-bordered dark stripe running diagonally through the eye. The young are similar to the adults in color pattern.

Sign: Shed skins, discarded broken rattles.

Vocalizations: Generally silent. Tail vibrates with a buzzing rattle when agitated.

Lifespan: Up to 20 years.

Diet

Carnivorous. Primarily nocturnal hunters, *Crotalus adamanteus* and its western cousin prey on small mammals, birds, reptiles, amphibians, large insects, and sometimes fish. Larger snakes may take larger prey, sometimes as large as a rabbit or muskrat.

Adapted to prey especially on small, warm-blooded animals, eastern diamondback and other pit vipers detect these animals through minute differences in body and air temperatures by employing the thermally sensitive sensory pits. Prey is also detected by scent using the forked tongue, which flicks outward almost constantly when the snake is actively hunting.

Once detected, food mammals are stalked quietly by slithering in close, then swiftly lunging forward with mouth open and fangs exposed. Striking distance is up to 75% of the snake's body length, meaning that an 8-foot rattler may accurately strike its victim from as far as 6 feet. Fangs are driven into a prey animal's body, where they immediately inject a dose of venom into its tissues. Venom flow is controlled by voluntary muscles surrounding the glands where it is manufactured, permitting the snake to meter dosage in relation to the size of its prey, but target areas are not specific, and there appears to be no preference about where a bite is administered. Fangs are sometimes broken off and remain in the victim, but rattlesnakes can replace lost teeth up to four times per year from reserve teeth carried in the upper jaw.

Once bitten, prey animals are typically released, and the fangs return to their resting position against the upper jaw. This practice helps to insure that the snake isn't injured by holding onto a struggling victim that may bite or scratch. The released prey then attempts to escape, but is quickly overcome by effects of the venom. The neurotoxic component acts immediately to paralyze a stricken animal's heart and respiratory system, while hemotoxins break down blood vessels and cause acute internal hemorrhaging. The hemotoxin's action also serves to break down and literally soften a prey's tissues, making it easier to swallow and digest.

In most instances, death comes swiftly to the rattler's prey, although it might run several yards before collapsing. The snake follows using its acute senses of smell and heat detection. The dead prey animal is swallowed head-first and whole in typical snake fashion, a process that may take several minutes to more than half an hour, depending on the size of both animals.

After ingesting prey, the now lumpy and somewhat sluggish snake retires to a secluded hollow to digest its meal. Like all snakes, the diamondback's digestive processes are very slow, but very efficient, assimilating bone, hair, and other body parts that would pass intact through the intestines of most predators. Presuming a prey animal was as large as the diamondback could swallow, 2 weeks or more may pass before the snake needs to eat again, and during that interval the rattler will remain in a sedentary state unless disturbed.

Habitats of the eastern diamondback generally provide an access to water that isn't available to their desert-dwelling cousins, but either species can survive an entire year on an amount of water equivalent to its own body weight. More water is required during a snake's seasonal molt, when existing skin is shed in response to body growth, and new skin loses moisture through dessication as it toughens. As with the western diamondback, much of the water needed to survive can be absorbed from the bodies of ingested prey.

Mating Habits

Eastern diamondbacks of either gender reach sexual maturity at 3 years. Like most snakes, mating occurs in the spring soon after adults emerge from hibernation. Ritualized territorial fights aren't uncommon among male diamondbacks, but the combatants rarely bite one another. Instead, they engage in a wrestling match by entwining one another with their upper bodies in a contest of strength. When it becomes obvious that one of the snakes is the stronger, the weaker diamondback retreats and leaves the area.

The female diamondback is passive during courtship, remaining almost inactive while the male slithers in jerky movements on top of her body, flicking his tongue continuously. Copulation occurs when the male forces his tail beneath the female's tail and she accepts the advance by raising her tail to allow insertion of his forked hemipenis. Intercourse typically lasts for several hours, with numerous resting periods between.

Gestation is comparatively long, lasting an average of 167 days. Being an ovoviviparous species, diamondback young are hatched from eggs carried within the mother's womb. The 10 to 20 young break free of the thin membranes encasing them and are born in a process that may last up to 5 hours. Newborn snakes are born both fanged and venomous, and remain with the mother for no more than a day before striking out on their own. Mothers provide no parental care or protection.

Being born at the onset of autumn, the young snakes must immediately learn to hunt and find a suitable shelter—an existing rodent burrow or hollow—in which to spend the coming winter. Probably most will become prey to birds, lizards, toads, and other snakes. The young grow fast, achieving a growth of roughly 1 foot per year until reaching puberty, at which time they have little to fear from most predators.

Behavior

Like western diamondback rattlesnakes, eastern diamondbacks are quick to take a defensive posture when threatened, but often prefer to lie motionless in the hope that an enemy will pass them by without notice. Ironically, this passive reaction increases the danger they pose toward humans, who might inadvertantly walk closely enough to the hiding rattler to panic it into striking. As mentioned previously, a walking stick used to gently probe shadows where a snake might be hiding provides sufficient warning of a rattler's presence before trouble can occur.

Diamondback rattlesnakes are often touted as causing more fatalities than any venomous snake in North America, but the truth is that those casualties are infrequent enough to be nearly insignificant, and nearly all snakebites are caused by their victims. No snake considers humans as prey, and none is willing to risk certain death in conflict with an adversary who may be more than 20 times its own size. An old proverb states that the best way to avoid a coiled and buzzing rattlesnake is to take one step backward, which remains sound advice for anyone faced with any species of venomous snake.

The rattles that give diamondbacks and other rattlesnakes their names are actually the terminal scales of a snake's tail, left behind each time a growing snake sheds its skin. Rattles were once thought to be a means of communication between rattlesnakes, but we now know that snakes are deaf to sounds, able only to detect vibrations through the ground. Instead, it appears that rattles were evolved mainly as a means of avoiding being stepped on by larger animals.

Frequency at which the rattles are shaken indicate their owner's level of fear: a slow shaking like that of a maraca (a rattle used in music) is used to alert potentially dangerous animals to the snake's presence. Rattling increases in frequency as the snake's level of agitation increases, until the sound becomes a buzzing at about 50 cycles per second. This latter sound, which has been described as cicadalike, or like the sizzling of bacon, is always accompanied by a coiled body that presents an enemy with a smaller target, and a tongue that flicks rapidly to gather as much scent as possible from the surrounding air.

A successful predator in its own right, the eastern diamondback, like all snakes around the world, also serves as prey to a number of fellow carnivores. Hatchlings are eaten by toads, frogs, larger snakes, many species of birds, and even ants. Larger individuals up to 3 feet in length are preyed on by hawks, owls, and eagles, and at least some coyotes have a limited immunity to venom that permits them to consider rattlesnakes as food. Perhaps most dangerous to snakes of any species or size are pigs, both wild and domestic; swine are especially resistant to snake venoms, and any serpent unlucky enough to attract the attention of a pig is almost certain to be killed and eaten.

While neither eastern nor western diamondbacks inhabit regions that normally receive snow in winter, they tend to gather together in communal dens, called hibernacula, during the coldest months (January to March). Suitable hibernacula include small caves and rock cracks, hollow logs, and animal burrows. The snakes don't actually hibernate during this period, but gather together in a lethargic mass that uses little energy, but helps to keep all of its members warm enough to survive until warm weather returns in March or April.

Although demonized by Old World immigrants, the eastern diamondback and its rattlesnake cousins were revered by most tribes of American Indians. Rattles were used as religious and ceremonial icons, and some tribes practiced rituals in which a vision-seeker would antagonize rattlesnakes into biting him in the belief that illness induced by their venom would carry him to the spirit world. While few accidental snakebites prove to be fatal, allowing oneself to be bitten numerous times by several rattlesnakes was very dangerous, and some of those who traveled to the spirit world in this manner remained there.

While not subjected to the carnival-like "rattlesnake roundups" that have depleted western diamondbacks from much of their historical range, eastern diamondbacks also face danger at the hands of humans. Continuing destruction of their habitat from housing and other development is forcing the reptiles to occupy increasingly smaller areas, while widespread fear of this species evokes an unwarranted kill-on-sight response from people who find an eastern diamondback near their homes. Eastern diamondback populations also face danger from commercial snake hunters who gather them (under permit in Florida and North Carolina) for sale as pets.

TURTLES

All turtles and tortoises belong to the order Testudines, which includes all reptiles that have a hard, plated carapace over a bony shell on their backs, and a hard, plated underbelly, called a plastron.

Tortoises spend their lives on land, have vegetarian diets, and are equipped with flat feet that are better suited to walking and digging. Turtles spend most of their lives in or near water, have webbed feet adapted for swimming, and eat a more carnivorous diet.

Like all reptiles, turtles are considered to be cold-blooded animals, but at least one, the Blandings turtle *(Emydoidea blandingi)* has been observed swimming under the

This exceptionally old and large Blandings turtle is a good example of why every tracker needs a camera.

In lieu of a proper measuring scale, trackers can use items whose dimensions are known as expedient field references.

ice on frozen ponds. All turtles and tortoises are hatched from eggs that have been buried in soft soil, then abandoned, by their mothers.

Families that comprise the order of turtles include: family Carettochelyidae (pignose turtles), family Chelidae (Austro-American side-necked turtles), family Cheloniidae (sea turtles), family Chelydridae (snapping turtles), family Dermatemydidae (Mesoamerican river turtle), family Dermochelyidae (leatherback turtle), family Emydidae (pond turtles and box turtles), family Kinosternidae (mud turtles and musk turtles), family Pelomedusidae (Afro-American side-necked turtles), family Testudinidae (tortoises), and family Trionychidae (softshell turtles).

Turtles, like the painted turtle shown, are reptiles thave have evolved bony exoskeletons to protect them from predators.

Northern Snapping Turtle *(Chelydra serpentina)*

Second only to the painted turtle *(Chrysemys picta)* as the most widespread turtle in North America, the northern snapper is the dominant aquatic carnivore in most habitats where it lives. In size, this species is second only to the alligator snapping turtle *(Macroclemys temminckii)* of the southeastern United States.

Snapping turtles, and the northern snapper especially, also differ from most turtles and tortoises by having a carapace and plastron that are too small for the animal to retreat into completely. Whether a too-small shell is the cause or the result of this species' legendary ferocity when cornered on land is a matter of conjecture, but an adult northern snapper has little need to fear any animal except humans.

Geographic Range

C. serpentina's northern range extends from southern Alberta, Canada, eastward to Nova Scotia. To the south, the species' range covers all the United States from the Rocky Mountains eastward to the Atlantic coast, and along the Gulf of Mexico into central Texas.

Habitat

Because they spend most of their lives in water, northern snapping turtles require a body of freshwater in their

An adult snapping turtle in its defensive posture. Note algae growing on carapace.

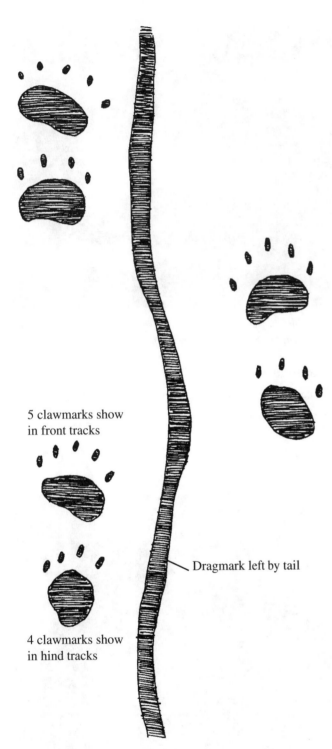

5 clawmarks show
in front tracks

Dragmark left by tail

4 clawmarks show
in hind tracks

Snapping turtle (Chelydra serpentina) *walking track pattern.*

habitats. The species is not found in saltwater, nor does it inhabit swift running streams or rivers. Most preferred are backwaters and beaver ponds, where muddy bottoms and an abundance of aquatic vegetation provide good places to hide, forage, and hibernate.

Physical Characteristics

Mass: Up to 70 pounds, but typically 35 to 40 pounds at maturity.

Body: Comparatively large head that cannot be withdrawn under the carapace, as with most turtles and tortoises. Carapace length up to 19 inches. Obviously powerful jaws and hooked beak. Long neck is normally kept retracted, the skin on its upper surface covered with bumpy projections (tubercules). Legs thickly built and powerful, covered with scaly skin and tubercules, and terminating in large, webbed feet. The plastron is small, covering only the vital organs in the belly, and leaving extremeties exposed.

Tail: Nearly as long as the carapace, thickly muscled, and covered along its top with saw-toothed keels, reminiscent of an alligator's tail.

Tracks: Five toes on forefeet, four toes on hind feet, each toe tipped with a thick, sharply pointed claw.

Tracks generally not perfect, but show scrapemarks where the foot slipped as the turtle's heavy body was pushed forward, usually with clawmarks evident. Tracks tend to print individually, without overlap, and in pairs, hind print behind front print. In soft mud or sand, the carapace drags intermittently, leaving a shallow trough. The tail also drags, leaving a serpentine channel between tracks. Straddle is variable, depending on the turtle's size, but always comparatively wide because of the snapper's plastron. Stride is also variable, depending on size, but equates to roughly one-half of the carapace length.

Scat: Misshapen and with a jagged, uneven surface. Color varies somewhat with diet, but is usually dark brown or black. Adult scats generally 1 to 1.5 inches long. Scats are usually deposited in water, but may be found along shorelines and on large, partially submerged logs where the turtle basked.

Coloration: The shell ranges in color from dark brown to tan and can even be black in some individuals. Snapping turtle necks, legs, and tails have a olive or yellowish color, with the head being a darker shade. The plastron is white or yellow.

Sign: In spring, usually May or June, look for narrow excavated holes, or large disturbances in sandy soil where egg-laying females buried a nest. Trails of flattened grasses near shorelines indicate a snapper's passing. Clouds of silt under streambanks tell of a snapping turtle burying itself in mud after being alerted to an observer's presence.

Vocalizations: Nearly always silent unless cornered on land. When threatened, the turtle may hiss and snap its jaws.

Lifespan: Unknown, but at least 40 years. Attempts to determine a snapping turtle's lifespan have been unsuccessful, and in some cases the turtles have outlived their owners.

Diet

Like all turtles (and unlike most tortoises) snapping turtles are omnivorous, and will eat nearly anything organic. Dietary components are dictated in large part by which foods are most available, but northern snappers eat large amounts of aquatic and shoreline vegetation, as well as carrion, and nearly any small animal that comes within reach of their powerful jaws. Being able to subsist on a broad variety of foods increases the snapping turtle's chances of survival under changing environmental conditions that might have detrimental effects on edible plants and animals.

Northern snapping turtles are surprisingly efficient hunters. A typical hunting technique is to lie in hiding while buried in silt at the bottom of a pond or quiet backwater, waiting for a prey animal to pass. Favored hunting spots include undercut banks and beneath sunken logs, because these places offer concealment for the turtle, and are also preferred hiding places for the small fish and crayfish that serve as its food. Although an air breather with lungs, snapping turtles, like frogs, can absorb much of the oxygen they require through their skins while submerged, although most will raise their snouts slightly above water to breathe air from time to time.

Unlike its larger cousin, the alligator snapping turtle, which lies in wait with mouth open wide and its pink, wormlike tongue waving as bait, the northern snapper

Its body submerged under a log, this large snapper breathes by raising its nostrils above water.

relies on motionless stealth and camouflage. When a fish swims within range, the snapper's powerful jaws shoot out, powered by its long extendable neck, and its beak snaps shut on the prey's body. Small prey is swallowed whole, but larger animals are gripped tightly by the jaws while strong, sharp-clawed forefeet shred its body into smaller pieces. This snapping behavior appears to be an ingrained instinct, because captive turtles raised from hatchlings also lunge with their jaws at even inanimate foods.

The size of a snapping turtle's prey changes as it grows; hatchlings subsist on insects, fish, and crustaceans, but large turtles have been witnessed snapping ducklings and goslings from the surface of shallow waters, along with snakes, frogs, and an occasional young muskrat.

Snapping turtles grow continuously throughout their lives, with some very old individuals achieving a carapace length of 2 feet or more. Their feeding habits are more voracious than most other reptile species, and snappers appear to be always hungry.

Mating Habits

Male northern snapping turtles reach sexual maturity at 5 years, but females generally don't reach breeding age until 7 years. Mating takes place in April or May among northern populations, but may occur as late as November among snappers living in the southernmost part of the species' range. Sexual maturity appears to be dictated more by size than by chronological age, and individuals that are malnourished may take longer to reach puberty, whereas those that are especially well-fed may breed earlier.

Likewise, mating season is initiated more by warming temperatures than by dates, and an unusually cold spring will delay procreational activities. Because snapping turtles, like all turtles, incubate their eggs in an underground nest, it's imperative that the earth be warmed enough to maintain a constant temperature between 60° and 70°F.

Just how male and female snapping turtles are attracted to one another is still under study, but pheromonal scents contained in urine probably play a large part in drawing the sexes together. Even so, females may not mate every year, but may carry live sperm from a previous mating within their reproductive organs for several years before laying eggs. This process of delayed implantation is seen in numerous other species, and is an adaptation that helps to insure that females are physically strong enough to withstand the demands of their part of the reproductive process without draining their own bodily reserves.

When snapper pairs do mate, copulation generally occurs at or near the water's edge. Mating is fairly conventional, with males mounting receptive females from behind. The female, if she accepts the male's advances, pushes her long tail to one side and allows him to climb atop her carapace, where he uses his strong, clawed forefeet to take a firm grasp on the edges of her shell. He then curls his own tail downward until their genitalia meet, and deposits his sperm within her body.

There is no lasting bond between snapping turtle mates, and as soon as a female is impregnated, she abandons the male. Precisely how long is required for an egg clutch to fully develop within the female's body is dictated by her own state of health, but 3 to 4 weeks is about average, and always coincides with warm weather.

When she's ready to lay her eggs, most often in late May or early June, a female leaves the water to find a suitable nesting place on dry ground, always well above the water table. Preferred nesting sites are in sandy soil along shorelines, but females have been observed laying eggs as far as a half-mile from open water, sometimes even crossing paved roads. Loose soil is an imperative, because nests are excavated by the turtle's strong hind feet to a depth of roughly 8 inches, but cinder-filled railroad grades that pass through wetlands appear to be among the most favored nesting places.

Nests begin as a broad, shallow hole wide enough to accommodate the female's rear, then abruptly taper to a narrow, downward-sloping tunnel about 2 inches in diameter. At the bottom of this remarkably consistent tunnel is an enlarged chamber that will contain the eggs. Elapsed time from start to completion may take 4 hours.

When her nest is ready, the female settles her rear over the hole and begins laying her clutch of round eggs, each about the size of a ping-pong ball. Clutch sizes depend on the size of the female, averaging about forty, but one clutch of more than one-hundred eggs was recorded from an exceptionally large turtle in Nebraska. Eggs are creamy white and covered with a flexible shell, again much like a ping-pong ball, but softer. Their flexible covering permits the eggs to roll down the tunnel-like nest opening and land atop one another without sustaining

Snapping turtle eggs.

damage, the way more brittle-shelled eggs would. After depositing her eggs in a process that may take several hours, the female refills the nest with loose soil and returns to the water. She may return to the same nesting site to lay eggs in subsequent years, but once deposited, each clutch is abandoned.

Although hundreds of eggs may be laid within a single square mile, few of them will hatch. With a taste and texture very much like a small chicken egg, snapping turtle eggs are a favorite food for every carnivore capable of reaching their incubation chamber. Strong diggers, like raccoons, skunks, badgers, and bears take a heavy toll by eating whole clutches, and I've personally been guilty of eating a dozen fried snapping turtle eggs for breakfast while backpacking. Despite heavy predation, snapping turtle populations remain healthy enough to indicate that a sufficient number survive.

Most snapping turtle eggs hatch after an incubation period of about 9 weeks, usually in late July or August, but abnormally cool weather has been known to delay hatching by as much as twice that, sometimes until September or October. The hatchlings, about 1 inch in diameter, tear free of their eggs using a typically reptilian "egg tooth" (also seen in snakes) that later falls off, and dig upward to the surface. For their first 2 weeks, the newborns carry a fat-rich yolk sac under their plastrons to give them a nutritional head-start as they learn to forage for plants and insects.

Like hatchlings of every turtle species, young snappers face a host of predators that range from muskrats and snakes to raccoons and most birds. Instinct compels the little turtles to immediately head for water, where they'll find sanctuary from most terrestrial predators. But even in the relative safety of a pond, hatchlings must hide from large fish, watersnakes, herons, otters, and larger turtles for their first 3 years of life. Presuming an abundant supply of food is available, a good rule of thumb for growth is about 1 inch of length per year for the first 5 years. At 5 years of age, and with a typical length of as many inches, few predators pose a danger to the snapper's powerful beak and strong armor.

Behavior

No turtle species is gregarious, but northern snapping turtles are perhaps the least social of any. With the exception of brief sexual encounters during the breeding season, neither juveniles nor adults of either sex are tolerant of one another. Obedient to the rule of nature that prohibits willingly killing one's own kind, territorial battles between snappers are seldom more than slightly injurious to either party. Lacerations from claws, and bites to the tail or hind legs of a retreating, vanquished adversary are common, but combatants are loath to use their powerful jaws as effectively as they might.

The same consideration does not apply to other turtle species. As some researchers have noted, large painted turtles especially are frequently found decapitated along shorelines during the spring mating season. These beheadings are the result of a decidedly lopsided territorial battle in which dominant painted turtles stand their ground against snapping turtles over a dispute of territorial or nesting rights. Because the painted turtle heads are never found with the body, and are apparently eaten by the snapping turtles who bite them off, some have suggested that this practice might stem from "inefficient feeding behavior." The fact that decapitated turtles are typically found with their meaty legs and tails intact indicates that this behavior is most likely territorial.

Researchers should note that snapping turtles on land can be very aggressive, and will bite hard given an opportunity. In the water, snapping turtles are almost docile, and swimmers need have no fear of them, but a snapper cornered on land will likely stand its ground, and may even attack. With a top running speed of about 1 mile per hour, there's little danger of being overtaken by a charging turtle, and most such attacks are simply attempts to escape, or to frighten an adversary into withdrawing.

Handling a snapping turtle is not recommended, largely because snapping turtles are a known vector for salmonella bacteria. If research demands handling a snapper, the safest method is to grasp it firmly at either side of the carapace, keeping hands, fore-arms, and any other parts of the body away from its sharp claws, and especially away from its long, extendable neck. Turtle hunters who take snappers as meat for the pot (turtle soup is a delicacy), or for sale to restaurants, recommend carrying the animal by its tail, but many researchers consider this method inhumane. However a turtle is handled, the handler should always wash his hands thoroughly afterward, and especially before eating.

PART THREE

COLLECTING FIELD DATA

CHAPTER 8

FINDING, RECORDING,
AND PRESERVING TRACKS,
SCATS, AND HAIR

CUTTING SIGN

Before a field researcher can collect data about an animal in the wild, he first has to find evidence of that animal's presence. This procedure, known generally as "cutting sign," is defined as looking for disturbances and other clues that all species leave behind as they go about their daily affairs. "Sign" is a collective term for tracks and trails, shed hair, scat deposits, scratchings, beds, or any other physical evidence of an animal's passing.

Begin by using Part Two of this book to determine whether an area offers suitable habitat for the animal you want to find. As mentioned in Chapter 1, a tracker can use the illustrations contained herein to identify prints and other sign when he finds them, but to actively seek out and follow any wild animal requires more detailed knowledge about the species' habits and lifestyles in different seasons. Grassy fields frequented by feeding deer during the summer months are poor places to cut deer sign when winter snows cover them and send the animals into secluded yards, where they subsist on tree browse until spring thaw. Likewise, May is usually a poor month for locating terrestrial toads and tree frogs in their normal wooded habitats, because they will have retired to local waterfronts to mate and lay eggs in the water.

Looking for sign in deep snow.

Hiking trails are good places to cut sign for most mammals, especially carnivorous species, which are almost universally territorial. Bears, bobcats, coyotes, and other species that hunt or fish for food regularly patrol and mark the boundaries of their territories with scats, especially where the boundary intersects another trail. A scat left on a hiking trail marks the place where a usually well-worn territorial trail crosses, and that territorial trail is a good place to find tracks, shed hair, and other sign.

Likewise, every animal must drink, so shorelines offer good prospects for cutting sign. Wet sand and mud are among the best tracking media, and they often yield foot impressions that are deep and detailed enough to make a plaster cast from. Because waterholes are visited daily by nearly all species in an area, their shorelines can provide a wealth of information about the number and variety of animals living there.

Seasonal foods also offer good potential for cutting sign. From late summer through autumn, wild blueberries are a favorite food of numerous species, from ravens and coyotes to raccoons and bears, as evidenced by scats that are almost incongruously purple in color. Spring spawning runs of trout and suckers attract bears and otters, while a good rain that brings earthworms to the surface precipitates increased activity from woodcocks and other birds that eat them.

So, too, do man-made food sources and habitats attract a variety of creatures. City dumps were once popular evening gathering spots for people who wanted to see bears foraging food scraps from human trash, and campground dumpsters are visited nightly by raccoons, opossums, and the occasional coyote or fox. Golf courses have become preferred nesting and molting places for geese, muskrats, and squirrels; they have learned to live in close proximity to people because those places are typically avoided by the carnivores who prey on them.

Cutting sign in the deep woods is a little more involved, but, again, well-worn trails are the most obvious evidence left by the animals that live there. The trick here is to "look wide," not allowing your eyes to focus on any one object, but viewing an area in its entirety. When you use this technique, your brain naturally selects features that are

Winter waterways are good places to find tracks and sign. Photo by Cheanne Chellis.

different from the surrounding terrain, and your eyes are drawn instinctively to faint trails and other sign that you might otherwise overlook.

How to "Walk Indian"

Trackers should also learn to "walk Indian." More than a few woodsmen have looked up from a trail of fresh hoof or paw prints to see their maker hightailing away from them—and even more never see the animal at all, because it heard them coming. Humans are inherently noisy when they walk. A human's body weight is supported by only two feet, so it's less well-distributed than with four-legged animals; and our long, plantigrade feet also compress more area underfoot. Both of these factors increase the probability that our steps will produce snapping, crunching, or grinding sounds as we walk.

"Walking Indian" is a learned gait that differs from the straight, forward, heel-to-toe walk most humans who walk over flat, level surfaces have become accustomed to using. To walk Indian, first raise your foot higher than normal when stepping forward; this will enable it to clear the many stumbling hazards encountered on natural, uneven terrain. Then bring your foot down on its outer heel, and roll it inward toward the big toe as you bring your rearward foot forward for the next step. This method helps to distribute your body weight more gently over a greater area, lessening the chances that a twig will snap or a stone will roll underfoot to reveal your presence.

Remote roadways are often traveled by wild animals for the sake of convenience. By looking closely, we can see that this one was used by both a gray wolf and a raccoon just hours before.

CASTING TRACKS

The best method of recording a track is to make a cast of it. This essentially means that the negative impression made in soil displaced by an animal's weight is filled with a material that flows into and molds itself to the print cavity, then hardens sufficiently to be removed from the impression and transported elsewhere for more detailed study. A well-made casting is an accurate three-dimensional representation of the object that made the print, whether that object is a wolf's paw, a hiking boot, or a radial tire.

Not all readable tracks are good enough to cast. Fresh prints left in the soft, wet soil of a riverbank or lakeshore or in new snow will frequently be deep and well-defined enough to provide a clean cast that accurately replicates the foot that made it. Sometimes, however, there will be discernible tracks in packed soil or snow that are plain enough to the eye, but not impressed heavily enough to clearly show many of the track's features in plaster. In such cases, you may need to follow an animal's trail until it crosses a place where footprints are deeper and better defined.

Making a Track Field

A "track field," also called a litmus field, is a simple and useful tool that works well when conditions make it difficult to get cast-quality tracks. The theory is to take a section of animal

Tracking is a puzzle: by assembling information about size, shape, and other factors, we know these tracks were made by a coyote weighing about 40 pounds. These clear tracks left in the slush around a beaver pond, then frozen hard, are very good for plaster casting.

Clearing a "litmus field" so that it will register the tracks of an animal walking over it. The headnet is to ward off black flies.

trail that's too hard or otherwise poorly suited to being impressed by footprints and turn it into a patch of earth that will show a clear track when walked over.

The process is simple: A small rake, a stick, or another scraping tool is used to rough up and loosen a section of trail to a depth of about 1 inch. Being fluffed-up, so to speak, the loosened area will compact under the weight of even small creatures walking over it, and it will yield clear track impressions that are ideally good enough to cast. You can use this technique with hard-frozen snow, debris-strewn humus, and hard-packed dirt. You can get dry sand to work by thoroughly wetting the cleared area with plain water, preferably water taken from a natural source nearby.

Note that foreign objects or smells left on or near the cleared area can negate the field's effectiveness by making animals go around instead of walking over it. Like ourselves, animals that use the same route every day are quick to notice even subtle changes, and especially anything that might indicate danger. Since it is composed of material that was already there, the track field almost never evokes a reaction, but something as small as a gum wrapper or the latent scent of deodorant soap is likely to cause animals to avoid it altogether.

The reverse is also true. A track field that has been judged safe to walk across by one animal will probably not arouse suspicion in those that arrive later, even different species. Soon, the disturbed area of trail will be considered to be just a normal feature, and it will be ignored entirely. This allows a researcher to use the same track field repeatedly by simply smoothing over previous tracks in preparation for the next passing animal.

Choosing Your Casting Material

Plaster-of-paris is the traditional casting material. It takes its name from the French city where it was first manufactured, and it has been the standard medium for casting tracks since the practice began. Best known as an artist's sculpting medium, this finely powdered form of calcine gypsum (calcium sulphate) is essentially a softer form of quick-drying cement that you can blend with water to achieve a desired viscosity, then form or mold to take on and hold a given shape.

An arguably superior alternative to plaster-of-paris is the "mud" that drywall hangers use to finish corners in a room, usually known by the brand name Durabond. Durabond hardens almost as quickly as plaster, it is a bit more water-resistant when it sets, and it's tougher and more flexible than plaster, so that casts poured with it are more tolerant of being handled in a classroom setting. The only real drawback is that drywall mud needs to be mixed especially well before pouring to help prevent the formation of voids, or unfilled air pockets, within the cast.

All-Weather Casting Techniques

In some instances, you can make a good track casting simply by pouring the casting medium into the impression. A track left in firm mud, in slushy snow that has since frozen hard, or in moist soil that has dried or frozen hard can be cast without preparation to the impression. But on some terrain, such as melting snow or very wet mud, a track's dimensions must be encased in a harder shell to keep distinguishing characteristics from being deformed when the plaster is added. Here are several methods for doing that.

Casting wax: Because casting media are semi-liquid when they're poured into the mold of a track, they can sometimes deform tracks made in snow by melting away the track's surfaces. To prevent erosion of what may be critical features in a print, surfaces of the depression are often coated with a spray wax prior to pouring in the plaster mix. (This spray wax, called casting wax, is sold at police supply stores.)

Ironically, casting wax works best in a warm, dry environment, where it usually isn't needed. In cold weather, it tends to congeal around the spray nozzle, spurting into the print in gobs instead of as a fine spray, and sometimes marring a track to the point where casting it would be useless. Carrying the spray can inside your jacket where it will be kept warm from body heat helps, but whenever possible it's best to avoid using casting wax at all.

Water spritz: In subfreezing weather, you can harden the surfaces of a track impression simply by spraying a fine mist of plain water over them. After a few minutes, depending on temperature, the water spritz will form an icy glaze over the print that leaves its details unmarred, and helps a cast to release more easily from its mold.

Spritzing a track only works when air temperatures are below the freezing mark, which means that trigger-type spray bottles are themselves in danger of freezing—especially around the nozzle. Carrying the bottle next to your body is sufficient to keep it unfrozen, but an air-activated handwarmer packet duct-taped to the outside of the bottle will keep it unfrozen when carried in a daypack.

Aerosol paints: Paint products packaged in aerosol spray cans offer probably the best method both for hardening a track prior to casting and for highlighting a print so that its contrasts are enhanced enough to photograph. Yellow or orange paint colors seem to work best for the latter, but almost any acrylic or enamel spray works to harden a track impression. Spray cans perform well in cold temperatures if kept relatively warm by body heat, but they should never be heated otherwise because their seams can split and leak paint onto other equipment.

A problem with using spray paint is that the ketones contained in it aren't at all environmentally friendly. For that reason, spray paints should be used only when needed, and any earth or snow onto which the spray falls should be removed and carried back to civilization for proper disposal.

Mixing and Pouring the Casting Medium

As with orienteering and first-aid, it's probably best to think of your casting tools as a kit. (See page 406 for a complete list of casting tools.) One of the most functional tools in your kit is a stoutly molded ½-quart plastic dish with resealable cover. When not in use, the dish contains plaster in a resealable plastic bag and stirring tools with which to blend it with water. The plastic dish itself serves as a mixing bowl, and afterward you can use it to safely contain the cast while it rides in your pack.

Mixing powder and water together isn't a complicated task, but neither should it be taken lightly. Too thick and your mix won't flow well into the nooks and crannies of the print. Too thin a mixture will cause the cast to take longer to set up, and when it does dry completely the cast will be overly brittle.

A proper casting mixture is roughly 50/50 by volume for plaster and water, but a simpler method is to blend the two ingredients until they have the consistency of cake batter. You can stir the mix with a plastic spoon, a wooden tongue depressor, or just a large twig from which all debris has been removed, but the end result should be

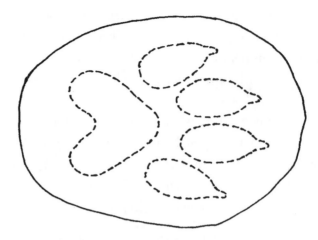

View from above

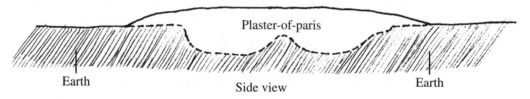

Earth

Plaster-of-paris

Side view

Earth

Making a plaster cast of a track.

a creamy blend with no lumps. In non-baking terms, the mixture should run smoothly from the stirrer when it's raised out of the bowl.

Ideally, you'd like to mix precisely the amount of plaster needed for the job at hand. In fact, you'll probably mix too much or too little the first few attempts. Either mistake is okay, because you can immediately mix and add more plaster, and excess can be packed out in a sealed plastic bag (plaster-of-paris does no harm to the environment).

When the plaster mix has been blended to the proper consistency, simply tip the bowl and pour it into the track impression. For best results, overfill the print slightly, allowing plaster to spill over the sides. Don't try to press the plaster down or work it into the corners, as this will almost certainly disfigure the track.

When the print has been filled with setting plaster, mark its location with a foot-long stick shoved several inches into the earth or snow. A 6-inch strip of orange or pink plastic surveyor's tape tied around the stick's top makes it visible from a distance, and helps to prevent accidentally stepping on the cast.

Removing and Transporting the Cast

After the cast has hardened, whether through drying or freezing, it must be removed so that it can be transported. This is always a delicate procedure, because any stress against the plaster can break, and possibly ruin completely, the still-fragile cast. Whenever possible, the safest method is to remove the entire track by taking the soil or snow into which it's pressed. This is most easily done by using a knife to make a continuous inward-angled cut all around the cast, then removing the entire cone-shaped divot. You can then gently break away excess earth or snow from the cast's edges; but if possible, it's best to take the track and cast together.

Plaster casts are fragile—in fact, they are softer than blackboard chalk. They are brittle, they tend to crumble with just a slight wetting, and their defining edges become rounded and worn with even gentle handling. Transporting casts seems like an even dicier proposition when you consider that the wildest animals are often found in remote, rugged terrain where a tracker must wade marshes, clamber over wind-felled trees, and remain constantly alert for tripping hazards.

Plastic food storage-type containers are possibly the best means of carrying plaster casts safely through rugged country. The containers themselves are tough, lightweight, and watertight with their lids snapped in place, and you can buy them in a variety of shapes and sizes to closely match the dimensions of the cast you are transporting. A variety of colors are available, too, so you can color-code the contents and identify them without opening the container. The container's rigid construction keeps the delicate plaster from being broken by other items in a day- or fanny-pack. Inside the container, you can surround the cast with plastic bubble-wrap, cotton batting, or even paper towels to help absorb the shock of travel.

ANALYZING CASTS: FINDING SPECIFIC ANOMALIES

Often, an individual animal can be identified by its track, or, more specifically, by physical anomalies that distinguish one animal's track from those of its brethren. Like people, wild animals collect an assortment of scars and disfigurements during their lives; and sometimes, injuries to the feet and legs show up as repeatable marks in their tracks. Most common is damage to the toes. In places where trapping is allowed, there may be individuals who are missing all or parts of toes. Missing claws are not uncommon, and sometimes there are scars in toe and heel pads that reveal themselves as smooth or raised areas in the normally rough surface of the pads.

PRESERVING CASTS

After you've made a cast and transported it intact to a place where it can be properly studied, it will as a matter of course be handled, perhaps by several people. Being made from a soft and brittle material, track casts wear quickly when handled with even the utmost care. Their edges get rounded from abrasion until details like claws and scars are marred beyond recognition or erased entirely. Even worse are casts that have absorbed moisture from exposure to rain or humidity, because these are likely to crumble into a handful of small pieces.

Probably the simplest method of preserving and protecting a plaster cast from damage and wear is to coat its fragile outside with a more durable coating that seals it against abrasion and moisture, but isn't so thick as to obscure the original details of the cast. An aerosol preservative is ideal here.

Least complicated of these coatings is spray enamel applied in two or three light coats, allowing each coat to dry thoroughly before adding the next. Once dry and hardened, the paint protects the cast's integrity so that it can be handled without degradation—important in a classroom setting where a cast may pass through many hands during its examination. Spray paint also makes it easy to color code plaster casts into whatever categories are needed, and to help prevent confusion between similar casts.

To maximize a cast's resistance to abrasion, add two or three light coats of clear acrylic spray to encase it in a plastic shell that stands up well to handling, makes the plaster impervious to moisture, and adds a little strength. An acrylic finish can be sprayed on over enamel, but take care not to use lacquer or any spray coating suspended in "hot" solvents, as these will react with enamel and cause it to wrinkle, possibly obscuring the cast's finer details.

MAKING A TRACK FROM A CAST

In some instances it may be desirable to reproduce a track from the cast—sometimes called "tracking a cast." A cast can show the details of an animal's foot in positive relief, but imagination is needed to mentally reverse its dimensions and picture it as a track once again.

In principle, turning a plaster cast into a hoof or paw print is as simple as pressing the cast, which represents the animal's foot, into wet plaster. In practice, however, there are a few methods for making that process easier.

First, the cast being used to make a track impression must be coated with a "mold release," which is nothing more complex than a slippery coating between the cast and the wet plaster that will keep the two from adhering to one another. Presuming that the cast has already been painted, the mold release can be as simple as a light coat of vegetable oil wiped onto its outer surfaces.

The wet plaster in which the track is to be reproduced should likewise be contained in a vessel that will permit it to be removed easily after it hardens, with as little stress to the delicate material as possible. A bowl filled with damp sand into which a track-size depression has been excavated is nearly ideal. Locate the depression at the center of the bowl, pour in the plaster mix, and gently seat the cast into the center of the plaster with an easy downward pressure until the track features are impressed into the medium.

When the plaster has set, gently pry the cast loose from the track with a knife tip or small screwdriver, leaving the reproduced track in the bowl surrounded by sand. Gently loosen the track from the sand in the same way and remove it from the bowl. After drying completely, the track can be coated with spray paint and used to show what a track should look like.

Note that some exaggeration will occur in the reproduced track. Typically, the copy will be slightly larger than the track cast, so the reproduction should not be used for taking precise measurements, as it won't exactly duplicate the original track. It will, however, adequately represent the configuration of a track from the species that was cast, and in that sense a replicated track impression is a valuable training tool.

PHOTOGRAPHING TRACKS

Light and contrast can pose special difficulties when photographing tracks. Even the highest-quality photo taken under the best conditions using the finest camera produces only a two-dimensional picture, without depth or thickness. Tracks that appear clearly to our eyes, with their binocular vision and good depth perception, often become featureless and unrecognizable in a photograph.

You can enhance animal prints for the camera by highlighting their contrasting features so that shadows increase the appearance of depth sufficiently to show up on film. The photo will still be two-dimensional, but by making the difference between light and shadow more pronounced, a track that might otherwise be indistinguishable from its background can be made distinct enough to take precise measurements from it.

Lighting can often make the contrasting features of a track more visible to a camera. A powerful wide-beam flashlight or a mantle-type gas lantern will often be enough. Conversely, shading a print from direct sunlight can also enhance its contrast, and frequently, a combination of shading and artificial light can be used at the same time to accent track features that would be difficult to see in natural light alone.

Track features can also be accented with color. Perhaps most effective is chalk dust, like that used by carpenters in chalk-line tools. Chalk dust is available in several colors (most commonly blue and red) from builders' supply and home improvement stores, and it's packaged in squeeze bottles that lend themselves well to lightly dusting tracks with color. The cost is low, the dust does no harm to the environment, and a single bottle will dust dozens of tracks.

SCAT AND ITS SIGNIFICANCE

Repulsive as it might seem, the study of scat, or droppings, left by an animal can be crucial to determining its seasonal diets, its habits, and even its range. By knowing the characteristics of scat, you can very often identify the species that left it, and even the relative size of an individual animal. By identifying the contents of its scat you can see what it ate, then extrapolate from known facts to predict when and where that animal might be found as it travels to or from a preferred feeding area.

Scat (and urine) also plays an important role in the social lives of most animals. Most predators use their own scat as a boundary marker, leaving deposits that are regularly refreshed along well-used trails, and especially at intersections, to warn off others who might compete with them for food.

Animals that have adapted to the role of prey, like whitetail deer, rabbits, and squirrels, use their scats to confuse the sharp olfactory senses of predators. A deer that can get a 100-yard head-start from a pack of hunting wolves will instinctively head for the thick forest and swamp where it makes its bed. As the deer penetrates further into the sanctuary of its bedding ground, the trails used by it and other deer become more numerous, all of them spotted with randomly sited scat deposits of all ages. In the thick cover of a whitetail yard it's easy for a predator to lose sight of running prey, while even the most discriminating sense of smell is likely to be entirely befuddled by the scent of so many animals.

Scat even has a purpose in the breeding rituals of most animals. Like urine, scat carries with it a number of hormonal odors that not only identify its maker like an olfactory fingerprint but also help to broadcast its sexual disposition, its age, and even its size during the mating season. Beavers and muskrats use scat to help make the mound-like mud scentposts they build along the shorelines of ponds and streams more noticeable; bull elk roll their bodies in bathtub-size mud wallows that have been scented with their own scat and urine to make them easier to detect by both receptive cows and contentious bulls; and breeding whitetail does dribble a trail of urine-borne pheromones down their hindquarters as they walk.

Aging Scat

Knowing how old a scat is can be critical to determining the whereabouts of an animal. The fresher the specimen, the better the chances that the animal you're seeking is nearby.

A fairly universal characteristic of scat is that it lightens in color and weight with age and decomposition. Fresh scat is composed of undigestible organic material with high moisture content, almost as if it were designed by nature to decay rapidly and return to the environment in as little time as possible. As exposure to bacteria, insects, and the elements turns the scat from organic materials into what is essentially dirt, its moisture content decreases through evaporation, and it begins to lighten in color. Hair,

An important element in determining when a scat was deposited is knowing that all scats become drier and lighter in color as they age, regardless of species. Rate of decomposition varies with content and environmental conditions, but scats of various carnivores contain flesh that breaks down quickly, while cellulose contained in herbivore scats remains intact for a longer period.

bone, and plant fibers that decay more slowly become more apparent, and the scat decreases to some extent in both diameter and mass.

Temperature and humidity can have a significant effect on how quickly a scat exhibits the signs of decomposition that help to determine its age. In hot, arid places, a coyote scat can become dry and grayed within a day, while that same scat in a deep forest might take several days to reach the same stage of decomposition. Throw in snow and subfreezing temperatures, and a scat may remain almost unchanged until spring thaw.

All of these variables must be considered when attempting to determine the age of a scat, which means that most estimates are going to be ballpark guesses. Presuming an average 70°F day without rain, a scat that appears wet and feels warm to the touch through disposable latex or nitrile gloves has been there for less than 2 hours. At about 4 hours the scat will have dried on the outside and will have cooled to air temperature, but will still be soft and wet inside. Barring rainfall, the scat will continue to dry from the outside in for about the next 5 days, becoming harder on the outside as it loses mass and shrinks roughly 10% through evaporation. By the time a week has passed, the organic materials within the scat will have begun to turn gray and powderlike. At 2 weeks, the entire scat will be gray and will crumble to the touch, but tufts of fur, coarser hair, and bones will still be in evidence. At 3 weeks, the deposit will have been reduced to a small pile of coarse gray dust, although bones and especially fur may remain for several months—usually until they're kicked or blown away.

Too, bear in mind that snowy terrain can make it impossible to determine the age of a scat beyond a few hours. As it does with food, freezing halts the decomposition of organic material, so a scat left at the beginning of winter can remain fresh until spring. Latent body heat will cause the scat to melt down into the snow until it reaches ambient temperature, which may take only a few minutes in subzero temperatures.

Seasonal Differences

While the contents of a scat sample can reveal much about an animal's diet, it's also true that the diet of nearly all animals will vary with the seasons. One remarkable example of those changes comes with the ripening of blueberries from late July through October, when scats from many carnivores literally turn purple. Blueberries are one of nature's richest and most nutritionally complete fruits, and bears, coyotes, raccoons, and other carnivores eat large quantities of them in season to put on body fat against the coming winter. The same phenomenon can be seen in the scats of birds and herbivores that rely on blueberries as part of their pre-winter diets.

Other seasonal dietary changes are less spectacular. In winter, deer scats are typically dry pellets that contain coarse plant fibers, the result of a rough diet of buds, bark, and dead grasses. In summer, the scats are also pellet-shaped but more moist because the animals are feeding on succulent green plants that aren't available during the winter months. The spring transition between those two types of browse is marked by scats that are watery and diarrhealike, much like miniature cowpies, as the deers' digestive systems adapt to richer, more easily assimilated foods.

COLLECTING SCAT SAMPLES

Although much can be learned from a scat in the field, it's sometimes necessary to transport a sample back to civilization where it can be examined using more sophisticated equipment.

Most important is to avoid contracting an illness from any parasites or germs that might be contained in a scat. Always handle scats while wearing disposable gloves, and exercise caution to avoid contaminating clothing or equipment. Whenever possible, wash your hands thoroughly after handling scat, and never eat anything until you've washed.

Some biologists prefer to wear a paper surgical-type mask to guard against airborne pathogens while handling scat. Added protection is never a bad idea, but in reality the incidence of sickness caused by airborne germs has so far been virtually nil. If you'll be handling scat in an enclosed room, though, wearing a surgical mask is prudent, especially if the animal under study is suspected of having a disease.

Carrying a scat sample from the wild demands a container that will seal it away from other equipment, both for reasons of hygiene and to keep the scat from picking up contamination that might ruin it for study. In cases where maintaining a sample's shape isn't a concern—solidly frozen scats or deer pellets, for example—a resealable plastic bag suffices nicely.

If you want to preserve a scat's physical integrity and shape during transport, you'll need a stronger container with stiff walls that will protect the sample from being deformed. Here again, a plastic dish with resealable airtight cover is perhaps the best choice.

PRESERVING SCAT FOR STUDY

Freezing is the most effective means of preserving organic material. A frozen scat maintains its shape, dimensions, and nearly all of its original mass for years, and you can thaw it any time for study with no loss of scientific integrity.

Many biologists have found it necessary at one time or another to store animal scat in their kitchen freezers. The practice, though repulsive, is safe so long as samples are kept solidly frozen in airtight containers. If possible, a freezer dedicated solely to scat storage is best.

COLLECTING HAIR SAMPLES

An animal's shed fur can tell a lot about its owner. The fine insulating winter underfur that keeps most species warm during winter months in snow country is shed every spring, usually from April through June, and within its fibers are many clues about the state of an individual's health. Mange mites, fleas, and other dermal parasites are evident from hair samples, although—as in the case of mites—you might need to view them under an ultraviolet light or microscope. These can provide important clues about the state of health for an entire population.

Hair samples are often overlooked by people who aren't looking for them. During the spring shed there may be tufts of underfur caught in foliage near where an animal passed, but other times hair might not be so obvious.

Rough-barked trees like maple, oak, and red pine growing at the sides of a well-used trail are among the most productive places to find discarded fur from spring through late summer. Mammals with thick coats, like wolves, raccoons, and especially bears, use the coarse trunks as scratching posts to dislodge shed hair. They rub their backs and sides against the bark to alleviate itching and leave some of their fur caught in the rough surfaces, or glued to sticky pitch exuded from the trunks.

IDENTIFICATION FROM HAIR AND FUR

Identifying fur taken from tree bark by its appearance alone can be difficult in the field, even with a microscope, but reading other sign left by the animal can help to determine its species. Tracks are the most obvious clue, because a scratching animal must stand heavily on at least two of its paws or hooves to lean its weight against an itching post. A 4-inch canid track next to a tree that has grayish tufts caught in its bark identifies the creature as a gray wolf, even if the details of the track aren't clear.

Scratching posts can also provide information about an animal's size. Black hairs caught in bark to a height of 6 feet reveal that a mature black bear used that tree to scratch between its shoulders while it stood upright on hind feet and rubbed against the trunk. The same hairs trapped at a height of 4 feet indicate that the bear was smaller, probably a 2-year-old recently ejected by its mother.

Animals sometimes lay claim to favorite scratching trees by leaving scat near them, thus providing another means of identifying their species and size. If we find a small, cylindrical scat with flat, untapered ends next to a tree that has gray and black fur in its bark, and with humanlike tracks too small to have come from a bear, we can tell that a territorial adult raccoon has claimed that particular tree as its own.

Sticky Traps

Taking a lesson from nature, field biologists attach small patches of fabric with very sticky outer surfaces to trees and shrubs at the sides of a trail, where they pull loose hairs from the coat of any mammal that rubs against them while walking past. These "sticky traps" are effective at all times of year because they don't rely on the animal to scratch itself, and they collect hairs from all types of animals at any point along a trail, not just at tree trunks.

Sticky traps need not be expensive or complex to be effective. You can fold a 6-inch strip of duct tape or plastic boxing tape onto itself to form a loop, and tack it adhesive-side out to a tree using a roofing nail. Alternately, you can fasten a foot-long strip to an overhanging branch, where it will be brushed against by passing animals. This hanging method also allows you to adjust the height of your sticky trap to more closely match the height of the animal under study, excluding species that are short enough to walk under the hanging tape without touching it.

As with any type of passive data collection device, the sticky trap's effectiveness relies heavily on its unobtrusiveness. An animal alarmed by the trap's presence is going to avoid it, and that of course means the trap will collect no hair. Yet, at the same time, the trap must be someplace where an animal will brush against it, and it must be secure enough that it won't come loose when that happens.

PASSAGE INDICATORS

Collecting data from an animal's trail depends on knowing whether or not that trail is being used regularly. A trail, by definition, is a ribbon of terrain on which normal plant life has been prevented from growing by the pressure from many feet. But sometimes it's tough to know what kind of animal made that trail, or how often it's used. A well-sited and concealed sticky trap placed on a trail that has been abandoned because of human presence, or because something on it has changed enough to create caution in species that used it, is a waste of time. And of course, abandoned trails are also bereft of fresh tracks, scats, and other sign.

There are a number of electronic devices that can be fastened alongside animal trails to tell us that an animal passed by, some with clocks that record the time of passage, and some with cameras that will snap an animal's photo as it walks past. All of these have their place in a field researcher's arsenal, but they can be prohibitively expensive and bulky when circumstances demand that several trails be monitored at the same time.

One simple and inexpensive method of monitoring a trail for animal activity uses nothing more complicated than a spool of sewing thread. By tying off one end securely to a sapling or branch at trailside, then stretching a length of thread across the trail and wedging it lightly into the crack of a split twig, the rough bark of a tree, or just weighting it with a small stone, you have a tripline that will easily be pulled free when pressed against. And unlike the simpler electronic monitors, the thread will even tell you in which direction the animal was traveling, because the loose end will be pulled in that direction as it crosses the animal's body.

Although not as precise as an electronic device that records the time of day that it was tripped, thread monitors can also be used to determine an animal's timetable, depending on how often they're checked, because, like ourselves, most animals fall into daily routines. By reattaching the loose end of a thread that has been pulled free, and then checking it frequently, resetting it each time it's tripped, you can progressively narrow the interim until you know within an hour or two when the animal will pass through.

Thread monitors can even help to determine the size of a passing animal. Larger species will pull the thread free at all levels, but by placing the thread higher you can rule out smaller animals, thereby narrowing down the choices about which species uses that trail to at least the taller ones.

CHAPTER 9

THE TRACKER'S FIELD KIT

A biologist-tracker gathering data in the field needs a specialized set of tools to efficiently perform a wide variety of tasks. Collecting scat samples, casting tracks, taking photos, making and documenting measurements—doing all these jobs properly demands the equipment of a woodsman and the precision instruments of a scientist. Good books that cover putting together a wilderness kit include The Outdoors Almanac (Len McDougall, Burford Books, 1999), but our focus here will be on the essential tools that every field researcher needs to conduct business in a sometimes unfriendly environment. The first section below, "Tools of the Trade," gives an in-depth look at a few of the most important items in the tracker's field kit. The second section, "Tracking Kit Equipment List," begins on page 406. It's a quick but comprehensive checklist that you can take shopping if necessary.

TOOLS OF THE TRADE

This list is generic—a roster of items that experience has shown are most useful in a variety of environments—but it shouldn't be followed blindly. A tracker in arid desert where animal tracks are formless depressions in dusty sand will have little need for a plaster-casting outfit, just as a dayhiker on established trails would probably not need a water filter. Determine what the objectives of your outing are, then use the summaries and checklists here to select the tools you'll most likely need, subtracting from or adding to them as a situation demands.

Equipment Bags

Despite the seemingly long list of equipment given here, all of it will fit into a large daypack with room to spare for bedroll, bivy shelter, and other tools that make working in a wilderness as comfortable as it can be. Called a "day-and-a-half pack" by some, suitable daypacks in this category have more than 2,000 cubic inches of storage, an internal frame, padded shoulder straps, a waist belt, and a sternum strap, and are comfortable enough to carry all day.

I especially prefer models with lots of pockets because they help with organizing loose gear into dedicated kits. If you need more pockets, you can add them by clipping GI-style compass and ammunition pouches to the waist belt or other straps. A few manufacturers make add-on accessory pouches that fit not only their own but also other brands of backpacks.

Resealable plastic food bags: These are a great way to protect even ungainly items such as cameras and radios from the environment. They are fairly durable, inexpensive, and lightweight. Sandwich-size bags help to keep smaller items, such as bone samples or rabbit droppings, in a convenient package. You can label the bags with permanent marker, leave them in the rain, or freeze them without fear of cross-contamination.

Water Bottles

Mixing plaster to cast a track requires water—and so do trackers. This makes a tightly sealed container of water necessary to any backcountry outfit. If a stream, pond, or even a relatively clear mud puddle is available, its water can be used to mix plaster, but people prefer water they know doesn't contain infectious organisms. In either instance, a container holding at least a quart of water should be considered required equipment for even short outings.

There are a number of good water bottles on the market, most made from rugged polyethylene or the less odor-absorbent Nalgene, some with poppet-tops, some with screw-tops, and most priced low enough to afford more than one.

My own most-necessary water bottle is the old-fashioned GI canteen outfit, with thick plastic 1-quart water bottle, a folding-handle metal cup that can be used on an open fire or stove for sterilizing, drying, or cooking, and an insulated case that can be carried on a belt or backpack strap. In hot weather, the case can be saturated to keep water in the canteen roughly 15°F cooler than the air.

If a secondary water bottle is needed, collapsible plastic water bladders are a handy choice. The bladder is essentially a rugged plastic bag with a molded-in screw-cap top. It can be rolled up when empty to conserve space, and a variety of capacities are available that can hold 2 liters or more.

For more specific information on water for casting and drinking, see "Casting Kit" on page 400 and "Clothing and Other Necessaries" on page 402.

Observation and Measurement Tools

Binoculars: Binos have real importance to even casual visitors to the wild because they allow us to see as well as or better than the sharpest-eyed bird of prey. Your chances of viewing animals casually going about their normal affairs are very much enhanced if you can see them first from a distance beyond their usually nearsighted visual range.

Good to very good binoculars are common today, but there are a few features that every fieldworthy model should have: waterproof, argon gas-filled construction that keeps lenses from fogging inside; at least 8x magnification; good optical clarity; light weight; and quality high enough to make it a rugged and reliable piece of equipment. I prefer roof-prism binoculars for their flat design that makes them carry almost unnoticed and always handy tucked inside a shirt or breast pocket.

Field microscope: Very close inspection of hairs, scat contents, vermin, and other sign may yield valuable information that's not apparent using the naked eye. A magnifying glass is good for many close-up observations, but there are times when more extreme optical power is needed—for instance, to see parasite ova or to identify insect parts in a scat sample, or to closely inspect tufts of shed fur.

There are numerous good microscopes but not many that are suited to field work. Prerequisites include pocket size, lightweight, good optical clarity with enough magnification (25x or more) to be useful, rugged construction, simple design, and—as important as any of these—a cost low enough to prevent heartbreak should the instrument be lost or broken. (See the Tracking Kit Equipment List on page 406 for specific recommendations.)

Ruler: A scale is one of the most basic tools for any wildlife researcher. Most fundamental is a 6-inch ruler that can be laid on the ground to measure tracks, scats, bone fragments, and other objects that cannot or should not be disturbed. The ruler needn't be complicated or expensive, but it should be marked with large numbers that contrast well with its color and can be seen clearly in a photo, and it should be scaled in both inches and centimeters. Crime scene rulers available from police supply catalogs are made for this type of use, but good candidates can also be found in most office supply stores.

Tape measure: For longer measurements, like the leaping distance of a deer, you will need a steel tape measure with a retractable blade. Again, the tape should be clearly marked with large numbers and graduations that show clearly in a photograph, and it should be scaled in both inches and centimeters. The blade should have a length of at least 25 feet to permit recording jumping lengths in a single measurement, and it should have a locking mechanism that allows the tape to be left extended for photographing. Many of the wide-blade carpenters' tape measures sold in hardware stores are well-suited to this purpose.

Casting Kit

Plaster-of-paris can be found priced inexpensively in most hobby or arts-and-crafts stores, while the slightly coarser patching plaster (or Durabond) used by drywallers is available almost anywhere home improvement supplies are found. Depending on the size and depth of a print, 1 pound of plaster carried in a resealable bag inside a snap-top plastic container will suffice to cast about five large tracks. The plastic bag helps to keep the plaster powder dry, while the plastic dish serves as a mixing bowl.

One problem encountered while casting tracks in snow is that the water needed to mix the plaster can freeze. A workable solution is to carry a water bottle zipped inside your jacket where the garment's waist cinch or the waist belt of a daypack keeps it from falling out, while your own body heat keeps its contents from turning to ice. Drawbacks are that this carry method isn't very convenient or comfortable, especially when the trail dictates travel through rugged country.

A better solution that Odawa tribal biologists and I stumbled onto while tracking gray wolves in subzero conditions is to duct-tape a palm-size or larger air-activated chemical handwarmer packet to the outside of water bottles. This method offers the convenience of being able to carry bottles inside your daypack, where there's enough air to keep the packet activated, and enough warmth generated by it to keep water well above the freezing mark for twelve hours or more.

Some track-casters carry plastic stir sticks for mixing plaster, but most environments will provide a convenient stick.

Plastic food storage containers: Plastic snap-top dishes of the type used for food storage come in handy for transporting both fragile items such as track casts and organic specimens that you wouldn't want to touch. Look for containers that have rugged construction and a leakproof, airtight seal between lid and dish. You can often find inexpensive dishes that meet these criteria in the housewares aisles of hardware, grocery, and department stores. Some containers even have multicolored lids so you can color-code their uses. This way, the contents can be identified without unsealing the cover.

Paper towels: Field biologists and trackers routinely need to wipe away mud, water, plaster, or worse from their hands, clothing, and equipment. A roll of household paper towels, carried inside a plastic bread bag to keep it dry, can be very handy for those situations. Flattening the roll's cardboard core makes it take up less space, while those taken from the kitchen towel holder when a roll is half-used are even more compact.

Orienteering Devices

The popularity of satellite-linked Global Positioning System (GPS) devices has prompted a waning interest in the old-fashioned compass, but the truth is that a field researcher needs both instruments, particularly if his route leads well off the beaten path. Both compass and GPS provide valuable navigational information, but each does that in a very different way.

A **compass** is essentially a magnetic indicator that is drawn toward Earth's magnetic north pole through electromotive induction—basically, it just points north, and all other orienteering techniques evolve from that single function. By knowing where north lies, an outdoorsman facing that direction knows east is right, west is left, and south is to the rear. A tracker entering even the most un-tracked wilderness in a westerly direction always knows that the way back lies east, and if the point of entry was from a road, riverbank, or some other large hard-to-miss landmark, it becomes pretty difficult to get lost.

A quality compass is an integral part of every tracker's field kit. This is the Brunton 8099 Elite. Photo courtesy Brunton USA.

Unlike a GPS, a compass works very well with any map. Orienting both map and compass to north provides a pictorial layout of the terrain around you, providing a pre-view of the type of country you'll encounter before you reach it. Being armed with this information makes it easier to avoid canyons, swamps, swollen river rapids, and other natural obstacles before they force you to backtrack and find a way around them.

Because a compass has so much value, particularly in terrain or weather where obvious navigational landmarks like the sun or moon are obscured, most savvy back-country veterans carry two: a simple pocket compass that's worn around the neck and never removed, and a more sophisticated map compass with prismatic or lensatic sights, map scales, and a clear base that permits features to be read with the compass sitting on top of a map. Both should be liquid-filled, with strongly magnetized indicators that move easily with no sign of being sticky; and neither should have a bubble inside the indicator capsule, as this is a sign that the capsule has a leak.

GPS: Just as a compass uses the magnetic north pole to give orienteers a single fixed point from which to reference location in terms of latitude and longitude, a GPS receiver uses microwave signals from satellites in stationary orbit above earth to triangulate its user's position on the planet surface.

Advantages offered by the GPS include an ability to precisely fix, or "waypoint," the precise math coordinates of some point of interest—a bear den, for instance—within a perimeter of 50 yards. The coordinates can then be transferred to a map to provide a visual representation of data that may in time reveal behavioral patterns.

GPS units also feature a "trek" mode that records a hiker's location every 5 minutes or so, then remembers those waypoint locations to lead him back out, then in again if he desires, on a kind of connect-the-dots course that leads from one recorded coordinate to the next.

Drawbacks of the GPS include the lack of reliability inherent to most battery-operated digital circuits when they're exposed to the environment. Battery life can be greatly diminished by cold; frost can form on contacts and prevent buttons from working properly; and getting the unit wet inside is virtually guaranteed to take it out of action until its circuit boards have dried completely.

And because GPS coordinates are taken from artificial satellites, not the magnetic north pole, the way they translate to a map is different than it is when using a compass. For example, GPS coordinates cannot be applied directly to a conventional latitude-longitude map because those maps aren't sectioned and scaled using the relatively new Universal Transverse Mercator grid system. And without that, an orienteer has no point of reference from which to calculate everything else.

Maps: Fortunately, there are good maps available that are marked for use with both compass and GPS. The U.S. Geographical Survey offers detailed topographical maps that may be used with both navigational systems, and even snowmobile maps from local chambers of commerce are being printed to work with either unit. Maps may be ordered online at www.usgs.gov for $5 each, plus $4 shipping and handling per order (so it pays to order several at once).

Clothing and Other Necessaries

Handwear: Gloves are important to field work in every season. In warm weather, a pair of sturdy work gloves can protect hands from cuts, abrasions, and other injuries. In cold weather, a rugged, insulated shell with synthetic fleece or knit wool liner can provide all the warmth needed to endure subzero cold.

Plastic gloves: Dirty hands are to be expected when working in the great out-of-doors, but for some things, a pair of inexpensive disposable gloves are a very good idea.

Handling scat and collecting bone, carcasses, and hair is much safer and more hygenic if you have a layer of rubber or plastic protecting your skin.

Thin latex (or non-allergenic nitrile) gloves like the kind worn by paramedics are an ideal choice, because they block direct contact with all infectious organisms or toxins while allowing the wearer to retain good dexterity and tactile senses. A less expensive but more slippery and slightly less tactile alternative is the clear plastic glove worn by food-service workers. In either case, soiled gloves should be stripped off after use by pulling them from the wrist toward the fingers, turning the glove inside out as it's removed from your hand. Used gloves can be stored in a resealable plastic bag. This way, they won't contaminate other items in your pack before you can dispose of them properly.

Water filters: Having clean, potable-quality water on hand is important not only for drinking but also for washing hands, cleansing wounds, and cleaning tools. Pump-type water filters designed for hikers have become a fundamental part of the basic backpacking outfit. Most filters are capable of producing a liter of clean water with about a minute of easy pumping, and all must pass EPA-mandated standards for removing parasites, cysts, and bacteria.

A new, state-of-the-art water purifier, like the MiOx from Cascade Designs, provides a smaller alternative to the pump-type filter. About the size of a small flashlight, these useful gadgets use ordinary salt and watch batteries to super-oxygenate a small amount of water, which is then added to a larger volume of untreated water to kill every living organism within. Also subject to EPA standards, these purifiers retail for about the same as a good filter (roughly $80).

Warm-weather boots: A tracker is by definition on his feet most of the time, and a comfortable, properly fitted pair of boots built with backwoods-use in mind can have a significant effect on how you feel at the end of the day. They should have shin-high uppers to guard and support the ankles, cushioned insoles with firm arch support, flexible but aggressive lug soles, and waterproof construction.

Many makes and models can meet those criteria for under $100, especially if you shop around for discontinued models. Always try on a pair of boots before buying them, and always try them on while wearing hiking socks, because they're thicker than other socks. And never take to the woods with a new pair of boots until

Proper footwear is essential for researchers who spend long periods of time in the wild.

you've walked at least 10 miles in them to crease the lowers, making the boot "break" where your joints flex and eliminating most pinch or rub points.

Cold-weather boots: Field researchers spend a lot of time outdoors, and since snow country offers the best possibilities for finding cast-quality tracks, they can expect to spend whole days or longer walking and working atop frozen hardpack. Cold toes are a common complaint when there's nothing but snow underfoot, and cold feet means loss of heat that can lead to frostbite, which kills tissue and can eventually lead to gangrene. The journey through each of these stages is extremely painful.

Cold feet are an unpleasantness that no winter outdoorsman need tolerate. Modern pac-boots carry comfort ratings down to –150°F, making them equal to any

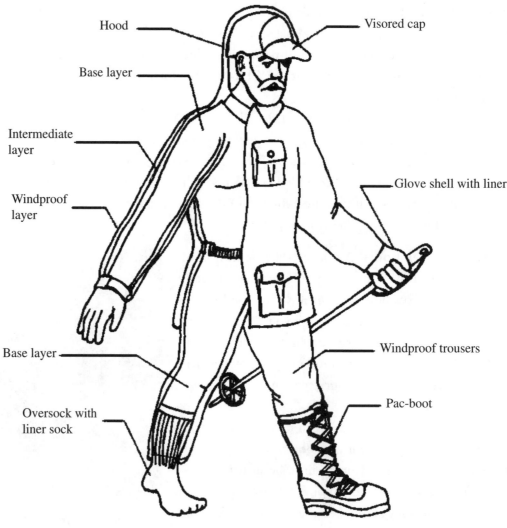

Layered cold weather outfit.

cold on Earth. Features to look for include removable liners and footbed that can be replaced in the field, waterproof construction, lace-to-toe design for a custom fit between foot and boot, and an aggressive lug sole for traction. Ideally, the boot should provide the walking comfort of a hiking boot, yet retain sufficient body heat to keep your toes warm during long spells of inactivity on snow—such as observing a carcass or photographing otters on a frozen lake. A number of name-brand boots can deliver those features for under $200.

Socks: Proper socks complement a good boot, and they can make a mediocre boot much more comfortable. The wrong socks can make a good hiking boot feel uncomfortable and a warm winter boot feel clammy.

Cotton or cotton-blend socks of any kind should be avoided. Cotton soaks up more water than any other fiber, losing whatever loft it has when airspaces are filled with water, then drying very slowly—and constantly cooling any body part it lies against.

Probably the best all-around, all-season sock is a two-sock system consisting of a thick woolen or wool-synthetic blend oversock worn over a slippery nonabsorbent acrylic liner sock. The oversock provides an insulating, cushioning layer, while the liner sock serves as both a friction barrier to prevent blisters and a wicking layer that keeps feet feeling dry.

Hat: In the wilderness, a hat is more than an adornment for the head; it's a vital piece of equipment. A visored ballcap is useful in all seasons for keeping rain and snow off your face and bright sun out of your eyes. It keeps deerflies from becoming entangled in your hair, and you can soak it in water to keep your head cool under a hot sun.

In driving snow or freezing wind, the ballcap can be replaced by a knit ski mask worn as a mask or hat as conditions require. You can carry the mask rolled-up in a jacket pocket when it's not in use. A parka shell or jacket hood thrown over either hat provides an added layer of protection.

Bug protection: From spring until midsummer, and even longer in some habitats, there are biting bugs in sufficient numbers to make working among them unpleasant or even impossible. Most important is keeping those clouds of blood-craving blackflies, mosquitoes, stable flies, and deerflies from getting into eyes and facial cavities, and the most effective method so far has been to cover the head from hat to shoulders with a large mesh bag made from no-see-um netting.

Headnets are cheap and simple to sew from no-see-um material, or they can be purchased ready-made at most army surplus stores for around $8. You can see through the mesh well enough to wear it all day. And a good headnet, held away from the face by a hat brim or ballcap bill, can reduce bites to the head and neck to zero if worn tucked inside the collar to prevent bugs from coming in underneath. This pocket-size necessity also camouflages the head quite well, and it even cuts glare to prevent headaches or snowblindness when you are snowshoeing in bright sunlight.

TRACKING KIT EQUIPMENT LIST

Following is a list of equipment that has proved to be most essential to gathering data, making track casts, and just plain comfort in the field. This list is meant to be comprehensive so far as essentials are concerned, but it cannot be complete for every application in every environment, so it should be added to, and sometimes subtracted from, as activities demand. Equipment recommended by name is given as an example here, meaning that products listed by their brands are more indicative of the level of quality and performance needed than they are an endorsement of particular models (which can be counted on to change or be discontinued from one year to the next anyway).

Equipment Bags

Daypack: 2,500-cubic-inch capacity, outside pockets, internal frame, waist belt, sternum strap, padded shoulder straps, hydration pocket; Exponent Otero by Coleman.

Stuff sacks: nylon, drawstring with cord-lock, colored for coding individual kits.

Observation and Measurement Tools

Binoculars: 10x28 roof prism, Leupold Gold Ring.

Camera, 35mm: with 200 or 400 ISO speed film; Pentax K1000 or better.

Lenses: 70–210 zoom for animals, 50mm for close-ups of scat or tracks.

Camera, digital: Kodak EasyShare CX4200 or better.

Microscope: 25x or 50x pen type, Edmund Scientific Co., packed inside a plastic toothbrush holder for protection.

Tape measure: 10 feet, locking tape, belt clip, graduated in both inches and centimeters.

Ruler: 6 inches, flexible, marked clearly in both inches and centimeters.

Casting Kit

Plaster: 1 pound minimum, in a resealable plastic bag, carried inside mixing bowl below.

Spray wax: 1 can or more, kept warm by body heat, used only if necessary (wet snow). Available at police supply stores or online at www.evidentcrimescene.com.

Plastic surveyor's marking ribbon: brightly colored for marking cast locations, 6 feet or more.

Spray bottle: filled with water, for spritzing an icy glaze onto tracks in snow before casting.

Plaster mixing bowl: with snap-down cover, Tupperware type, 2-cup capacity or larger.

Resealable plastic dishes: low-wall Tupperware-type, at least 4x4 inches, for carrying casts.

Paper towels: partial roll, flattened, carried in plastic bread bag, for cushioning casts in dish.

Belt knife: 5-inch blade, sharp, for loosening casts, skinning; Ontario Knives SpecPlus.

Gloves: disposable, medical or food service type, for handling scat, carcasses, 4–5 pairs.

Air-activated handwarmer packets: to keep water bottles and hands unfrozen, 4 packets.

Duct tape: a dozen feet wound around a pencil.

Bar soap: in dish for washing hands, small tub of waterless hand soap if water is unavailable.

Orienteering

Compass, primary: prismatic-sighted map compass, liquid-filled; Brunton 8099.

Compass, secondary: pocket compass, liquid-filled, worn around neck; Brunton Tag-A-Long.

GPS: 12-channel, AA-powered, lighted screen, replacement batteries; Eagle Expedition II.

Map: U.S. Geographical Survey topographical, gridded with both Universal Transverse Mercator and latitude-longitude coordinates for use with GPS and magnetic compass.

Clothing and Other Necessaries

Water bottle, drinking: Platypus 1-liter water bladder.

Water bottle, casting: any 1-quart plastic bottle will do.

Water filter: MSR (Mountain Safety Research) Waterworks. Available at www.msr.com.

Boots, spring and winter hiking: waterproof, internal liner, LaCrosse Snowdrift PFT.

Boots, summer: hi-ankle, lace-to-toe, waterproof; Lowa Biomex Vertex.

Boots, winter: waterproof, comfort rated to at least -100°F; Rocky Snow Stalker.

Socks, all seasons: wool or synthetic oversock with acrylic liner sock; WigWam Mills.

Base layer, winter: synthetic, matched to temperatures, top and bottom; Medalist X-Static.

Parka shell, all seasons: hooded, large pockets, rainproof, breathable; Columbia.

Trousers, all seasons: six-pocket, ripstop weave, GI-type, dark color or camouflage.

Gloves, summer: leather or leather-and-fabric work gloves, gauntlet-length, most brands.

Gloves, winter: shell gloves with ComforTemp insulation, synthetic Fleece liners; Wells-Lamont.

Snowshoes, heavy load: 10x36 backpacking type, aluminum frame, crampons; Redfeather Powder.

Snowshoes, hiking: 9x30 backcountry type, aluminum frame, crampons; Tubbs Pinnacle.

Headnet: no-see-um mesh, worn over ballcap for bug protection, glare protection, camouflage.

APPENDICES

GLOSSARY OF TERMS

Accipiter: A genus of hawks characterized by short wings and a long tail.

Alar: A wing, winglike, or pertaining to a wing (alar extent = wingspan).

Altricial: Naked and helpless at birth, usually refers to the newborn of mammals and birds.

Amphibian: A cold-blooded hairless, featherless animal that is hatched in water and lives part of its life as an aquatic creature.

Animal: A living creature capable of actively migrating from one habitat to another.

Animalia: The taxonomic kingdom of so-called higher animals—those with an actual brain, nervous system, and some form of limbs to propel them from one habitat to another. Always multicelled, with specialized cells forming everything from internal organs to skin to hooves and feathers. All cells have a nucleus, all share the same basic genetic structure, and none can live outside the organism.

Archaea: A taxonomic domain of single-celled organisms that resemble bacteria but have a notably different DNA-management process.

Artiodactyla: The order of even-toed hooved animals, including deer, pig, and cow families.

Bacteria: A taxonomic domain made up of single-celled organisms that have no cell nucleus and are capable of survival without being part of a multicellular organism. With an entire physiology contained within just one cell, these creatures are tiny, and can't usually be seen without the aid of a microscope.

Beard: The tuft of hairlike feathers (mesofiloplumes) on the breast of an adult male turkey.

Benthos: The bottom of a sea or lake; also, the organisms living at the bottom of a sea or lake.

Binomial system: A labeling system developed by Carl Linnaeus in which a specific type of animal is identified by a two-part species name consisting of a first, genus, name, and a second, species, name. All names are in Latin, which has become the universal language of biologists of all nationalities. Example: The coyote is known as *Canis latrans,* its first name identifying it as a member of the canid (dog) family; the second name further identifying it as a unique individual within that family.

Bovidae: Cow family, characterized by having two hollow forward-facing permanent horns atop the brow, cloven hooves, heavy bodies, and an herbivorous diet with multiple stomachs.

Bovine: A member of the cow family.

Carnassial: Teeth that are adapted for tearing flesh, specifically the last premolar and the first molar in carnivorous animals.

Cast: A positive molding of a negative impression (track), usually made by pouring a viscous mix of plaster-of-paris and water into the impression, then removing it after it has hardened.

Casting: Bird dropping (noun); also the act of making a plaster track cast (verb).

Catamount: A mountain lion or lynx.

Caudal: Of, at, or near the tail or posterior parts of an animal; as in the caudal fin (tail) of a fish.

Cecal, or caecal: Of or relating to the cecum, at the beginning of the large intestine.

Cephalic: Of, at, or relating to the head or skull.

Chordata: The phylum of animals having a spinal cord.

Class: The taxonomic category that falls between phylum and order.

Cloaca: The genital-excretory cavity of a bird, reptile, or amphibian of either sex.

Cougar: A mountain lion.

Crepuscular: Mostly active during the twilight hours of dawn and dusk.

Delayed implantation: The ability of females in some species to carry a fertilized egg for a period of time before it becomes attached to the uterine wall and begins to develop. This phenomenon helps to insure that females are healthy enough to withstand the drain on their own bodily resources that gestation demands; if a female is underfed or in poor health, the egg will spontaneously abort.

Diapause: A period of quiescence between insemination and pregnancy; also called delayed implantation.

Digitigrade: The practice of walking or running with the weight forward, on the toes; a characteristic common to four-legged animals, both predator and prey, that are designed for running at high speeds.

Diurnal: Active during daylight hours.

Domain: One of the three most basic groups that all life is grouped into, consisting of eukarya, bacteria, and archaea.

Estivate (Aestivate): The practice of spending all or a portion of the summer months in a state of energy-conserving torpor to escape heat and drought.

Eukarya: A taxonomic domain made up of living things that are comprised of multiple, usually specialized, cells that have nuclei. This domain encompasses all plants, fungi, lichens, and animals. Being multicellular, the species within the Eukarya domain are sometimes very large, like the sperm whale, and most are visible to the human eye.

Family: The taxonomic classification below order and above genus, which groups animals by their most common shared characteristics. For example, the dog family (family Canidae) shares numerous physical characteristics that separate it from the cat family (family Felidae), even though both families share many common traits, like four toes, long tails, and canine teeth.

Fecundity: In animals, a seasonal period of fertility in which males develop active spermatozoans and females can become pregnant.

Frass: Caterpillar droppings.

Fungi: A kingdom of one-celled or multicelled organisms that have cell nuclei, but are usually not able to live or reproduce freely. Reproduction is usually via spores that are carried by the forces of nature to a suitable habitat, or sometimes a host, but some single-celled fungi are asexual and can reproduce by cellular mitosis. Fungi include mushrooms and toadstools, yeasts, molds, and mildews. Some scientists also place lichens in this kingdom.

Gait: The speed, or pace, at which an animal is traveling, evidenced by differences in the way tracks are grouped. The three gaits consist of walking, trotting, and running.

Gamete: A mature sperm or egg capable of participating in the fertilization process.

Genus: The taxonomic category of shared characteristics that ranks between family and species, usually the first name in a two-part species name.

Granivorous: Animals that feed primarily on seeds and grain.

Hibernate: An instinctive habit of animals that spend winter denned and in a state of deep sleep, their metabolisms and heart rates slowed to conserve energy until warm weather returns.

Hoof: The hard lowermost portion of an herbivorous animal's foot, actually modified claws that have evolved to give hoofed species like deer, horses, and bovids good running speed on firm ground.

Interdigital: A physical characteristic, usually a scent gland in animals, that occurs between the toes or fingers.

Iteroparous: A gestation process, seen especially in snakes, in which fertilized eggs are carried within the mother's body, but not nurtured by her, until the self-contained ova hatch and live young emerge.

Keratin: A fibrous protein in mammals that forms claws, horns, hooves, and fingernails.

Kingdom: One of the five basic groups into which living organisms are grouped, consisting of monerans, protistans, fungi (mold, mushrooms), plants (trees, all plants), and animals (fishes, mammals, reptiles, amphibians, birds).

Linnaean System: *See* Binomial system.

Lobe: A peninsular extension from a larger growth, like the lobe of a human ear, or the rounded portions of an animal's paw that extend rearward individually from its heel pad.

Mammal: A warm-blooded creature that gives birth to live young, nurses its young, and has hair or fur. Only bats can actually fly, and only the duck-billed platypus defies this classification by laying eggs.

Mandible: The lower, movable part of the jaw in mammals; either the upper or lower part of the beak in birds.

Manus: The end of the forelimb in vertebrates, as in fingers or toes.

Meiosis: A cell division in breeding animals that reduces the number of chromosomes in reproductive cells, thus causing fertile sperm or eggs (gametes) to be produced.

Monera: A kingdom of one-celled microscopic creatures that are free-living or sometimes live in small colonies. They have no nucleus, and all are capable of independent life, including those that live in colonies. Found primarily in water, where some decompose organic materials, some are parasitic of larger host animals. Monerans include flagellates (Giardia), pseudopodium, and ciliates.

Monodactyla: The order of animals having a single claw at the end of each leg (lobsters, crabs).

Monogynist: The practice of taking only one mate at a time.

Monomorphosis: Both sexes of a species exhibiting the same colors and patterns.

Musk: An often pungent, skunklike aroma exuded through the scent glands of many species, especially mammals. The scent is carried in an oily liquid produced by glands that may be in the cheeks, near the anus, between the hind legs, or another portion of the animal's anatomy from which a scent can be rubbed or otherwise deposited onto a landmark. Components of a musk scent include information about their owner's gender, sexual disposition, physical size, fearfulness, and other characterics, some of which have yet to be quantified.

Order: The taxonomic grouping of animal similarities, between class and family.

Ovoviparous: Egg-laying creatures that gestate ova inside a chamber within their bodies, then give birth to live young; especially snakes.

Pad: The fleshy bottom portion of an animal's paw or hoof, usually consisting of toes and a heel pad.

Painter: A mountain lion.

Papillae: Tiny hooklike projections on the upper surface of a cat's tongue that are used for rasping flesh from bone.

Paw: (*See* Pes); the footlike part at the end of a forelimb, consisting of toes, a sole or heel pad, and claws.

Pelage: The coat of any mammal, consisting of hair, fur, or wool, distinct from bare skin.

Perineal: In animals, an area between the scrotum and anus in males, and between the posterior vulva and the anus in females, which contains scent glands from which pheromones and other hormonal odors are emitted.

Perrissodactyla: The order of hooved mammals having an uneven number of toes, particularly the horse family, which has a single hoof.

Pes: A foot or footlike part, especially the hoof or paw of a four-footed animal.

Phylum: The taxonomic category of animal similarities that falls between the rankings of kingdom and class; the highest category in animal taxonomy.

Piscivore: Fish.

Plantae: A kingdom of multicelled organisms consisting of sometimes billions of cells that have a nucleus and are not free-living. Many of the cells within these organisms are highly specialized (such as cells that form roots and cells that form leaves or seeds), but all work together to maintain and propagate the organism. Most use photosynthesis to provide life energy. Plantae includes all plants, from true mosses, ferns, and grasses to bushes, shrubs, and the largest trees. Some scientists place lichens in this kingdom; others consider them fungi.

Plaster-of-paris: A finely powdered form of calcine gypsum (calcium sulphate) that can be mixed with water to achieve a desired viscosity, then formed or molded to take on and hold a given shape; used for casting tracks in soil or snow.

Pollex: The innermost forelimb digit; a thumb.

Polyestrous: A phenomenon in which females come into heat several times during a mating season until they become pregnant.

Polygynandrous: An individual of either sex having more than one mate at a time.

Polygynous: Having more than one female mate at a time.

Polygenesis: The derivation of a species of animal from more than one ancestral species. Example: The red wolf *(Canis rufus)* is thought by some to be a hybrid between the gray wolf *(Canis lupus)* and the coyote *(Canis latrans)*.

Precocial: Maturing at an early age, as in moose calves that can stand and begin walking almost immediately after being born.

Print: An impression left in soil or snow, usually by an animal's feet, but sometimes by its tail or nose.

Przewalski's horse: The last remaining breed of wild horse (*Equus caballus przevalskii*), formerly found in Sinkiang and Mongolia, but now surviving primarily in zoos.

Protista: A kingdom of free-living microscopic creatures that are most often one-celled, with a few living in colonies. Unlike monerans, protistans have a cell nucleus. Usually found in water. Members include plankton, paramecia, algae, amoebae, spirogyra, diatoms, volvox, euglena, and dinoflagellates.

Puma: A mountain lion.

Raptor: Largest of the birds of prey, including all eagles.

Reptile: A cold-blooded, hairless, featherless animal that is born, and often lives, on land.

Riparian: Of, on, or pertaining to the banks of a natural waterway.

Rostrum: A beaklike or snoutlike projection, usually in reference to nasal passages.

Scat: Solid or semi-solid excrement; feces.

Scent: A usually hormonal exudation from various glands that can serve to warn, advertise, or sexually excite others of the same species, usually accompanied by an enduring musky odor.

Scentpost: A urine- or musk-scented landmark that serves as a territorial marker and is refreshed with new scent periodically by its owner.

Sign: Any of a variety of markings that indicate the presence of an animal, including tracks, scats, scents, and disturbances to the area where an animal passed or lives.

Species: The most specific category in taxonomy, consisting of two Latin names that identify an animal's genus and its particular species (*see* Binomial system). Example: The bobcat is known as *Lynx rufus,* or wild cat (genus *Lynx*) that is red (species *rufus*).

Spermatogenesis: The maturation of a new generation of sperm cells, especially in annual breeders.

Spoor: Any sign, usually a scent, that an animal leaves to mark its passing.

Straddle: The average distance between tracks made by an animal's right legs and its left legs.

Stride: In this book, the distance a walking animal's foot travels from the point where it leaves the ground to the point where it again makes contact.

Subphylum: A taxonomic subranking that falls beween the categories of phylum and class.

Superclass: A taxonomic subranking that falls between the categories of class and order.

Talon: A large, sharp claw located at the end of an animal's toe, used for tearing or gripping flesh.

Taxonomy: A ranking system that categorizes data about animals and other topics into logical categories.

Territory: An area of land that is claimed by an animal as home, usually bounded by established trails, scent or scat posts, and defended against intruders that might infringe on its resources.

Track: A mark left on the earth by an animal's foot, usually an impression in soil or snow.

Trail: A ribbon of earth that has been trampled or otherwise disturbed (as a furrow through tall grass) by the passage of an animal. In most cases a trail is used regularly because it permits easy travel, at a fast gait if the need arises.

Vertebrata: A biological category of animals that have a bony spine, including mammals, reptiles, and fishes, but excluding insects and worms.

Vibrissae: In mammals, the whiskers at either side of the nose; in insectivorous birds, the modified feathers at either side of the beak.

Viviparous: A gestation process in which living young develop within the mother's body, nurtured from her own resources, before being born alive; not born from an egg.

GLOSSARY OF SCIENTIFIC NAMES

Antelope, pronghorn: *Antilocapra americana*

Armadillo, nine-banded: *Dasypus novemcinctus*

Badger, American: *Taxidea taxus*

Bear, black: *Ursus americanus*

Bear, brown: *Ursus arctos horribilis*

Bear, polar: *Ursus maritimus*

Beaver: *Castor canadensis*

Bison: *Bison bison*

Bobcat: *Lynx rufus*

Bullfrog: *Rana catesbeiana*

Caribou: *Rangifer tarandus*

Cat, house: *Felis silvestris*

Chickadee, black-capped: *Poecile atricapilla*

Chicken, domestic: *Gallus gallus*

Cormorant, double-crested: *Phalacrocorax auritus*

Cougar, or mountain lion: *Puma concolor*

Coyote: *Canis latrans*

Cow, domestic: *Bos taurus*

Crane, sandhill: *Grus canadensis*

Deer, mule: *Odocoileus hemionus*

Deer, whitetail: *Odocoileus virginianus*

Dog, domestic: *Canis familiaris*

Duck, domestic: *Anas boschas*

Duck, mallard: *Anas platyrhynchos*

Duck, wood: *Aix sponsa*

Eagle, bald: *Haliaeetus leucocephalus*

Eagle, golden: *Aquila chrysaetos*

Elk, American: *see* Wapiti

Ermine: *Mustela erminea*

Fisher: *Martes pennanti*

Fox, gray: *Urocyon cinereoargenteus*

Fox, red: *Vulpes vulpes*

Goose, Canada: *Branta canadensis*

Grouse, ruffed: *Bonasa umbellus*

Hare, snowshoe: *Lepus americanus*

Heron, great blue: *Ardea herodias*

Horse, domestic: *Equus caballus*

Jaguar: *Panthera onca*

Loon, common: *Gavia immer*

Lynx: *Lynx canadensis*

Marmot, hoary: *Marmota caligata*

Marmot, yellow-bellied: *Marmota flaviventris*

Marmot, woodchuck: *Marmota monax*

Marten, pine: *Martes americana*

Mink: *Mustela vision*

Moose, New World: *Alces alces*

Mountain lion: *see* Cougar

Mule deer: *Odocoileus hemionus*

Muskox: *Ovibos moschatus*

Muskrat: *Ondatra zibethicus*

Opossum, Virginia: *Didelphis virginiana*

Otter, river: *Lontra canadensis*

Otter, sea: *Enhydra lutris*

Peccary, collared: *Dicotyles tajacu*

Peeper, Spring: *Pseudacris crucifer*

Pig, wild: *Sus scrofa*

Porcupine: *Erethizon dorsatum*

Rabbit, Eastern cottontail: *Sylvilagus floridanus*

Raccoon: *Procyon lotor*

Rattlesnake, Eastern Diamondback: *Crotalus adamanteus*

Raven, common: *Corvus corax*

Skunk, striped: *Mephitis mephitis*

Skunk, Western spotted: *Spilogale gracilis*

Snake, common garter: *Thamnophis sirtalis*

Snake, corn: *Elaphe guttata*

Snake, Eastern hognose: *Heterodon platyrhinos*

Snake, Massasauga rattlesnake: *Sistrurus catenensis*

Snake, Northern water: *Nerodia sipedon*

Snake, sidewinder: *Crotalus cerastes*

Snipe, common: *Gallinago gallinago*

Squirrel, fox: *Sciurus niger*

Squirrel, gray: *Sciurus carolinensis*

Squirrel, red: *Tamiasciurus hudsonicus*

Toad, American: *Bufo americanus*

Turkey, American wild: *Meleagris gallopavo*

Turtle, Blandings: *Emydoidea blandingii*

Turtle, Northern snapping: *Chelydra serpentina*

Turtle, painted: *Chrysemys picta*

Vulture, turkey: *Cathartes aura*

Wapiti, or American elk: *Cervus elaphus*

Weasel, least: *Mustela nivalis*

Weasel, long-tailed: *Mustela frenata*

Weasel, short-tailed: *see* Ermine

Wolf, gray: *Canis lupus*

Wolf, red: *Canis rufus*

Wolverine: *Gulo gulo*

Woodchuck: *Marmota monax*

Woodcock, American: *Scolopax minor*

TERMS FOR MULTIPLE ANIMALS

antelope: herd

ants: army, colony, swarm

apes: shrewdness

asses: herd, pace

bacteria: culture

badgers: cete, colony

bass: shoal

bears: sleuth, sloth

beavers: colony

bees: grist, hive, swarm

birds: congregation, dissimulation, flock, volary

bison: herd

bitterns: sedge, siege

boars and pigs: sounder, singular

bobolinks: chain

bucks: brace, clash

buffalo: herd

buzzards: wake

caterpillars: army

cats: clowder, clutter, pounce

cattle: drove, herd, team

chickens: brood, peep

chicks: clutch, chattering

clams: bed

cobras: quiver

colts: rag, rake

coots: cover

cows: kine

coyote: band

cranes: herd, sedge, siege

crocodiles: float

crows: murder

cubs: litter

curlews: herd

curs: cowardice

deer: herd, leash

dogs: kennel, litter, pack

dolphins: pod

donkeys: drove, herd, pace

dotterel: trip

doves: bevy, cote, dole, dule, paddling, piteousness

ducks: paddling, raft, team

eagles: convocation

eggs: clutch

elephant seals: pod (adolescents: weaner pod)

elephants: herd

elks: gang

emus: mob

ferrets: business, cast, fesnying

finches: charm

fish: catch, drought, haul, run, school, shoal

flies: swarm

foxes: lead, leash, skulk

frogs: army, colony, knot

geese (flying): gaggle, skein

gnats: cloud, horde, swarm

gnus (wildebeast): implausibility

goats: drove, herd, tribe, trip

goldfinches: charm

goldfish: glint

gorillas: band

greyhounds: leash

hares: down, husk

hawks or flacons: cast

hawks (soaring): kettle

hens: brood

herons: hedge, sedge, siege

herrings: shoal

hogs: drift, passel, parcel

horses: herd, harras, stable, team, troop

hounds: cry, mute, pack

house cats: clowder, cluster, dout, nuisance

jackrabbits: husk

jays: party, scold

jellyfish: smack

kangaroos: herd, mob, troop

kittens: litter, kindle

lapwings: deceit

larks: ascension

leopards: leap, leep, lepe

lions: pride, sault, troop

lizards: lounge

locusts: plague

magpies: tiding

mallards: sord

mares: stud

martens: richness

moles: company, labor, movement

monkeys: cartload, tribe, troop, troup

mules: barren, pack, rake, span

nightingales: watch

otters: bevy, family, romp

owls: parliament

oxen: drove, herd, team, yoke

parrots: company

partridges (also grouse or ptarmigans): covey

peacocks: muster, ostentation

penguins: colony, huddle

pheasants (on the ground): nide, nye

pheasants (when flushed): bouquet

pigeons: flight, flock

piglets: farrow

pigs: herd, litter, sounder

pilchards: shoal

plovers: congregation, wing

ponies: string

porpoises: herd, pod

pups: litter

quail: bevy, covey

rabbits: bury, colony, down, drove, husk, leash, trace, trip

rabbits (young): nest

raccoons: gaze

rats: colony, pack, plague, swarm

rattlesnakes: rhumba

ravens: unkindness

rhinoceros: crash

roebucks: bevy

rooks: building, clamor

rooks, ravens, crows: storytelling

seals: bob, colony, crash, harem, herd, pod, team

sharks: shiver

sheep: down, drove, flock, fold, hurtle, trip

skunks: polecats, chine

snakes: den, nest, pit

snipe: walk, wisp

sparrows: host

squirrels: dray, scurry

starlings: murmuration

storks: muster, mustering

swallows (also doves, goshawks, cormorants): flight

swans: bevy, herd, wedge

swans (or geese, flying in a "V"): wedge

swifts: flock

swine: drift, sounder

teal: spring

tigers: ambush

toads: knot

trout: hover

turkeys: raft, rafter

turtledoves: dule, pitying

turtles: bale

vipers: generation, nest

walruses: herd, pod

whales: gam, herd, pod, school

wild cats: destruction

wildfowl: plump

wolves: herd, pack, rout, route

woodcocks: fall

woodpeckers: descent

zebras: crossing, herd

CREDITS

Illustrations on Pages 171, 180, and 283 by Bob Hines, courtesy of U.S. Fish and Wildlife Service.

The following illustrations courtesy of the U.S. Department of Agriculture: pages 58 (George A. Robinson), 69, and 83.

All other illustrations by Len McDougall.

Photos by Len McDougall except the following:

Pages 32, 38, 49, 61, 71, 103, 200, and 313: Courtesy of Bob Meyer.

Page 150: Photograph by Roger Barbour.

The following photographs courtesy of the U.S. Fish and Wildlife Service: pages 55 (Steve Kaufman), 65, 73 (Tom Stehn), 109 (Dave Schaffer), 113 (V. Bern), 123 (Larry Moats), 128 and 266 (John and Karen Hollingsworth), 136 and 156 (Erwin and Peggy Bauer), 140, 208 (Dave Olsen), 278 (Eastern wild turkey photo by Gary M. Stolz; Western wild turkey photographer unknown), 287, 293 (Lee Karney), 299, 304 (John Cossick), 311, 317 (Claire Dobert), 359 (Ed McCrea).